Hacking the Earthship

IN SEARCH OF AN EARTH-SHELTER
THAT WORKS FOR EVERYBODY

Rachel Preston Prinz
and Contributors

Archinia Press

ALBUQUERQUE, NEW MEXICO

Copyright © 2015 by Rachel Preston Prinz

All rights reserved. No part of this publication may be reproduced, distributed or transmitted in any form or by any means, including photocopying, recording, or other electronic or mechanical methods, without the prior written permission of the publisher, except in the case of brief quotations embodied in critical reviews and certain other noncommercial uses permitted by copyright law. For permission requests, write to the publisher, addressed "Attention: Permissions Coordinator," at the address below.

The views and opinions expressed within are those of the listed authors and do not necessarily reflect those of the other authors and contributors. The author, contributors, and publisher accept no responsibility, nor liability, in any manner whatsoever for any error or omission, nor any loss, damage, injury, or adverse outcome of any kind as a result of the information contained in this book or reliance upon it. Readers are advised to seek professional advice prior to design or construction of any building.

The publisher accepts no responsibility for the accuracy of the URLs referred to in this publication, and does not guarantee that any content on those websites is, or will remain, accurate or appropriate. Nor do we have any control over the removal of that information. If a link is broken or removed, and you find it, please let us know for future publications.

Archinia Press
410 Solano Drive SE
Albuquerque, NM 87108
Tel: 505-906-1146
Email: intentiondesign@gmail.com
http://www.archinia.com
http://www.HackingtheEarthship.blogspot.com

Original Book Layout ©2013 BookDesignTemplates.com
Cover design by Arianna Shewfelt
Photos unless otherwise noted are by Rachel Preston Prinz

Hacking the Earthship/ Rachel Preston Prinz. —1st ed.
Genre: Non-Fiction
Keywords: Earthship, Architecture, Design, Sustainability, Green Design, Natural Building
ISBN: 978-0-9861155-2-3

Contents

Introduction 7
    Background and Methodology 11
Engaging with the Process: Part 1 15
The Earthship Reality Project 17
    The Mythos 19
    "Just the Facts, Ma'am" 41
    Earthships are not for Everybody 50
    Motivation: Why we have to do something MORE 51
The Science: Academic Research and Tire Off-gassing 53
    Academic Research on Earthship Performance 54
    Research Conclusions 61
    Tires and Off-gassing Research 62
Engaging with the Process: Part 2 65
A Way Forward 67
    Earthship 2.0: Reinventing 67
    Working towards a Better Definition of Sustainability 72
    Cost Effective Sustainable Features 74
    From Vision to Reality 79
    Where is the Money? How to Afford to Pay Cash for Your Home 83
    Insurance for the Non-Traditional Home 94
    Planning a Build 98
    Regulatory Forces – The Code 101
Design 105
The Building's Context and Site 107
    Land Uses 108
    Choosing a Building Site 111
    Vernacular Design Principals 131
Designing for Thermal Comfort 143
    Passive Solar Design 145

- Thermal Mass versus Insulation 151
- Earth-Coupling and Earth-Sheltering 101 153
- Natural Ventilation Strategies and Indoor Air Quality 155
- Thermal and Moisture Protection 159
- Acoustics - Sound Insulation 164

The Structural System 167
- Foundations 169
- Floor Structures 172
- Framing 173

Engaging with the Process: Part 3 175

The Enclosure System 177
- Secrets of Great Curb Appeal 179
- Walls 180
- Traditional Earthship Building Blocks 183
- Other Types of Walls 196
- Roofing 226
- Doors and Windows 236

Rooms, Spaces, Colors, & Textures 241
- Create an Efficient Floorplan 241
- Entrance 249
- Courtyards 250
- Hallways & Hidden Hallways 252
- Living Room 252
- Dining Rooms 252
- Great Room 253
- Kitchens and Baths 253
- Bedrooms 260
- Second Floors and Lofts 261
- Storage 261
- Laundry Room 261
- Garage 263
- Root Cellar 264

  Stairs and Towers 266

  Standard Furniture Dimensions 269

  Details of Design 271

  Planning for the Long Game 275

  Universal Design 277

  Finishes 280

Engaging with the Process: Part 4 291

Mechanical Systems 293

  Mechanical Heating and Cooling 294

  Electrical Systems 303

  Plumbing 317

  Final Notes on Mechanical Systems 327

Imbuing Space with Spirit 329

  What is Happy, Anyway? 329

  Your Core Desired Feelings 331

  Locating "Power Spots" 332

  Creating Sacred Spaces 333

  Correct timing 334

  Vaastu & Feng Shui 336

Conclusion: A New Set of Earth-shelter Building Criteria 341

Overwhelmed? Need Help? 345

  Hiring an Architect or Designer 346

APPENDICES 349

New Home Design Worksheet 349

Site Design Checklist 367

Participate! 373

Suggested Reading 375

Earthships around the World 377

Index 381

About the Author 387

Contributors 389

"This hour in history needs a dedicated circle of transformed nonconformists.
Our planet teeters on the brink of annihilation; dangerous passions of pride, hatred, and selfishness
are enthroned in our lives; and men do reverence before false gods of nationalism and materialism.
The saving of our world from pending doom will come, not through the complacent adjustment
of the conforming majority, but through the creative maladjustment of a nonconformist minority."

—MARTIN LUTHER KING, JR.

ACKNOWLEDGEMENTS

*There is no way that this book would have come together without my amazing contributors.
I am so thankful for their participation and am honored to count them all among my friends and inspirations.*

*I also want to thank Professors David Woodcock, Joe Hutchinson, and Charles Graham
and architects David Puckett, Randy Byers, Doug DeChant, and Barbara Felix
who all taught me new ways of seeing the architectural world.*

*I thank my mom for taking me to Paris and gifting me with my passion for architecture,
and my dad for showing me how doing good work by hand makes better buildings.*

Special thanks to Illac Diaz who challenged me to make a real difference for people with this work.

*Thanks also to the many people who contacted our office to ask for and inspire us to help
as well as all the people who contributed their knowledge, expertise, and experiences
through our surveys, interviews, and research.*

*I would also like to thank my husband, my family, and my friends for always standing by me,
even when I do crazy things like disappearing for 6 months to write a book.*

Next Page: Figure 1. Earth Wall Detail at Carole Crews Workshop Site

Introduction

This project started with one idea: Share the answers to the questions I got asked day after day about improving Earthships. What started out as 3 pages on the Archinia website a few years back has now grown into a coalition of designers, engineers, sustainability experts, and people in-the-know all sharing their knowledge so that we can try and help make the world a little bit better place.

We love the organic forms of earthen architecture and the idea of living freely and in concert with nature – growing our food, reducing our need for systems, rising and setting with the sun – these are noble, sustainable, and mindful ways to live.

Living in Taos, New Mexico at the epicenter of the Earthship phenomenon, we are impressed by these structures every time someone comes to visit, because they inevitably want to see them. We have many friends who have lived in them. We have visited them, interviewed their builders, and even gone to workshops about them. While we celebrate the Earthship's successes… like the glass bottle walls that radiate a mosaic of blue, green, and amber light… we also see… and hear people's frustrations over… their flaws.

We are often asked whether the Earthships are as good as the hype around them suggests. When we started posting about common problems on our website, people took notice and started asking us not only to help solve the issues they were having with their existing Earthships, but also to help them hack the design to make a more natural version. As a designer, I was intrigued by this idea because I also wanted to see if the Earthship could be done with natural materials. So, I rallied my team and we started working. We found research, collected data, took tours and made observations, and… in order to build a new paradigm… we got back to basics.

This return to basics started for me when I moved to New Mexico seven years ago. Previous to my move, I lived in Vail, Colorado and worked as a project manager for an architect who designed $7million+ homes in the most prestigious areas of the Rocky Mountains. Working on projects of that scale and quality gave me one set of values around architecture: the bigger, the prettier, and the more expensive… the better. I was quite literally at the top of the residential architecture game. I got to work on some of the most magnificent residential spaces there are.

Here in New Mexico though, I got back to my roots – in the earth – and I found my way back to great design for real people again. I realized that everyone deserves to live in a place that is safe, warm, requires little energy input, and is a space that can make their lives a little brighter. I also realized that the most efficient way we can change our world to a more sustainable one is to impact as many peoples' homes as possible. Because for every new cruddy building that gets built, we all pay for the bad design by losing our incredible wealth of natural resources, which are mined, extracted, cut down, and otherwise abused in order to support these bad buildings.

I went back to what I consider the heart of great architecture. I re-read Christopher Alexander's <u>A Pattern Language</u>, which investigates the forms of architecture and landscapes designed by people of different cultures in different places. I re-read Kenneth Frampton's essays on Critical Regionalism, which discuss designing buildings that are of their place and time and culture. I re-read Sarah Susankah's <u>The Not So Big House</u> so I could remember how to do small-scale design well again. I joined the Architecture 2030 movement and the SEED movement so I could commit to sustainability goals that support our earth and its people too. I learned how to make adobes, install and repair earth plaster, and build naturally. And I started a 5-year research project on sustainable and natural earth-centered design in New Mexico and around the world.

Here in New Mexico, people have been living off the land and designing and building in concert with nature for more than 1,000 years. Many of our historic buildings work as well today as they did when they were built. I thought this might be true as I visited the many archaeological sites where our original architectures still exist intact. I confirmed it when Archinia was hired for two projects that allowed me to survey more than 500 historic buildings in Taos County – many of these adobe buildings were still in relatively good shape after 100 years! It became clear rather quickly that these natural buildings are a tangible offering that we can pass on to our kids. That is important because it is truly sustainable.

The story of how all of it worked together became a part of me and informed how I relate to every space now. And who isn't looking for a deeper, more meaning-full connection to their place in the world? This is why I want to share so much of what makes great vernacular architecture work with you – I want to help you find your special connection to your Place. Connecting to Place has become important again for many designers around the world. In fact, now there is an entire discipline in architecture called PlaceMaking. PlaceMaking is less about making things than it is about honoring the Places we build in. I think this idea can help us build better buildings in general. And better Earthships in particular.

Forty years have passed since the earliest Earthships were dreamed into existence. In that time, Mike Reynolds – the father of Earthships – and visionaries like him have played a fundamental role in expanding ideas about sustainable design and natural building. This has helped to create a new generation of would-be home builders that are better-versed in sustainable strategies. Those who can afford Earthships also have a more discerning eye, as the price point of the buildings has risen dramatically, and with that comes a more sophisticated consumer.

THE NEW GENERATION OF EARTHSHIP ENTHUSIASTS:

- Does not want to cart questionable building materials long distances in the name of recycling and call it "green".
- Wants to build locally and naturally… and they want to build it themselves.
- Wants their buildings to be cool in summer, warm in winter, the humidity to be predictable and regular; and they want to minimize pests and allergens in their environment.
- Wants to be able to get a permit, and insurance, and resell their homes if they want to; or pass them on to their children if they can.
- They might have been influenced by the tiny house movement, and they want a smaller home that is "just right"… for their budget, time, ability, energy use, and maintenance.
- Oftentimes, they want to be able to spend the rest of their lives in their home, which means they want to make their home easy to manage, maintain, and get around in, even if they are in a walker or wheelchair.
- They want their home to feel like it is made from and relating to the earth: in views, in light, in fresh air, in the ability to grow food, and in a beautiful landscape that supports the function of the home.

Finding the balance between all these desires is a delicate and sometimes lengthy process of discernment, study, and goal-setting. That is what this book aims to help you do.

Chapter 1 THE EARTHSHIP REALITY PROJECT addresses the Earthship ideal as it exists today, discussing the science behind the Earthships, as well as issues and resolutions of the design over the past 40 years.

Chapter 2 THE SCIENCE: ACADEMIC RESEARCH AND TIRE OFF-GASSING reviews some of the best academic and scientific research on Earthship design and performance, and then offers interpretations of what must be addressed to remedy the issues raised.

Chapter 3 A WAY FORWARD begins to lay out a path for those who want to utilize earth-sheltering and Earthship ideals as a basis of design for a truly sustainable home. In this chapter, we discuss designing a sustainable home, obtaining financing and insurance, tax credits, cost effective sustainable features, minimizing waste, managing the complexities of the build, visioning, and Code requirements.

Chapter 4 THE BUILDING'S CONTEXT AND SITE addresses design techniques for the site and landscape, and discusses methods for how to put both to work for you.

Chapter 5 DESIGNING FOR THERMAL COMFORT addresses natural, mechanical, and design options for improving thermal performance. Topics covered include passive solar design; using thermal mass versus insulation; using earth-coupling versus earth-sheltering; designing for thermal and moisture protection; and natural ventilation. We also touch on acoustics.

Chapters 6 through 8 are a three-part series on the basic building blocks of a building.

Chapter 6 THE STRUCTURAL SYSTEM specifically addresses the ways we can form the building's structure.

Chapter 7 THE ENCLOSURE SYSTEM outlines methods for the construction of the building's envelope or skin. We discuss traditional earthship building blocks like tire, glass, and can walls, as well as alternative systems like adobe, cob, rammed earth, earthbags, wood block concrete forms, timber frame, log, cordwood, and strawbale buildings. We also cover various roofing options as well as doors and windows in this chapter.

Chapter 8 ROOMS, SPACES, COLORS, & TEXTURES discusses the spaces within the building envelope and how we can decorate those spaces in order to create a home we love.

Chapter 9 MECHANICAL SYSTEMS outlines basic mechanical, electrical, and plumbing considerations for various systems, including and especially on-grid systems since those are what make an Earthship most affordable.

Chapter 10 IMBUING SPACE WITH SPIRIT is affectionately titled "The WooWoo Chapter." This chapter addresses the psychological and spiritual aspects of design and covers a wide range of topics including psychology of space and color, locating power spots, astrologically-correct timing for cutting wood and other building tasks, and we even talk about Feng Shui and Vaastu. While my intellectual approach to design has always been rooted in the science of building, my heart resides in another place – one that is inhabited with a little bit of magic. While there may be overtones throughout the text, this chapter makes no attempt to reign in magical thinking. I hope that for those of you who are called to create spaces that are spiritually "more", these tips are of benefit.

Chapter 11 CONCLUSION: A NEW SET OF EARTH-SHELTER BUILDING CRITERIA presents my conclusions about the kind of earth-sheltered home I want, after having gone through the process of asking myself the same questions you will as you design your home using this book. I am not offering a general conclusion that will work for you, because that is not possible for me to do. We will get into the reasons why a conclusion that works for me cannot work for you in the sections where we discuss how there can be no Global Model of design. I do hope that seeing the results of my investigation assists you in determining what works for you.

Chapter 12 OVERWHELMED? NEED HELP? discusses some helpful tips if you hire an architect or residential designer to help you design your space.

The APPENDICES offer lists of resources and worksheets designed to help you manifest a space you will love.

The opening photos of each chapter were selected with the intention of offering inspiration. For me, these photos represent the best of Earthships as well as earthen design… and abundance… which is what I wish for all of us.

We will post a list of links for the sites we mention here on our blog and we will post new and revised content as it becomes available between editions. Follow us at http://hackingtheearthship.blogspot.com/ for updates!

Finally, I want to offer that there were two other motivations for me writing this book. The first is that I have gone partially blind and there is a pretty good chance that I will end up totally blind eventually. I wanted to document all the tips and tricks I have learned in my career before I cannot see the words on the mountain of pages of sticky notes, notebooks, and files that I saved anymore. So I wrote down all I could remember and transcribed every tidbit of design advice that I could find in my files. Plus, I have this crazy idea that Architecture (the good stuff, with a capital-A) should not be reserved for the rich. Modern homes for regular people are rarely designed to last or work properly for their climate. This demands more resources and results in higher monthly fuel costs. These homes require still more resources when they must be repaired or rebuilt because they are poorly constructed... and on and on it goes. I want to help stop this crazy cycle that people, myself included, are getting trapped in. I want to help bring design back to the people. That is why, when my first editor told me on Christmas Eve that she couldn't finish the book, and the second editor told me in late February she couldn't finish it either... I kept writing. I care less about perfect wording and citations than I do about getting this information in your hands so you can make your spaces shine and start saving your money and resources NOW.

The second motivation is that I want what I suspect all of our readers want – a place of my own that fills the void created by living in a world that is not in alignment with my values. I want my own perfect little oasis that is of-the-earth and that feeds my body and soul. I have a solid background in this, as I have worked for many years to help people design and build their own perfect spaces. But there were things I did not know myself about some of the kinds of building that I have not already worked with. What I didn't know, I learned, and shared here... so you don't have to spend countless hours researching it all yourself.

This book is also a bit of an homage to the people and organizations who inspired and taught me through this process, and who joined in in this effort to help us identify truly sustainable ways of doing earth-sheltered buildings. There are so many extraordinary people doing amazing work out there. Their work can change the way we approach architecture and design! I want to celebrate that and help people to use design to improve their lives. So I will also share stories about the people who inspired me and include links to their work so you can get inspired too!

With all of my heart, I hope these pages help you manifest your dream home too.

We wanted to make this book totally open-source. However, publishing books is not free. So we are charging a little something to cover our expenses. We do ask that if you can, you contribute to the effort in whatever way you are able, like buying a copy, reviewing this positively if it was useful for you, shooting us an email and offering suggestions of things you wish were here for future editions, or even sharing your own success stories so we can share them with our readers! With a little help, we can continue to make this book and the documentaries, articles, and websites we will develop alongside it... better. Portions of the proceeds raised will go to our not-for-profit architectural education programs ARCHITECTURE FOR EVERYBODY and BUILT FOR LIFE. If you believe in this work, please consider making a tax-deductible donation through our fiscal sponsor, Albuquerque's RIO GRANDE COMMUNITY DEVELOPMENT CORPORATION.

Background and Methodology

An Earthship is a trademarked building type introduced in the 1970's and designed by architect Michael "Mike" Reynolds through his firm Earthship Biotecture (previously known as Solar Survival architecture). Because of the worldwide dissemination of the concept since, the term Earthship... generally accepted as meaning something to the effect of "underground house with a solar wall"... has become part of the common lexicon. It is as synonymous with calling a drink that is sparkly, sweet, and caramel colored a "coke" even if it is not the original Coca Cola product. We are going to use the common parlance in this book, and use the term Earthship to refer to any building built on the methodology, even if it is a modified version of the original trademarked design.

IN PRINCIPLE, EARTHSHIPS:

- Use recycled waste tires, glass bottles, and cans along with natural materials and concrete to construct a structure that is intended to have minimal impact on the environment.

- Make their own water using the roof's gutter system to direct rain and snow to cisterns where it is stored. Then a gravity-fed Water Organizing Module filters, pressurizes, and pumps the stored water to sinks, showers, bath faucets, and sometimes to solar thermal hot water heaters.

- After the filtered rain water is used once, it is directed to rubber-lined greywater planters to be filtered and aerated. A pump panel at the end of the planter moves the water to the toilet tank for flushing. The blackwater from the toilet goes outside to a septic tank, and possibly a blackwater planter which cleans the effluent before delivering it to a septic field.

- Produce their own heat and cooling, through using a combination of passive solar design, natural ventilation, a photovoltaic solar array, a wind turbine, and/or a gas generator.

- Produces food via a "food forest" and "salad bar" grown in the indoor greywater planters.

An Earthship's exterior walls are typically constructed of used tires filled with dirt to provide thermal mass "cooling and heating". Interior walls are constructed of a honeycomb of empty aluminum drink cans or glass bottles set in concrete. Earthships are artistically beautiful and the houses appear to rise out of the earth as if by natural commandment.

However, there is a disconnect between how the Earthships are intended to work and how they actually work. Around the world, groups and forums discuss the design's many issues. In order to identify patterns within the issues, in early 2014, we started case studying Earthship builds around the world as well as here at home in New Mexico. We catalogued the issues and resolutions that expert builders and other researchers were finding. We studied the data collected from Earthship builds in 15 countries and visited 20 sites in the US... from the smallest tiny house Earthship to some of the largest and most palatial Earthships in the world. We read commentaries from builds, builders, and systems; digging ever deeper into the data - what research has been done? If not on this wall system, what do people know about the materials? What are the pros and cons? What is the embodied energy? We designed surveys and conducted interviews of owners, builders, and renters to find out what issues they were having and how they solved them. We started collecting weather data to see what tweaks make the homes work well in what climates.

Then we branched out, finding scientific research and data to support both sides of every debate, conducting more interviews... we started collecting enough data to start to identify patterns in what techniques worked where and why. That the Earthships have some issues is an established fact. What was not fully established are the reasons or patterns that explained why. We analyzed the data and tried to figure out what it did, and maybe did not, say. Academic research is especially difficult to digest, so in as much as we were able, we translated that into plain English. We also found some places in the Earthship website and literature that were confusing, and we attempted to explain more of what was happening there.

Our next goal was to document what design tweaks worked for people, and pair those tips and tricks with some solid design advice so that we could empower readers to design a space that meets their physical needs of food, shelter, and water; fiscal needs of value, budget, and schedule; and psycho-emotional needs of a space that supports you in becoming who you dream of being.

Then, we kept going, cultivating the list of "people to watch" in Earthships in particular and Natural Building in general. We checked out the websites, blogs, research, forums, and Facebook fan pages of the foremost experts in their fields. Some were professional designers and contractors and some were hobbyists who had learned by doing. We paid careful attention to their advice and problem solving tips, and then dug into the next level of data… the comments… sometimes hundreds, even thousands, from invested readers who were sharing their own stories of triumph over common issues raised. Too hot, too cold, just right - what they did and how they did it - we wrote it down.

Then, after reading <u>Earthship</u> Volumes 1-3, we realized that what people really needed was help a) deciding what systems worked for their climate and values, and b) learning how to utilize them. Finally, we consulted experts - architects, engineers, landscape architects, and researchers - to help us offer better clarifications and more useful design tools.

It is our goal to supplement the standard Earthship literature with helpful principles of design that can help elevate the Earthship ideal into its next generation, and hopefully help to make the process as painless as possible for would-be builders along the way.

Our Earthship Survey

In 2014, we started collecting information from Earthship owners, builders, and renters in an online survey. The questions we asked were:

- Have you owned, rented, or built an Earthship?
- What is the Zip Code of your Earthship? (We collect this for climate analysis)
- Was your Earthship designed or built by Earthship Biotecture?
- In what year was your Earthship finished?
- If you built your Earthship, how long did it take you to build it?
- How long have you lived in or did you live in your Earthship?
- Do you still own or rent your Earthship?
- If you do not still own or rent your Earthship, why did you sell it or move?
- Is/was your Earthship a standard or custom design?
- Did you purchase drawings? If so, how much did they cost?
- What was the cost to build your Earthship? Does this include your own time?
- Is your Earthship oriented due south?
- If your Earthship has slanted glass, does it tend to overheat in the buffer zone/greenhouse? If yes, what is too hot by your standards?
- If your Earthship overheats, is it doing so year round or certain months only?
- Does your Earthship have the buffer zone/greenhouse separated from the body of the house by windows and doors?
- If the buffer zone/greenhouse is separated by windows and doors, are they pre-fabricated exterior grade doors and windows or custom made doors and windows?
- Do you use custom diagonal shades on your slanted front windows?
- If you look out from your slanted windows, is the ground higher than the floor you are standing on?
- Did you have any issues with the aluminum cans in your build during construction or after completion?
- Do you know how many tires you used?
- Did you have any issues with the tires in your build during construction or after completion?
- Did you have any issues with the glass bottle walls in your build during construction or after completion?
- What type of finishes did you use on your wall?
- Do you have pets? Have they had any impact on your use of the home?
- Does your Earthship utilize a cistern or is it connected to city water? Is it an open cistern or closed?
- Does your roof work like a teacup (have a V in it for water collection) or is it a shed roof draining to one side of the house?
- Do you utilize a solar electric system?
- Are the planting beds at or below the ground level?
- Are you able to grow all the vegetables you would like in your Earthship?

- Do you have any pest issues in your Earthship?
- Are you using composting or flush toilets?
- Are there any issues with your systems?
- Does your septic include an exterior blackwater recharge area?
- Do you find your earth-bermed rooms in the habitable area to be cold or dark?
- Are your rooms on multiple levels? Has that ever not worked for you? (i.e. have you had trouble while on crutches or in a wheelchair, tripped, etc.?)
- Are you as satisfied with the Earthship today as when you moved in or decided to build it?
- Do you feel like you got a great deal on your Earthship?

Would you like to be made aware as new questions get asked, or as we collect the data from these surveys and share it? Read: Would you like to be added to our mailing list?

- Is there more you would like to share? Do you have ideas you think would make them better or tweaks that you used successfully that you want to pass on?

Asking these questions allowed us to collect and analyze the data on the Earthships, including climate data, without assuming that we knew what the outcome would be. This gave us access to unbiased information which we used to build upon the foundations of our research.

Engaging with the Process: Part 1

What are your concerns about the Earthship ideals now that you know more about them?

What tweaks do you want to make?

What are your favorite parts of the design?

Chapter I

The Earthship Reality Project

by Rachel Preston Prinz, Pratik Zaveri, and Asha Stout

An Earthship is constructed of three exterior walls (west, north, and east, in the northern hemisphere; west, south, and east in the southern hemisphere), of used automobile tires rammed or compacted with 300-400 pounds of soil, and stacked, bricklike, to a height of 8 feet or so. The floor plan of an Earthship averages about 1700 square feet (SF) or 160 square meters (SM). Interior plumbing walls are traditionally-framed and the remaining walls are most often constructed of salvaged aluminum drink cans or glass bottles placed in concrete. The houses are large and feel organic in their form.

In most Earthships, there is a slanted glass greenhouse on the south face of the structure which opens to the main body of the house. Due to the overheating this causes, in the newest models, the greenhouse - which now has nearly vertical or true vertical windows - is separated from the main body of the house with a wall of windows and doors. The greenhouse hallway between the outside window wall and the interior window wall is used for growing plants and vegetables year-round and it is intended to perform the function of a solar thermal battery.

The metal panel roof collects rainwater and an underground piping system funnels it to cisterns usually located in the sloped earth berm behind the house on the north. The water is filtered and pressurized to provide running water for sinks, showers, and baths in a system called a Water Organizing Module. If the water is stored for long periods of time, it is treated to prevent microbial growth. Greywater from sinks and showers is cleaned via a grease trap and delivered to interior planters, and then to toilets. Water is then moved outside to a septic tank or a blackwater botanical waste treatment cell and then, if required by Code (most often it is), to a septic field.

In the Earthship concept, photovoltaic panels and/or small wind turbines store enough energy to supply all the houses' power needs. In principal, the Earthship's main heating source is the sun, captured via the greenhouse on the south face of the structure, and cooling is provided by natural ventilation. A berm on the north side of the structure is intended to provide thermal improvement, helping to maintain the Earthship at or near a comfortable inner-earth temperature near 58 degrees. A recent addition to the model - long vent tubes passing through the berm - are intended to bring fresh air into the structure to improve occupant comfort. These passively-inspired design techniques sometimes work, and sometimes do not... requiring additional heating and/or cooling depending on location... which we will explain in some detail in later sections.

Previous Page: Figure 2: Earthship Ceiling at Greater World

Figure 2. The Phoenix Earthship

According to the Earthship website and literature, Earthships are sustainable, use recycled materials, will work anywhere in the world, and will give us everything we need to survive. They also aim to be the most adaptable, affordable, fastest, and easiest to build building in the world, and they will give you the best resale value of any other options available.

However, if this was accurate, we would not be writing this book.

IT CAN BE SAID THAT THE PROS OF THE EARTHSHIP MODEL ARE:

- Energy efficiency: the buildings utilize solar and/or geothermal heat, cooling and hot water, and provide rain and greywater harvesting.
- Self-sustainability: you can grow veggies inside, use and reuse water, and minimize impact on the environment.
- Ease of construction: in principle, anyone can build an Earthship. If you can pound dirt, you can do it.
- "Recycling": some of the materials used come from waste products that would otherwise fill up a landfill, or are made from recycled materials.
- Natural light: these buildings have it in abundance.

Not all of these pros are as pro as they seem. In principle, when only these words are applied to them, they are pros. But as we come to learn more about what the underlying processes are, maybe not. What follows through the end of this chapter may be considered the Earthship's cons.

We should mention here that many of the titles that follow are in quotes. When that happens it is because we are quoting the various theories presented in the Earthship films, website, and literature. When you see something in italics, it is a direct quote from the listed source. Also, because this book is written from the point of view of a conversation between friends, we use the term "you" when what we are talking about is something we cannot help you with here, and "we" when it is something this book can help you with or is an approach we take in our offices. I use "I" when sharing something from my own life.

Please also note that because many of the Earthships are in Taos, we talk about the Taos climate in detail. We do that because we want to show you how the design works in this climate, so you know what to look for in your area. But we focus on helping out most… in the place we know best.

The Mythos

by Rachel Preston Prinz and Pratik Zaveri

MYTH·OS

Noun: *mythos*; plural noun: *mythoi*

1. myth or mythology.

    A set of beliefs or assumptions about something.

The term mythology used in reference to a type of building may seem surprising. But it is really not so far of a stretch. The Earthship is just that – a building ideal based on beliefs and assumptions that are passed on by the use of traditional storytelling elements.

Mike Reynolds and Earthship Biotecture have used traditional storytelling in the form of sharing both established and new myths to illustrate their story to their fans since the beginning of their efforts to birth Earthships into the world. These stories have become part of the mythos of Earthships worldwide.

Reynolds says in *Garbage Warrior* that his hero is the Biblical character Noah. This may explain why Earthship Volume 1 opens with the story of Noah and the Ark. In the relating of the story, the book talks about "the fact" that Noah saw the clouds before the great flood and knew he needed to build a ship before the coming deluge.

This is relevant, when we start to ask questions about how the Earthships work. Because, like the Noah story, the factuality of which has been debated since that story was written down hundreds and maybe even thousands of years after it happened, if it happened at all… what IS – how the Earthships work and if the buildings do what they aspire to – and the ideals they are inspired to make happen … are not yet in agreement.

But that is the beauty of inspiration: it leads to salvation. At least, in the Noah story it does. Hopefully, eventually, the Earthships and other sustainably designed buildings will help us to achieve a better lifestyle than that which we have been offered.

And that is the whole point of having an ideal, and a story, isn't it?

The Myth of "The Most Economical Building Design in the World... (which will) cost about the same as a conventional non-sustainable home..."

The Earthships are legendary for being ultra-affordable and doable by anyone, which is exactly what Mike Reynolds hoped they would be and this ideal... this story... is what gets passed on from each generation to the next. The issue is that the data does not fully support the noble idea that adopters of this technology wanted to be true.

There is no way around this but to face it: Earthships are one of the most expensive, most labor-intensive, most technologically demanding, and time-consuming structures out there. They are also not as sustainable as they are reported to be, which we will go into further detail about throughout this chapter. The Earthships of today cost $225+ per square foot (PSF). This is confirmed in a 2007 study by researchers Kruis and Heun (see Chapter 2 for details about this study), which found that the cost to build an off-grid Earthship at that time averaged $162 PSF, a grid-tied Earthship averaged $107.50 PSF, and a standard stick-frame home cost $97.75 PSF. Adding in 7 years of inflation brings those numbers close to the $225 mark of today's builds. Several designer/builders have confirmed that their Earthships cost around $200 PSF. This data belies the assertion that the Earthships "cost about the same as a conventional home", since a conventional home costs from 1/2 to 2/3 of that depending on the techniques used.

The cost myth is further exacerbated by other means as well. While tires, glass bottles, and aluminum cans may be "free"... the plans and permits, excavation, tools, concrete, wood framing and vigas, roofing, cooling tubes, insulation and thermal wrap, cisterns, interior finishes, glazing for two walls of windows, shades, glass doors, appliances, and the systems... are not. Plus, nearly every piece of an Earthship is custom-fabricated and therefore comes with the delays of custom construction and often, a higher cost. If you are a do-it-yourselfer, this can be OK, but if you are paying for labor and you are on a budget... maybe not so much.

REALITY CHECK: BASE COSTS OF AN EARTHSHIP

When we ran the numbers on a Global Model 3 bedroom Earthship, and then compared them to build budgets from our research, the base price for an unfinished building was $179,000 in U.S. dollars.

Excavation	$ 20,000
Tools	$ 5,000
Roofing	$ 35,000
Concrete & Rebar	$ 17,000
Front wall framing + Windows	$ 20,000
Cooling tubes	$ 5,000
Cisterns	$ 7,000
Thermal wrap and poly sheets	$ 10,000
Systems Package	$ 60,000
	$ 179,000

While these base prices may seem high, and they are... many homes need these items. Building a home costs money, no matter how you go about it. Some homes cost more than others. The off-grid Earthship is one such home.

The cost issue is even further exacerbated because "early adopters" of any technology often pave the way for future builders. It can be quite expensive for the early adopter to test an idea, as they have to become a scientist: they first devise a theory – the design and plans – and then find the funding to prove the system works. Even strawbale construction, which has been around for a very long time, has only recently been accepted for use in seismic zones. This approval only came once full scale structural testing of the system had proven it to work. The change came from people taking a chance and building and then testing the system to prove it could withstand the loads. The good news is, in leading the charge for more sustainable and natural design, we improve the chances for others to get to use what we prove works.

We offer these initial costs considerations here because budgeting data for Earthships, overall, is pretty lacking or outright avoided, which might explain why so many builds run over budget. These cost considerations are also why we decided to cover building types in this book that are a bit more expensive and/or a bit more "out there". If you are going to spend this amount of money, you should get exactly the kind of home you want.

So let's address some of the cost aspects of the materials typical to Earthship builds...

LAND

One of the factors that people often miss when planning a build is the cost of the land. The Earthship has a huge footprint of up to 3,500 square feet including the berm (this high density per square foot ratio is part of what makes it non-sustainable) which means you really need an acre to place it on. Land can cost anywhere from $5,000 to $100,000 an acre depending on where you build. To combat this, many have made the mistake of buying cheap land for their building, but cheap land usually is not ideal for settlement. We will cover why this is a bad investment and what makes an ideal build location in Chapter 4.

TIRES

An average Earthship requires about 900 tires for its back wall. But those tires are most likely not located on your building site. Or within 10 miles of your building site. Because, most likely, you are going to be "out there" where it is still okay to do experimental architecture. To get the tires to your site, you will need to make time to go select them out of a tire dump, which can take 20 hours or more, and then transport them the however many miles between the dump and your land. One option would be to get them all in one load on an 18-wheeler, which can carry 800 tires. But there are road access issues to address, rental and fuel costs, and driver hire issues with that. So, let's look at a more practical option... you can get up to 50 tires piled and tied into the bed of a standard pickup truck and get it done in 16 loads. (PS Have you budgeted to sell your fuel-efficient hybrid and get a pickup truck?) How much mpg does the truck get? What is that cost per load? Times 16 loads? According to the EPA report, "Scrap Tires: Handbook on Recycling Applications and Management for the U.S. and Mexico" from December 2010, the cost of transporting one tire in an average 25 mile haul (12.5 miles each way) is nearly $0.50. Multiply that by 900 tires and we have a fuel cost of $450 for tires. A horse trailer would be another great option for this work. Know someone who has one you can borrow?

There is a lot of debate on whether the tires are a good idea or not because of potential off-gassing of dangerous chemicals. To learn more about this debate, see Tires and the Off-gassing Issue and Chapter 2.

CANS

The average number of uncrushed soda and beer cans used in an Earthship is 10,000. You can drink all that yourselves, but it comes at a price - buying the drinks - which you may well do for a two year build using volunteers. But you can get creative too! One of the most ingenious ways we have heard of is from a renowned Earthship build in Canada. Manitoba Earthship Project partnered with the Winnipeg Folk Festival to collect the cans from the recycling bins at the festival! That garnered them more 12,000 cans in one week. However you get the cans, if you do not get them delivered, you need to get them to the site. If you pack them well, you can get 4,000 cans in the bed of a pickup truck. That is three loads, for planning purposes. Then, you want to budget time and water for washing them out so the house does not reek of beer and soda or attract pests.

GLASS BOTTLES

You will need 2,000 bottles to make the standard 1,000 bottle bricks for the beautiful bottle walls. Those easily fit in one truckload if you pack them tightly and organized like a honeycomb. More likely, however, you will do it in several less organized truckloads as you are able to go to the recycle center and sort them. Predict three loads minimum for that. Plan 2 hours for sorting and bagging per load. You will want to plan for enough water and cleaning time to get these cleaned up as well. An easy way of getting all the bottles you need in one day might be to partner with a local wine festival and take all their empties. You might not get the colors you want, but you will get a lot of bottles quickly. Like with the cans, the number of loads and gas required to bring them back to your site will depend on the vehicle used and distance traveled.

CEMENT AND CONCRETE

We did a takeoff off of plans for a Global Model Earthship to help budget for cement and concrete costs. Contrary to popular belief, concrete makes up the majority of the materials used in the build. Here is the overview of how much concrete might be needed: (Please note that haul numbers do not include sand or aggregate.)

GLOBAL MODEL CONCRETE TAKEOFF

	# Bedrooms (without vestibules)			
	Studio	One	Two	Three
Interior Footings	0.68	1.13	1.58	2.70
Can Walls	1.71	1.71	6.84	15.40
Front Face Footing	2.39	3.66	4.00	5.79
Stem Walls	0.40	0.40	0.27	0.50
Exterior Footing at Doors	0.37	0.37	0.37	0.37
Bond Beams	4.07	4.95	5.18	6.42
Buttress & Footing	1.31	2.43	1.97	2.35
Cubic yards required	10.92	14.65	20.20	33.53
concrete truck loads at 8 CY/truck (or # of logical pours)=	3	3	4	5
or, Bags of cement at 90 lbs. each = x lbs.	66	88	121	201
to move to site	5897.88	7912.62	10909.08	18104.58
x 1,000 lbs. per truckload = # of hauls	6	8	11	18

HIDDEN COSTS

One thing we noticed in the research – mileage and time is not included in the budgets for most builds. Now add volunteer's driving time and mileage, plus the mileage for family and friends who help, inspectors, and near daily trips to the hardware store or into town for more water. Fuel costs and time involved are real hidden costs that can make or break a project. When added to the cost of feeding, watering, and insuring volunteers, these hidden costs can derail a build.

ADDITIONAL COSTS TO PLAN IN ADVANCE FOR:

- Propane costs for cooking, clothes drying, space heating, and on-demand water heating.
- Backup water supply.
- Backup power supply.
- Re-mudding the earth plaster each year.
- Re-staining or oiling the exterior wood each year.
- Periodic septic cleanouts.
- Periodic cistern cleanouts.
- PV battery banks should be replaced every 15 years.
- PV panels should be replaced every 25 years

EMOTIONAL COSTS

One of the negative factors that came up repeatedly in our research is the emotional cost of building an Earthship. A build can negatively impact a person's: sense of privacy, financial stress, employment, physical state, happiness, and sense of comfort and safety. A build can also have an impact on a person's relationships with people in general, and their relationship with their spouse in particular. This is something to consider for those who might want to build a home inspired by the Earthship model, especially for those who may be especially sensitive to these energies and emotions.

There is more to discuss about the affordability equation and it deals with more of the legends around the Earthships. Bear with us as we try and explain...

The Myth of "A Radically Sustainable Home Made of Recycled and Natural Materials…"

by Rachel Preston Prinz and Carrie Christopher

Just because it is organic in form does not mean it is natural.

The Earthship literature states that 45% of a typical Earthship is made from recyclable materials. That means; a) that 45% of the materials used are removed from the recycling stream where they would be used until they cannot be used anymore, and; b) that 55% of what constitutes the Earthship is virgin material, which must be harvested, mined, manufactured, and/or transported to the site.

Only the soil used in the berm and the earth plasters, framing, and vigas are natural. The roofing, thermal protection and rigid insulation, gutters and downspouts, EPDM, aluminum cans, plumbing, wiring, glass bottles, tires, cisterns, cooling tubes, tools, concrete, glazing for two walls of windows, window shades, glass doors, appliances, rebar, and the mechanical and plumbing system are not natural. Of these, the concrete, plumbing, and windows can amount to twice the number of those materials used in a traditional stick-built home.

Figure 3. Earthship bottle brick build site

Looking at the natural angle a bit deeper, the modern Earthship relies heavily on the use of concrete, which has been documented as contributing between 5% and 10% of the world's greenhouse gases. Concrete also removes oxygen from the air we breathe as it cures over its life. This can be a real issue if we have breathing issues or allergies.

In some ways, Earthships are even more polluting than other building types. They introduce toxins to oftentimes virgin land, are generally junkyards during construction, and they remove materials from the recycling stream.

We have to be careful in how we talk about the Earthships, or any other building type. Using wishful thinking, passing on legends that are not true, and using buzzwords people have an emotional reaction to in order to trigger a belief that these buildings are recycled and natural… does not lead to better or more sustainable design. It does, however, lead to frustration for would-be builders.

We point these issues out only because we want to help address the real concerns that people have.

The Myth of Earthships and Recycling

by Rachel Preston Prinz, Pratik Zaveri, Asha Stout, and Carrie Christopher

Nature operates on the principles of zero waste. Trees make flowers and fruit in order to germinate and grow new versions of themselves and keep growing. Excesses of flowers and fruits are consumed by other species - they fall on the ground, decompose, feed various organisms and microorganisms, and enrich the soil. Animals and insects exhale carbon dioxide, which plants take in and use for their own growth, and then the plants release oxygen which helps us and the animals and insects with our own survival. Nitrogen from plant waste is transformed into protein by microorganisms, animals, and other plants. This continuous cycle is a symbiotic relationship: they feed us and we feed them.

The Earth's major nutrients—carbon, hydrogen, oxygen, and nitrogen—are CYCLED and, then, once they are used and discarded to be used again, RECYCLED. Industry altered the natural equilibrium of the planet. We took substances from the Earth's crust and concentrated, altered, and synthesized them into vast quantities of modified materials that cannot safely be returned to the soil or to the earth's original biological cycle because they are no longer made up of the primary constituents of life. We have to think of another way to make use of these used materials.

So when we want to talk about true sustainability, we begin with the familiar "Reduce, Reuse, Recycle" philosophy. First, we REDUCE our use of materials insofar as we are able. Some people would say that having an exterior and interior window wall, as is common in the newest Earthships, is a violation of the REDUCE principle. These walls are not necessary. You can have the greenhouse via other means - like a stand-alone greenhouse that can be built of all recycled or reused materials. Another way we can reduce our footprint is to literally reduce our footprint. The Phoenix Earthship, for instance, has a total area of about 5,400 square feet, of which about half is unusable because the space is devoted to greenhouse and mechanical rooms. A 5,400 SF house is not sustainable, especially when only half of it is usable. Is it really necessary? Well, that is up to you.

RECYCLING is the process where used materials are remanufactured into new products by taking the material, breaking it down, and then using its raw ingredients to build something new. This prevents the waste of useful materials, reduces the consumption of virgin materials, lowers energy use, decreases air and water pollution, and lowers gas emissions.

Downcycling converts used materials into products of lesser quality and reduced functionality. Making rags from old clothes and using cardboard boxes as packing or insulating material are examples of downcycling.

Upcycling, or returning the used materials into original raw form and reworking them into new forms, is what happens when we recycle aluminum and glass. Aluminum is melted down and made into new cans, saving over 90% of the energy required to make new ones from scratch. Glass works in the same way. This cycle can continue in perpetuity. Upcycling reduces the amount of waste that we produce and reduces the need for new virgin material to be mined, fabricated, or harvested. In the case of plastic, this means fewer oil wells drilled. For metals, fewer mountains mined. For paper, fewer trees felled. All around, this means less expended, or embodied, energy. The goal of upcycling is to prevent wasting potentially useful materials by making use of existing ones.

REUSE takes a used item and reuses it, rather than putting it into the waste stream. This helps in exploiting the full potential of a material before it is discarded. So, as in the case of the tires, bottles, and cans used in Earthships, we are REUSING them, not recycling them, because we use the intact item as filler for the walls. None of those materials are going back into the production cycle; they are just making the recycling chain longer.

The Myth of "The Most Efficient, Easy to Build Construction Method on the Planet"

Earthships require extraordinary amounts of time, patience, self-education, and physical labor to build. One builder noted that he could tell if people were "real prospects" to build an Earthship by testing them on a build site. He said, "I just let 'em pound one tire full. It takes 3 wheelbarrows of dirt and a good pounding, and the first time they do one, it can take up to two hours that will rock their entire body. If they are standing at the end of it, they might be a candidate for building their own." How many would-be builders are really prepared for this? Several of the people we interviewed ended up injured from all that pounding. There is a price for that, too.

While Earthships might be "easy to build", there is no promise of producing a well-built result. This is an issue inherent in using unskilled labor, no matter what the building project type. People who have never built anything will not know what not to do. This can turn your home into a giant craft project. That might be okay for the hidden stuff, but what if you really care about your home being well-built and beautifully so? Several builders in our research noted that even with years of experience in constructing other types of buildings, the Earthship proved to be a monster project to both manage and learn the techniques for.

The most concerning part of the "most efficient" issue is that the time needed for building the home is either devoted to, or sacrificed from, daily activities. If you are not independently wealthy and require a source of income, you have to sacrifice your time to build a home (which can be a full-time job in itself); in addition to having a job to make the money to pay for the home you are building. When this happens, the sustainability of the process comes into question.

Sometimes we need help – an expert – to get things built. But it is difficult to find an expert in Earthship building who can provide the help you need and that you can afford. We heard time and again... a lack of professional assistance can totally derail a project for unseasoned builders.

THE ABANDONMENT PHENOMENON

Figure 4. Abandoned build in Taos.

Nearly a third of the people who contacted us after hearing about this project wanted us to share that they had given up on their Earthship dream, sometimes in mid-build. They felt like they had lost time, money, and even faith from their Earthship experience. Some had been injured. Some ran out of money. Others ran out of patience for trying to train building inspectors in something they barely understood themselves. Others could not figure out the systems, which, as one interviewee commented "required German language knowledge or an engineering degree to make work." Still others gave up because other teams wanting to build Earthships in their area had failed to obtain permission. The most disheartening part was that the prospective builders who were forced to quit seemed depressed and demoralized by the experience. Once we knew to look for it, this sentiment was quietly echoed in the message boards and forums. Several sources in our research commented that people they knew had spent years pouring every penny and thousands of hours of sweat equity into their Earthship, and when the project was finally complete... they lived in them for a while and then sold their home at a loss just to "get out from under it."

The Myth of Build-Out Time

While the legend is that an Earthship can be built in a few weeks, that does not seem to be most people's experience. Most often, builder-led projects take from a few weeks to 2 months. When doing it on your own, an Earthship can easily take 2 years to build.

The design and permitting process can also take years - first, learning for yourselves, then training the local code enforcement officials. With planning and permitting, a build can as long as 5 years. Are you ready for a multi-year camping adventure? Can you afford a hotel/rental for that time? Regardless of HOW you do it, you need a plan as well as cash flow to pull it off.

The Myth of "Will Perform as Expected in Any Part of the World, in Any Climate" or, Reality Check: There is no such thing as a Global Model

We love the idea of a convenient one-size-fits-all approach to design. However, the Global Model promise is one that fails to deliver, in Earthships, and an every other kind of architecture. The reality is: Not every building works in every climate. There is a thousand years of architectural and archaeological evidence in New Mexico that backs up this fact, and tens of thousands of years of evidence from around the world. Cultures migrated and modified their own home designs as they went. They did not do so because they were trying to be stylish or to merge with the new culture. They adapted to the new conditions because they needed to stay warm in winter and cool in summer. The only things they had to work with were natural forces like the sun and physics (gravity, thermal and liquid dynamics, etc.), the materials and tools they had available to them, and history. It was anything but convenient to have to adjust, but they did, because they needed to in order to survive.

Let's try an exercise. We are going to give you a new religion. We will not tell you what religion it is, but it is not from here, and we do not care what you were brought up as. We just want you to start being that religion, today. OK? Ready Set Go! What? You do not love that idea? Good, because we are not going to ask you to do anything of the sort because it is preposterous. It is, however, a decent metaphor to illustrate just how absurd the concept of a Global Model of design is for architecture. Many of the underlying reasons why a Global Model is infeasible are the same as why we cannot adopt a new religion from somewhere else around the world on a whim.

First, there are cultural concerns. People around the world are building on traditions that have been developed over 10,000 years of their own settlement and technology patterns. They would be wise to be reticent to adopt a new building technology that is not proven, culturally appropriate, or technologically feasible. I think back on several projects I have worked on where sophisticated technology-based systems like water filtration systems, have been donated to worthy charities in third world countries. At first, wow! How they changed things for the better! New school uniforms were purchased from the proceeds from the sales of purified water, and a bustling business was born. But, then, a tiny plastic part broke. Suddenly, that awesome system turned into an expensive piece of wall art because the people who were gifted the technology did not have the knowledge, parts, access to alternatives, or technical know-how to repair it.

Another great example to technological appropriateness in design came for me on a project I worked on in Peru. A non-profit organization wanted to build a 20,000 square foot multi-level concrete building and ceremonial space in a jungle that is only accessible by a 2 hour powered canoe ride. I kept asking, "How are you planning on building that?" knowing that cranes and a pump truck would be required. Someone would justify how it could happen using experimental technology that was not available in Peru. We could always have tried - spending huge amounts of money and effort to buy and ship the systems there and experiment with making it work. Finally I quit the project because I realized that my approach to design was too "traditional" and it would be an uphill battle to go simple within the context of these very big dreams. I stayed in touch, however, because I love the organization's work. A year or so ago, I received a newsletter that announced they had finally built their facility in the jungle. When it came down to it, they built a 1,500 square foot building out of local materials and that was built by locals. However, it took them 2 years to break away from the big idea and back to something that truly worked for its place. The best news of all (for me) was that humble little building supported local crafts, culture, economies, and because of all that – it was both affordable and easily maintainable. That was good design. And it was sustainable.

Climate is another important criteria for why there can be no Global Model of architecture. There are different climates around the world and different microclimates within those climates. While ideas that work in Iran may a great place to start for ideas what might work in New Mexico, because they share similar climates, the wind directions, snowfall and rain amounts, soil types, and geography play important roles in differentiating how the designs perform. We can see this illustrated quite easily. In New Mexico, where many presume we are "all in the same climate", there are actually 6 diverse bioregions that have different water, climate, agricultural, soil, and architectural properties. The architectural systems especially cannot be made to "fit" in all these regions. In the flat and hot desert, our traditional adobe homes with flat roofs placed directly on the ground are ideal. But in the mountainous regions, they utilize small easy-to-heat log buildings on sturdy foundations that elevate the homes out of the snow in winter. To ignore the sun or landscape is to risk overheating and/or water infiltration.

Figure 4. REACH Homes

Few Earthships seem to place an emphasis on site selection for anything other than solar access and views. In one example of how this can go wrong, several Earthships were built at the Rural Earthship Alternative Community Habitat (REACH) near the Taos Ski Valley. The REACH community, despite the assertion otherwise in *Garbage Warrior*, is not entirely a success. Some of the Earthships at REACH are only used by the interns at Earthship Biotecture or as rentals during summer. Most often, the people staying there have no idea there are issues with these buildings because they are so happy to be part of the movement and living in the beautiful spaces with the stunning views in the summertime when the site is accessible. They most often do not recognize that those buildings are available to them for a reason – the spaces do not work for homebuyers. Homes in this prestigious area can sell for $300,000 or more – an expensive dorm room indeed! But the builders did not follow some basic but necessary design principles and thus, the buildings were difficult to sell. Not everyone wants to climb stairs in the dark to get into bed, to be colder than comfortable in winter, overheated in summer, or to go down a dark set of stairs into their closet. Or to listen to your neighbor's conversations because the site acts like a natural amphitheater and the houses are placed too close together. Or have to abandon their essential veggie growing planters because their cat will not stop using them as a litterbox. Or to use the wench on their 4WD to drag themselves up an impassable snowboarding-worthy hill in the winter. REACH is an experimental dream that did not end up manifesting so well. Once it was removed from the Taos Plateau to a hillside just a few miles away from the original Greater World development, the weaknesses in the one-size-fits-all approach of the Earthship concept began to be revealed. Some of the issues were due to limited design understanding and poorly designed building details by novice builders, and some were due to the unique mountain climate and landscape that the design was not modified to respond to.

This is just one close example of how even small microclimatic variations can undermine the performance of a building. With every mile traveled away from Greater World, these issues become more challenging and more important to resolve. Once we get into the hot/humid regions, the idea implodes, and not just for Earthships. Buildings that work well in the high arid desert do not work well near the equator. Earthship Biotecture will go into areas hit by natural disasters to help them out by quickly building micro Earthships to try and assist in the rebuilding efforts. That is an awesome thing to do. The people in those areas need help now and they can assist, as well as attempt to work the Global aspect of their design out by modifying it for tropical climates. The only issue is that observers and users of these facilities report that the tropical models have issues, including lack of humidity control, lack of ventilation, poor lighting, wind channeling, mold, darkness, and worst of all... acting as a reservoir to capture hurricane water while shedding hurricane winds.

We need to utilize architectural tools here in New Mexico that you may not need where you are. In his article "Earthship Hype and Earthship Reality" on GreenBuildingAdvisor.com, building expert Martin Holladay points out that while a cistern may be required in New Mexico where we struggle to have enough water, a place like New England may not need the cistern because of the natural wetness of the climate and the predominance of springs and wells. Issues like this are why we need to pay attention to climate and not blindly follow the standard design when that standard does not work FOR us.

There are specific issues in the design of the Global Model Earthships. There are Code-compliance issues of not having a means of egress from every bedroom without passing through a secondary space. The new earth vents can render the berm dysfunctional and are, in some locations, wrought with snow, mold, and maintenance issues. The cisterns diminish the earth-sheltering benefits of the berm. Hidden hallways and an uninhabitable greenhouse account for an average of 50% of the space being unusable. Openings in the south wall in the living room render the greenhouse part of the space and thus create humidity and overheating issues which can rot furniture. This causes a demand for additional ventilation. The over-sizing of rooms and under-sizing of functional spaces, and the inclusion of the mechanical room and all of its noise and heat as part of the main body of the house are yet more design challenges faced by Earthship dwellers. We can do better.

The overwhelming evidence does not support a global model of design... and it is not a bias towards Earthships... neither Earthships nor any other building type works for everybody in every place. Evidently, Earthship Europe agrees, based on this quote from their website,

> *"...concerning the Global Model (one model for everywhere) I can only say:*
> *'Would you built an igloo in the desert?'"*

Earthship Europe has modified the designs extensively to make them work for European climates, and their spinoff Flagship Europe has walked away from the Earthship concept entirely. That is one way that we can know if Earthships or any other new build type works in an area. We can ask how many more got built after the first one. And, if they changed things, what got changed? In many cases, Earthships are modified heavily so they perform adequately, often at great expense and over a long period of time. That fact is not advertised, or for that matter... even acknowledged.

The most important factor we can suggest for those who really love this idea and want to make it work is to study everything you can about the vernacular architecture in the place you want to live. Visit every historic or archaeological site you can. Learn from these buildings and their relationship to their place, and adapt the design of your home to fit the area's climate and existing building traditions. Then, think small. Design only what is needed for space, and then plan ahead for additions to make them easy. The Earthship firms will not guarantee that anything they design for you will be permitable, so you might as well tweak the design and make it work for you.

The Myth of "Will Provide You with What You Need to Survive..."

The Earthship greenhouse is not just designed to provide a space to collect natural heat and light from the sun. It is also intended to be used as a greenhouse for growing your own food. The plants in the greenhouse are fed by a greywater system that uses reclaimed shower and sink water to water the plants, which then clean the water for use in toilets later. That is a cool idea! In the Earthship literature and books, it is emphasized that that the Earthship greenhouse can grow "all the food you need to survive."

Figure 5. Greenhouses at the Greater World Visitor's Center, The Phoenix, and most people's homes...

Of the people whose Earthships we surveyed, who we interviewed, who commented on blogs or forums, or who answered our surveys... none were able to corroborate this ideal. Certainly the greenhouses can provide some food. But, the people we spoke to said that they could not grow their own food in sufficient supply to say they were provided all they need. They used grocery stores, farmers markets, or CSAs as their primary source of food. The Earthship greenhouse served as a supplemental resource, and only seasonally, in many cases.

An architect who blogs anonymously was in the audience at one of the Earthship lectures in Australia. Afterwards, he reported in his blog that he struggled with the lifestyle and thermal performance data presented, as the presentations implied the information presented was an "undisputed truth" when in fact some of the data presented showed clearly that there were issues with performance. But, people would have to know what to look for in order to determine what parts were concerning. (This is why we attempt to explain the width and breadth of the research in Chapter 2.) He went on to question if the fish or water plants in the pond systems used for aquaponics were edible. He then calculated that in order to eat fish in the recommended dietary amounts of three times a week, you would need to harvest at least 12 fish each month. Clearly that would require a large and sophisticated system, which would put this ideal out of reach for the scale and budget of most Earthships.

This vision of providing all we need through maximizing the value of our space is awesome. We get it. We do. But it does not seem possible to produce enough food working at the scale of a single Earthship to meet this ideal.

According to the research completed by Kruis and Heun in 2007, a family of four living in an Earthship would require 98 gallons (370L) of water per day, or 37,500 gallons (135,000L) of water per year. They identified in their research that the water requirement was totally achievable in a wet place like Michigan, but those quantities could not be achieved in Hawaii, New Mexico, or Alaska. This corroborates our experience in Taos where most of the Earthship owners we know have to buy water. This makes a backup dependable water supply essential for many locations.

The Myth of Thermal Comfort

In the "Earthship 101" slide presentation, the second slide says, "Imagine... living in a home that cost you nothing to heat or cool..." The problem with this statement is that it is wishful thinking. The base water and power systems required to run Earthships cost $60,000. Systems for heating, cooling, humidity control, and ventilation are required in almost every circumstance, but they are omitted from the Earthship design and therefore budgeting, because the "Earthship controls its own temperatures." While this is an admirable ideal, it is not accurate, or even physically possible, which we will explain in some detail throughout this book. Regardless, a traditionally-built home's system for mechanical, electrical, and plumbing costs around $35,000. So in buying an Earthship systems package, the owner has paid a $25,000 premium to "pre-pay" for water and power. The problem is... an owner of a traditionally-built home will spend somewhere around $20,000 over the life of their home to buy water, gas, and electric from utility companies. That means an Earthship owner pays a $5,000 premium over and above what a regular grid-tied user will pay over the lifetime of their home, plus they still need backup heat, additional solar panels and batteries for some locations, as well as humidification controls and cooling in many locations. Furthermore, Earthships commonly use propane for domestic hot water, cooking, and supplementary heating, as well as some form of gas generators for backup power for cloudy days. These are not free and those costs are not factored into the vast majority of budgets.

Because Earthships are not designed for their specific climate, they tend to have hot and cold spots. The Earthship literature tells us that "the average temperature in an Earthship is 70 degrees." That sounds really comfortable, right? Except that temperature is based on an average of 365 days. The research and experience of many owners tells us that up to 70% of those days will include extended periods of over and under-heating - an Earthship is often hotter than comfortable between 10am and 7pm in summer and colder than comfortable between 7pm and 9am in winter.

PRINCIPLES OF A SOLAR OVEN – WHY EARTHSHIPS OVERHEAT

There is no other way to say it: Earthships, especially those with slanted glass and no overhangs, tend to overheat. Even in the winter. Many Earthship owners will say that even when it is -10°F outside and snow is blowing sideways in 40mph gusts, they will have to open up all the windows to cool their home off enough to be comfortable. That might be okay for a while. However, as we get older, or as our hands cannot crank windows and vents anymore, as we tire of stopping what we are doing to get up to open and close windows twice a day, or when we have to get snow off the windows when its freezing cold... this becomes a relevant maintenance issue.

A substantial amount of scientific research has been done on thermal performance of Earthships in varied American, Australian, and European climates. We will share some overviews of the findings by these researchers later in Chapter 2, but the consensus is that Earthships overheat as much as 9 months a year, depending on location. Earthships also under-heat in northern latitudes due to cloudy conditions, colder inner-earth temperatures, and the fact that earth-sheltering is designed to be used for passive *cooling*. That means supplementary ventilation, dehumidification, and/or heating need to be considered basic requirements for the Earthship to work. Most of the time, these additional systems are installed after the build, which can lead to unsightly additions that were not accounted for in budgeting. Acknowledging this early allows us to address these issues in the design phase, where we can make the intrusions fit beautifully into the home and plan for the financing to make it all work.

We know now why the buildings overheat, which is great because it means we can do something about it. Earthships, when they use slanted windows and no overhanging roof, are designed like solar ovens. The buildings are oriented to true south, and the slanted windows allow in too much sun. In the summer, the greenhouse can be stiflingly hot and humid. The heat is not quite as sweltering in winter, but neither is it comfortable. The temperature in the greenhouse can be "unbearable" as some owners have stated, swinging between 45°F and 95°F depending on the season. A shade cloth is often required on the greenhouse in the summer to prevent overheating. If we design this critical area correctly from the outset, we do not need that shade cloth and can avoid overheating.

Many early Earthships did not use wall insulation. This is a problem, even in Taos. Some builders these days are insulating their Earthships, and/or putting a line of insulation as a secondary wall 4 feet outside the tire walls. The extra insulation costs money, uses more unnatural and unsustainable resources, and takes more time to build. Plus, it is yet another system that can fail. The issues that cause the need for these extra materials can be addressed with good design that speaks to your climate.

In the winter, because there are not many windows in the north-side living spaces, the north ends of the rooms stay at or near earth temperature, which is around 58 degrees in Taos, but is much lower in other parts of the world. So you have to have a sweater in part of the house and then strip to your skivvies to pass through the greenhouse to another part of the house, where you will need your sweater again. We also know now that supplemental heat is needed in winter, especially in areas where it freezes. Earthship builders in cold climates who prefer comfortable indoor temperatures are likely to a) install floor and foundation insulation, and b) install a heating system. Foundation insulation is critical because the cold can seep up from the earth and make spaces uncomfortable for anyone not wearing socks and sometimes even insulated winter boots too. Radiant floors, wood stoves, fireplaces and furnaces are all common additions in colder-climate Earthships.

Even in the winter, non-vented Earthships with the greenhouse open to the living areas can be stiflingly hot. Supposedly, roof venting, and the new earth tubes (which are not able to be retrofitted) helps prevent overheating in the summer. However, this natural ventilation cooling technique only works in areas where humidification is of no concern. In humid or dry areas, we also need to supplement the tube and vent system with dehumidification (in humid areas) or humidification (in arid areas). Otherwise, in a humid environment, an Earthship will collect water along their interior wall surfaces, forming a vertical pool for molds and algaes to grow. This often occurs on the walls of the planting areas and edible plants end up being infected or overwatered. This is an epidemic issue among the many Earthship dwellers who do not live in an environment as arid as Taos.

This is why we discuss both active and passive thermal comfort strategies in this book.

The Myth of Performance: Known Issues in Earthships Worldwide

It seems that Earthships have been somewhat stymied in their evolution due to the assertion that because they are "experimental", they do not need to work. We believe you should have a home that does work. We want you to know that "better" is easily achievable if you approach the design armed with good information.

We know that there are issues from decades of documentation of problems at builds around the world, as well as from Earthship research. See "Earthship Research Overview in Plain English" in Chapter 2 for more on this.

Here is a summary of what has been documented as having gone wrong with some of the larger and more well-known builds around the world:

EARTHSHIP FIFE in Scotland had moisture issues because of using wet soil when filling the tires, which at the time was thought to improve compaction. This trapped moisture inside the building. Once it evaporated and moved out of the tires, the moisture led to rotting problems with the wood framing in the roof system.

Figure 6. Welcome Sign

The VALENCIA SPAIN EARTHSHIP is known to suffer from summer overheating. This was resolved by adding external block-out shades over the south-facing windows and utilizing shading over the skylights in summertime. The greywater system was modified - a typical retrofit in many Earthships. Removing the kitchen sink from the greywater system seemed to resolve smell issues. Modern Earthships use a grease trap to attempt to combat this issue, but commentary from people utilizing the new systems suggests that because of the regular and "gross" grease trap cleanouts required, removing the kitchen sink from the system is ideal.

EARTHSHIP ZWOLLE in the Netherlands was built on a concrete slab to accommodate a high water table, yet still had significant water infiltration issues. Another issue with the design was using a north entrance, which contributed to thermal performance issues, as well as unanticipated weather loading and impacts on the structure. The failure of thermal performance has led to the building being closed during winter. Due to high humidity in the Netherlands, moisture became a real issue as did mold. A lack of construction expertise in the build team has also contributed to cracking in the concrete around the tires, contributing to degradation of the building envelope, as well as moisture infiltration and thermal performance issues. There are also issues in the building's water catchment and filtration system, so these systems have been abandoned.

The STAR COMMUNITY lies at the end of eight miles of rugged unpaved roads nearly an hour from Taos. The community is so remote that many people will not even travel out there, let alone attempt to live that far out. People who have lived there will tell you this neighborhood is only really viable for a specific kind of person with a deeply self-reliant can-do attitude.

The Earthship built in 2007 in BRIGHTON, ENGLAND is a "cottage" of over 1300 square feet built for half a million dollars. The Brighton Earthship been studied extensively, and various remedies applied for its thermal performance issues, which include regular under-heating for extended periods, as well as periodic overheating. This Earthships' greenhouse does not extend the full width of the south façade. It appears that a lack of thermal insulation at the floor, which is applied over a chalk soil substrate, is contributing to continued coldness during the winter. Evidently thermal bridging is a substantive issue in this building. Thermal Bridging has been documented as an issue in other Earthships at higher latitudes, including EARTHSHIP GER in Switzerland. A case study performed by EcoOpenHouses.org on the Brighton Earthship notes several improvement suggestions which might be useful for our readers, including using compact fluorescents in lieu of the undersized LEDs; replacement of the wood pellet stove in favor of a multi-fuel type stove to offer more fuel options; replacement of the less-than-ideally functioning wind turbine with additional solar PV panels (at considerable expense); using lime plasters in lieu of cement in the walls; and using adequate insulation.

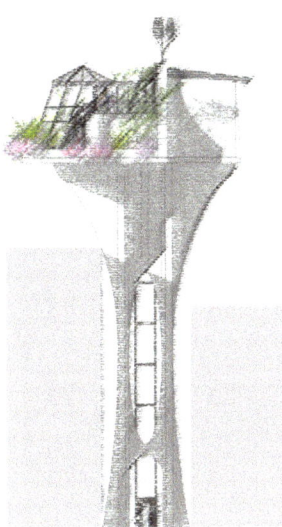

Figure 7. Earthship in the Sky sketch

One future product that we are compelled to address here is the EARTHSHIP IN THE SKY design for New York City. One of our pre-order readers sent the drawings for this Earthship to us and we promised we would talk about it, if only briefly, here. So here it is. Hoisted on a triumphantly arched concrete wedding cake topper, this fantasy Earthship requires more concrete for its base than many entire buildings. The design loses the berm, which makes it more of a concreteship than an Earthship, it will likely require OSHA compliance in the build which eliminates all those who would want to work on it unless they are certified for high-rise construction, and… it blocks out the light for neighboring buildings. This is illegal in many countries, as older buildings were designed to harness the light and heat of the sun. This Earthship raises itself above its neighbors and steals their sunlight and airspace, while also preventing the truly sustainable response to housing in a city where every square inch has value beyond measure. The sustainable thing to do here would be to house as many people and businesses as possible in the space below just as the neighboring buildings do.

The entry at the new Earthship Visitor's Center at GREATER WORLD COMMUNITY has its own issues, not the least of which is the incredible number of wooden materials used. The design of the framing structure on this building, as with most Earthships, means thermal bridges that invite cold air into the building. The huge number of pieces of bent wood used presents challenges of building and maintenance for the less-than-expert carpenter. The vestibule wall shades the entrance area from the sun, which is great in summer, but it also allows snow and ice to remain in winter. The benches are not deep enough to sit on for most people. Each piece of glass in this door and sidelight detail is hand-cut and comes with that time, maintenance, and cost. The water-stained wood on the interior of the skylight assemblies suggests there are water intrusion issues in this Earthship as well. The last and most frustrating issue for visitors is that it seems like no-one ever bothered to plan for how the space would be used. The greenhouse is a dead-end when the movie viewing room at the end of that corridor is being used for its intended purpose. More than once, we have had to direct guests to walk back around through the greenhouse, or to gently push them through the dark space while people were using it. This made our guests uncomfortable; several noted they felt as if they were "interrupting someone". The functional aspect of design… is exactly what we want to help you do better.

The Earthship that everyone wants to point to, to say "Hey look, these CAN work" is THE PHOENIX. It is gorgeous! It is also for sale, and you can make it yours for $1.5Million, or $277 per square foot. It has some of the most beautifully detailed work ever done on Earthships. This palatial Earthship has 1/3 of its 5,400 SF floor area devoted to food production. An 1,800 SF greenhouse that costs $277 per square foot is an expensive greenhouse, indeed – that adds up to $498,000! We cannot help but ask - will the amount of food it produces ever add up to a half a million dollars' worth, and thus justify the cost of this feature? Similarly to the awkward room arrangements at the visitor's center, the Phoenix has one bedroom big enough for a king and a full bed, and then another bedroom with a built-in headboard that results in a closet/office space behind the bed that is so squished and dark that a normal person cannot even use it. There is also limited privacy in the house as nearly every room, including the baths, has an open ceiling. Would someone really pay $1.5Million for a home that does not work for the way people live? Or that isn't comfortable? And affords no privacy? Or where half of the floor space isn't usable? We overheard someone say that they "had probably invested around $1.4 million in making the house work." If the Phoenix cannot achieve a high return on the huge investment that was made in it, what does that mean for yours?

The Myth of Custom Design

Not everyone wants to, or can, pay upwards of $50,000 for the fully custom design of their home. If we had the money to spend on exactly what we wanted, we likely would. But many of us cannot afford that, so we don't attempt to.

To offer a more affordable alternative, Earthship designers (Earthship Biotecture is not alone in this any longer) make standard plans available for sale that are essentially kits that you tweak in the same way as when buying a "custom home" in a suburban development. Maybe the plans are customized with your name and a few choices in materials or finishes, upgrades like a vestibule and that is it. These plans can cost up to $10,000 themselves.

Here is a list of available custom upgrades available as of this writing, and an explanation of what they are and do:

OPEN END

This essentially creates an enclosed quarter circle vestibule on one end of the greenhouse. This allows light in and expands the greenhouse capabilities, while helping to keep some of the dirt and dust and snow outside. This option adds functional square footage to the greenhouse for growing, but does not increase habitable space.

GARAGE

The garage in Earthships is constructed by the same means as the Earthship itself, often even utilizing vigas for the structure. This is an expensive addition due to the large vigas required to span the space, concrete for the floor, and the garage doors. Up to an additional 200 tires may be required. Additional heating may be required, and windows should be provided along the south and/or west walls if a greenhouse is not.

AIRLOCK / VAULTED ENTRY

In the old days, this was called a vestibule. Vestibules are used in climates where to want to offer a "buffer" between the inside and outside. Vestibules are a great design element for use on the west side of buildings in Taos. The reason being that the prominent wind direction in the summer is from the west, and that wind carries heated dust from Arizona across the desert and straight into your house. A vestibule traps some of that dust and cools the air before it gets inside. A vestibule is also a great idea when used as a mudroom in the primary entrance of the house. As designed, the vestibules available at this time are too small for that use. Make them a bit deeper, add shelves and hooks for storing tools and boots and coats, add a bench for taking off your snow or work boots, and enjoy the many benefits of this space.

The vaulted entry adds a sheltered vault to this vestibule. It is pretty and prevents some snow and ice buildup right at the door. It can have a detrimental effect on the amount of light coming into this end of the structure, so plan for an exterior outdoor light in the vault.

DUPLEX

An Earthship plan is mirrored down the middle to make one Earthship into two separate functional spaces.

SPLIT LEVEL

Split level Earthships work better when building on a sloping site, as long as you are and remain fully able. However, there are good reasons that split level houses were abandoned years ago – they make maintenance and regular cleaning harder; they require additional structure that is harder to build and more likely to require a structural engineer's or architect's stamp to get past permitting; they make carrying your baby and groceries and laundry and vacuum cleaner around the house more difficult; and they lead to injuries from people falling down stairs and steps. They are also not accessible unless you are perfectly abled and remain so – no twisted ankles, surgeries, broken bones, blindness, or wheelchairs allowed.

The "custom plan" option, being largely un-customizable, has left some people we talked to wondering what they were really getting for the many thousands of dollars they are paying for these plans, especially when those plans are not guaranteed to get permitted. The permitting issue is something that takes me aback a little, from working in the design profession for nearly 20 years now. If I designed a home for someone that they could not build, I would be taken to court and have the pants sued off me. The common response to this concern is, "The Earthship is an experiment." But if I put myself in the shoes of a potential buyer, I cannot help but to think "…but my life savings is not an experiment for someone else to make *for their cause, with my money.*"

One of the issues that people have mentioned to us regarding Earthship plans is that if you already have a plan set - if you bought a copy from a previous builder or bought stock plans - to get those plans modified is going to cost quite a bit. One of our sources shared that they were quoted an upfront cost of $150 per half hour for a phone consultation. If that is indeed true, that is an astronomical price. To assume that anyone can provide great service at that price point over the phone is to presume a lot. Further, that meeting does not promise any results. All you are buying is time. In architecture firms with some of the top architects in the country, for actual face-time with the lead architect, one might pay $200 per hour. Most architects and designers will come into a meeting with both of you knowing what the expected deliverables will be after that meeting. Progress will be made. That is why you meet. A phone consult with no end result does not sound like a good investment.

A good designer will help you to get you a home that you will love. That is part of the reason why we believe a buyer is better off to contact a regional architect rather than an Earthship designer to get your plans, especially if you want to use alternate materials. An architect or established residential designer will get you to plans that will work. That is their job. It can cost more but it works the first time. The expert gets to share their recognized wealth of knowledge to persuade the permitting authority that the system they are building with works. It takes all of the pressure off the client. That is how design is supposed to work. Plus, humans have been building earth-sheltered structures for 10,000 years. It is not like an Earthship designer has the market cornered on how to do great earth-sheltering.

We will attempt in later chapters to help you answer many of the questions a designer would and should answer, so that you can get the best design possible with or without professional help. The key is to know exactly what the designer needs to figure out in order to maximize the value of the time spent on your project. It is easy to dramatically cut a design budget just by minimizing the amount of preparation and research the designer has to do.

The Myth of Education

According to Wikipedia,

> *"A degree is a college or university diploma... which is usually awarded in recognition of the recipient having either satisfactorily completed a prescribed course of study or having conducted a scholarly endeavor deemed worthy of his or her admission to the degree. The most common degrees awarded today are Associate, Bachelors, Masters, and Doctoral degrees."*

The most basic degree, called a Bachelor's degree, consists of a course of study of 3 to 4 years. To call oneself "architecturally trained," one must have a 4 year degree at an accredited University and then also pursue an additional specialized course of study over an additional 2 years, towards a professional terminus degree usually known as a Master's of Architecture. Or, alternately, one must do the 5 year Bachelor's in Architecture that some colleges offer. At the minimum, an architecturally-trained designer will have spent 5 years of 50+ hour weeks studying their field. That is 12,500 hours of design study. To become eligible to be tested to become a licensed architect, another 5+ years of internship are required, often at 50+ hours a week for 50 weeks a year. That is another 12,500 hours of training. So the minimum for a new designer fresh out of school is 12,500 hours of experience, and the average for a well-trained architectural designer ready to take the exams and with some real experience is 25,000 experience hours.

Why, one might ask, is this relevant? The Earthship website states that there is no time limit for interns in obtaining their degree, which they get from attending the Earthship Academy, a $2,500 on-site building education program that requires a minimum of a month-long commitment.

The major issue here is that one cannot get a "degree" in 4 weeks. Even if super-students work extra diligently in such a program and stay on for say... 3 months... those graduates are coming out with MAYBE 600 hours of experience.

WHAT SOUNDS LIKE A BETTER INVESTMENT IN YOUR HOME DESIGN? HIRING A DESIGNER WITH 25,000 HOURS OF EXPERIENCE OR 200 HOURS?

The internship would be more accurately called a "workshop" or "certification." This issue is compounded by people who have completed the Earthship training and are calling themselves "degreed" in Biotecture - something that sounds a lot like Architecture. Except they are missing critical knowledge about the core components of good design: basic structures and systems, site orientation, landscape, thermal action, etcetera... Not that a degree is required to do good building, but call it a degree implies that the graduates have special knowledge, training, and/or experience - when they only have a workshop's worth. Would you let a person with one workshop worth of accounting manage your IRS audit? Probably not. So why would you let someone with one workshop's worth of Earthship training design your house?

I do not say this lightly. I am an architecturally-trained designer and researcher with 16 years (around 40,000 hours) of experience. I am not trying to protect that tiny piece of the pie that licensed architects are keen to keep me from feeding off of - the 2% of all buildings that licensed architects design. But I am fully trained, and was certified in 2006 to take the Architects Registration Exam. I believe that you should expect from a "degreed" designer more than a Biotecture graduate can possibly get in that speck of time. Architecturally-trained designers know how to protect your health, safety, and welfare; we understand climatic impacts on design; and we know when to call in a licensed architect and/or an engineer. Working with someone who knows about design is like medicine: you want the best trained designer you can find, just like you want the best doctor you can find.

We believe that the better solution for those who are looking to get a solid foundation in Earthships and other natural building techniques is to check out the UNM-Taos Green Technology Program, which offers University-level courses in CAD, Tiny Houses, Southwest Landscapes, Solar Design, Building Science, Wiring and Plumbing, Sustainable Systems, Solar Thermal and PV... in addition to the Earthship Design class taught by Earthship

Biotecture's own renowned expert Phil Basehart. The diversity of the UNM-Taos program will help you to be ready for many of the questions you may need to answer if you want to design yourself an Earthship-inspired home that diverges from traditional models.

There are specialized classes on natural building that would be a great asset on this journey as well. Some of them could easily be paired with a visit to Taos to check out the Greater World site or attend the workshop or visit UNM-Taos. We will talk about several of them in more depth in later chapters, but you might want to look into studying Earth Plaster with Carole Crews, or Cob and Strawbale Building with Sigi Koko, Adobe Making with Cornerstones Partnership, or Cordwood with Richard Flatau. Our friend Oliver Swann's Natural Homes website is the largest online natural building resource in the world, and he has a list of workshops that might be a bit closer to you. For those in or wanting to attend an accredited architecture program, I would recommend the sustainable design class at CU-Boulder where they come out to Lama Foundation north of Taos and design new modern style sustainable tiny-house inspired buildings. The buildings they design are extraordinary. Paired with Lama's training in permaculture, this opportunity offers an exceptional alternative for those who would love to see natural done in modern, design-oriented, ways.

The Myth of Getting it Built by People who are Willing to Pay

Asking people to pay for the opportunity to work on your home is one common way of attempting to raise money and feed and house volunteers. If you are really organized, then pay for the traditional Earthship training, and then pay for the insurance and food for the volunteers to come to your home and help build, this might be feasible for you. Do not get discouraged if volunteers are hard to find at the start, or if people want to help but cannot pay. Many people who have enough disposable income to pay will often go to Earthship Biotecture to get a certification. After some time, and some publicity of you project, hopefully more volunteers will come help. We will get more into planning for volunteers in the section Planning a Build: Managing Volunteers.

The Myth of "A Higher Resale Value."

A research study conducted by the website RealAssetsJunkie.com noted that the resale cost of an Earthship averages $191 per square foot (PSF). Being as the cost to build an Earthship starts at $225 PSF, this means that a builder stands to lose up to $34 PSF if they choose to resell their home. An average Global Model Earthship is 1,700 square feet, which results in:

COST TO BUILD	1700 X $225 =	$382,500
(-)RESALE VALUE	1700 X $191 =	$324,700
NET LOSS =		**$ 57,800**

To help address these issues, a great floor plan, an inviting home, and thus, great detailing, is required. Start with our section Secrets of Great Curb Appeal for more information about how to build a home people will pay more to buy.

The Myth of Awesome Community

Okay so maybe the title for this section isn't entirely fair. The vast majority of the Earthship owners we have met are good, hardworking, people. Some of them are a little idealistic and maybe are not as interested in the actualities as the ideals, but that is the kind of attitude that drives change and we appreciate that. We are idealists in our own way, daring to think that that our team can... and has a responsibility to... make good design the norm for The Other 98% (of people who cannot afford to hire an expert to design their dream home). So we are not throwing stones in our glass house here...

But when we hear about the issues of owning an Earthship... many of which center around privacy, safety, and protecting the sense of sanctuary people have worked so hard to create, well... then we think those realities are worth addressing.

We had heard tales around Taos of people coming up to Earthship windows and peering in at people as they painted, fed their kids, laid in bed naked and afraid to move... and of the constant hum of traffic along the Taos streets where the Earthships are clustered. I myself have done all those things, that is part of how I came to learn about the buildings. It never occurred to me that I was but one in a parade of people that invades Earthship owner's privacy day in and day out.

When we started researching for this book, we found the extensive and informative Darfield Earthship website, and it really began to gel for us that people who live in Earthships do not always get respected by would-be builders. In one of their many blogposts, Darfield's owners posted a photo that showed a whiteboard they had written a message on for stoppers-by. It says something to the effect of, "Yes, we love our house of bottles and cans, but we are an active family and do not always have time for visitors, so please do not come up to the house if the gate is closed. Please join us for one of our regular tours by signing up at our Facebook page. Please don't pee or poop or discard your little one's diapers or other junk in the driveway." And it goes on. Another post commented that one of their kids was just... done... with showing the house. It was just too much to constantly open their lives up to strangers. I think it is probably too much for most adults too. Definitely do yourself the favor and check out their website at http://www.darfieldearthship.com/ to find out more about the blessings and curses of a publicly-attractive build.

These sentiments of overwhelm and frustrations echoed across message boards and in our own research – people's homes and lives are being invaded. That is not cool.

So, for all the adventurers who are leading this charge and trying to find a way towards truly sustainable design: Please, if you want to go see the Earthships, or any other kind of experimental house type, do... but do it in places you are invited. Please do not invade people's privacy. Take a tour. If you find yourself in a place where you just cannot help yourself but to stop and take a photo, please do not litter, and please be quick about it and be on your way. Please be a respectful visitor. Thank you.

One other thing... one of the consistent comments we hear about Earthships, which are promoted as being pro-community... is that, as one neighbor put it to us, "They are pro their own community and they could care less about their neighbors". This is something worth thinking about when building your home. What are your values around that? How can we make this better?

"Just the Facts, Ma'am"

by Pratik Zaveri and Rachel Preston Prinz

One of the most difficult aspects of talking about the Earthships is addressing issues around the data presented as supporting evidence for the idea. The Earthship website and publications are a bit "fuzzy" and we want to clarify what we can so our readers can have solid information when making decisions regarding a potential Earthship home.

We call some of what happens in the Earthship books, website, and philosophy a "One-Way View." Without realizing it, the literature points to reasons to use the model… that actually point to problems with the model. We have touched on some of these already. Earthship Volume 1 and the Earthship website both talk about indigenous materials being available around the world and then go on to point out that shipping materials great distances uses a lot energy and is therefore not sustainable. This statement, while looking towards an ideal that we all really want to meet, fails to address the economic and energetic inputs required to obtain and transport the materials required to build an Earthship, as we identified in The Myth of "The Most Economical Building Design in the World" section. It forgets that Earthships require triple or quadruple the energetic inputs of a standard building. It only sees what it wants to see – the ideal. This is a perfect example of a "one-way view" and it is based on a concept called "cognitive anchoring". From Wikipedia:

> "Anchoring or focalism is a cognitive bias that describes the common human tendency to rely too heavily on the first piece of information offered (the "anchor") when making decisions. During decision-making, anchoring occurs when individuals use an initial piece of information to make subsequent judgments. Once an anchor is set, other judgments are made by adjusting away from that anchor, and there is a bias toward interpreting other information around the anchor. For example, the initial price offered for a used car sets the standard for the rest of the negotiations, so that prices lower than the initial price seem more reasonable even if they are still higher than what the car is really worth."

The many issues of not depending on traditional systems that the Earthship literature attempts to address are absolutely valid, as every day we seem to get nearer to an economic and cultural collapse that renders alternates not only ideal but necessary. However, the "better world" the Earthship ideal promises cannot be delivered through ideals and wishful thinking. It has to come from actions… and those actions need to be based on good science and good design.

Issues with the Data

UNDERLYING SCIENCE

Especially in Earthship Volume 1, solid science is used to understand the movement of the sun and other natural processes. Yet, some of the most important details that could help builders to make the design more successful are omitted. For instance, soil is mentioned only briefly, stating the Earthships "must be built on undisturbed earth", and yet, to build them, we disturb the earth. There is also no mention that thermal performance is degraded when the soil used in the berm is naturally wet, or that the Earthship needs extra design consideration when the inner-earth temperature is lower than that of Taos. This inner-earth temperature issue has led to critical issues in Earthships around the world.

Let's look at this a little more deeply.

The Earthship website points out that the Earthship's technology is based on the sun, the earth, and the efforts of the people themselves. That is sortof true. The passive solar aspects of the design and the photovoltaics use the sun. There is earth in the berm. People build the Earthships. Earthships also use a huge number of solar panels, batteries full of toxic acids, and countless manufactured goods, many of which have extremely high embodied energy equal to and even well beyond that of standard buildings. As well, sophisticated engineering skills are required to design, install, and maintain the Earthship so that the technologies can work. So the ideal is really based on simple natural AND complex manufactured processes.

AFFORDABILITY AND DO-ABILITY

The ideal is that the Earthship is financially accessible by the common person, but experience does not bear that out, as we have illustrated previously in The Myth of "The Most Economical Building Design in the World" section.

It is stated in the Earthship literature that the Earthships are specifically designed with the intent of being built by unskilled people. While the methods of construction may not necessarily require skill, they most definitely require ability. Pounding tires is not for the faint of heart and building angled walls is really only work for a master carpenter. This is one reason why you may really want to consider using Earthship Biotecture's teams to build your home if you can afford them - they are second to none in these skills.

PASSIVE SOLAR AND WIND ORIENTATION

The Earthship books stress the importance of orientation towards the sun, but neglect that orientation is only relevant when you live in a place with ample sunshine. Cloudy days, which are not mentioned at all, can render the Earthship just another failed building, as we will see in Chapter 2.

Earthship Volume 1 talks about facing the Earthship north in Taos. How would a north-facing design even work? It would be a snow magnet and would hold ice and snow against the house when it needs to be in the sun to melt! Sure, large north windows are not unusual in Taos… when the artists arrived they wanted that pure north light so they built huge windows facing north… but these were not used in Taos until the late 1800s, because in order to pull off a completely nature-ignorant design, you needed a large wood stove to compensate for the cold north wind. The books do not address this needed heat source. The book goes on to propose a roof garden, in an area with a 140 day growing season, high winds, and tendency for drought. This is not the recipe I would follow for a house in Taos. Evidently, they figured out not to do that as well, because the Taos Earthships face south and there are no rooftop gardens that we know of.

The wind diagrams in the book show wind coming from one direction, and it looks like it is usually assumed as from the south. The problem is… the wind in Taos comes from the North in winter and West in summer. Showing it coming from a direction it rarely does suggests that the ventilation will not work effectively. The research and commentaries from users indicates that this is accurate - many Earthships have ventilation issues, especially those where predominant winds come from less than ideal directions for the design. For the greenhouse's low awning windows to functionally draw air into the space and up through the skylight there has to be some wind pushing into and away from the building from the right directions to force enough draw.

MATERIALS OF CONSTRUCTION

The Earthship website's Construction Materials page talks about how for the vast majority of human existence, our homes were built of found indigenous materials including stone, earth, sticks, and grasses. That is true. But unlike tires, concrete, aluminum cans, and glass bottles… stone, earth, sticks, and grasses have extremely low embodied energy, as they can be found at just about any good potential building site. To add to that, the embodied energy of concrete, which makes up roughly half of the building materials used by volume in a modern Earthship's construction, is staggering. (Refer to the Concrete section for more information.) Concrete is not a by-product of our civilization. It is a mined product that rapes the environment and diminishes our ability to breathe.

Indigenous is typically understood to refer to locally-sourced, raw materials, or local peoples. Indigenous is the epitome of simplicity. Tires, concrete, bottles, and cans are not simple, nor are they indigenous to anyone's site that we know of. Shipping tires, concrete, cans, and bottles from wherever they are to your build site uses energy and removes these materials from the recycling stream. These misconceptions help to illustrate why Earthships are not truly sustainable.

The literature talks about wood being less than ideal as a durable material for building, as it is natural, lightweight, and porous, which will lead it to decompose quickly. The people of Bavaria, who have lived in some of their wooden houses for 400 years, may disagree with that. As would the builders of the Hōryū-ji temple pagoda in Japan, which still stands after the wood was felled in 594AD! That is nearly 1,500 years old! Wood can last a long time when it is felled at the correct time, is the right species for its use, and is well cared for over its life. And not all wood is light and porous. Generally, we use heavy and dense deciduous hardwoods on the exterior of a building and evergreen softwoods for interior framing. Plus, to be fair… Earthships use a boatload of wood.

The literature goes on to complain that manufactured materials dictate the way buildings are built, and then goes on to suggest that the reverse should be true, implying that housing should dictate the nature of materials. And yet the primary building block of an Earthship is the tire – a highly manufactured material.

EMBODIED ENERGY

What the Earthship literature offers as a means of explaining embodied energy is not a complete picture of what embodied energy is. Embodied energy is the amount of energy it takes to take a raw material, get it to a manufacturing site, manufacture the finished product, and then get it to you. Embodied energy can be high – aluminum, a common component of solar panel installations as well as an Earthship's can walls, contains an enormous amount of embodied energy – it has to be mined, to the tune of 8 tons of ore per 1 ton of usable material; shipped great distances for manufacturing; designed; then takes a great deal of heat to produce a usable product – which also means a great deal of fuel; then it must be shipped to a warehouse, to the supplier, and then to the build site. Whether that aluminum is in a reused can or a brand new window, it still had to have all of those processes applied to it. There IS embodied energy in an Earthship. Just because we are reusing the embodied energy required does not negate its existence. In fact, the reality here is that reusing cans in walls requires more materials to be mined and manufactured because the first-generation cans are being removed from the recycling stream.

The literature also states that one of the main goals of the Earthship ideal is to use materials that require little or no manufactured energy. And yet, the building blocks of Earthships… the tires, cans, bottles, concrete, wood framing and vigas, roofing, cooling tubes, insulation and thermal wrap, cisterns, interior finishes, glazing for two walls of windows, shades, glass doors, appliances, and the mechanical and plumbing systems… have manufactured or embodied energy… and lots of it.

The literature makes the case that the Earthship is using such simple materials that it makes sense for large-scale production for low-impact living. Except, large scale production of the currently extremely oversized Earthships is not sustainable. Earthships have gigantic footprints, in terms of the amount of land required to build on, as well as square footage, as well as embodied energy. They are also too expensive to be viable for large scale development.

RELIANCE ON "THE MACHINE"

The literature goes on to discuss the ideal of not relying on natural gas, but many Earthships at latitudes above and including Taos have been retrofitted with propane or gas to stay warm enough in winter.

The importance of not relying on modern food systems is discussed, yet the food growing system as designed most often cannot provide the quantity of food that makes self-reliance possible. What is offered is an extraordinarily expensive system that cannot provide in grocery savings what it adds in cost.

SYSTEMS

The literature speaks to the common house using "monstrous systems" and states that the modern house cannot function without systems. Reynolds likened the standard home and its large systems to being a patient in ICU being "plugged in" at a hospital: If the lines were cut, then what?

Yet, nothing is ever mentioned of the standard systems used in an Earthship, which deplete resources, cost a great deal at outset, are prohibitively complex to maintain and repair, and still do not work when something goes wrong. All of this costs money and resources. To compound that, backup heat and power are required in nearly every build because most Earthships do not work as intended. Systems are a reality for the vast majority of owners.

CARS

The literature goes on to discuss the Earthship in relation to a car, addressing the very real concern that reliance on cars is part of what is wrong with sustainability in our world. Yet, Earthships are often located out in the distant expanses and do not work as intended, forcing users to depend on a car far more than the average homeowner – to get materials, water, groceries, gas, to get the kids to school - and, because they are "out there" where it is legal to build experiments, oftentimes owners must travel further distances to do these things. My grocery store is 2 miles from my home. I travel four miles total to get down to the store and back. Greater World is 15 or so miles from the grocery store. That is 30 miles total. Even if we both only need a carton of milk, my cost and time investment is dramatically lower. Multiply that mileage times 40 trips to the store a year. Now multiple it by the number of trips into town you must make to get supplies, get water, take the kids back and forth to school...

SAVING THE RAINFORESTS AND OXYGEN

The literature notes that when we cut down the rainforests, we cut off our own oxygen supply. This is such an important issue and that fact cannot be argued. The first book goes on to imply that Earthships are minimizing the impact on deforestation to resolve this issue. However, Earthships use huge amounts of wood, which results in forests being cut down. Is this ideal really being met here?

Earthships also use as much or more concrete as that used in a traditionally constructed home. Concrete uses oxygen to cure over its life and it gets that oxygen from the air we breathe. The manufacture of the Portland cement used in concrete contributes to between 5 and 10% of the world's greenhouse gases.

So, in principle the Earthships are saving the rainforests, while in practice they are making them work harder.

IMPACTS ON THE WATER SYSTEM

The literature addresses the issues of the global water supply and its impact on the ecosystems that affect fish. This concern is justified, as we continue to poison our oceans with untold numbers of toxins. Yet, the leeching of the tires and the septic systems in an Earthship build has the potential to affect the health of the aquifers from which we all drink. A common admonishment in the professional and academic tire research is that the places we store tires are supposed to be isolated from any contact with the water supply via sealed EPDM pond liners.

THERMAL COMFORT

The commonly held belief that Earthships are comfortable is supported by the Earthship literature stating that the temperature ranges from 65-76 degrees with no backup heating or cooling. This is just not accurate, as we have described in the Myth of Thermal Comfort section.

The Thermal Mass section of the Earthship website states that a lightly-built house (presumably one without earth-sheltering) "obviously" takes more energy to heat and cool. Only, that is not accurate. A light house with good insulation and located in the right climate needs less heating and cooling than an Earthship.

LANDSCAPE

Landscaping is critical to great design, for important tasks like turning winds into breezes; turning sunlight into food energy and shade; and for minimizing the reflection of the sun off the ground. Yet, the only hints of how to address landscape that are provided in the literature are effectively "do not puncture the roof", "slope the berm away from the building", and "do not plant trees within 20 feet of the tire wall". But this makes the building more dependent on systems to perform and offers no advice on how to make these ideas work.

It is suggested that locating the building on a sloping site can keep water from the inside, but there is no guidance on proper site design for this. In fact, the Hut designs create major water ponding issues right at the front door. Positive drainage - the design of a site to shed water away from the building - is a challenging thing to do even for an architect or designer with lots of experience. We have spent days designing a site for positive drainage before. See our Landscape chapter for tips and tricks to resolve these issues.

There is a section about harnessing the power of natural springs, but no mention is made about how springs can become rivers with rainfall, or how water tables rise and fall though the moon's cycles. These are all manageable with good design.

EARTHQUAKES

The Earthship website talks about the Earthships in regard to Earthquakes. This section specifically addresses horizontal movement, and suggests using "rubbery" and resilient materials for building rather than brittle materials like concrete because they crack.

So, a little Earthquake 101 here: an earthquake's source, or epicenter, is always located along a geologic fault line. A well-known example is the San Andreas Fault in California. The fault line occurs where two tectonic plates meet. The plates are moving at different rates and different directions, basically grinding against each other along the fault line. But the fault line is not perfectly smooth, so the line 'holds' the plates from sliding against each other. When the forces along the fault line become greater than the ability of a part of the fault line to resist them ... boom! The energy is released explosively as an earthquake. The energy is released as waves through the earth, very much like a wave in the ocean. When the waves reach the surface of the earth, where your Earthship might be perched much like a ship on the sea, your Earthship (or any structure) is tossed horizontally *and vertically*. We generally think of buildings as static – they don't move about. When the earth moves beneath it, a building resists the movement. This is called inertia – put a salt shaker on a napkin and yank the napkin away – the bottom of the shaker is attached to the napkin and has to follow. But the rest of the shaker tries to stay where it was, and the shaker topples. The same thing happens to our buildings.

Earthquake-resistant buildings (anyone that tells you a building is earthquake-proof is uninformed or misleading) are generally both strong and resilient. Strong enough not to shatter under the earthquake forces, and resilient enough to "give" a little without breaking. It is a little counterintuitive, but it is that resiliency that usually helps buildings survive smaller earthquakes with little damage, and in a big earthquake, resiliency allows a building to bend rather than break, to tilt rather than topple, so people inside can get out.

The Earthship's interior walls and the buttresses for the back tire wall are concrete. So the brittle material argument is moot. As to the insinuation of the "rubbery" quality of the tires... once they are packed with earth, the wall acts more like concrete than rubber. So this is moot too.

WALLS

The Earthship books cover using wood for framing, but offer no clarification on the size or types of wood to use, or when it should be harvested.

The website suggests that the aluminum can walls are very strong. However, the strength of the walls is not achieved by the aluminum, but by the cement that holds the cans together. While aluminum itself is strong, in this application, it has a smooth surface. There is no way the bond between cement and metal is stronger than that of, say... porous bricks, to which the cement can bind at the pore level... and hence it is not as easy to build a truly strong wall by this means. Also, the way the walls are built requires you to crush the can a little, decreasing the amount of space that is taken up by the can, and requiring more cement.

ROOF

The roof design from Earthship Volume 1 is not well designed and uses a huge number of resources. Plus, roof framing should really follow the pitch of the roof for the best structural performance. Gutters should have a minimum slope so they work.

FLOORS

Earth floors are recommended, but earth floors only work in some climates and they do not always work for passive solar design, which needs to be modified for the installation type and climate. Many Earthships now use flagstone or brick flooring.

WINDOWS AND SKYLIGHTS

Awning windows at the base of the greenhouse against the ground can get buried in snow and cannot provide adequate ventilation unless they are cleared at every snowfall. That is a maintenance nightmare in cold climates, where some of our respondents noted that they had to remove snow as many as three times a day to insure adequate ventilation. There are some design issues with the standard skylight details too. They must be opened and closed by the occupant in order to regulate ventilation and solar heating. If left closed all day they can cause overheating, but if accidentally left open on cold nights they can vent too much heat. Both windows and skylights are also notorious for condensation problems. This often contributes to rot and mold issues.

MAINTENANCE

There is just no way around it: Maintenance-wise, Earthships are on par with any naturally-built building, if not more so. Day-to-day maintenance on an Earthship can easily be double or triple that of a traditionally-built building. Earthship systems also require specialized repairmen that charge a lot for their knowledge and are sometimes difficult to locate.

PETS AND KIDS

Your pets may not understand that the planters are not their personal litter box or entertainment center. Or that the cistern, if left open to the building, is not their swimming pool or bathtub. Sometimes, kids may be equally susceptible. (I know I would have been.)

PESTS

In the video *From the Ground Up*, there is a moment where we see someone using earth to plaster the wall and you can see bugs milling about in the plaster. That does not stop once the plaster dries. In fact, now the bugs have awesome places to build colonies - in the tires. You might as well prepare yourself early... centipedes, jerusalem crickets, moths, spiders, snakes, rats, mice... they will all be your friends in an Earthship. That is totally okay for some people. For others, it is a terrifying nightmare.

PRODUCTS OFFERED

The books, especially Earthship Volume 1, are woefully out of date. Some of the products offered, like the Dynasphere wind turbine, are investments in less than ideal technology (see our Wind Power section for an explanation why). There are other places to look for more up-to-date solutions, and the majority of them are free online. Check out our Resource Guide at the back of this book for books, websites, workshops, and connections.

The Tire Issue

The Earthships use tires based on the ideal that tires are a plentiful resource which can be used for building in order to keep them out of landfills. According to the EPA report, "Scrap Tires: Handbook on Recycling Applications and Management for the U.S. and Mexico," in one year's worth of calculations, 275 million tires were already stockpiled in the United States, and approximately 290 million new scrap tires were generated. There is a very real need to address this issue.

The problem with the tires is that many people are concerned about them off-gassing toxic fumes.

The Earthship literature talks about how many materials are unsafe and we often do not find out until it is too late. This is true. Yet, the very real health concerns which arise from the use of the tires are treated as if this topic is irrelevant and people are being ridiculous to ask for more information.

Because of some of the research we did several years ago when we first posted on our website about tire concerns, many fans will call our office to ask the question "Is there really an issue with off-gassing?" The answer is simply... we are not sure. We do not assert that we have smelled any vapors in the many Earthship homes we have visited. We have not. However, in addition to our role helping to design sustainable homes and communities, we are a historic preservation firm. We deal with lead-based paint and asbestos abatement in our day-to-day work. We are also aware of many people in modern times too whose cheap gypsum board walls imported from China made them sick. You cannot smell any of the contaminants in any of these applications. These products have been banned because they are toxic whether you can smell them or not. The price paid for that knowledge was tens of thousands of lives, because they did not test the materials before approving them for use in construction. We do not want to see anyone repeat those same mistakes, least of all... you.

The Earthship website has an article that attempts to assuage concerns with a transcription of a front page of a scientific report that offers "proof" that tires are not an issue. Outside of the report's commentary being disturbingly unprofessional, it should also be noted that this report is from 1995. To accurately state their position, the "40 years of research and development" should read "the 20 year old research" if the only thing it can point to in refuting people's concerns is this one old report.

More than a few people consider this an issue. A commenter on the website offered that seriously addressing people's concerns was essential if they wanted to legitimize their assertion that the tires are okay. He pointed out that being busy didn't justify ignoring people.

We agree.

A great deal of research has been performed regarding the use of scrap tires since 1995, and overwhelmingly, researchers recommend using tires in civil engineering - not architectural - applications. The research and best practices guides are very clear that when tires are used, that they not be installed without an EPDM pond liner installed beneath them so they do not leech toxins into the earth and water below. Further, they recommend that recycling rates be increased in the U.S. as they have been in the EU.

Let's face reality here, head on: By using tires in construction, these materials are not being recycled. They are only being reused in such a way that those materials cannot go back to supply chain, which results in further extraction of virgin raw materials. So, in using waste tires for construction, we are increasing demand for more mining, extraction of petroleum, and manufacturing... which requires energy and transportation... which requires more petroleum... and time... and wears down our already crumbling infrastructure. That is not sustainable.

Let's go further here, and imagine a less than ideal scenario... your little one, or your beloved, gets sick from the off-gassing "non-issue". Something like that can destroy you emotionally and financially. Is it worth the risk? In our digging into the data, we have heard of several people who developed "allergies" living in Earthships that they did not have before. A couple of those people moved out and have returned to good health after some time. Was it the Earthship? Was it the tires? No one can be sure. To be fair, we also have a friend with severe chemical sensitivities whose health was restored while living in an Earthship.

Regardless, we do not take chances with people's health. If there is any question at all about the health, safety, and welfare of the client, or their friends and family... we say no. As far as we are concerned, the tires are an unacceptable risk. You can check out the research we have collected in The Science: Tires and off-gassing section in Chapter 2 and make that choice for yourself.

What is exciting is that many Earthship building organizations also agree that tires are not necessary. Some are not even allowed to use tires because of laws in their countries that prohibit use of tires in building. Others have decided for themselves not to use tires. Those that have abandoned the idea have moved towards other earth-sheltering technologies like earthbags and rammed earth.

One final note here: While it is a commonly held belief that "the tire walls provide thermal mass", it is the thick earth berm and rammed earth wall that gives thermal mass. The tires are not required for that wall system to perform that function.

The Earthship at the End of its Life

What happens to an Earthship when it dies? All buildings do eventually. What will be left is a flagstone floor (in most cases), glass panel windows, some concrete filled with cans and bottles, wood framing and beams, cabinetry, plumbing, cisterns, metal flashing and roof, and the earthen tire berm.

The flagstone will be reusable. It will just need chiseling out. The glass could be reused intact for other projects, or recycled outright if it is broken. The metal flashing of the greenhouse and the metal roof system will most likely be reusable or recyclable.

Plumbing probably will not be recycled due to health concerns and deterioration of the PVC. The concrete filled with cans and bottles will not likely be good for anything. The bottles and cans will likely break or be too encased in the concrete for salvage or even recycling. The cabinets in all but the most sophisticated Earthship are plywood, so there is no point trying to save them. Those materials – about 10 dump truck loads worth – will most likely be taken to the landfill. Footings and buttresses, if they are present, will add another 5-10 dump truck loads. There is some possibility they can be reused in non-structural landscape walls, though the presence of exposed rebar, which rusts and causes the concrete to spall, will likely render those unusable.

Concrete cisterns will also be discarded - another dump truck load or two for the landfill... as will the raised interior planting beds – another 2-3 loads. If the cisterns are plastic, chances are no-one will want to reuse them because of deterioration, but maybe by the time they are abandoned we will have figured out how to manage recycling them.

Maybe some of the wood that was covered with metal can be salvaged, though likely not from the greenhouse, as it will likely be rendered unusable due to moisture damage. The vigas, and the roof decking if it is solid wood, should be reusable.

Tires have a life of 30,000 years, so the berm, while it may deteriorate, will likely be left to degrade and become a mini dumpsite of toxic materials that may threaten the water supply. Or, the tires can be returned to the landfill.

Earthship Life Cycle Cost Assessment

We talk about aspects of the life cycle cost of Earthships throughout this book, breaking down embodied energy and cost, including maintenance. We do not provide an accounting for regional differences, as there are too many to calculate. We use the U.S. dollar and local costs in New Mexico as the basis for our calculations.

Life cycle cost is a comprehensive assessment, and since that is not our purpose, we did not want to include a whole book about it here. What we did want to do was offer an overview so that our readers could focus on the parts of sustainability and life cycle cost that matter to them. If you do not care about embodied energy, skip those sections.

What follows was the easiest way we could put the cost of the Earthship into perspective for ourselves. We hope it works for you too!

Comparing the Earthship to a traditionally built home:

A three bedroom home of the same size as the Global Model Earthship requires approximately 13,000 board feet of lumber for framing. If laid out end to end, this would make a line of wood nearly 2.5 miles long! We would need 14 tons of concrete. Sheathing would add up to somewhere around 6,000 square feet, as would drywall. Roofing material, exterior siding, and insulation would cover an area nearly 10,000 square feet. We would need 15 windows, 12 doors, toilets, kitchen sinks, bathroom sinks, cabinets, fireplace(s) or stoves, and garage doors. We would also need food, water, electricity, fuel, and household products.

The Global Earthship still requires thousands of board feet of lumber and vigas for framing. It needs 9 tons of concrete. The roofing material, exterior stucco, and insulation would still cover an area nearly 7,000 square feet due to extra levels of insulation required at the berm's cisterns, thermal wrap, and tubes. We would need 40 windows and 9 doors - double that of a normal home - since there are two layers of windows and doors at the greenhouse, plus the same toilets, kitchen sinks, bathroom sinks, cabinets, fireplace(s) or stoves, garage doors, etcetera... as a regular house. We would pay a premium charge for the systems and their maintenance and require backup power and backup heat, plus we would need special soils for the greenhouse, soil amendments, and insect control. We would also still need food, water, fuel, and household products.

Does the Earthship model actually end up increasing financial and material requirements? The math suggests that the answer to this is yes.

Earthships are not for Everybody

We can use this list of common concerns in Earthships (including the ultra-simple Hut designs) as a checklist to make sure these items are thought through in our new designs:

- Managing garbage.
- Getting enough potable water, which might mean trucking it in.
- Salvaged plumbing fixtures are sometimes really gross and do not work that well, plus they use more water than new ones.
- The old, hand formed bathtubs are painful "scrubbing machines that will eat your flesh off."
- Maybe having half-finished construction for years as you earn enough money to pay for completion.
- Shadows because lights are too short for the light to clear the big vigas.
- Refrigerators have to be hidden behind a wall or deep in the space so they do not overheat in winter because of the passive solar.
- Incomplete and/or undersized kitchens and cabinets / lack of a pantry.
- Lack of privacy.
- Lack of thermal comfort / requirements for clothing layers (and their regular, active, use).
- Lack of indoor plumbing / potty.
- Lack of a hot shower if systems are not complete.
- Kitchens and baths in the greenhouse part of the house can be sweltering and develop mold issues.
- Earth walls that weep water and/or dissolve.
- Yearly re-plastering.
- Mold issues due to greenhouse thermal bridging, poor ventilation, and unchecked humidity.
- Bucketing water for plants if the greywater is not working.
- Opening and closing vents, twice a day every day.
- Clearing the snow off the front windows and roof so ventilation can happen correctly.
- Cleaning out the grease trap – yuck!
- Not being able to black out the sun when you want to sleep.
- Lack of storage.
- So much sunlight can create glare for TVs/computers.
- Less livable space.
- Greenhouse watering, plants, and pests.
- No drying clothes inside in humid climates else humidity can become intolerable.
- Fixing leaking systems.
- Roof leaks.
- Water hammer "thunks" in poorly designed plumbing systems when they are turned on and off.
- Not being able to leave because the systems require daily use and regular maintenance to function correctly, (i.e. Monitoring solar systems, greywater recharge so the plants survive).
- Issues with the layout of the Water Organizing Module (WOM) and Power Organizing Module (POM) design for making repairs.
- Needing specialized (read: $$$$) help for repairs.

Motivation: Why we have to do something MORE

We are excited to see Earthship Biotecture pioneering change. In addition to their standard designs, when there is a disaster somewhere in the world, they mobilize their team to get on-site quickly and build something that can help the victims weather the storm. They are taking Earthships to places around the third world where experimental architecture is a benefit and Codes are more lenient. This allows them to experiment and improve the designs.

We hope they succeed!

We believe that fans should not totally abandon the Earthship idea, but they should be informed and know what is really involved so they can make informed decisions.

We cannot really say it better than Martin Holladay, a resident expert on GreenBuildingAdvisor.com, who said,

> *"... I was once young and poor and idealistic and interested in building a house in the wilderness. Young people who get together to smash dirt in old tires have a lot of fun. They have smiles on their faces. At the end of the day, they share a six-pack and pass around a joint... some of them may fall in love. Later... they will remember their Earthship project fondly. Let them build their Earthships. If they have read all of my caveats, and still want to pound dirt into old tires, by all means they should."*

Next page: Figure 8.
Earthen kitchen at Rancho de los Golondrinas

CHAPTER II

The Science: Academic Research and Tire Off-gassing

What follows is an accounting of the most important academic and professional Earthship research we were able to locate over many months of tracking research studies.

Some people have asked why we do not include "the good parts" found in the research. This perception issue is not entirely accurate - there is supporting data included as well as non-supporting data. We are focusing mainly on the problems because these are the parts of the design that we can work to fix.

THE SUMMARY OF THE FINDINGS OF THE RESEARCH IS AS FOLLOWS:

- Earthships can overheat up to 8 months a year and under-heat up to 3 months a year. The techniques for natural ventilation used in typical Earthships are inadequate. Supplementary heating and cooling are required.
- Natural ventilation in a humid climate is not adequate. Dehumidification is required.
- Most people cannot collect enough water for average consumption with their roof catchment. A well or grid-tied system is usually required.
- Photovoltaics are cost prohibitive in many high-latitude climates due to large battery requirements.
- Passive solar is not effective as the only means of heating in cloudy climates or high latitude climates where days and nights may by 24 hours long. The same is also true for photovoltaics.
- Earthships are not an appropriate building technique for tropical, equatorial, or hot/humid climates.
- The greenhouse is not suitable for habitation.
- The Earthship uses many more manufactured materials than not. It is therefore not as sustainable or natural as most people believe.
- Tires, cans, and bottles are better suited to true recycling than reuse in Earthships. Reusing them instead of recycling them increases demand for virgin materials.
- Thermal bridges are one of the major factors in under- and over-heating.
- Tire walls are structurally sound.
- Using an attached greenhouse is an excellent way to minimize thermal loading for many building types.

Here is the deal about academic research, though: studies can be easily manipulated to say whatever people want them to. That is how Monsanto gets research that supports the use of GMOs; how pharmaceutical companies get permission to release drugs we later end up taking off the market; and how almost everything gets passed by Congress... the powers-that-be just make the limits of the study so that they do not include the things they do not want people to know. Then they can say "that is outside the scope of this study."

That is why modern medicine doesn't recognize, say... Chinese Medicine. The powers-that-be do not put money towards research on things that might keep them from making more money. An herb (that anyone can grow) is harder to make money off of than a pill (when you control the supply). And here is what is important about that: even 100 years of research does not equal the 2,500 years of experiential evidence that supports the validity of Chinese Medicine. Do you think anyone who goes to a Doctor of Chinese Medicine cares about the research done on that practice? Not likely. They care about feeling better and chances are they know that it works from experience. The doctor can feel safe applying his knowledge too - there are thousands of years of knowledge and experience to back up his efforts. We do not need research to show us that bio-climatic vernacular design works... we have 10,000 years of examples that show us that it works. Billions of people around the world know climatic design works. If they want to know what kinds of building work for their area, they just look around, see what buildings are left standing, and then they do that. It is that simple. This is why developing a sense of Place around where you build your home is essential.

We point out some of the challenges and limitations of research in our commentaries that follow. An incomplete picture creates a space for doubt. Doubt offers an opportunity for misunderstanding. If there is a space for interpretation, and we are able to find it, we have attempted to let you know. Not because we are trying to find flaws in studies, but because what is missing or not discussed might matter to you.

While it is important to note the limitations of research's applicability, the findings of the people building Earthships around the world have echoed the findings of the research. So, we are not proposing to throw out the research. Rather, we believe that we should look at the issues raised in it from multiple viewpoints.

Academic Research on Earthship Performance

We selected only those studies to cover here which offered some evolution of the Earthship idea. We found hundreds of studies on Earthships that would be more correctly described as "papers" - they reviewed the Earthship literature, the movies, or the concept but added nothing to the discussion of what works, does not work, or could be done to make the design work. Finding tangible, verifiable, and useful data was something of a challenge.

For this book we wanted to include the best available, so we clipped the relevant parts of the study conclusions to include here, and added some explanations in simple English since academic studies are some of the most boring and difficult things to read on the planet.

Analysis of the Performance of Earthship Housing in Various Global Climates

Nathanael J. Kruis and Matthew K. Heun
Proceedings of ES200; Energy Sustainability 2007; June 27-30, 2007, Long Beach, California.

This 2007 study was conducted from two engineering PhDs at Calvin College in Michigan. Their report was formulated to determine whether the 3 bedroom Global Model Earthship design meets the comfort, electrical, and water demand for several North American locations. The research team studied actual values as well as theoretical values from simulations on industry-standard software. They also determined the financial implications of Earthship construction compared to the same floorplan expressed as a standard wood-framed house with batt insulation in each of the areas studied, which included Alaska, Hawaii, New Mexico, and Michigan.

This study established thermal comfort levels as within the range between 21°C (70°F) and 28°C (82°F). The research findings indicated that the theoretical energy simulations were more forgiving than the measured Earthship temperatures, and temperatures were routinely 3 degrees more comfortable in the simulations than in actuality during noon heat peaks and rainy periods.

The results of the study indicated that the Earthship really does not perform to expectation except in summer (in the northern hemisphere). This lends credibility to the assertion many have made which suggests that the pitched window wall is detrimental to the design. The reason the window wall works better in the summer is because the greenhouse is shaded from the sun, which is too far north in this season to overheat it. It seems safe to assume that the plants assist by providing additional shading as well. Once the sun starts moving south again, those spaces will overheat in latitudes below Anchorage, for at least 1 month in Grand Rapids, and for as many as 8 months in Albuquerque. Many say that opening the windows can fix that, but some of those months include winter, and when you have below freezing temps and blowing snow to contend with, opening windows is not always a viable solution. Especially for your greenhouse plants which may not do well in the tropical temperatures sandwiched between freezing periods that occurs when the space is opened and closed up. The research also indicates that the design fails to perform in winter in high latitude areas, requiring backup heat and additional insulation at the perimeter of the building, on the greenhouse, and under the foundations and floors.

The staggering cost of installing adequate PV as delineated in the findings illustrates a negative economic impact of the build-out. The PV required to power an Earthship in Anchorage costs nearly $105,000 for the vast solar array and batteries required to support the extremely cold and dark winter, as compared to the $29,700 required for solar PV in Albuquerque. This is in 2006 dollars, but the range remains the same even if we update the costs. These calculations are somewhat limited in that they address equipment but not installation, labor, or maintenance.

The study determined that a family of four living in an Earthship would require 98 gallons (370L) of water per day, or 37,500 gallons (135,000L) of water per year. This suggests that the Earthship is only really saving water insofar as it is able to use greywater for toilets. The use of water for faucets, washing machines, and showers... are all equal to that of regularly "efficiently designed" buildings. The study confirms that rainwater collection is achievable in a wet place like Michigan, but not in Hawaii, New Mexico, or Alaska. This makes a backup water supply essential.

One of the most surprising findings from this research was the determination that the most affordable Earthship to build is a grid-tied one. In each of the locations they studied, grid-tied Earthships performed similarly, or even better, than a stick-built house. The only slightly higher additional cost at build-out of the grid-tied Earthship over a stick system was fundamentally attributable to the additional catchment and greywater systems. Off-grid Earthships tended to cost 30% more over their lifetime in Albuquerque and Hawaii, 50% more in Michigan, and as much as 200% more expensive than stuck-built over the lifetime of the home in Anchorage.

Some considerations:

- The assumption that the earthen walls perform the same as concrete did not take into account the voids where the walls use applied earth stucco in lieu of rammed (most often between the tires). These areas likely have different thermal behaviors.
- The seasonal moisture content of the soil - the earth is more thermally conductive when wet - was excluded from consideration.
- The assumption that Earthships had double-pane windows might be too favorable. We have not seen that many Earthships with double-pane windows.
- Issues of air leakage and infiltration have major implications on actual heating and cooling loads.
- The use of Energy Star appliances was assumed. These appliances are used almost exclusively in high-end Earthships, based on our data, and thus this benefit is inaccessible to many.

Thermal Comfort of Global Model Earthship in Various European Climates

Martin Freney, Veronica Soebarto, and Terry Williamson
Proceedings of BS2013: 13th Conference of International Building Performance Simulation Association, Chambéry, France, August 26-28.

This study was completed by three academic researchers from the Australia University of Adelaide in 2013. Their efforts were an expansion of previous studies cited herein, and evaluated the Global Model Earthship in both actual and simulated thermal performance scenarios in Taos, New Mexico; London, England; Paris, France; and Albacete, Seville, and Valladolid in Spain.

This Earthship study was based on a 2 bedroom Global Model Earthship oriented at 10 degrees east of south. The area of the building is 1,720 Square Feet (SF), or 160 Square Meters (SM). Of that, 645 SF or 60 SM (38% of the floor area) is greenhouse. The Earthship in this study has upgrades including a western covered entry and eastern vestibule entrance, and it uses rigid insulation vertically in the berm approximately four feet, or 1200mm, from the tires. Of particular note in this study was the use of an accepted international standard for thermal comfort that is more stringent than those used in previous studies.

The study identified that:

In London and Paris, additional heating is required for half of the year and the greenhouse is too cold to grow plants. This cannot be addressed by adding a heat source without addressing humidity as well. Also in Paris, the greenhouse also requires supplemental cooling for several months of the year.

In Valladolid, the greenhouse is too hot for more than half of the year and additional cooling and/or ventilation is required. Additional cooling is also required in the main body of the house from September through November.

In Albacete and Seville, the greenhouse is too hot throughout the year and additional cooling and/or ventilation is required. Additional cooling is required in the main body of the house from October through December.

The study identified that simulations did not predict the extremes of temperatures measured in on-site testing. It also noted that up to half of each day, thermal comfort was not achieved. The coldest periods measured were between 6 and 8 am, followed by a steady rise to comfortable temperatures. This implies that an automatic or timed system is ideal for maximizing comfort and minimizing heating loads. The study also identified that the greenhouse was not suitable for human habitation due to these extremes.

One of the most important impacts of this study was to confirm what many were already saying - that the inner-earth temperature that Reynolds assumed was 58 degrees everywhere actually varies dramatically by region, based on factors including local temperatures, water table, soil type, wind, humidity, and rainfall. In places where the inner-earth temperature is lower, this temperature difference requires a build-out utilizing extensive insulation under the slab and around the foundations and exterior walls.

The researchers noted that schedules for opening and closing the vents in the greenhouse had been provided through occupant surveys and the advice given to them by Earthship Biotecture. This confirms what some owners state - that the natural ventilation systems trend towards being maintenance-heavy on the day-to-day.

SOME CONSIDERATIONS:
- The Earthship studied in Taos was not occupied during winter of the on-site case study. Functional use patterns in previous studies indicated additional large spikes of cold and heat due to occupant use.
- The research team tightened the requirements for comfort over most studies.
- The simulations did not account for thermal bridging effects.
- The impact of the earth tubes in the north wall of the greenhouse was not modeled.
- Comfort assessments were based on daily average temperatures rather than the range of daily temperatures modelled, thus skewing perceptions of actual comfort.

Learning from 'Earthship' Based on Monitoring and Thermal Simulation

Martin Freney, Veronica Soebarto and Terry Williamson
University of Adelaide, Adelaide, Australia. 2012.

This study was conducted by the same research team that conducted the previous study. This study provides a comprehensive review of Earthship thermal performance in the Adelaide area of Australia.

The study identified that heating and cooling loads were minimized when using thermal mass was utilized on interior walls. It also identified that a greenhouse can be used to minimize overheating on the south wall for nearly every possible building type. The wall types most benefitted are brick, timber frame, rammed earth, and brick veneer. Interestingly, they also identified that the Earthship has the least to gain from the use of the greenhouse, saving energy of only 505kWh annually.

To put this in perspective, the US Energy Information Administration puts the cost of a kWh of electricity at $0.13 as of August 2014. That equates to a savings of $65.65 per year over traditional power. However, that savings is easily eaten up in the $40+k cost of the greenhouse.

The researchers modeled other wall types for the berm and identified that an insulated concrete block berm wall provides equal thermal performance to the rammed earth tire wall. They also identified that without the berm, thermal performance is nearly equal for walls constructed of rammed earth tires, concrete block, strawbale, and insulated rammed earth.

The issues raised in this study echo the findings of the previous studies and also identified an opportunity to utilize alternative wall types to achieve similar thermal performance to an Earthship.

The Sustainability of Conventional Houses, Passive Houses and Earthships, Based on Legislation, Environmental Impact Energy and Operating Energy

Elena Kuil
University of Groningen. 2012.

This report compared traditional construction to the PassivHaus and Earthship in terms of sustainability and recycling.

The report is extremely helpful in understanding the impact of removing the Earthship's recycled components of tires, glass, and cans from the recycling stream. In Europe, they are nearing a 100% recycling rate for these items as well as steel. This removes any benefits from using tires, cans, glass, steel, or aluminum in the building.

Interestingly (and perhaps surprisingly), the report identified that the conventionally constructed home actually has a lower environmental impact than either the PassivHaus or the Earthship. PassivHauses use more insulation, and the Earthship's use of dirt and clay is actually considered an environmental impact. This is the first study to acknowledge this that we have found. The study also identified that the Earthship has a higher environmental impact due to the use of rock wool, steel, and rigid insulation as well as flagstone, which must be quarried.

In order of sustainability, the report identified that traditional construction has a lower environmental impact than PassivHauses, which in turn have a lower impact than Earthships.

Earthship Performance

Earthship Europe
2012. Digitally available at: http://Earthshipeurope.org/index.php/Earthships/performance

STUDY CONCLUSIONS:

"Reynolds explains... in 'Comfort in any climate' is that the temperature of the outer few feet of earth heat up and cool down in response to surface weather. However at about 4 feet (1.2 m) the temperature is more constant, around 58oF (14,4oC)... it sure is not the case in most European situations... you can take the years average temperature of your location and that is about the temperature of the earth at 1,5 m deep. The average temperature in Belgium is 9,8oC (49.6oF). So tapping into the earth will give you the uncomfortable feeling of 9,8oC, when you probably want at least 19,8oC... I expect this tapping into the earth has a negative effect on performance in many European countries. To me it made more sense to insulate underneath the entire Earthship (walls included) instead of just insulate the thermal wrap."

"...huge thermal bridges. To most construction engineers in Western Europe it is well known that thermal bridges can cause moist and mold problems. The difference in temperature between the insulated and not insulated part causes moist to gather at that point. This is not prevented by completely sealing of water from the outside since the (moisture) comes from the inside. In time, when not properly handled, it will turn into mold."

"Ventilating in summer when it is warm will not give a great deal of problems the Reynolds way. But winter time in cold and moist climates do need another way of ventilating.

"...thermal mass. It is clearly made for a New Mexico situation. Longer days in winter, probably more clear sky days and less days with a grey sky no sun coming through... the few ours of sunlight on a short winter day in Sweden (cannot) make the thermal mass work, provided the sky is clear blue and without any clouds. The amount of heat lost through the windows should be investigated, as should the amount of heat gained though them and those should be compared..."

Case Study Report: The Brighton Earthship: Evaluating Thermal Performance

University of Brighton
Centre for Sustainability of the Built Environment

This study was conducted by the University of Brighton at the Brighton Earthship just before the building was occupied. The study identified that internal temperature conditions in the build were consistently warmer than outside. They attribute that to the thermal battery effect of the berm not having reached its balance point temperature, which some believe can take up to two years. Later research on this build has identified that the inner-earth temperature, a lack of adequate insulation, a lack of adequate ventilation, and thermal bridging are contributing to the thermal performance failure of this build. It seems that part of the misunderstanding about the issues in this design are attributable to the design intending to use the berm for heating, when in fact earth-sheltering is a natural cooling strategy. That is not addressed in any of the research we have seen.

Earthship Ironbank

Martin Freney
Digitally available at: http://www.Earthshipironbank.com.au/research.html

Freney is well regarded as one of the foremost researchers in Earthship design. He has conducted a great deal of research on Earthship Performance. This study compares the workings of Earthship Ironbank to various other types of building systems.

It is somewhat difficult to discern the performance based on the figures provided, however. Figure 8.157 Whole House Weighted Score, compares the off-grid Earthship and an off-grid adobe house against other wall types that are all on-grid. Items labeled "gas for cooking", "miscellaneous", "water and wastewater", "food production", and "gas for hot water boost" appear to show strong relationships across all building systems, and thus can be eliminated for clarity. The only pieces of the performance equation that are comparable then, are "thermal envelope", "heating and cooling", "household electrical", and "waste".

The chart shows favor to the performance of the Earthship, however, some might argue that off-grid build performance should be compared against other off-grid builds using various building materials, not to alternative systems in on-grid builds.

The major difference in the "household electrical" seems to be grid-tied versus off-grid systems. However, we believe that the tricks for minimizing electrical use used in Earthships can easily be applied to other systems. So, for our review, we eliminated considering power requirements for the various systems, comparing only the remaining four components - "thermal envelope", "heating and cooling", "household electrical", and "waste".

SOME OBSERVATIONS:

- Building type ES1 is an Earthship made of insulated adobe. It has no berm or greenhouse. This construction is compared to uninsulated adobe. That skews the perception of the uninsulated adobe's performance unfavorably and doesn't meet Code. In the U.S., adobe requires thermal wrap and insulation to be Code-compliant.

- There is no mention of the timber frame infill or insulation. Whether the infill is an insulating system or a thermal mass system is relevant when comparing systems. The thermal performance of the infill can range greatly depending on the infill type.

- We believe that for a true comparison, wall systems should be built on the same assumptions: the same passive solar orientation; rainwater harvesting; water and power provided by thermal solar and photovoltaics; greenhouses which allow for food production; insulation... must be factored in for all systems to accurately determine whether they are similar or different in performance.

- None of these systems appears to factor in maintenance costs.

To us, the most important piece of this research is in this quote:

"Bottom line: build an energy efficient, water efficient house anyway you can - and get off the grid..."

The missing piece here, for us, is that the techniques used in making Earthships work... can be used across systems to make all architecture work better!

Testing and Analysis of Modified Rammed Earth Tire Walls

Aaron Zimmerman, Eric Burger, & Jared Nolan
Swarthmore College. Department of Engineering. May 6, 2011.

This 2011 study set out to determine the loading and structural capacity of the tire walls in order to determine if they were indeed stable enough to build with. Their test results revealed that the walls are indeed suitable for single story construction. They also determined that a structural foundation was not required for that area, but that the foundation requirement would vary based on specific site conditions.

Earthship Biotectures: Experimental Subdivision in Taos, New Mexico: The Greater World Earthship Community

Ann Schmidt
Sustainability and the Built Environment Class Report. 2006.

While this study could easily have been lost alongside similar efforts overviewing the Earthship concept, Ms. Schmidt visited Greater World herself and made an astute observation that offers an important insight into the Earthship ideal:

> "There are many questions I have after investigating the Greater World Earthship Community. There is no doubt that the Earthship exceeds the general expectation of a sustainable building, but the Greater World Community does not meet the criteria described as smart growth. Dwellings are arranged too far apart. Individually owned cars are still the main source of transportation. Currently, the nearest retail center is twelve miles away. Residents of this community must either telecommute for work, or drive to places of employment. How could this community be modified to increase densities without compromising the way an Earthship works? Further, would a developer take on the task of the labor-intensive rammed earth tire?"

ND HACKING THE EARTHSHIP • 61

Research Conclusions

This research points to several issues that must be resolved if the Earthship ideals are to be realized:

The current Earthship concept cannot provide a consistently comfortable environment solely through passive solar.

- VENTILATION
  - Solution: Provide for additional means of ventilation
    See section: Natural Ventilation Strategies and Indoor Air Quality

- DEHUMIDIFICATION
  - Solution: Add humidification or dehumidification depending on climate
    See section: The Reality: Humidification Matters

- OVERHEATING
  - Solution: Provide shading and design according to accepted passive solar strategies
    See chapter: Design for Thermal Comfort
  - Solution: Minimize glazing on the south
    See section: Earthship Sloped Window Greenhouse

- UNDERHEATING
  - Solution: Installation of backup heating.
  - Solution: Use slab and foundation insulation

The current Earthship concept cannot provide an adequate supply of electricity through a PV power generator at a reasonable price.

- Solution: Use a grid-tied system. The cost of PV will come down over time.
- Solution: Minimize floor space and loading
  See Section: Create an Efficient Floorplan
- Solution: Smarter electrical loading
  See Section: Mechanical Systems: Electrical: Power

The current Earthship concept cannot provide a consistent supply of water solely through catchwater and greywater systems.

- Solution: Address water issues as appropriate to your climate. Provide a well or grid-tied system. Use best practices in water management
  See Section: Rainwater Harvesting and Collection

A tropical wet/dry climate does not need such intensive design of the thermal envelope. An equally sustainable and comfortable environment can be achieved with less material and a lower cost than the Earthship design.

- Solution: Use a different building system.

Tires and Off-gassing Research

We do not have a vested interest in saying that the off-gassing of the tires is a "non-issue." We do not believe that your health is a non-issue. Neither do the countries that have banned the use of tires in buildings. Because of laws prohibiting the use of tires, groups like Earthship Belgium are using earthbags instead of tires for their Earthships.

Just a few months ago, the tire off-gassing issue was raised again when The Washington Post did a story on a number of soccer goalies who have contracted cancer. Scientists and doctors began studying the unique subgroup, which led them to pose a link between the incidents of cancer and goalies who had played extensively on athletic fields paved with a form of AstroTurf that used crumb rubber from recycled tires in its makeup. While in its early stages now, this may ultimately prove to be fruitful research to the tire off-gassing issue.

Here is what we DO know, from the scientific studies and best practices promoted by experts in the many fields which influence our assertion that the tires are dangerous, so you can decide what works for you!

THE LAUNDRY LIST OF VOLATILE CHEMICALS & HEAVY METALS USED IN TIRES IS ALARMING:

- Benzene inhalation causes cancer.
- Toluene inhalation causes cognitive dysfunction.
- Arsenic inhalation causes organ failure.
- Acetone inhalation causes irritation of the throat and lung.
- Nickel inhalation causes sinusitis and cancer.
- Copper inhalation causes nausea and suppressed liver function.
- Cadmium inhalation causes kidney disease and an increased frequency of kidney stone formation.

Organic compounds in tires break down more quickly than the vulcanized rubber. Criteria which determine breakdown rate include: heating, friction (from movement), water trapping and freezing, and evaporation of plasticizers.

But here is where it gets really interesting. Here are scientific studies done for several different materials, all of which are constructed of recycled tires.

SCRAP TIRES: HANDBOOK ON RECYCLING APPLICATIONS AND MANAGEMENT FOR THE U.S. AND MEXICO

According to this EPA report from December 2010;

"These (tire) piles pose a public health concern. They are breeding grounds and havens for mosquitoes and other vectors, resulting in the spread of dengue fever, yellow fever, encephalitis, West Nile virus, and malaria. Improperly managed in stockpiles, in illegal dumps, and scattered along road sides, scrap tires are a significant border environmental problem as a result of the leaching process, fires hazards, and water contamination. Once ignited, tire fires are difficult to extinguish. When water is applied to fight the fire, serious air, ground water, and surface water contamination may result. Toxic emissions from tire fires, such as sulfuric acid and gaseous nitric acid, can irritate the skin, eyes, and mucus membranes, and can affect the central nervous system, cause depression, have negative respiratory effects and, in extreme cases, cause mutations and cancer."

ARTIFICIAL TURF: EXPOSURES TO GROUND UP RUBBER TIRES ATHLETIC FIELDS, PLAYGROUNDS, GARDEN MULCH

This 2008, but constantly updated, report from by the firm Environment and Human Health, Inc. for the Canadian version of the EPA states that:

> "The metals zinc, cadmium, and lead were also identified as contaminants from tire rubber released into ground water. With the exception of zinc, there are insufficient data to assess the health or environmental risks of any of these metals. It appears clear that the zinc levels are high enough to be phytotoxic if they enter the ground water or soil. It is doubtful that there is any human toxicity from zinc at the levels reported, but such a conclusion would have to be tested by more careful study."

> "The particulate exposures due to tire dust and chemicals contained in the dust that can be released in the lungs are especially troublesome. Nearly every test adequate to assess the risk that was reported found one or two dozen compounds released from particulates. There are processes in the body that can release the chemicals contained in the rubber particles. Moreover, potent carcinogens are found in the tire dust. Only the assumption of limited exposure could support the conclusions of low cancer risk."

> "In summary, the toxic actions of concern from the materials... include: Severe irritation of the respiratory system; Severe irritation of the eyes, skin and mucous membranes; Systemic effects on the liver and kidneys; Neurotoxic responses; Allergic reactions; Cancers; Developmental effects"

CAL RECYCLES REPORT ON TIRE BREAKDOWN

This 2012 report states:

> " Natural rubber alone poses a dangerous fire hazard and when heated to decomposition emits toxic fumes of SOx. Base materials used in polymer rubber production, such as butadiene and styrene, are suspected human carcinogens, and many of the polymer additives can cause systemic toxic effects."

> "The tire filler, carbon black, is mildly toxic by ingestion, inhalation and skin contact."

> "Isoprene is a mild toxic by the pathway of inhalation. It also reacts with air and ozone to form dangerous peroxides. Butadiene is a confirmed carcinogen and teratogen in animals and a suspected human carcinogen. Inhalation of high concentrations of butadiene can cause unconsciousness and death. Human systemic effects of butadiene by inhalation include coughing and hallucinations. Styrene is a suspected carcinogen. It has been found to be poisonous by ingestion, inhalation, and intravenous routes."

> "Zinc oxide is added to tire rubber at relatively high concentrations. Zinc oxide is moderately toxic to humans by ingestion. Some human systemic effects associated with the inhalation of zinc oxide are chills, fever, tightness of the chest, and coughing."

DRAFT SCREENING ASSESSMENT FOR CARBON BLACK

The 2013 report produced by Environment Canada states:

> "Increased incidences of lung tumors were observed in female rats exposed by inhalation to the only or lowest concentration (of carbon black) tested..."

REVIEW OF THE IMPACTS OF CRUMB RUBBER IN ARTIFICIAL TURF APPLICATIONS

This 2008 report from Liberty Tire states about off-gassing:

> "The 2007 EEDEMS report mentioned above raised concerns about health effects on the crews installing crumb rubber athletic fields in poorly ventilated indoor areas and recommends a minimum air renewal rate of 2 vol.h-1. A 2006 study conducted in Norway drew a similar conclusion... These recent findings are consistent with those of a 1999 Taiwanese study that identified temperature and age of the recycled rubber material as the primary factors in VOC emission rates."

And then you read statements from industry professionals dealing with tire decompositions in their everyday lives, who say things like...

> "While the levels of chemicals off-gassing from indoor play spaces was considered below the threshold where the chemicals are harmful, it is worth noting that indoor spaces showed up to ten times as much volatile chemicals in the air. If you want to err on the side of caution, you may want to consider refraining from using recycled rubber mats indoors, where there is a minuscule but present danger that could deem recycled rubber unhealthy."
>
> - from "Are Recycled Rubber Mats Unhealthy?" by Lara Stewart at BrightHub
>
> "Minor off-gassing is an issue with rubber flooring. In some cases, products with recycled content are included with caveats regarding where they should be used. Rubber flooring made from recycled automobile tires is a good example--the caveat is that these products should not be used in most fully enclosed indoor spaces due to off-gassing concerns."
>
> from "Building Materials: What Makes a Product Environment Friendly?" at Earthwise.com
>
> "Do not use rubber flooring such as that made from recycled tires in enclosed areas because off-gassing can continue for years."
>
> - From "Healthy Indoor Environments" at The Sustainability Project.

To be fair, we cannot ignore this undated report from Humbolt State, which addresses the risks directly.

> "Reusing our worn out tires is of course better than throwing them into a landfill, but many of the current reuse applications found in our society come with significant environmental impacts. One appropriate use for old tires is in Earthship homes. A question we frequently receive ... is if the tires used in these projects pose health risks through off-gassing or chemical leaching. "it depends".
>
> The specific constituents contained in a given tire (e.g. arsenic, aluminum, cadmium, chromium, manganese, mercury, lead, sulfur, and zinc) are dependent on the tire's type, age, and manufacturer. The location in which the used tires are placed is a critical factor that determines how much of each mineral constituent is leached. Tires decompose when exposed to high temperatures, sunlight, or oxidizing agents. None of these elements are present when a tire is packed with soil and surrounded by a stucco barrier inside an Earthship. That being said, the tires used in Earthship walls are of minimal risk to inhabitants because they have little potential to decompose.
>
> ...used tires most likely do not pose a health risk if they are rammed with earth and sequestered in a location away from exposure to sun or moisture... EPA researchers have acknowledged that the current literature we have pertaining to the health risks that used tires pose is incomplete, and that further study should be conducted before used tires are used in applications where humans are exposed"

Is it worth the chance you take to use the tires? If your answer to this is yes, the tire chapter that follows in the design section has suggestions for making them work, as well as offering viable alternatives!

Engaging with the Process: Part 2

Draw your inspiration here!

Chapter III

A Way Forward

"In order to change an existing paradigm you do not struggle to try and change the problematic model. You create a new model and make the old one obsolete."

- Buckminster Fuller

Whether your dream home ultimately ends up being an Earthship, an earth-shelter, a natural home, a tiny house... or some variation or combination of these... the path ahead is one that can sometimes be difficult and overwhelming. In the chapters that follow, we will line out each step in the process of design to help you find your way.

Earthship 2.0: Reinventing

Since time immemorial, architects and builders have been imagining a new future into existence. We would not have had the Gothic Age, the Renaissance, the Arts and Crafts Movement, or Modernism without someone wanting to imagine a better architectural future for people. Many of these movements forged architecture that will stand the test of time and that will continue to influence designers for generations beyond our own.

The failure of modern design happened when we started developing future movements around the 20th century ideas of everything having to be entirely new instead of building on the past. We have seen countless homes of the future come and go since the Industrial Revolution... from Claude Ledoux' sphere home in the nineteenth century, to Disneyland's "House of the Tomorrow" made by Monsanto and built in 1957 (and abandoned because it was already outdated by 1967)... these interpretations of what we "needed" for the future depended on the technology and the materials of the moment to make their statement. This is a solid foundation on which to build, in principle... use what we have to work with. The problem is that technology becomes outdated more quickly with every passing year. When we build our ideas of home based on fad design techniques and trendy but untested materials and technologies, the vision for the future we just invested in is no longer relevant or useful when those ideas and materials change.

The Earthship suffers from the same handicap. Forty years ago, there was a real need to do something... anything... with old tires, cans, and bottles. Today, those materials can all be recycled for better uses rather than be reused as building materials. And we know now that the buildings do not meet the performance ideals to which they were designed in many climates. We can move past these limitations - we can take what is good from the Earthships and tweak the rest to make our home work better for our values and location. In fact, if we want to call ourselves truly sustainable, we have a responsibility to.

Several of the European Union (EU)-based Earthship organizations decided to look to science to see if the Earthships were truly viable from the standpoint of thermal performance, materials used, and liveability. When they determined that the buildings did not function adequately to meet their needs, they decided to abandon all but the line of separate rooms, the greenhouse, the south-facing wall of windows, the grey water system and rainwater harvesting systems. They then redesigned every remaining detail. We agree with this approach. We would even propose taking it a step further... we would abandon the tropical-style greenhouse as it is currently designed and add a window wall designed to passive solar guidelines and an attached production greenhouse instead.

This book is our attempt to share the best information we have learned about Earthships and other natural building ideas from projects, builders, forums, and designers around the world. We then added layers of best practices we use when designing buildings to meet or exceed the requirements of typical municipal green design ordinances, LEED, HUD, USAA, and even the Building Code... so that it is easier for your project to meet or exceed those standards from the outset.

We will incorporate some of the best design ideas gleaned from our own experience as well as from forward-thinking designs like Frank Lloyd Wright's timeless Usonian Houses, the "homes for tomorrow" he designed in the 1930s. The Usonian Houses used beautifully detailed natural materials and offered a living "heart" of the home in the living areas (often centered around a fireplace). They worked with and embraced nature and he incorporated people-scaled spaces in the home. We will also explore the underlying principles in the teachings of the first century Roman architect Vitruvius who called for buildings to be built on the principals of "firmness, commodity, and delight", so we will also address structural stability, designing spaces sized and oriented for the way we live, and designing spaces that feed our souls. Because that is part of what we see is missing from the general built environment... not just Earthships.

We have built several resources to offer you architectural inspiration from the rich history we all share. Check out our firm Archinia's Pinterest boards titled Usonian, Magic Cottages, EcoCommunities, and Archinia's Inspired Idea Book to find inspiration from projects around the world.

We also love our friend Sigi Koko's website http://www.buildnaturally.com and her Facebook fan page https://www.facebook.com/buildnaturally for the best of the best in great design tips for natural building.

As well, we love our friend Oliver Swann's Natural Home website at http://www.NaturalHomes.org.

Home Design with YOU in Mind

Designing a home is an enormous undertaking. Helping to design and manage these complex projects is one of the things we do in our office. It takes many hands and many months to pull together all the information needed to craft a design and then to detail a home so that it meets the client's quality and performance standards and makes our clients feel truly "at home".

We know that many people would like to design and create a space that they can build themselves or with their community. Their motivation might be being environmentally-sensitive, fulfilling the dream of designing a home of one's own, or it might be about getting the most home value for the money you have to invest. Designing a home can prove to be frustrating without any training or guidance. For some, it might even prove impossible. There is so much to know and learning it all can take a lifetime. And, just when you think you have it figured out, you meet someone from somewhere else and they do things exactly the opposite way of what you thought was "right". Or technology or science change and suddenly what was right is now wrong. With sixteen plus years of practice under my belt, I am only just realizing that beginner's mind is an essential element in design. It allows me to question all of my assumptions and go back to science to look for reasons to do something… or not to. So, please, do not lose faith. You can work your way through this too. It is all about taking your gut feelings and figuring out what they are really telling you, and then turning to people who are craftsmen, like the team we have brought on for this effort, to get their expertise to help you do it well.

In this book we want to share the resources as well as the ideas, tips, tricks, and rules of thumb that we have learned along the way. We want to empower our readers to achieve their home design goals in ways that support their lifestyle and their values, whether they use the Earthship idea fully or just borrow aspects they love from it. We will walk through our process of design in the next chapters so that readers have the tools needed to make their self-designed space shine. For materials, we will offer a broad swath of what is available, not depending solely on traditional Earthship design techniques.

Some of the biggest questions that you will need to answer in regard to how you want to build and live in your new home will require you to define your values. Sometimes there is no easy choice. There are pros and cons for every system and material. You will find reasons to use adobe and reasons for using strawbale instead. You will have to make a choice about which of those works for you. You may not want to use wood products because that may go against a deeply held environmental value that motivates you to save every bit of the earth and allow it to remain natural. So when it comes to choosing fiberglass windows versus clad-wood, you may choose fiberglass. Alternately, you may not want to use plastic products and support the oil industry that manufactures them. It is all about understanding your own values and determining what works for you. The same holds true for the aspects of design we will talk about here.

This book is not intended to deal with the technicalities of building. There are plenty of resources available outside of this work that excel in technical building details for various systems, but lack what we are trying to offer in design. We will also not cover the Water Organizing Modules, Power Organizing Modules, or equipment and appliances typical in Earthships here. Those systems are covered in Earthship, Volumes 2 and 3. We are going to cover some of what is missing from the standard literature as well as alternate options for those for whom grid-tied means affordable. We will also try to explain the underlying principles behind the different materials and methods so that you can make more informed design decisions and choose the methods and materials that will help you to live the life you want. Which of these materials and methods you go with depends on your values, your experience level, and your budget… and whether you build grid-tied, or off-grid. Hopefully, you will find a combination of resources that works for you!

This book is written from the point of view of New Mexico, USA. The issues that we discuss here are designed for the northern hemisphere. We try and provide guidance for southern hemisphere applications where appropriate.

We hope that this will be just the beginning, and that we will add to the book in future editions to make it better. It is all about bringing architecture to the People. And, hopefully, doing it in a truly sustainable way that makes life better for everyone. That is our mission.

Sustainable Home

by Rachel Preston Prinz and Carrie Christopher

Designing a truly sustainable home is an art, and when it is done well, it is an art that is based on science. Many people like to think that "going green" can be achieved via a checklist like LEED and trusting things that are labeled "green". In reality though, that is not enough because a lot of what is considered "green" today is really just "greener". Many modern "green" products use the same old technologies with a few less chemicals. That is not truly sustainable. Whereas some traditional techniques are thousands of years old and do not need chemicals at all, last longer, and support traditional craftwork. Because of the challenges in finding the right balance, in our office we developed a sustainability philosophy to guide our projects. These criteria will guide us as we talk through all of the aspects of design in this book.

We choose materials based on criteria that give our clients the most truly sustainable buildings:

PERFORMANCE WITHIN THE SPECIFIED CLIMATE

Some trees, when used in their native humid environments will naturally deter against pests and decomposition. These woods are far more sustainable than a single creosote-treated pine log, which is potentially toxic to everything around it, including the soil and water. Because of these types of considerations, we choose materials that are local to, or specifically selected to work with, as well as support, our environment.

TENDENCY TO DECOMPOSE / MEANS OF DECOMPOSITION

We prefer using materials that have a long history of good performance, are easily approved, and are superior performers in enhancing thermal comfort. Adobe, brick, stone, and timber frame are the most natural, resilient, and easiest to repair materials to build with. They are also the longest lasting building materials; they have a long history of successful use; and they are often accepted outright by building officials.

EMBODIED ENERGY

Embodied energy is the total amount of energy consumed to take a material from the cradle (the mine) to the grave (the build site). This includes the cost of obtaining the raw material, transporting it to the manufacturing site, making the finished product, and then transporting it to the build site. Embodied energy can be high. Aluminum, a common and predominant component of solar panel installations, contains an enormous amount of embodied energy. It has to be mined, shipped great distances, manufactured, which takes a great deal of heat to produce a usable product, then it must be shipped to the builder. Straw, on the other hand, is a waste product of wheat and grain production, and more than 200 billion tons of it are burned or otherwise disposed of in the United States alone each year. Thus, strawbale has a low embodied energy. Strawbale is an ideal material for the right climate and application.

TOXICITY

Many of today's newest technologies and materials, even some apparently benign ones, have not been tested in real living environments before they are enthusiastically adopted into design and manufacturing practice. We saw the hugely detrimental effects of mass installations of asbestos from World War II up through the 1970's. They finally discovered that asbestos was cancer-causing and a rush ensued to get those materials out of buildings. We are in no hurry to repeat such mistakes. One of the industries we look to for research on new materials is cosmetics. Cosmetics manufacturers perform research studies on the individual materials in their products and produce a publicly-available list of which of those chemicals cause harm. To discover which ingredients are healthiest for your build, check out http://www.cosmeticdatabase.com

Many of the materials we assume and have been told are "green" are actually dangerous. For instance, many bio-based plastics are toxic. They are just assumed to be less toxic because they support the sustainable renewables industry. Coca-Cola's PlantBottle, for instance, is PET plastic but with one ingredient from sugar cane. The rest of the bottle is made from p-xylene, a hazardous chemical linked to brain damage in newborn animal studies. So, the PlantBottle might be seen as a better option than the original bottle, but it is hardly safe or sustainable. We pay special attention to these materials.

MAINTENANCE / REPAIR-ABILITY

All buildings require maintenance. Green buildings require more than the average amount of upkeep. This is the beauty of truly sustainable buildings - if they are "alive", we must feed them and care for them so they can stay healthy. This brings us into relationship with our space - we become a participant in, as opposed to a user of, the space. Repair, on the other hand, is never a fun prospect. Repair of new materials and technologies is sometimes infeasible.

LACK OF DEPENDENCE ON TECHNOLOGY

Technology is not always the right answer for every family. Or for every society. While commerce and manufacturing profit greatly from it, many times it is not the right choice for the way we want to live. The bells and whistles... like automated & geared solar panels adjusters, programmable thermostats, and water filtration systems... often require the input of power. Imagine a massive storm shuts down the grid, the solar battery is broken, or our place gets struck by lightning... we want to be able to heat water, stay warm or cool, feed ourselves and the kids, and be safe despite whatever happens. When technology fails, we want to be able to keep living our lives. That is why our designs are not technology-dependent.

LOCATION

Where we get our materials impacts the area's commerce and industry, the health of the land, and minimizes the impact of energy consumption. As in the tree example in Performance within the Specified Climate above, location can also offer us a great opportunity to minimize the use of chemical treatments. We design our homes to work for and within our climates as well as to work with the land.

Working towards a Better Definition of Sustainability

by Rachel Preston Prinz and Carrie Christopher

Environmental sustainability is what most people think of when we talk about sustainability, but that is only one piece of true sustainability. When it is fully realized, sustainability addresses the ideas of social sustainability, economic sustainability, and environmental sustainability.

SOCIAL SUSTAINABILITY allows everyone within a community to prosper by providing opportunities to those who might want to develop themselves. One of the ways that community builds - where 20 or so people build a house together - support social sustainability is to allow the young, poor, or inexperienced an opportunity to learn new skills which they can use to improve their status and well-being. Social sustainability also encourages the mixing of different cultures and ideals so that all the participants grow in their understanding, and hopefully treatment, of one another. When social sustainability is applied to a community, it improves the quality of life of all of the community's members and encourages participation in governance through cultivating democratic means of communication and problem solving. When this ideal is fully realized, it achieves this without compromising the capabilities of future generations to do the same. Community builds accomplish this! Using techniques of building that utilize traditional techniques preserves our traditions for future generations. That also improves social sustainability.

A SUSTAINABLE ECONOMY is one in which our resources are not used up faster than nature renews them and if encourages the equitable sharing of economic benefits. Our build is sustainable economically when we a) use as little as possible to get as much as we need and no more, and b) when we use local agents, materials, and techniques so that we are investing money back into our communities. When we pay cash for our homes instead of getting a mortgage, it is a double bonus of economic sustainability.

ENVIRONMENTAL SUSTAINABILITY is the way we use materials to minimize the impact on the environment. Sustainable measures in design are not just about the Energy Star rating or the product's number of Volatile Organic Compounds (VOCs). In an environmentally sustainable building, the design:

- Is adapted specifically to a site.
- Does not rob from the needs of the environment.
- Is oriented to take advantage of sun, rain, wind, and other climatic benefits.
- Is sized exactly large enough to fit its purpose, and no more, so as not waste space (or resources).
- Uses regional materials, from no more than 500 miles and preferably under 200 miles away.
- Uses services of local artists and artisans for items like cabinetry, wall murals, and decorative metal work.
- Is built with materials that are low in embodied energy and high in performance.
- Operates pollution-free and waste-minimized during and after construction.
- Generates no wastes that are not useful for another process within the building or of benefit to the immediate environment.
- Is comprised of integrated systems that maximize efficiency and comfort.
- Is efficient: Reduces the energy required to function, harvests its own water and energy needs on-site, and then conserves those resources so they last.
- Promotes the health and well-being of all inhabitants.

Truly sustainable design starts with site planning, continues with building design and material selection, pays special attention to the methods and period of construction so as to minimize waste, and is finally achieved through the structure's life once operational. It considers energy, community, and conservation at every turn. From the energy required to transport materials; to the energy embodied in the materials; to the energy consumed by heating, cooling, lighting, plumbing and site drainage; and lastly - the costs and efforts required in maintaining a structure. It even considers the way we compost and recycle.

What is ironic about all this rigmarole about true sustainability is that it is fundamentally the common sense and low-tech solutions that are often the most sustainable. Designing a building with plenty of well-placed windows and that uses tube skylights to light inner rooms like closets and powder rooms makes daylighting an alternative to electric lighting for daytime use. Eliminating these power inputs reduces the number of resources needed. This type of approach is common sense, low-tech, and sustainable.

When we are talking about sustainable communities, the concepts of sustainability apply not only to the buildings, but also to the way the buildings and the people in them relate to one another. Sustainable communities are designed with people in mind. They are walkable and bike-able; it is possible to live, work, and play in the same neighborhood; there are goods and services available within the community; and the design preserves open space. It is even possible that sustainable technology is improved - a community cistern collects water off public buildings for landscaping, or maybe the curbs are designed to funnel storm water to trees. At this level, we can really make a difference and put ourselves on the path to achieving true sustainability.

We encourage using the *Principle of Appropriate Technology* in determining what you want to do in the build. This concept is really the ultimate "use what you have" philosophy: combine materials on hand using people power, spend as little money as possible, and solve a problem in your community in the process. Using this principle changes the way we live and build and participate in community. In principle, the Earthship concept attempts to do this. In practice though, it does not. For instance, using tires as building blocks wants to solve a problem. But unless you live on the edge of a tire dump, you are importing the problem. So, when you decide to build, consider what you have access to. What is a problem in your area that you can use to your advantage to make your home and your community better in the process?

Using passive solar design, building smaller, placing each room so that it has windows on at least two sides, looking to nature to learn how to live, understanding and working with our climate... all are techniques that you can use to address these principles.

Cost Effective Sustainable Features

by Rachel Preston Prinz and Carrie Christopher

We know we want to design a home that is truly sustainable, but we are not always sure how to make sustainability fit into our budgets. Here are some ideas for how sustainable investments stack up.

FEATURE	COST-EFFECTIVE	USER-FRIENDLY	NOTES
Non-toxic and native building materials	Very	Very	Protects from chemical sensitivities, reduces pollution, minimizes transportation cost
Passive solar gain	Very	Very	Methods: Direct gain through glass. Clerestory or high windows allow light to penetrate further into the structure. Trombe walls = masonry covered with glass. Greenhouse
Rainwater harvesting	Very	Very	Use harvested rainwater to water trees, shrubs, ponds; possible domestic uses include bathing, washing, and toilet tanks
Drip irrigation	Very	Very	Flexible tubing a few inches below the soil preserves water; watering can be put on a timer = effortless!
Solar hot water	Moderately	Very	Take an old water heater, paint it black, and hang it in the clerestory or greenhouse ceiling, allowing it to heat up to 90 degrees before entering the hot water heater.
Wind power	Moderately	Mostly	On sites with sustained winds. Costs up to $25,000.

Greywater harvesting	Not	Very	Best in arid environments. Many Building Codes require separate grey water sewer pipe and septic systems. Immediate distribution to landscape is possible.
Solar photovoltaic (PV) electricity	Moderately	Mostly	Photovoltaics require a great deal of technological gadgets to function. Failure of any = no power.
Constructed wetlands	Not	Very	Recycle black sewage water through septic, into pond lined with plastic sheeting, layered with gravel and sands, planted with aquatic plants. Cost $5,000.
Solar PV	Not	Very	Rooftop solar is clunky, and uses more embodied energy to manufacture the panels than will ever be produced by the panels over their lifetime, but manufacturing processes and technologies are getting more and more efficient. Alternatives include purchasing solar power from your utility, which may be partnered with a solar farm designed for that purpose.
Composting toilet	Moderately	Not So Much	Not everyone enjoys being this in touch with their potty. Might be off-putting in use and maintenance if not designed correctly.

Minimizing Waste and Pollution

by Rachel Preston Prinz and Carrie Christopher

Construction projects produce seven to ten pounds of waste per square foot. This is one of the reasons why construction projects are one of the largest contributors to landfills. To reduce or eliminate construction waste, plan your purchases so that you use all of your materials, then reduce waste, reuse, and recycle what is left.

GOING GREEN DURING CONSTRUCTION

Materials and products that are benign and can easily be managed through construction either by recycling, reuse, or other means, include:

- Woody and plant materials
- Concrete
- Gravel, aggregate, stone and rock
- Masonry and rubble
- Metals (ferrous and non-ferrous)
- Wood
- Plastic
- Glass
- Doors and windows
- Asphalt roofing
- Gypsum board (also called sheet rock)
- Carpet and carpet padding
- Cardboard and paper
- Plumbing
- Lighting fixtures

SUGGESTIONS FOR PREVENTING BUILDING SITE WASTE:

- Provide recycle bins for wood, drywall, cardboard, plastic, glass, aluminum, and metal (including steel framing).
- Store lumber on level blocking and under cover to minimize warping, twisting and waste.
- Set aside lumber and plywood/oriented strand board (OSB) cut-offs that can be used as fire blocking and spacers in header construction.
- Set aside large drywall scraps for use as filler pieces in small hidden areas.
- Reuse joint compound buckets for tool or material storage.
- Stack and cover loose brick and other masonry materials to prevent staining or loss.
- Branches and trees from site clearing can be stored separately and chipped for use as landscaping mulch and erosion control during construction.

- Clean concrete chunks, old brick, broken blocks and other masonry rubble can be used as backfill along foundation walls as well as in landscape gabion walls.

- When remodeling, separate metal radiators, grates, piping, aluminum siding, and old appliances for recyling.

- Use leftover insulation in interior wall cavities or on top of attic insulation.

- Collect clean sawdust for use in compost piles, around planting areas, or for outhouses. Avoid sawdust that might contain painted or treated wood.

- Use biodegradable trash bags for actual trash. Compost what you can!

- After construction is complete, donate unused materials to the local building component recycler (often Habitat for Humanity ReStore) or to neighbours.

TO MAXIMIZE THE RECYCLING BENEFITS OF BUILDING MATERIALS, ALSO CONSIDER:

- If using a contractor to pour foundations, make sure that they use reusable aluminum forms rather than wood forms, which are most often thrown away after one use.

- Use the more natural 30-year roofing materials like slate, clay, or metal.

- Use finger-jointed wood windows, trim, top and bottom plate material, and studs (ask at your lumber yard).

- Avoid large dimension solid lumber.

- Minimize material cuts.

- Use engineered wood "I" joists for flooring.

- Use trusses or "I" joists for roofs.

- Use structural insulated panels for walls or roofs.

- Use engineered wood studs, beams, joists or headers.

One of the more subtle ways we can have a positive impact on our sustainability footprint, especially when we are building the home ourselves, is to think about how we get materials to and from our site. The first instinct for most is to use the vehicle we have. But if our vehicle is a Toyota® Prius, that could be a problem. Many people buy an old truck for the purpose of the build. The issue with that is... lots of gas and exhaust in most cases. So we are building green but polluting during construction. That does not make sense, does it? To combat this, we suggest that if an alternate vehicle is required, consider one powered by renewable fuels. Buying new is always an option, but if funds are not readily available for that, consider that many governmental agencies auction their fleet vehicles. Check sites like autoauction.gsa.gov or your state's fleet services sites for public auction dates. Government fleet auctions are a great place to find a first-generation biodiesel truck for getting your construction materials to your site in the most environmentally-friendly way possible.

REUSING BUILDING MATERIALS

Using old building materials in our builds keeps them out of a landfill. We also love the look of richly textured and colored salvage materials in our buildings. As preservationists, we know that the best woods and the best materials were used in the old days, and there are lots of cool and innovative ways to use these materials in our home today! For reusing historic building materials, we have found that the most dependable ones to use include:

- Hardwood doors and windows, transoms, and shutters
- Roofing and flooring bricks
- Hardwood beams and roof decking
- Pine wood floors
- Hardware, including latches, locks, and hinges
- Stone and ceramic tiles
- Tin ceiling tiles, shingles, and siding
- Metal elements like anchors and stirrups (structural framing pieces)
- Cast iron railings, balusters, screens, trusses, and ornaments
- Historic lighting (though this can be a bit tricky if you do not know what you are doing)
- Rubble-masonry material from infilled veneer walls. May include stone and brick fragments for the foundations or rubble walls.
- Other historic building materials may be salvageable, but they really need to be evaluated on a case-by-case basis.

Our number one rule of thumb on building materials is never fully trust anyone trying to sell you something. They may be on commission or trying to move something out of their warehouse, so they may not be as forthright as we would like them to be. Always think it through and be willing to walk away, especially if they exert pressure on an expensive item because they "do not know if it will be there tomorrow". It is doubtful that there is going to be a rush on anything at a home store, even a Habitat ReStore, though things will certainly move unexpectedly sometimes. Any doubts? Just don't do it. Ask if they will take a refundable deposit to hold it if you are nervous about anything at all.

Our second big tip on this is do not use someone else's old lumber scraps in anything structural, or in interior applications. It is not possible to know how well those were stored. Can you confirm that they were kept dry, or in a place with no water issues? If they were overheated or stored without laying them out flat and supporting them along their entire length, they may split or be bent, and if they were kept where there was high humidity, they may bend, or, and maybe more importantly, they may have invisible molds growing in them that could make you sick.

From Vision to Reality

What does our house really want to look like? What qualities will it have? How big will it be? In this section, we will walk through the process of putting your vision down on paper. That way, you can have a light to guide you when things get busy and confusing, as they do on every build.

DEVELOPING A COMMON LANGUAGE

Towards the end of writing this book, I was happily basking in the sun making notes from a phone conference with contributor Sigi Koko, and we started talking about a common experience we have as designers, when people come to us and say "I want _____". What they fill in the blank with here could be "an Earthship"; "a cob home"; "a strawbale home"… pretty much any building that could be considered sustainable, and in many cases… natural. The challenge for us as designers is that the person asking for our help may not actually want to design a home that is the type they say they want. They saw a photo of something on a website or Pinterest board, or even on one of our blog posts about our practices, and they want THAT. The words used to describe what they saw become part of their language and it is really the only way they have to describe what THAT is. But THAT, be it strawbale, or cob, or even Earthship… may not be right for their climate. It might not be right for their lifestyle. It may require more maintenance than they have an interest in doing. It may not be right for their budget. Or it may give them weird shaped rooms. THAT might not make them feel how they want to feel in their space. So, much of what we end up doing as designers is asking questions that help our clients to get to what they really mean when they say "I want THAT." This finessing of ideas is part of why we love our jobs. It is also part of what makes doing what we do challenging for those that may not be trained to do this, as we are.

Many times, when someone comes in and says they want a "cob cottage", what someone really wants is to feel cozy in a smaller home than they might be in now or that they think is "normal". They may want to have rich textures like whitewashed walls and sculpted plaster surrounding them. They may want exposed wood that looks like timber framing. But they may not want to pay for real timber framing. When people come to me and say they want "an Earthship, done better", they usually mean that they want windows that bathe a room in light and warmth. They want pretty stained-glass-esque walls. They want a greenhouse so they can grow their own food. They want greywater recycling. They want textures and colors and to be independent of the grid and all the yuck that represents to those of us who seek the ever-evasive "More. Better." And most of the time, they want it built more naturally than that which they are offered… and with a minimum of maintenance required.

Where Sigi is more of a master craftsman, my expertise is really in finding new criteria for doing old things in better ways. I am more of a design problem solver and idea connector. The same will hold true for everyone on your build. We all have different strengths. The biggest key for getting the home that you dream of is to be willing to see exactly what it is you are looking for, to learn as much as you possibly can, and then to assess your strengths and weaknesses (and those of your team) regarding materials and systems, and then to modify your ideas as appropriate to your value, climate, and budget. That is what the following exercises aim to help you do.

Where You Live Now

One of the best ways of knowing what you really need for spaces in your home is to take an objective look at the home you have now and use that understanding to determine what spaces you really need for the long term.

HERE IS HOW:

- Make a list of each space in your current home.
- Measure the length and width of each room, then multiply those by each other to get the square footage for that room.
- Then list what all that space is used for. Does the guest room double as an office? Or off-season clothes storage? Is it used daily? Weekly? Annually? Who all uses the space? Is the room too big for all of its uses? Too small? Write it all down. If the space is too large or too small, how much extra room do you think you need? And finally, if you only need a part of the room - the closet, for instance, or the office area – how much space does that take up?
- Lastly, number each room by how much it gets used.

Now you have set your priorities and have an idea how much space you need to design your new space!

Wish List

What are your visions and dreams for how your new home will be and feel? Make a list of everything you see when you imagine yourself there – from textures, to views, to colors, to room uses. Write down everything, even if you know you cannot afford it.

Once you know your vision, go through the list and underline everything that is a "must have". Then, put a star or a heart next to items you really want but do not need. Finally, make a new list for each underlined must item and describe what underlying meanings that item entails. Does each bathroom have to have natural lighting? Or does the living room need to have a workspace for the computer? Write it down.

Making these lists and clarifying what you mean will not only help to quantify the spaces you need, but it will also help to determine the qualities of those spaces.

We have included another helpful exercise for this effort called Your Core Desired Feelings in Chapter 10. This section is about figuring out the essence of what you really want to feel in your space. Maybe doing that now will help you too.

Setting a Vision

Giving your vision a name is one of the most helpful things you can do to help guide your design and share it with others. Call it your palace, your cottage, your casita, your tropical paradise, your hermit's cave, your hobbit house... What is the vision you have for your future home? What does it want to be? What does that mean to you? Write all this down. Start thinking about the parts of whatever you are attracted to. Do you love the hobbit houses' round doors? The casita's deep-set windows? The big bank of windows on the Earthship that provides a warm nesting spot to bask in the sun? A big wrap-around porch like on southern plantations? Whatever it is, take some time and give it a name. Then define it, inside and out. What are you really looking for?

Idea Book

It is what it sounds like. A good designer will make one for you or ask you to make one. So, let's make one! All you need is a pile of our favorite magazines, a 3 ring binder, and some dividers.

Have you ever made a vision board? Here, you will do the same thing... dream a life into being... only this time, for your house! Just tear out pages of magazines that have pictures of things you would love to have and put them all in the binder. Use dividers to make sections for each room so you can find things easily. Then, you can show what you want to our designer, your build crew, or the gal at the hardware store who is blending your paint and know they get exactly what you mean for what you want for the space.

We recommend at least 3 hours for this and that everyone in the home participate. Do not be surprised just how clear things become from working this process! For those that are digitally inclined, a Pinterest board is a great place to do this exercise. We have started several boards which may provide some inspiration, which we shared in the Earthship 2.0 section.

Good luck and happy collecting!

Site Diagram

A site analysis is a great tool for helping you to come to know your site intimately. When we do them for our clients, we do casual sketch versions like the one seen here as well as detailed analyses on topographic site plans. We will walk you through all of the information you want to include in the site section. This is a tool for you, and you may also find that it helps you to communicate with your designer, your build crew, and/or your contractors. If they know why you are doing something, they may be able to help you see ways these ideas might be improved, or keep things from happening that could be detrimental.

A typical site analysis uses a sketch or a copy of the site plat, adds a scale, and adds a north arrow. You can find North with a compass, but you also can do it by doing nothing but sitting on the site at dawn and dusk one day. This ancient method of wayfinding uses a *gnomon* - a sundial of sorts - at sunrise and sunset in order to determine where north is. Just hammer a sturdy straight stick or rebar into the ground. Make a mark on the ground from the stick along the outside edge of the shadow at the first rays of the sunrise. Do the same at the last rays of the sunset. Divide the triangle-shaped space between the two marks in half equally and draw another line from the stick through the halfway point at the center of the angle. This middle line is not only noon, but North. (Reverse this to find South in the southern hemisphere.)

Draw a sun in the south, if you live in the northern hemisphere. (Reverse this if you live in the southern hemisphere.) If you have mountains within 2 miles of your home, draw those in the directions they are in. If there is a valley or a split in the mountains that points at your house, show that too, as cold air will travel down this valley and cool your home by a few degrees. Mark the directions of nearby water and big stands of trees. Also, note the views!

Then add the primary movement of hot summer winds... you might draw these in red. That is the hot air we want to shed. Then, draw in the way the wind moves in winter in blue. That is the cold air we want to shed. These are the directions we want to locate berms in if possible. This is one place where the standard design of an Earthship lacks... sometimes we want our berm to be on a side wall even more than the back wall if we really want to use earth-sheltering to our most advantage to shed the hot and cold winds.

Then, draw in natural drainages and swales. Add rises and natural berms. Watch how these flow across the site. Where is the water coming from and where is it going? Many times, you will be able to determine the pitch of the land, and then easily determine the direction you want to pitch the ground away from your house to get rid of groundwater which might threaten the foundation.

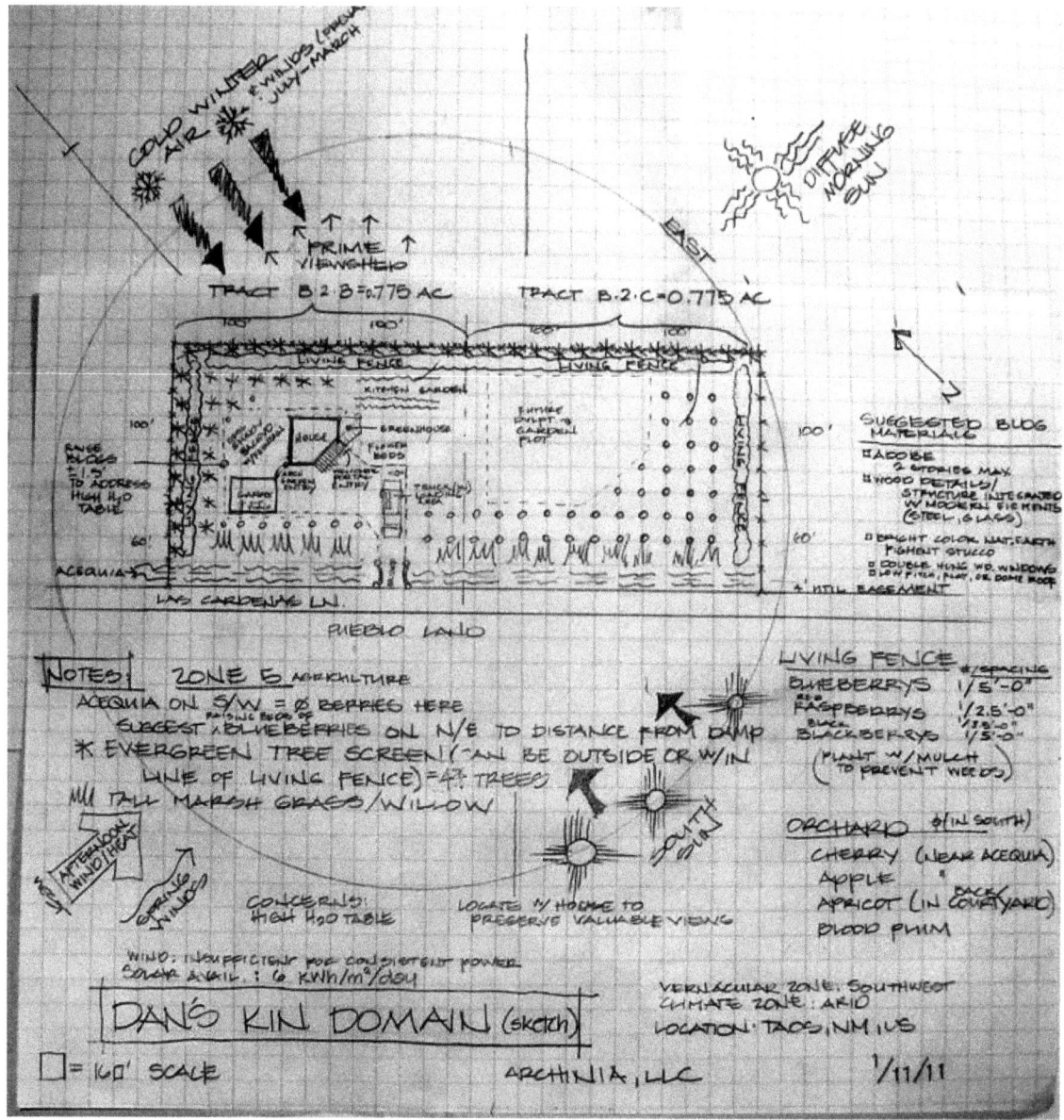

Figure 9. Typical Site Diagram

Another thing you might consider if you live on your site for a bit is to study your rain- and snow-shadows. You can tell which way your storms typically come from by watching where there is a "shadow" cast by whatever you are living in that does not get wet or have snow on it. The rain and snow shadow location is a great place to put the entrance to your home if you want to minimize the amount of shoveling you have to do. It is also a great place to put steps that will not be covered for weather protection.

Where is the Money?
How to Afford to Pay Cash for Your Home

"If you do not have $20-30,000 in cash, only in rare cases should you start building."
- the Darfield Earthship

One of the issues with the Earthships, and any other kind of home we might want to build to be free (of debt, especially…), is that our dreams tend to live larger than what we can afford. No matter how crafty and creative we are, if we want to live debt-free and are not independently wealthy… we need to have a plan.

Mortgage Financing

by Steve Scott

In acquiring or remodeling a home in a rural location or using sustainable materials, there are fewer choices when it comes to financing than a conventional home loan. When you get into sustainable or renewables 'green' building, the sources funding is even more difficult to find.

That said, home financing is predicated on the level of risk to the lender and ultimately the investor on those loans, whether it's Fannie Mae, Freddie Mac, FHA, VA or USDA.

The GSE's or Government Sponsored Enterprises such as Fannie Mae and Freddie Mac as well as the government insurance funds FHA and VA do not lend in rural locations where there is a lack of market activity, lack of comparable sales, lack of community and public services, or a scattered low density residential population.

The criteria for location and property types include things such as distance, paved or gravel access roads, electrical power and proper method of sewage disposal/treatment. For instance on distance, most conventional lenders will require that comparable sales be within a few miles and within a few months of closing to establish a market value. The property must have paved or gravel roads to the property so as to have year round access to and from the property. There must be potable water on or to the property by either service or well. Also considered are methods of handling waste such as septic or sewage.

In meeting their requirements, you may obtain a conventional loan secured on that property, but you'll be required to meet the other qualifying criteria regarding credit and your ability to repay the mortgage. These loans can be obtained from many different sources such as banks, credit unions or mortgage companies. These sources may also offer either FHA or VA (provided you are a Veteran with an eligibility certificate) loans.

For those properties that are considered 'rural', the USDA has lending programs where lack of comparable sales or the distance may be a factor in not being able to obtain conventional financing. You can find out more by searching online at http://www.rd.usda.gov and 'browse by state' or look under 'programs & services'.

FHA does have Energy Efficient Mortgages or EEMs that provide mortgage insurance to lenders for an acquisition or refinance of a principle residence to incorporate the cost of energy improvements. This type of loan can be used in conjunction with a FHA 203(k) rehabilitation loan which is for purchasing or refinancing a primary residence that needs repairs.

HUD does provide Title I Home Improvement Loans with a maximum loan amount of $25,000 on a single family dwelling. This is for existing construction that is not being purchased or refinanced.

When thinking in terms of a 'green' home with amenities such as rammed earth or strawbale walls, financing is more difficult to acquire. Most people that buy or build these types of homes usually do so with private money sources such as family loans, personal loans against pledged assets or loans secured against other properties. However, it must be noted that even upon completion, it may be difficult to obtain financing for either a refinance or a buyer of the property.

One option is to contact local or regional banks and credit unions to find community lenders who may be willing to loan on 'green' or rural properties.

As 'green' becomes more mainstream, which we are seeing not only in rural but urban areas, systems such as solar photovoltaic and solar thermal can be financed through special programs utilizing rebates, grants or tax credits or loans to defray the initial costs of installation. Typically, most financing for solar energy is calculated on a ten year repayment plan with a cost of $15,000 and no down payment. To find out more; you can search online for the U.S. Department of Energy 'The Borrower's Guide to Financing Solar Energy Systems'.

There is also a 'Consumer's Guide for Small Wind Electrical Systems' page 24 explains a 2002 Farm Bill – Wind Energy Development Provisions which covers incentive types and eligible technologies. Just be aware that Congress may have made changes to the funding of these improvements in recent years.

Generally speaking, financing a 'green' home purchase or construction which may be off the grid, will be a challenge but not an insurmountable one. It may even take an amalgam of different programs to achieve one's goal of living green.

The rule of thumb is to do your homework to make sure all of your cost estimates such as materials, labor and any delays or other cost overruns are factored into the loan, so that you aren't put into the position of running out of funds needed to complete the project. This is probably the most important piece of advice anyone can give a potential homeowner that is building or remodeling a home.

Tools to Facilitate Financing

A project plan is a useful tool to take to your prospective bank or mortgage company. People who choose to go the professionally-designed home route will have some of this at the ready, as their designer or builder will work to get some of these things compiled for the building permit. A project plan should include plans and specs, a project budget broken down by phases, a letter from the building & planning division confirming the project has been approved for a construction permit, and a letter from your insurance carrier stating that they are willing to cover the home.

In our research, we found that many times, people got a loan for the land, then obtain an owner/builder construction mortgage. Sometimes, these unconventional homes can cost slightly more to finance because of a higher interest rate due to higher risk.

Getting financing will be easiest if the title for the land is absolutely clear; if you have established a solid credit history previously, especially with the bank you are looking to borrow from; and if you have at least 20% to put down in cash. 20% down offers better rates, eliminates the need for private mortgage insurance, and gives access to larger and more diverse types of loans.

If they agree to cover your loan, the lending institution will give you a letter of credit.

Cost implications of the financing effort include the building permit, which can easily cost $1,000 or more; plumbing permit; electrical permit; grading permit; design and/or engineering fees. These most often cannot be charged to the mortgage and can easily add up to $20,000; plus you will also pay for appraisals and origination costs. Be sure to ask your lending advisor to clarify all costs from their end.

For those that want to purchase and complete an unfinished Earthship, please be aware: according to John Kejr, Taos' Earthship sales expert, one of the issues with buying existing Earthships these days is appraisals. New federal laws say that lenders cannot choose the appraiser. That means that it is likely that the appraiser assigned to your project will not understand off-grid experimental housing. This can lead to the Earthship being under-valued. This can be great if you are a buyer, but challenging if you are looking to sell. John has a ton of great information at his blog at http://taosearthships.com/blog.htm

If you are successful in getting financing, understand your bridging loan requirements to make draws available at certain points in your construction.

One of the aspects of design we perform for our clients is planning for the reality of building, including ongoing maintenance costs. This kind of attention to the financials is needed if you want to be sure you can afford your dream home. If you cannot afford it, you can then evolve the plan to make it work before you get to the point of having a half-built house that you have to abandon.

Creative Funding Solutions

GIVE UP ON GRANTWRITING

One of the hardest parts of my job, which has included working professionally as an architectural grant-writer, is telling people that forming a non-profit to build your home is not going to work. It just won't. That would be awesome. But the economy has made money harder to get and the foundations that might have money to give for eco-minded projects are looking at your project in relation to other projects. If they have to choose between building one family an Earthship and building a school for a whole class of under-privileged kids, they are most likely going to choose the school because it makes the biggest impact on the most people. If there are grants out there for which your Earthship would be eligible, each proposal would have to be adjusted so that it meets each grant-maker's funding guidelines and priorities. That is no small task. A grant can easily take 1,000 hours to prepare, then another 100 hours to change for each foundation. Because of the community impact criteria most grant-makers require, the likelihood of your grant being funded is extremely small. We have watched many well-planned projects in well-funded organizations with huge potential positive community impacts work for years and make no progress in obtaining grants to fund their building projects. Unless you can afford a staff of grant-writers and your building will be for the public good, do yourself a favor and write this idea off and make a plan for funding your project another way. If you are extremely good at marketing, you might be able to get sponsors for a few parts of the project.

SAYING YES TO THE GRID

The single biggest cost consideration in Earthship builds appears to lie in the decision to go grid-tied versus going off-grid. The grid-tied Earthship still has simple greywater and rainwater catchment systems, but omits the solar photovoltaics, Power Organizing, and Water Organizing Module of traditional Earthships, saving up to $100,000 and sometimes even more. This brings the cost of a grid-tied Earthship to only a few dollars more per square foot than a conventionally-built home. The grid-tied Earthship gets its water and power from the grid, which means a couple of small bills each month. Preparing for future off-grid use by wiring for future connections would add another few thousand dollars to the cost at the build-out, but will facilitate easy upgrades down the road. We will cover much of how to do this in the coming sections.

MINIMIZE YOUR FOOTPRINT, MAXIMIZE USABLE SPACE

Part of the affordability plan for any build has to be to eliminate wasted space, unnecessarily large (or small) hallways, and invisible hallways so we can maximize the use of space. More than half of the traditional Earthship is invisible hallway and uninhabitable greenhouse. Cut that out and you can cut the build cost by up to a third. Why not half? Because there are certain start-up costs that will not change if the building gets a little smaller. We call these "mobilization" costs. That includes getting all the equipment including tools to the site, getting your building materials on-site, getting permits paid for and approved, getting contractors lined up, setting up a campsite or buying an RV, getting water to the site … basically anything and everything we need to get going on the build. These are required for every build, and the scale of them changes only slightly whether you are building a 200 square foot house or a 2,000 square foot house.

This idea is not limited to Earthships. In any house, we can minimize cost outlays by minimizing the square footage. Planning for building only the space we need is a critical first step, and we will guide you through this process in Chapter 8.

DO NOT RUSH!!!

UNIQUE WAYS OF INVESTING IN THE BUILD

When thinking about how to live while you are building, it may seem most logical to stay in a tent. But think about this for a second: If you buy a small RV, a gypsy wagon, or one of those cute log cabin trailer houses, even used, and make and keep it nice so you can really enjoy being out on your site throughout the build, you can then sell your temporary home at the end of the build and use that money to pay off anything you put on credit. Or rent it out for income later. You can use your temporary housing as an investment, and since you might be there a year or more, be more comfortable with that extra layer of weather, privacy, and financial protection. Check out our Gypsy Wagon Pinterest Board for Tips and Tricks for how to make living small during the build fun and beautiful.

Another great option is to look at portable tiny houses. Some of the best manufacturers for these are Bear Creek Carpentry Company of Woodgate, New York; Heirloom Tiny Houses of Oregon; or for those with luxe taste, Wheelhaus. For those who want a tiny home made of local, natural, and salvage materials, check out Humble Hand Crafts.

Another way we have found in our design practice for getting an "instant" home is to buy a cute little historic house that is somewhere they do not want it anymore and have it moved in. While the purchase price of the home can often amount to nearly nothing ($20,000 is normal, though $1.00 is not uncommon), the move can cost up to $50,000. But once it is on site, you have got nearly instant valuable property. Build a foundation, put the relocated home on it, fix it up, live in it while you are building your home, and if you have enough land, sell it to someone you want to be neighbors with. Again, investment at the outset can be realized as investment in your hand-built dream home after construction. You can find free old houses at http://circaoldhouses.com/move-me-love-me-free-houses-for-anyone-who-can-move-them/

HOUSING PRICES - ALTERNATIVES TO CAMPING AND/OR UPGRADES TO SITE

200SF Self-Built Cabin	$20,000
200SF Tiny house	$50,000
200SF Pre-built Cabin or RV	$60,000
400SF Geodesic Dome	$11,000
Shower, Outhouse	$3,000

BUYING UNFINISHED

One of the ways that you can save money on an Earthship is to buy one that is unfinished and finish it out. If you have great carpentry skills and know your way around construction or can verify that the tire walls are not shoddily built, this may be a viable option. We suggest ripping that angled front wall out, straighten it up, and build a shed roof from the top of the now higher wall to pitch onto the shed roof over the rooms which will render a single pitch to the north shedding water from the front face to the back. You will be doubly benefitted if you add a 2 foot deep overhang over these windows to shade them and prevent overheating the 8 months a year Earthships tend to get hot. If you do this, remember, you will need to get insurance for living in the house while you are redoing it.

GETTING HELP

STUDY, STUDY, STUDY. Make sure there is an internet-connected laptop with access to Google and YouTube on-site and study every build action before starting. Ask the volunteers to watch with you a second time. Learning the hard way costs money, time, and frustration. Get everyone on-board early and save yourself that.

Minimizing mistakes and having adequate supervision by someone who knows what they are doing means minimizing cost. Sometimes hiring a construction manager, even if they come out only every few days, is worth every penny. Oftentimes, they can spot corrections that should be made before they become real problems.

Another great tip we gleaned from our research was to rally the local community around your build. Look to find new friends who are building or who have built a natural and/or sustainable home in your area. They may know of resources you may otherwise not find. They may have made tweaks to their design that you can use to make yours work better. They may have figured out issues with designing for your climate that can save you time, money, and/or frustration. Most of all… they may have gone through the process of permitting and they might just save you some major headaches by sharing their experiences with you. Friends and allies are a critical aspect to any natural or hand-made build!

DO NOT RUSH!!!

SALVAGE MATERIALS

Saving money on building materials is not just about what can be found at the dump or in the neighbors' shed. Check with local construction, landscape, and demolition companies or visit local construction sites and see if they have waste materials you can take off their hands. Check with the telephone company to see if they have discarded telephone poles or even the train companies to find steel materials or even bridges for salvage! Get creative! Who has some version of what is needed that can be had on the cheap? Then, be sure to visit Habitat for Humanity ReStores, thrift stores, and peruse websites like Craigslist or Freecycle! Go to garage sales. Barter. Trade with other homesteaders… which means… get to know the neighbors and share tips and tricks.

BUILD ON A MATERIAL-RICH SITE

If building on a site with trees, you may choose a place to build that has an awesome feel or views, even if it has trees in the spot you want to build. Why? You can cut those trees and mill your own lumber. You will already have some of the tools you need for the build. Add an attachment or two and milling is easy.

Got rocks? Clear them off and use them instead of cans for building bond beams or interior walls. Hand-drill the well. Design a solar composting toilet. If you can dream it, someone has done it, and the instructions are probably on YouTube. Be sure to read the comments! There are often tips and tweaks that make a design better.

It all comes back to STUDY STUDY STUDY!

MAKE A PLAN

Have we said this yet? DO NOT RUSH!!! Make a plan. Prepare for people not to show up. Have a backup plan for when they don't. Have a backup plan for the backup plan. Have extra food and water in case extra people show up. Get the tools and materials you need before construction starts. Store materials well.

Start building in spring when the snow is melted. Do not build anything structural on rainy days - the ground shifts and wood fluffs up with weather and humidity. Wait until it is dry.

Do not start building in fall unless you are 100% sure you can get the building "dried in", or weather-tight, before the first freeze. Then you can use the slow winter months to hire contractors to do inside work. They are often hungry for work during the winter and might work for a better rate. Though, to be fair, if you cannot afford some type of supplementary heat if your system is not running yet and you live in a very cold place, this may not work either.

There are countless big decisions in building a home, and we want to be mindful of every one because they all affect each other. Do not feel rushed. Take the time to make sure each decision is the best way to proceed. Take each aspect of the project and break it down into bite sized bits to manage the pressure.

Pick the Right Materials

When we asked our friend Sigi Koko what she thought about which building materials were most affordable, she offered,

> *"I approach which material to use by asking: 1) what is available locally and 2) what performance characteristics are needed. Then it goes to labor cost and considerations. Really, the only expensive natural building materials are due to labor costs, not material costs."*

The aspects of building that you can do yourself will bring down the cost. What skills do you bring to the table?

The other part of picking the right materials is designing them to work for more than one purpose. A great example of this happens at Taos Pueblo. There are many free-standing and attached *latilla* (rough but straight branch) trellises out in front of the main buildings. These are great shade structures for when the summer heat gets to be too much and they are often used as a shelter for tribal groups during feast days. What most people do not realize is that these functional, usable, cool spaces are a bonus. The trellis' real purpose is as a drying rack for food, chiles, and herbal medicinals.

The same holds true for the Pueblo's massing. Massing is when you take a bunch of blocks and stretch and squish them to make different sizes, them put them all together to make a more interesting form. In the case of Taos Pueblo, the massing makes the building look like it has been added to and built up over time, which is true, and it also echoes the form of the sacred mountain behind the home block. This design allows for maximum exposure of the south-east facing Pueblo's roof and walls to the sun for solar gain during the winter. Using stacked massing allows them to share heat from floor to floor in winter via shared fireplaces and chimneys, and also renders the most interior spaces and bottom levels of the Pueblo cool in the heat of summer. This allows the people of the Pueblo to use these cool dark spaces for food storage just like a root cellar. The constant internal temperatures that result from using this unusual form of earth-sheltering allow the Puebloans to keep goods in storage for a stunning 7 years! They also use the massing and terracing of the Pueblo form to differentiate uses. The first floor is a public floor for shops and front doors. The slightly stepped back second floor is used as a living room and kitchen. The even more stepped back and smaller third floor is used as a bedroom, where the heat that rises and the fireplace that heats the much smaller space can keep the occupants warm through the night. (With an added bonus of extra security, plus an amazing view to wake up to.) Using a tool like massing can help us to plan for additions, raise the roof on one special room, as well as integrate chimneys, stair towers, atriums, tower skylights, or buttressing into the form of the building in beautiful, smart, ways.

Learning how systems can work together can help us to achieve the highest levels of sustainability with the smallest financial and physical footprint possible.

Homeowners Bill of Rights

We believe in the Homeowners Bill of Rights. Most of the time when people use this term, they are referring to a document protecting a homeowner from negative lending practices. The version we use, from Homeowners Against Deficient Dwellings, is based on the idea that we all deserve a place to live that works for us:

When consumers buy a new home or contract for additions and/or remodeling of an existing home:

They have the right to safe and sound, quality construction.

They have the right to expect that their new home and/or any home improvements are built in compliance with all existing local, state, and federal Building Codes and ordinances.

They have the right to expect that only quality, performance-proven building products are used in their homes and that all such products are installed in accordance with manufacturers' specifications.

They have the right to expect that the Architect's and Engineer's designs are completely and accurately followed.

They have the right to expect that the home will not leak or breed toxic mold(s), is structurally sound, and that all mechanical systems and structural components will perform properly.

They have the right to receive, in a timely manner prior to signing a sales contract and/or closing documents, complete information regarding their purchase contracts, warranties, disclosures of agencies, and any and all relationships and/or partnerships their real estate broker and/or builder may have with all agencies involved with the home buying process. This includes, but is not limited to: home inspectors, lenders, title companies, builders'/subcontractors' insurance carriers, products' manufacturers, realtors, and home warranty companies.

They have the right to access records, public and private, regarding performance and complaints pertaining to their builder, subcontractors, home warranty companies, lenders, manufacturers, realtors, title companies, insurance carriers, and any other entity associated with the home building/home buying process.

They have the right to full disclosures in regard to new housing.

They have the right to a trial conducted by their peers, rather than to be forced into contractual binding arbitration.

They have the right to peace of mind concerning the safety of their family.

- *From http://hadd.com/bill-of-rights*

Tax Incentives for Green Design

The national governments in the United States and other nations support energy savings through programs for individuals, communities, and organizations. In the US, the Database of State Incentives for Renewables and Efficiency (DSIRE) offers a comprehensive listing of information on state, local, utility, and federal incentives and policies that promote renewable energy and energy efficiency. Their website is at: http://www.dsireusa.org/

Here are some other programs to check out:

U.S. FEDERAL GRANT PROGRAMS

- Tribal Energy Program Grants
- U.S. Department of Treasury - Renewable Energy Grants
- USDA - Rural Energy for America Program (REAP) Grants

U.S. FEDERAL LOAN PROGRAMS

- Clean Renewable Energy Bonds (CREBs)
- Energy-Efficient Mortgages
- Qualified Energy Conservation Bonds (QECBs)
- U.S. Department of Energy - Loan Guarantee Program
- USDA - Rural Energy for America Program (REAP) Loan Guarantees

PERSONAL EXEMPTIONS AND TAX CREDITS

- Residential Energy Conservation Subsidy Exclusion
- Residential Energy Efficiency Tax Credit
- Residential Renewable Energy Tax Credit

To find federal tax credit opportunities in the US, visit: http://www.energytaxincentives.org/

CANADA

The Office of Energy Efficiency at Natural Resources Canada offers grants and incentives through its ecoENERGY Retrofit program to homeowners, businesses, large industries and public institutions to help them invest in energy- and pollution-saving upgrades. Selected provincial and municipal entities also offer incentives.

Budgeting for a Contractor

> *"People who haven't built "things" really should not expect to learn to do so while building an Earthship. Hiring somebody is difficult when building an Earthship because there are so few people who have done it who are for hire.*
> *We had 10 years experience designing and building log homes and it was still difficult for us. Only if you are one of those rare individuals who can do "anything" should you embark on a project like this without a fair bit of construction experience."*
>
> \- From The Darfield Earthship blog

Sometimes you get to a point where you realize you just need some extra help. It is time to find an expert to help work out the details. Hiring a contractor can be a complex process. Our best advice here is to find someone with a good reputation who works day-in and day-out with natural materials. Do not get a specialist, like a rammed earth home contractor, unless you are using their preferred system.

A home built by a contractor will cost more than what we can build it for ourselves because they will add taxes, labor, bonding, overhead, and profit. These are not things to get mad about or frustrated by. Taxes, we all have to pay. Labor is what it costs to get it installed. Bonding protects us from predatory business practices. There is nothing a contractor does on site that is not managed by someone else before they do it - getting orders on paper, picked up, tracked, and to the build site takes time and attention to detail which they will often pay someone to do. We want to pay for someone else to do that so the professional help we need – the contractor – is available for us when we need them. Anyone who is in business has to make a profit to keep growing. That is also how a company will have the money to pay in advance for our materials. We like profit. It helps us get good buildings built and helps to grow worthy businesses in our community. Taxes, we can figure easily… in New Mexico, they are around 7%. Labor we can predict as approximately 27%. Bonding should be around 2%. Overhead should be around 12%. Profit should be limited to around 10%. So, if we all up all the percentages we get to 58%, which translates to… for every dollar we spend on materials, we can add $0.58 for a contractor to purchase and install everything associated with that dollar. Your local area will likely have different number but this is a place to start if you want to consider whether hiring a contractor might be an option for you.

One note here: hiring a budget contractor is not always a good idea. In our work, we have found consistently that mid- to high-end contractors use better materials, better tools, and are more likely to complete the project in a timely manner. We have had repeated experiences with budget contractors who skip the submittal process and then use unspecified materials that degrade building system performance; they suggest alternates to "save you money" that will not last as long or perform as well (and you will replace later thereby reducing your real "savings"; and they tend to deliver contracts late. It is our experience that what you do not pay for in regard to quality means it takes more time and/or it may not work out as well. So you are paying either with cash, or mediocre materials and a longer build time. Sadly, "You get what you pay for" is an appropriate adage here. It really comes down to the Quality/Cost/Quantity equation we will talk about in the next section.

Deciding Factors

There is an old idea that rules many aspects of life that says that there are three choices that govern our decision making. In most cases, those choices are Cost, Quality, and Quantity (in this case - space). The general rule is that of three choices, we can only get two. So we can have Low Cost but we have to sacrifice a little in Quantity to get better Quality. Or we have to sacrifice a little Quality if we want more Quantity. Or, we can have all the Quantity we need and high Quality finishes, but we should be prepared for a higher Cost. We have discovered this rule to be true for all but the wealthiest clients. So, you want to think about where your priorities are. Which two of the three factors are your priorities? Write them down and come back to this when you need to remind yourself.

There are decisions you can make at the outset which will help keep costs down. A square or rectilinear house is easier to build and less expensive than a rounded or angled house. Complex shapes have higher ratios of surface area per square foot, so to keep costs down, make shapes, especially roof shapes, simple. Use straight walls, because curved walls can cost substantially more. Eliminate bump-outs on the exterior of the building, because corners cost money. Same with the details. If you use common square or rectilinear windows, doors, and cabinets in lieu of handmade, angled, or rounded ones, the cost will come down. The manufacture time and build time, as well as maintenance cost and time, will also come down

The less distance the roof joist or viga has to span, the smaller those members have to be, and costs will come down. The fewer finishes you use and joints between materials you have, costs will also come down. The fewer the number of deliveries from the building store, costs will come down.

Combining the living room, kitchen, and dining room can save us up to 500 square feet. That is whatever your cost per square foot is, times 500, in savings.

If you design ceiling heights around common "pre-cut" stud lengths, gypsum board sizes, or adobe brick thicknesses, you will need to trim fewer pieces, and thus... costs will come down.

Putting energy into the design before you start building is one of the best ways you can work the Cost aspect of design in your favor.

Insurance for the Non-Traditional Home

by Debra Bailey of Brown and Brown Insurance of Taos

You may have already discovered that finding a company to insure non-traditional homes, including Earthships, strawbale, or berm-homes, can be a challenge. That is because insurance companies promulgate their rates based on statistics and use the law of large numbers. Thus far, we do not have a population of these homes adequate to provide the necessary supporting data required by our state's admitted carriers.

There was a time when it was impossible to insure these homes, but we have made progress. Currently, there are a few Surplus Lines Carriers that will insure these homes on either a Dwelling Fire Policy or a Homeowner's Policy. We will provide more information regarding these policy types further in this chapter. Here are the questions you need to ask your insurer:

How do I know if my home is properly insured?

Quite often, Earthship clients come to me asking that I review their current policy, and I find that they do not have a Homeowner's Policy, but rather the more limiting Dwelling Fire Policy. For the policyholder, it is important to know there is a difference in the Dwelling Fire Policy and the Homeowner's Policy. If you do not see these words on the policy's declaration page, look at the policy form numbers for these identifiers: DP-1, DP-2, DP-3, HO-2, HO-3, HO-5. The DP forms represent the Dwelling Fire Policy forms. The HO forms represent the Homeowner's Policy forms.

HO Policies provide broader coverage than DP Policies. If the insured home is OWNER occupied as either a primary or secondary home, purchasing a Homeowner's policy is required. If the home is tenant occupied, then it is appropriate to insure it with a DP Policy.

Why is my agent asking me to sign a disclosure statement acknowledging that my home is insured with a non-admitted carrier? What does that mean?

An admitted carrier is an insurance company that has been approved by the state's insurance department. The insurance company must comply with state insurance regulations, and in the event the insurance company fails financially, the state will step in to make payment of states. A non-admitted carrier is an insurance company that has not been approved by the state and does not have the backing of the state's guaranty fund in the case the company becomes insolvent. By law, if an agent places your insurance through a Non-Admitted carrier, they must inform you of this and the agent will document their disclosure by having you sign the disclosure statement.

Is being insured by a non-admitted carrier a bad thing?

Not necessarily. While it may seem as if admitted carriers are the clear winner between the two types, there are other issues to consider as well. Insurance companies are given letter grades form A++ to F. The grades are calculated by a credit firm called A.M. Best, which has been rating insurance companies since 1906. The A++ is the best and highest rating, while the F is the lowest rating a company can receive. So, though a company may be a Non-Admitted Carrier (such as your Lloyd's companies), this company could have a financial rating of A++. And, you may have an Admitted Carrier with a C rating. Which would you prefer? I would definitely prefer to take my chances with the A++ Non-Admitted Carrier. Any carrier with an "A" rating or better is a good bet.

What is the right amount of insurance to purchase on my home?

Home value can be a confusing subject. If you look at a home appraisal, you will find that most appraisals reflect the current market value. This is a reflection of the economic conditions for "resale value" of homes in a geographic location. Often times, however, people who build non-traditional homes participate in the building of the home, and do not know what it would cost to have a professional contractor build the home. The bottom line is this: Your home should be insured for the current REPLACEMENT VALUE. Should you sustain a loss, the insurance company is obligated to pay a professional contractor to restore or rebuild your home. Due to the current economic climate in most areas of the US, the market value of an existing home is lower than new home construction cost.

It is wise to have your insurance agent complete a Replacement Cost Estimate on your home. After providing facts about the features of your home, including square footage, exterior wall material, interior wall material, flooring, ceiling, number of bathrooms, special features such as skylights, solar panels, water filtration systems, heating and cooling systems, etc... your agent can determine the replacement value for your property.

What if I do not want to insure for full replacement value?

Most insurance policies require that you insure your home for full replacement value because contractually, if your home is a total loss, they are required to rebuild the home in its entirety. Additionally, personal property insurance policies contain wording in the contract called the Co-Insurance Clause. This states that, if your home is insured for less than 80% of Current Replacement Cost, at the time of the loss, the insured's claim can be penalized proportionate the amount the home is under-insured. You purchase insured to be fully protected. You do not want to discover, at the time you have a claim, that your home was UNDER-insured, and you will be penalized in your claim settlement.

If my home were destroyed, I would not rebuild anyway, I just want money to help me start over somewhere new. Is this possible?

It is rare to find a property insurance policy with a cash-pay-out feature. And the few that exist are home-owner's policies where it is a stipulation that the home be insured for full replacement value. Ordinarily, the Homeowner's and Dwelling Fire Policies state that the insurance company will rebuild or repair the home, and at the same property location. If you are interested in a policy with the cash pay-out feature, discuss this with your agent.

Does it matter if I shop for insurance online, go to an exclusive agent or an independent agent?

I love shopping online and once I have done all my research and I KNOW my product, I feel confident to see where I can get my best deal: Amazon vs. E-Bay vs Best-Buy vs Target, etcetera... This works for price comparisons on a staple product. But, when I need professional guidance and consultation, I prefer to seek counsel with a professional. A consultation with a personal insurance agent is far more than "just getting a quote." You can obtain a price quote on-line or by phone. But, I highly recommend that when considering insurance, you do more than get a quote. Schedule a visit with a licensed agent to discuss your assets, your exposures and your financial/insurance needs. Let this agent provide counsel that will provide choices and a range of coverages to best meet your needs.

Having said that, let's talk exclusive agents vs independent agents. The exclusive agent is licensed and authorized to write with one specific insurance company. The independent agent is licensed and authorized to write through a variety of companies. This may be advantageous, especially with the non-conventional homes. An independent agent my offer a wider variety of choices to meet your insurance needs.

I am ready to insure my home. What type of information will I need? How do I get started?

Before you waste a lot of time disclosing details, ask the agent outright, "Do you have a market to insure an Earthship home?" (Or, whatever type of non-traditional home you may own or be about to build.) Many agencies do not, and this will save you a lot of time. If you are working with a builder, they may work with an insurance agency that has already worked out how to work within the constraints of the kinds of homes they build. As the leading agent in New Mexico for insuring Earthship homes, we are listed on the website for Earthship Biotecture.

Once you have found an agent that has a market, dig a little deeper. If you need to insure a home that you intend to occupy as a primary or secondary home, ask, "Can you provide a homeowner's policy or only the Dwelling Fire Policy?" If this agent can only provide a Dwelling Fire Policy, you may want to keep searching. If you intend to occupy the home yourself, you should be able to find a Homeowner's Policy.

Seek an insurance agent who has knowledge of sustainable home design and is working to educate the insurance underwriters about these homes. Once you have identified the agent that has an insurance market that might meet your needs, you will need to present the following information about your home: Year Built, Square footage, Exterior Wall construction type, interior wall construction type, shape and type roof, flooring type, ceiling type, Heating type, supplemental heating sources, garage – detached or attached, location address, distance to nearest responding fire department; is there a fire hydrant within 1,000 feet of the home? Do you have dogs? Breed of dog.

Any business on premises? List of special features, such as skylights, special filtration systems, etcetera... Have you had prior home insurance? Name of your prior carrier? Any prior states/losses? The underwriter will also need your personal information: name, date of birth, occupation. You will usually need to provide at least two color photos of the home: Full view of front and full view of back. Some carriers may request additional photos. If you have construction drawings of your home, they may prove useful. If there are additional structures such as storage buildings, outbuildings, detached garage or carport, photos of these structures may be required as well.

How do I choose a deductible?

Property policies include a deductible applicable to physical loss states. I would recommend choosing the highest deductible you can afford to incur at the time of a loss. I recommend that people think of their home insurance as their back up plan in case of a catastrophic loss. So, if you know you can afford to repair your home for damages within say $5,000, why pay the higher insurance premium for a policy with a $1,000 deductible. Purchase a policy at a lower premium with a $5,000 deductible. Everyone has their own comfort zone. For some it is $1,000, for some it is $2,500 or $5,000. For some it may be as high as $10,000. When shopping for insurance, you should find a range that is in your comfort zone and ask your agent to provide quotes using a deductible range that falls in your zone. For example, compare the insurance premium on a policy with at $1,000 deductible, a $2,500 and a $5,000. Then, you can make an informed choice.

What do the policy types mean?

The HOMEOWNER'S POLICY will include a Declaration of Insurance which will reflect your name, mailing address and the Property Location. It will list your coverage limits. These are comprised of the following:

- Dwelling – The limit of insurance applicable to the main dwelling structure.

- Other Structures – The limit of insurance applicable to the other structures on the premises such as a detached garage, a storage building, fence, chicken coop, dog house, well shed, fence, statue, water fountain, etcetera...

- Personal Property – The limit of insurance applicable to everything inside your home that is not attached to the structure, such as furniture, rugs, clothing, electronics, etcetera... Important note: Every policy has limitations written into the contract that provide limitations on certain classes of personal property such as jewellery, oriental rugs, property used for business, and more. Read your contract and/or discuss these with your agent to learn how to extend your coverage to meet your personal needs.

- Personal Liability – The limit of insurance applicable to pay others in case you are held liable for injury to another person or damage to the property of others.

- Medical Payments – The limit of insurance applicable in case someone, other than you or members of your household are injured on premises. There are special provisions and limitations concerning employees, contact labor, etcetera... Discuss these special circumstances with your agent.

Policy forms vary. Some are written to provide Replacement Value on your home and applicable to your personal property. Others are written to insure for Actual Cash Value (replacement cost less depreciation). Discuss this with your agent to be sure you know what you are purchasing.

DWELLING FIRE POLICY FORMS are most often used for homes that are tenant-occupied. The dwelling and personal property may be insured for either Replacement Value or Actual Cash Value for perils such as fire, smoke, windstorm, hurricane, hail, vandalism, and burglary/theft. Do not assume each of these perils is included in your policy. The perils coverage provided must be stated in the policy. The Dwelling Fire Policy is not a comprehensive package, but rather a policy that is built line by line. For this reason, it is not safe to assume that one policy is equal to another. You must be certain that each coverage has been added and rated into your package.

It is important that you look for your Personal Liability coverage on this policy. I have reviewed a lot of policies where the agent did not include this protection and the customer was unaware. Failure to include this protection will result in a serious gap in your insurance protection.

How much personal liability insurance should I purchase?

That is like asking, 'how high is high?" There is not definitive answer. Any of us are at risk of the unknown, unexpected. The basic Homeowner's or Dwelling Fire Policy will offer coverage options ranging from $25,000 to $500,000. The increased premium for the higher limit is nominal. Therefore, I strongly recommend the maximum liability available through your carrier. For added protection, you may wish to speak with your agent about a Personal Umbrella Policy that provides excess liability over your basic policy. Should you find yourself in court as a result of an accident that led to a serious injury or fatality, the dollar amount of the settlements can easily add up to millions.

"You cannot get blood out of a turnip," is a phrase I have often heard spoken by the individual who believes his assets do not warrant concern or the need for higher limits of liability insurance. Most often this person does not realize that if the court awards a settlement of, let's say, $1million, and his personal liability limits $50,000, the insurance company will pay out the $50,000 and the court will hold the individual liable for the remaining $950,000. This places your assets at risk, which will include your savings, your retirement account, and future earnings.

If you are considering your need for higher limits of insurance, please consider these facts:

Have you ever hosted a party at your house? You could be held responsible if a guest is injured on your property or causes an auto accident after being served drinks in your home. If a lawsuit is brought against you, your current assets and part of your future earnings could be at risk.

The following incidents affected real customers who were protected with a Personal Umbrella Policy:

- An insured was a chaperone for his child's field trip and one of the children was seriously injured resulting in a payment of $850,000.
- An insured lost control of their vehicle during a rain storm and caused two fatalities resulting in a payment of $2 million.
- A swing set broke at a birthday party and injured a guest resulting in a payment of $1 million.
- An insured's son got into a fight at school injuring another student resulting in a payment of $1 million.
- An insured was skiing and collided with another skier causing an injury that resulted in permanent paralysis; resulting in payment of $5 million.

Now, look at what can happen if you DO NOT have a Personal Umbrella Policy. If you have only $300,000 liability coverage and you are sued for a $1 million claim, without a Personal Umbrella, you could personally be on the hook for $700,000. A Personal Umbrella policy protects you and your family with:

- ADDITIONAL LIABILITY coverage from $1 million to $5 million for your primary and secondary homes, rental properties, automobile, motorcycle, watercraft, recreational vehicle and more
- LEGAL DEFENSE FEES – even if it is a frivolous case, the defense cost alone could add up to thousands of dollars

The information provided within this chapter merely scratches the surface on the subject of personal property insurance. It is not intended to replace the counsel of your personal insurance agent, nor replace your policy contract. The bottom line is that you should choose your insurance agent as carefully as you would your medical physician or legal advisor. Your financial future is at stake. Plan to set up at least one meeting per year for an insurance review with a trusted insurance consultant. Discuss any pertinent changes in your property and/or lifestyle that might warrant a change in your insurance protection needs.

Planning a Build

One of the best aspects of Earthship design is the culture. Bringing together a community to build a home is a beautiful thing. People help you, they grow their skills… and you get a home.

When Mike Reynolds and Earthship Biotecture go out onto a build, they come with an expert 12 person crew. A 12-15 person crew of volunteers, which may be revolving, rounds out the team. Supposedly the Global Models can be built by a good crew in 8-9 days. We have yet to hear of that happening in practice, but in principle it can be done. Do not plan for that though… read on and we will try and help shine a light on why. Plus, not everyone can afford to have that level of expertise or that number of people on their team. So, we adapt.

Here are a few tips we have gleaned that can help facilitate getting into a new home as quickly as possible.

- Plan for at least a 6 month build.
- Start in spring when people are fresh and the weather is nice, and snow is melted off for a minimum of 2 weeks. Do not start in fall if it freezes or snows. If anything goes awry, we will have an exposed building under snow! That is no good!
- Do not expect a project that can be done in a day in spring to happen that way in the heat of summer.
- Make a plan for volunteers. (See: Getting it Built: Managing Volunteers)
- Have an up-to-date, extensive, first aid kit. We also learned from surveys that trying to bring on someone with EMT or Paramedic status as one of the core crew is ideal.
- Notify participants before they come that they need health insurance.
- Make sure participants sign a waiver stating they have insurance and understand the risks of working on a build site.
- You will need insurance too.

One note we would like to add here: Using local skills allows ideas and techniques to continue to be passed on. So if you live in a place with rich local building traditions, please consider including them in your design, and building a community around your build that includes the community beyond the site as well. That is one way to improve social and cultural sustainability on your project, and it gets your neighbors on your team.

Getting it Built: Managing Volunteers

One of the things we were not expecting to come up as part of our research was the issue of working with volunteers in building an Earthship.

Many of the people who show up on Earthship builds really DO love and live the ideals. They are believers in this big audacious goal we all share... the holy grail of affordability and off-grid living... and a simpler way of being and living in concert with nature. Some volunteers have been WWOOFers, worked on farms, or volunteered at Habitat builds or disaster relief efforts. Oftentimes, they travel and work in exchange for room and/or board. Many have left regular jobs to do what they can to live their ideals of living lean and growing through experience. They have heard that anyone can build an Earthship, so they come. The community of volunteers can oftentimes start to act and feel like a family.

But as we all know, even family can be a lot to manage... and it may have issues.

The reality is that some volunteers are just not going to be up to the wrenching physical labor of pounding tires. Or they will have no building experience. Or they have no money and need a place to stay. There needs to be a plan for them to stay, how to train them, and a plan for everyone to have a place and way of contributing with the skills they DO have. Several of the builders we talked to noted that planning for the interns is a full time job in itself. That is time, space, money, and planning we need to prepare for. A few of the questions to answer for a build plan include:

HOUSING QUESTIONS

- How will we house our guests? Do we share our space with them?
- Will we provide electricity? Gas? Wi-Fi?
- If they are camping, where? What happens when it gets too cold? What happens when there are storms? Snow?
- Where do they pee and poo? Who maintains this?
- Is there enough water for our family, the build, and our guests? If not, what do we do to get it? Remember to double the amount of water per participant in summer to be sure three is enough. Tip: The U.S. Army and OSHA say that while working outside, a person requires 2 gallons of water per day.
- Where do guests park?
- What about pets?
- What days are we working? What about off days?
- What are "the rules"?
- How do the family and guests interact? Do we ever want "just family time"?
- Do we need a "group space" for people to congregate, eat, and chill out together?
- What do we do with the kids during the build?
- What do we do with volunteers if it gets too cold to camp?

FEEDING QUESTIONS

- How will we feed our guests?
- Who is cooking? On what? Where?
- When do they prep meals?
- Do they need additional support? How many crew can we let go from the build site to get people fed? For how long?
- Where do we get food? Does that require town runs? If so, how often?
- What is our budget for food?
- Who determines the recipes? Have we included vegetarian, vegan, and gluten-free options?
- Who determines the food buying list?
- Who is responsible for the money?
- Whose car is being used?

FINANCE QUESTIONS

- Will we charge an internship fee to help cover costs?
- How much will cover our costs?
- What about people who show up and cannot afford the fee?
- What insurance do we need?

BUILD QUESTIONS

- How do we figure out what a volunteer's Knowledge, Skills, and Abilities are before they get here so we can put them to work in a way that suits what they can do well?
- Will we have a daily or weekly meeting?
- How often will we bring in new guests? Tip: According to our research, builders find it often works better to bring on teams for specific build dates rather than allowing anytime volunteers, which can take a lot of time in training people to get them up to speed by one of the "principals" which should be spent on working on the build itself
- How will we structure the day to train interns?
- What do we do with people with no building experience?
- What do we do with people who cannot pound tires?
- Is there someone here who can be the go-to person for questions?
- Is there a "supervisor" who checks work? (Many builders commented that oversight is a huge issue)
- Who's in charge? Who can make decisions? Who can approve changes?
- What will happen when a volunteer gets injured?

This is just a first taste of what questions will come up as part of a community-built project. Hopefully this will help you to get started.

Request: As you evolve this list, please share your additions with us, as we would love to share what you did to make your build plan shine!

Regulatory Forces – The Code

by Rachel Preston Prinz and Michael Curry

Compliance with zoning, land-use, and building ordinances is a normal part of designing and constructing a building. Nearly designer, builder, or homeowner has to deal with some combination of Land Use, Building, and/or Zoning Codes. Which ones you are subject to can vary by location. These regulations may dictate the acceptable use of your site; the height, allowable floor area, and shape of our building(s); where you may locate the building and how far it must be from the property line(s); and of what materials it may be constructed. They may limit the size of balconies and decks; dictate how many parking spaces you need for guests; how you must construct your access to the road; the size and construction of fences, decks, and accessory structures; and even where you may put your septic field.

When you are on the receiving end of these Codes, it is easy to get frustrated by "getting told what to do." But when the Codes are turned around and applied on our behalf, they may keep our neighbor from building a 7 story tall house, keep a permitable monstrosity a distance away from our property line, or keep toxic materials out of our aquifer. So, despite that the Codes limit us in some ways, they also help us in many ways.

Sometimes Zoning Codes will talk about the percentage of allowable lot coverage, and since this seems like a tricky calculation, we thought we would explain it here: just divide the floor area of the house (its length times width) by the area of the property – and be sure to use the same units for each (square feet for example).

CODE COMPLIANCE: CRITICAL FEATURES OF A SITE PLAN

If your local building department requires you to provide a site plan, be sure the following items are included:

- Your name, mailing address, and contact phone numbers and/or email
- Physical address of the building site
- Legal description of the property
- North arrow
- Drawing scale
- Property lines and dimensions
- Names of adjacent streets
- Lines of required setbacks and easements
- Existing structures with areas to be demolished dashed
- The proposed new building, showing roof overhangs and balconies as dashed lines
- Driveways, sidewalks, parking areas, accessory structures (i.e. shed, outhouse),and garage
- Utilities
- Fencing and trees
- Water features, including natural creeks

GETTING A BUILDING PERMIT

Earthships, in many cases, are considered "experimental architecture." Building Codes do not often know what to do with experiments. Many locations do not allow wiggle room in the interpretation of the Code at all. If an Earthship is allowed, it will most likely be limited to use as a residential structure. An Earthship will most likely not be approved for an Assembly Occupancy like a school or community center due to stringent requirements to address safety concerns. However, with perseverance, and adaptation, it IS possible to obtain a building permit.

Building permits are good for you too. They prevent contractors from cutting corners that may affect the lifespan and performance of your building. They help to guide the process of building for do-it-yourselfers who might not know the ins and outs. They help you to get and maintain insurance for your build. Having a building permit even facilitates selling your home, because then the realtor and the prospective buyers know the means of fabrication were held to a certain standard.

Early on in the process of designing your home, you will want to check with the city and/or county planning and building departments to find out what submittals are required to obtain a building permit, so you know what to plan for in design. Most often a site plan to show the location of the build and setbacks from the neighboring properties, as well as building plans and elevations, are required, along with a permitting fee. The fee often starts somewhere around $500 for new construction, so you also want to plan for that for budgeting purposes. If you are going to use a contractor, they will often manage the permitting process and free you from that work, and they will obtain worker's compensation coverage which is required when using hired hands on the build.

Plumbing, mechanical, and electrical work is sometimes covered by a building permit and sometimes by a separate permitting process. Once your plans and other documents are in the hands of the permitting authority, obtaining a permit can take anywhere from a month to 3 months or longer, depending on location and the complexity of the permit submittal. As you plan your Earthship, anticipating this inevitable step and its associated wait will help make it a less stressful experience.

Tip: A means of escaping every bedroom without passing through another space is required by Code. This can be done easily by adding a window large enough for a person to get out of easily. Where the building is below grade (like a basement, or most of an Earthship), most people choose to add a window and exterior window well to an interior bedroom, which renders the berm somewhat moot at the location of the window well. Especially in the end rooms, you might hold the berm back from a portion of east or west end of the building and add an exterior door to an outdoor space. Whichever you do, it is critical to get this requirement added to the plan if approval is required.

GETTING A CERTIFICATE OF OCCUPANCY

Building a home usually requires several inspections by the permitting authority. These can be stressful and it is not unusual for work to get held up for a little while waiting for an inspector. The key here is to have backup plans for the work to be done each day so that should you be waiting on an inspection, work can continue. Oftentimes, footings, the foundation, and the framing are inspected prior to the next layer of the building being applied. Then, before the walls get their skin, there are electrical, fire alarm, and sewage inspections. A final inspection determines whether the building is safe enough for occupancy.

To get a Certificate of Occupancy (CO), most times the finishes on the exterior and any interior finishes that are part of the insulation system must be completed. The building has to be weather-tight and systems must be functional. Windows covered with sheets of plastic will not suffice here. Remember, the Code official has taken an oath to protect our health, safety, and welfare. That means you cannot get sick from the building being unfinished and open to weather. So figure that even if the structure is tires or pop cans, it has to be covered completely with its finished stucco, or whatever finish you are going to use. The heating, electrical, and septic systems will have to be complete and operational, though sometimes it will be okay if the blackwater cells are not operational yet.

Getting your CO usually takes at least a couple of weeks, so schedule your inspections well in advance of when you intend to start living in the space.

Tip: Do not try to fake anything to pass inspection and then remove it once it is approved to save money. That is a hugely expensive mistake and we have seen people busted for it, or pay the price with a broken system later, usually after everything is finished and everyone who can help has gone home. It is not worth losing the time, money, and materials invested to get caught. A red tag or a fine is not worth it. Less trouble = less money.

Next Page: Figure 10.
Beautiful earth-sheltered ruin converted to exterior space at Lama Foundation

Design

The design of a building includes planning for several major elements that make a building work:

- THE STRUCTURAL SYSTEM gives the building it is skeleton
- THE ENCLOSURE SYSTEM gives the building it's skin and insulation, and
- THE MECHANICAL SYSTEM acts as a building's lungs, guts, and veins.

Within these systems are other more subtle systems:

- The way we move through a building: the way the spaces interact, along with the halls and hidden halls we use to get from point to point
- The building's personality: its colors, textures, and the way light interacts within it, and
- The buildings context, or the way it relates to the world around it.

When all of these systems are integrated into a coherent whole, the building performs at its best.

Before we go down this rabbit hole, let's address some general considerations…

Planning a build of any magnitude is a complex process. The information in this book is intended to help you move through this process in an easy-to-understand and manageable way. We will offer tips and tricks and rules of thumb to help keep things moving. There are entire books written on every subject we will cover here, so please know that our attempt at describing them is to offer a general understanding of the system and to be able to compare systems. This is in no way meant to be a comprehensive analysis of every system, though every system we cover has been scrutinized from many viewpoints to try and make things easier and get you to the right answer, sooner.

One of the most important tips we can offer here is to understand that with nearly every building material, we will be working with something called nominal and actual dimensions. For instance, what we call a 2x4 today is not a true 2x4. That is its NOMINAL size. The ACTUAL dimension of a 2x4 is 1-3/4 inches x 3-1/2 inches. Windows and doors are the same. They have an "actual opening" size, and a "framed opening" size. Most materials and products have multiple dimensions to consider. So, verify your measurements three times and cut once. Then you can save yourself the headaches of re-doing. Also, always keep in mind that it is easier to cut framing to size than it is to cut gypsum board. It is also easy to trim adobes to the size you need. Build around the easiest thing to cut to minimize effort.

CHAPTER IV

The Building's Context and Site

"Cold logic dictates that if God created the Earth and the Nature that lives all around us, then every blade of grass, every tree and cloud, the water and the stars can only be His materialised thoughts." But we simply pay no attention to them, we trample them, break them, disfigure them, all the while talking about our faith. What kind of faith is that? Who are we really worshipping?"

- From Book V of the Anastasia (Ringing Cedars) series

Where we build our home has a substantial impact on how we build. We do not want to build where there is not enough water to sustain life, where there are regular wildfires, or we will get flooded out every time we get a big rain.

The way we work as human beings also impacts how we want to design our buildings. We need privacy, views, silence, and access to nature, among many other things. By paying careful attention to how we site a building, we can plan ahead to capture the view with windows and decks and we can use walls and vegetation to hide our neighbor's ugly junk truck or to dampen the sound of their barking dog. We can even use building materials and methods that help to soften the sound of the airport down the way, or alternately, that help to bring the sound of the rustling trees or a stream into our experience.

A site's location, geography, topography, vegetation, climate, orientation, and views are all critical factors that will help determine the size, shape, and style of what to build. In this chapter we will walk through the aspects of site design that you will need to know before you start to plan your building.

Previous Page: Figure 11.
Well-sited Northern New Mexican style home in Valdez Valley

Land Uses

The land we choose to make home on is a space for a sacred partnership between ourselves and the earth, the elementals, the animals, and the energies that occupy our space. We want to cultivate those relationships and to help all the beings affected by our participation with the land to thrive.

The earth is a natural organism that is alive in every way. Its rivers act like blood vessels and its oceans are giant filters. It is growing new parts of its body all the time. It expands and contracts as it breathes. Man is but one organism living on the earth, and each of us is like a cell in a massive system. The human cell can be detrimental to the earth in the same way that the cancerous cell is detrimental to us. Or we can choose differently, and work with nature. Using our resources in the most thoughtful, compassionate, and even useful way will allow us to progress as a species and minimize our impact on the earth.

The earth has certain zones within it that it uses to keep itself safe and healthy. We can utilize the natural topography and technologies that the earth has in place and minimize our impact on the system, thereby making it more whole. In order to accomplish this, we must allow certain places to remain pristine so that they may function by design. Here are tips for working within each of the earth's eight main functional zones.

WATERFRONT

Land uses that allow for the preservation of waterfront include harbor facilities, marinas, water treatment plants, water-related and water-using industries (i.e. a millhouse), and single-structure (1,500 SF footprint and larger) estates built upon several acres of land. Land uses that do not damage water resources include organic agriculture, forestry, recreation, schools, and residential open space. Leave 200 feet each side of existing waterways free from development or degradation of any type so the systems that naturally clean the water and protect us from flooding can do their jobs.

Negative ionization, a physical and emotional health benefit of watercourses, is produced by lightning and thunderstorms as well as fast moving water, fountains, waterfalls, and during rain. Using these natural elements in the design of your home and landscape is of great benefit. Make them a destination!

MARSHES

Grassy marshes serve the needs of flood and water storage, as well as providing wildlife habitat and spawning grounds for fish. These areas should be left alone for the most part, so they can do their jobs, but are usable for recreation and certain types of agriculture like cranberry bogs.

FLOODPLAINS

Floodplains allow rivers and lakes to overflow which clears out debris that chokes the flow of fresh water. Floodplains are a useful natural technology, though we can sometimes lose property in the moments when the edges are not so predictable. For that reason, it is best to use 50-year floodplains for uses that can withstand the deluge. Agriculture, forestry, open space, marinas, water-related and utilizing industries, and limited raised housing are appropriate here. A map of flood levels is available at most insurance companies and many libraries if you would like to find out where the floodplains are in your area.

Building near a stream is okay, just build within the open or forested areas away from the river or stream so that the grasslands and wetlands which filter the water are allowed to function correctly. Allow the low parts of stream, river, and lake areas, especially those with grasses but also those within the 50-year floodplain, to remain untouched to allow riparian access, give the water plenty of space to be cleaned, and allow hardwoods to grow.

AQUIFERS

Aquifers and their strata of rock, gravel, and/or sand are keys to clean water. Development in these areas should minimize the impact of sewage treatment. Industry and urbanization in these zones is more than detrimental: it has the capacity to poison the regional ecosystem. Agriculture, forestry, recreation, and low density housing are acceptable uses.

If you are building on your own home over an aquifer, use a blackwater enhanced septic instead of a straight septic system if you can. If your settlement is over an aquifer, use a community-wide sewer type system and single mass production plant to make methane. Many septic systems punching holes of effluent above the aquifer spreads contaminants over the entire system. Fewer septic fields producing water with less effluent in them allows the aquifers' healthy bacteria and natural bio-scrubbers to have a chance to defend the system.

AQUIFER RECHARGE ZONES

These areas occur at the intersection of surface water and aquifers. At periods of low flow, streams and rivers are often really just moving groundwater. If the stream or river is polluted, the aquifer becomes polluted. These areas are better left alone.

STEEP LANDS

The U.S. Soil Conservation Service recommends not building or farming on soils sloping more than 12% in order to minimize erosion and allow for natural flood control. Steep slopes are recommended for recreation and forestry, with some low-density housing. Plan for 1 house per 3 acres in steep terrain or in the deepest parts of the forest. Do not plow or plant more than 12% of available meadows unless you are using only locally-occurring plants, and even then only plant 50% of the available space. This is mainly for the safety and health of the wildlife who may not understand why your carrots are off-limits.

FORESTS AND WOODLANDS

Forests improve microclimates around all land use areas. They cast off heavy winds and allow breezes. They diminish erosion, sedimentation, flood, and drought. They offer wildlife habitat, and allow us a space for both recreation and scenic beauty. The forest is low maintenance and self-perpetuating. They are most effectively utilized for forestry, recreation, and housing densities of one unit per acre.

PRIME AGRICULTURAL LANDS

Prime agricultural soils are the most productive agricultural soils. Many people do not realize that they also recharge all of the topsoil in the area. These rich soils are worthy of our protection, if for no other reason than the ability to use them later. There are many areas of non-prime agricultural lands. These are perfect for large groupings of buildings. Preserve the best lands you can for cultivation and water/topsoil recharge. Use only deep, well-drained soils for row agriculture. Do not attempt to use rocky or swampy soils or steep sites without ecologically-minded terracing for agricultural uses.

If there are USDA Category 1 soils on your land, allow a portion of them to remain fallow in service the rest of the land. Use only at most an area equal to 35% of these soils, and use crop rotation techniques so that your topsoil stays healthy and can be recharged. Only build 1 large building (1,500SF footprint) per 25 acres in these prime soil recharge areas.

To understand your soils profiles, go to your state's page at the USDA, or your country's equivalent. The USDA page is located here: http://soils.usda.gov/sqi/

The Best Design of All: At the Intersection of Two Ecosystems

Building at the intersection of two ecosystems is often the most desirable. We can see this principle in action at the 600+ year old Taos Pueblo, which is built at the intersection of the Taos rift valley, the base of Wheeler Peak on the Sangre de Cristo mountain range, and at the mouth of the Rio Pueblo River and watershed. The valley at this location is suitable for agriculture and grazing; the mountains provide wood for vigas and ladders as well as superior hunting grounds; the earth at the site has a high enough clay content to be workable for making adobe buildings; the river provides a constant source of fresh flowing water; and the riparian areas around the river offer reeds for building, willows for making baskets, and small birds, insects, and other animals for naturally managing the ecosystem as well as staying in touch with nature.

Choosing a Building Site

Oftentimes, the land is one of the least workable features of a building site. You get to choose between property you have or property you can afford. However, the careful selection of your site before you build can allow you to dream bigger and better than you ever thought possible. Your real estate agent knows what generic home or land Buyer X wants, and they know how to answer questions about the following criteria:

SITE SELECTION CONVENTIONAL CRITERIA

BEAUTY
Views; Trees; Scenic Quality

QUALITY OF LIFE
Neighbors; Proximity to Police, Fire, & Medicine; Schools; Shopping; Recreation

INVESTMENT
Property Values; Security; Taxes

DESIGN
Codes and Covenants; Gas, Water, Sewer, Power; Roads & Transportation; Slope & drainage

These get to the meat of things. But what about the heart of things? What is missing?

In Japan, every landscape is designed to play host to the god(s) and ancestors. There are mountains, valleys, waterfalls, streams, and abundant plants, especially flowering ones which can delight the senses... in every home garden regardless of how small. There is something to this practice, and when combined with an attention to ecology and relationship, they create a way of seeing the site of your new home in an entirely new way.

How about adding these criteria to help you design the perfect space?

A NEW PARADIGM FOR SITE SELECTION

ENERGY FACTORS
Solar Exposure; Energy Sources; Greywater & Rainwater Harvesting; Location on Site

NATURAL FACTORS
Growing Season; Native Plants; Soil Conditions; Water Supply and Sourcing; Wildlife Habitat; Wind Exposure

MANMADE FACTORS
Development Potential; Light Pollution; Sound Pollution; Connection to Place, Community, and Spirit

A truly ecologically-based site design takes into consideration not just acquisition of the literal chunk of land, but also the relationship between your needs and the land's. In order to accomplish a truly sustainable site, we must let go the concept of a square or rectilinear boundary. As we know, nature does not often work in squares.

One rule of thumb for residential design is to spend 1/4-1/3 of your total budget on purchasing land. More than that and the home becomes less valuable, and thus, harder to sell.

Geography

It is important to understand the role geography plays in building design. Something as simple sounding as soil type determines the type of foundation required, the form of the building, our relationship to water, the kinds of vegetation we can use, as well as impacts the way we can use nature to help heat and cool the home.

SOILS

Every building ultimately depends on its soil for its foundation's foundation. Quite literally, it does not matter what you build, if you build it wrong for the soil type, it will fail. There are two major soil types that we need to know about here: coarse-grained, and fine-grained. Coarse-grained soils include cobbles, gravels, and sand. Fine-grained soils are so finely grained that most of the time they can really just be described as "dirt" - you cannot really make out the particles. Fine-grained soils include clayey soils, silty soils, and some very fine sandy soils.

It may seem intuitive that fine-grained soils are ideal, because they are more "solid". In reality, when these soils get wet, or are in places where there are earthquakes, which make the earth act like water, these soils tend to slip, which makes them less than ideal for building on. Coarse grained soils have lots of surface area and lots of chunky, irregular surfaces, so they tend to grab on to each other and hold together better.

To give an idea of what this means, roughly, the bearing capacity of the soil can range from around 1.5 tons per square foot in soft clays, which are susceptible to frost and have poor drainage, to sometimes even more than 6 tons per square foot in compacted gravels, which have almost no susceptibility to frost, and offer great drainage away from the structure.

Sandy loam type soils, which tend to shrink and swell with humidity and temperature fluctuations, can easily see 2 inch wide cracks over the course of a single day in drought conditions. That is enough to shift a foundation.

Soils are critical!

When we design a building's foundation, we want to make sure the soil can handle the load. Else... our walls will eventually crack and fall down. Coming back in to repair that after the fact can sometimes be a nightmare.

In cold climates, the freeze/thaw cycles of the seasons can make the ground "heave", so we want to have footings that go down below the frost line so they stay stable.

When we build directly on fine-grained soils, because they tend to hold more water, we can get water infiltration into the building. In fact, these soils can be so pesky in the way they behave that they suck water like a straw up above the water table and into the house! That is why, in places near the beach or near rivers where the soils tend to be really fine and water tables are close to the earth's surface, they build up high. It is not just about flooding during hurricanes and massive storms - it is about staying dry on the day-to-day too.

Topography and Climate

Our climate impacts our ability to use nature to help heat and cool the home. This aspect of design influences the shape, style, orientation, and construction of the home. The climate includes: access to the sun, which we use for heat, natural light, and energy in some cases; wind impacts our capacity for ventilation, the structure of the building, and how much heat we lose in winter; rain and snow impact our ability to collect water, the shape of the roof, how high we build off the ground, where and how water moves on the site, and what building materials we might use; and temperature impacts our thermal comfort – how warm we are able to keep the space in winter, as well as how cool in summer.

Topography plays an important role in our climate. Proximity to bodies of water impacts glare, temperature, and the direction of winds. Cool, heavier, air tends to flow like water down from the mountains and into the lowlands. So, valleys tend to be cooler than on the sides of hills and mountains. Hard-packed earth tends to act like a solar collector, and can even cause glare as the sun bounces off light-colored soils and into your windows. Large bodies of water tend to be warmer than land in winter and cooler than the land in the summer (which is why they are great for geothermal heating). As a large body of water warms up (really retains heat) at night, it generates breezes. Preserving natural drainages can keep us dry by moving the water away from our homes in the same way it always has, using gravity. It is important to know where the water table is, how that changes over the seasons, so we can build wells deep enough and stay dry inside throughout the year too.

On flat areas, some people build up, some build directly on or even into the earth, and some may even choose to raise the entire building on an earthen pad or piers a few feet above grade to stay away from high water or groundwater. You do not want to build on or into the ground unless your seasonal water tables stay well below the bottom of your foundations. If there are groundwater issues, you will for sure want to dampproof or waterproof your foundations or basement.

Piers are great when you are near water or where they may be flooding issues, or where the soils are not adequate. Houses in tropical areas are often raised above the ground, to get up into the trees, not for safety or security, but so that they can get access to breezes.

Definitely have a minimum 1% pitch on the slope away from the house on flat areas to get rain and snow away from the foundations. That means… for every 10 feet away from the building you go, the earth should also go down 1 inch. If the slope is over 3% (3 inches down per 10 feet over) and the soil is fine, use ground covers in your landscape to prevent erosion.

On slopes, we have the option of building above them on piers, cutting into the slope to build retaining walls as the back wall of our structures, or building our buildings all the way into the earth. Which we do depends on soil type, our preference for how we want the building to look… and most of all… budget. Because building in the earth is not an inexpensive prospect. A good rule of thumb for ease of construction is to use as much fill above as you cut from the earth below, and to align your road or driveway to natural grade to reduce cut and fill and then stabilize the cut sections with stone walls. We recommend not building on sites with a 25% or greater slope. (That means a site where you go 1 foot down for every four feet over.)

One other note about slopes in regard to earth-sheltered buildings in particular: When the Earthships are built on the Taos Mesa, earth is piled up behind the Earthship to make a berm. This is very different, functionally, from building against or on a sloped site. Because when we excavate the slope away from hill or mountainside, that landform has a way of being in the world - it has drainages, a certain water table, as well as ways that plants grow on it and animals use it, all of which are established. The natural water table of the site may pass through your excavation cut, which might bring water into your home. When you pile up earth behind your house, the major concerns around this goes away. The earth berm has to redefine its relationship with the world, and most often, it will adapt around your building's well-designed thermal protection system. Mostly, gravity is the biggest determinant for how the berm will behave. The water table will most likely not hop up into the berm. But on a sloping site, interacting with an existing water table can be a real issue. Just something of which to be aware…

Working with Microclimates

We already know that microclimates work - they are why we wear clothes. From the moment that Man decided to turn a bone into a needle, he began on the path to understanding how to personally regulate the heat and cold. He made clothes. They held the warmth close to the body so that heat was not lost to the normal evaporation, convection, and radiation cycles as it was when we were in full contact with the outside air. We began to control our environment so we could maximize comfort.

In The Best Design of All: The Intersection of Two Ecosystems, we talked about how the intersection of ecosystems is the richest place to build for a variety of reasons. We can also use a micro version of the multi-ecosystem technique on our building site to encourage plant growth and biodiversity, as well as to improve privacy, breezes, and the thermal performance of our building. All we have to do is learn how to work with microclimates and develop those to create ecosystems around our homes.

While I studied microclimates as part of my Master's thesis on bio-regional design in Italy, I had just about forgotten all that I had learned about them until I reconnected with some articles and lectures by designer Vishnu Magee of Archetype Design in Taos. His ways of working within the Taos climate on his build sites are profoundly effective at helping make his homes work in this challenging climate. It is not that complicated, either. Here is how he inspired us:

Because the sun is almost always in the south (in the northern hemisphere), the north side of our buildings are shaded up to 8 months per year. That means this is where the cool is most of the time. That is a great thing to know when you want to find a cool spot to sit in the summer. Alternately, four to five of those months in Taos... are in a deep freeze. That also means that the north side of the home is where the snow will stay for the longest amount of time, which means these areas can support water-loving freeze-tolerant plants. It also means that is where the water leaks will tend to be, so we should plan for a French drain on the north to get the snowmelt away from our homes.

If your home is at 7,000 feet elevation or higher, because of the shading, the north side of the structure may act more like an alpine climate at 9,000 feet elevation than a sub-alpine one at 7,000 feet. That means careful selection of plants is required, especially for windbreaks. On the north in these locations, it is best to plant alpine species like aspens and blue spruce, currants, and chokecherries, who all love cool and moist environments. Directing roof rainwater to the northeast will provide a wet area perfect for aspen.

The south side gets full sun 300 days of the year, and the walls hold heat, much as it does in the high desert at 5,000 feet. Anywhere in Taos, using fruiting deciduous trees on the south prevents too much solar gain in summer, and allows the full sun to warm the home in winter. Fruits like apples, pears, crab-apples, and pinons love this location and will flower and fruit in abundance. Using flowering shrubs who usually like a little more light on the south is ideal. Great plants for this location include roses, littleleaf, mock orange, apache plume, and campsis vine. A south side courtyard is perfect for climbing roses and trumpet vines. This also can extend the growing season for edibles and perennials and give them all time to flower and fruit! Container plants are great here. *Ramadas*, or trellises, on the south can provide cooler spaces for hanging out as well as prevent overheating of the outside space and the home.

Because of the bright cool mornings, we can use delicate flowering species on the east, like clematis. This will provide shade to keep from overheating in this area and surround us with flowers.

Sages, sumacs, and chamisa - all drought and desert-tolerant plants - love the west side where the sun is abundant.

Northwest patios are perfect for summer sunsets, as they are somewhat shaded by the house. The southeast is a perfect place to place a little table for breakfast, as it embraces the sunrise and is cool but comfortable.

Figure 9. Portale on right at entrance plus secondary trellis to buffer the heat

Pair these tips and tricks from Vishnu with another of New Mexico's traditional architectural responses – garden walls around the home and an entrance gate that points the way to the home's front entry - and you will create a zone of manageable microclimates that will not only serve your aesthetic and thermal performance needs, but will also offer you added security and the ability to grow a more diverse garden!

We hope that this illustration will provide some inspiration for you to create microclimates around your home!

General Site Design Criteria

The earliest human settlements occurred in subtropical regions where adequate food and water resources were readily available. As settlement spread to more temperate regions, staying warm during winter became of critical concern, and the choice of dwelling site became more important. Most of these early primitive dwellings show a strong sensitivity to local conditions. Out of necessity, the indigenous designers of these homes took maximum advantage of the natural amenities of terrain, geology, hydrology, and vegetation to gain increased thermal comfort and protection.

At Mesa Verde, the Anasazi built their dwellings into rock cliffs facing south to take advantage of the warming sun, and to shelter them from the cold northern cold winds. People who live near the mountains have been building on a rise in the landscape at the edge of a mountain for as long as anyone can remember, from Pakistan to Taos Pueblo. This allows the low-lying parts of the landscape to be used for agriculture and it takes advantages of breezes and offers protection from cold winds.

Our indigenous forebearers knew, and many modern architects and designers have rediscovered, that appropriate siting can greatly reduce unwanted environmental impacts. Here are our best tips and tricks for making the most of the building site:

LOOK FOR:

- A site with fresh water on the land or at the property line, with water rights.
- Evergreen trees to the north.
- An open face to south.
- Deciduous trees to west.
- If on a hill, it slopes more south or southeast, unless in a very cold climate, where southwest may be ideal for solar gain. Never choose a north-facing site on a hill unless you live somewhere hot that does not freeze, and you do not want to use solar power... then it is ideal.
- Access to building site should be easy from the nearest road, which should be located to the south if it consistently snows.
- Views to east or west are ideal for side porches.

SITE DISTURBANCE

Minimize site disturbance by following the contours of the land and by locating outlying and transportation-dependent buildings near existing roads and utilities. Minimize the length of your drive and center the house as much as possible on the land to keep everything close together. To minimize your negative impact on the land, make sure your construction excavation does not affect outside of 10 feet from the building footprint.

MINIMIZE BUILDING FOOTPRINT

One of the best things we can do for our site is to minimize the building footprint. We will get into much more detail about how to accomplish this in the section called Creating an Efficient Floorplan.

ORIENTATION

Locate the home's entrance and walkways on the south if you live where there is snow and/or ice. Use partial shading like portals and latticework on southern and western facades if overheating is a problem during the summer.

In hot/arid climates, consider a courtyard arrangement of multiple buildings for different purposes: in the Earthship model, this might mean kitchens on the west to take advantage of the early morning light from the east, classrooms south for good north light, living on the north so the south-facing windows warm up the space, and dining on the east so you can take in the sunset through west-facing glass when this space is most often used. This layout affords natural heat and cooling if the court is planted with deciduous trees or has covered walkways around it. Use water fountains in the courtyard to keep the water moving and clean while also providing natural air conditioning!.

VIEWS

Siting the building to capture the best views is a great way to design to encourage a deeper love for your space. Build on a little knoll if possible. You will find this a lovely place to build as the winds will carry away most pests, fumes, overly humid or dry air, and water can be directed away from foundations. This also offers the best views.

EARTHSHIP-SPECIFIC SITING ISSUES

As noted in our research chapter, some site parameters that affect performance of Earthships (and every other building, really) are consistent within climates, like solar radiation, outside air temperature, and precipitation rates. Other parameters that affect performance vary by the unique site, and can include the availability and direction of wind, the soil type, as well as vegetative, geographical, and architectural influences.

In areas where humidity is regularly higher than 50%, especially if the groundwater is high, you really do not want to build your Earthship into the ground. You really want to build your home with the floor system above the ground. Which belies using the Earthship model at all, really.

EXCAVATION

Try and leave 40% or more of the site as-is. This protects the soils and the way that nature uses the space. Excavate only what you absolutely must to install the foundations, so as not to pollute the water table or your streams with dust and debris. Building up, not down, reduces excavation costs. Use 100% of excavated fill on-site or give it to neighbors within a 3 mile radius for maximum sustainability.

We understand that the $12,000-$20,000 price tag for an Earthship's excavation is a whopper. You can sometimes save money by renting the equipment yourself, if you know how to use it and have a way of getting it to the site. But running a skid steer and a backhoe are not jobs for the inexperienced or worrisome. It is best to hire a pro for this challenging and important work.

TOPSOIL

Stockpile any topsoil removed from the building site for use in gardens. If there is an extensive area of soil relocation, and you have any slope on your land, provide erosion control like straw blankets so the soil does not get washed away in a storm. Lay mulch or plywood where large equipment may overly compact the soil.

BERMS AND SWALES

We can use swales and berms to provide groundwater recharge and direct water to ponds and natural drainages.

We do need to be mindful of diverting streams, or creating them. Water and the land are inextricably in relationship with one another, so mindful management is critical for the survival of both, as well as to the health and well-being of the plants and animals.

Swales are shallow low depressions either carved out of the ground or between two berms. They are designed to encourage the accumulation of rain during storms and hold it for a few hours to let it infiltrate the soil. Swales can be tree-lined on both sides to cover the area with shade. Swales lined with native trees are an extremely cost-effective water conservation technique.

Berms are raised areas that are usually planted and are used to direct water to swales. They are the equivalent of the tiny slope in nearly every road used to push water off the middle of the road toward the curbs. In most cases berms are at least 2 feet tall and can be as much as 6 feet tall. Berms can serve as a leach field for your septic system, allowing the higher ground to serve the filtration purpose before the effluent gets into the groundwater.

Using berms and swales together can help us to create microclimates in our exterior space that offers habitats for animals, encourages biodiversity, provides thermal control, and creates great outdoor space to play in and around.

WATER TANKS

Locate water tanks on the northwest if you live in a cold climate so they have a natural advantage to prevent freezing. Likewise, locate them in the northeast if you live in a warm climate to prevent overheating.

PONDS AND WILDLIFE

We choose the places where we build, oftentimes, because they have access to nature that we adore. And we want to keep it there instead of scaring it away. In order to do that, we want to maintain wildlife habitat. First, we can avoid environmentally sensitive areas or areas directly adjacent to a water source when we build.

Take a natural resources inventory – What lives there? How does it use the space? Is your wetland on a seasonal migration route? If you live in a wildlife-rich place, consider participating in a resources conservation easement. Especially if you have a wetland on your site, verify that your site is not critical to a species with the local wetland institute and verify that your site is not included in your jurisdiction's comprehensive plan.

If there is access from your land to running water – a stream, creek, arroyo, even a small pond or lake… this is ideal. But do not build within the floodplain of a river if at all possible. If you must, elevate the building on concrete piles or built-up landforms high enough to bring it outside of flood danger. Though remember… with rivers expected to modulate their flow rates and directions due to global warming, the landscapes around our rivers may be changed in ways that maps cannot predict. To build close to a river is to take a chance.

Tip: Use a constructed wetland, sand filter, and/or aerobic system to clean wastewater before pumping to septic.

IRRIGATION

There are big pros and big cons in irrigation systems. On one hand they use a lot of water. On the other, you can conserve water by using rainwater catchment to irrigate, as well as utilizing devices such as manual flow-control valves, drip irrigation, an automatic rain shut-off, and a timer with multiple start times.

Where landscape plants require watering, you might consider sloping the earth away from them towards a pond, swale, or drainage to harvest runoff. Another option is to use irrigation just to get young plants settled in and then remove it later. You might want to use soaker hoses and drip irrigation rather than a spray irrigation system to save water.

PAVING

Use porous paving surfaces that allow natural water cycles to continue functioning. Share driveways or parking areas if possible. This may create some maintenance issues so you may want a written, signed agreement between both parties as to the cost sharing and scheduling of periodic maintenance.

Plan for a 12 foot width for single driveways and a 20 foot width for double driveways. Any 90° turns in the driveway need to have a 10 foot radius on the inside of the curve to make the turn.

Place 3 inch PVC pipe sleeves to cross under sidewalks, drives, and patios if you plan to have outbuildings or will need power for pumps, ponds, or wells later. This will allow you to easily get wires to remote locations in the future.

OUTDOOR LIGHTING

Install motion sensors on outdoor lighting and use solar power on exterior lights if possible.

WINDBREAKS AND SNOW FENCES

Since people began building shelters, they have had to work with nature to address their thermal comfort. Part of these efforts extended into the landscape. The teepees of the Plains' Indians often used skin or blanket windscreens to protect the entrance from wind and snow. The same technique is used by the Inuit Indians on their igloos. Windbreaks and wind fences specifically address wind issues. They are designed slightly differently than snow breaks and snow fences, due to snow being heavier. Here are a few tips:

Windbreaks

Windbreaks are collections of trees or fences organized to minimize unwanted winds and maximize breezes. The best windbreaks are a mix of staggered evergreens and deciduous trees planted with berries and garden plants.

Evergreen trees offer year-round protection from gusting winds. Excellent choices for the evergreens in your windbreak include arborvitae, spruce, pine, or fir. Deciduous trees only work for hot summer winds, since they are bare in winter, but they do offer 60% of the wind protection that evergreens do.

Depending on your areas' specific climate and the direction of the prevailing winds, you might need to adjust this rule of thumb, but windbreaks are usually most effective when located on the north and west of structures, planted away from the house at a distance no less than 10 times the height of the tallest trees and no more than 15 times that height. You also want to plan for about 3 times the height of the trees for open space beyond the trees in the direction the wind is coming from. Wind velocity increases as it flows around the ends of windbreaks, so curve the edges slightly towards the home to provide a sheltered interior and minimize this effect.

Place deciduous shade trees to the south and west of your drives, patios, porches, and sidewalks to keep them cool if you live in a hot climate. Place evergreen trees to the north of paving if you live in a freezing or snowy climate. Deciduous trees are fine to the south as they lose their leaves in winter.

Snow breaks

To minimize snow piles and heat loss in winter, plant 3-5 rows of staggered evergreens in the in the north as well as the direction snow is coming from (if it is not the north), starting at least 10 feet away from the home. To figure out the best direction for your snow break, pay attention to snowdrifts and leaves that fall from the trees. Where do they end up? Put the snow break in between these piles and the wind. Place the snow break in the same way you would a snow fence, as described below, using the tree's full grown height as the multiplier.

Snow Fences

Position a snow fence away from the home at a distance 35 times the height of your fence, in the direction the wind is coming from. So if the fence is 4 feet tall, you will want to place it 140 feet away from the home.

RECYCLING AND COMPOSTING

Provide secure exterior locations for recycling and composting. Hand-built wood bins are often a good choice. Sheds offer the opportunity to store more weather-susceptible things like newspapers and magazines. Keep your compost out of direct sun so it does not dry out. Composting on the south and west exposures is not advised in hot climates unless there is plenty of tree cover in summer. Also, on that note, and not everyone lives this way outside of America, but while you are working towards your perfect little sustainable oasis… think hard about what you bring home. That cup from your favorite coffee shop – can you persuade them to use compostable cups? Can you take your own permanent cup? How can you make a difference here?

CHICKEN

Are you going to have a chicken coop? Free range chickens are great for clearing bugs! At night, they need a safe place to tuck in. Be sure not to put their home in the southwest if you are in a hot climate so it does not overheat and therefore smell. Placing it where it can get some sun but is shaded so it doesn't get too much, has access to ventilation, and is up on higher ground so it dries quickly after rains is best. Make it easy to collect the chicken poo for your compost pile or methane tank.

GOATS

Allow your natural weed management system, goats and otherwise, to free-range so that erosion is not localized and the plants have a chance to heal.

Landscaping

Vegetation impacts the way we can use nature to help heat and cool the home, our air quality, our ability to feed ourselves, our ability to create privacy, and it helps to diffuse sound. Grass and other ground covers can lower temperatures and encourage cooling, stabilize the soil and control erosion, provide better air and water infiltration into your gardens, as well as reduce glare bouncing off the hard earth into the home in places where vegetation is rare. Do not plant anything but grass and groundcovers within 2 feet of the outside wall of your home to prevent holding water against the foundation. Vines shade walls and exterior spaces when they are used on trellises, and they cool the environment through evaporation.

Trees do not just provide shade but they also reduce sky, ground, and snow glare; filter the air; help harness and hold rainfall; stabilize soils and prevent erosion; turn winds into breezes; and soften loud sounds by breaking them up with the many surfaces of their leaves or needles. Trees can even be used to capture a view and to screen our homes from prying eyes.

Think about susceptibility to fire and the desired interactions with wildlife (i.e. deer are notorious for eating flowers) when selecting vegetation for planting. Contact your local garden club to find out what Xeriscape plants grow well in your area, as these native plants will reduce maintenance and water use while enhancing wildlife habitat.

PROTECTING TREES AND VEGETATION

Trees often point the way to water. They create shade and points of outdoor destination. What can we do to protect and preserve these natural resources for the long term?

Minimize the clearing off of native vegetation. Native plants are more tolerant to drought, shade, and fire. However, clear as much vegetation as possible for the first 50 feet outside the house on all sides if you live in a forested area. This will help protect your home in case of fire.

Do not cut down or damage trees that you do not intend to during construction. It is all too common that a tree, meant to be left standing, sustains root damage beyond saving by careless excavators. Put orange cones or site fencing up to protect the tree for 5 feet beyond the drip line.

Consult an arborist if you can afford one to make sure the trees you want to protect do not need extra care.

If tree removal is required, mulch them on-site or mill them and use the wood for framing.

PLANTING TREES AND VEGETATION

If you would like to design your landscaping to work for your energy savings, locate five to eight deciduous or native fruit trees on the south and west so the home is partially shaded in summer and takes on full heat in the winter. This will help prevent overheating in summer and will keep the home warm in winter. Keep these trees a distance away from the building that will keep the roots away from your foundations and utility lines. Remember that trees have about the same size roots as they do canopy. A good rule of thumb for this is to find out how tall and wide the tree will get once it is fully grown, then set it far enough away from the building to accommodate its full grown size.

An evergreen or deciduous tree on the southeast corner will also help cool down hot mornings in warm and hot climates. This tradition has a long history, too... once upon a time in the northeast US, they used to place evergreens on the southwest and southeast corners to minimize solar gain in this way. These were called husband and wife trees.

Fill the space below trees with smaller deciduous and evergreen shrubs, plants, and small trees. This will prevent the ground from reflecting heat back up under your eaves, will provide shade, and will help cool the space around the house through evaporation. Flowering plants will love these places!

Grow hybrid native, organic fruits and veggies all around the house. They will use less water and fertilizer and produce better, and if installed correctly, will enhance natural breezes! For the best in landscape / privacy interaction, borrow an idea from the Russian Kins Domains movement… use a living fence made of berry bushes to serve as sustenance, provide habitat for birds, and provide a means of supporting yourself at the same time as dissuading people from coming onto your land.

Growing your Own: Dan's EPIC Garden

An important part of the original vision for the Earthships is that they be able to grow all the fruits and vegetables needed to support the family that lives in them. That ideal has not proven to work out so well for most people, so we wanted to get to the bottom of what could be done better so readers could be more successful at growing their own food.

Our friend Dan Jones is a renowned gardener and horticulturist in Taos. He works professionally helping people to cultivate and maintain their own gardens, trees, and landscapes. He built his own home a couple of years ago, and his personal garden has been such a resounding success that a few months ago he started a CSA to share his bounty with friends. I sat down with him over coffee one morning and interviewed him to discover how he did it.

Figure 10. Dan's Gorgeous Garden

His site is a little over an acre, and on that are his home, extensive vegetable gardens, a detached garage, a driveway, an irrigation ditch, and beautiful floral gardens crossed by walking paths and dotted with places of repose. He even has a little running stream powered by his rainwater catchment system in a cascading landscape he created at his front entry. He uses a combination of raised beds, ground beds, cold frames, and a greenhouse to grow enough food to feed at least ten people.

The success of his gardens is partially attributable to Dan's careful attention to detail as he was choosing the land where he would locate his home, and is partially due to his cultivating the plants in the way the plants want to be treated – an advantage a horticulturist may have over some of us. He assures me that this is nothing some studying, hands-on experience, and/or coaching with a professional cannot overcome.

Dan, being from the northeast, knew that without water, he would not feel at home. So he chose a piece of land along a traditional Hispanic-period irrigation ditch called an *acequia* that had been cultivated for decades and maybe as much as a century. The acequia watered his fields, which were originally grazed and used to grow hay. When he first walked the land, Dan noted that the land was liberally dotted with nitrogen-fixing clover and alfalfa, which told him that the soil would likely be nutritionally sound. The land also had a high water table and acted much like a wild meadow. It was filled with wild flowers in the summertime. It features an outrageously good 360° view of the Taos rift valley, punctuated by the beautiful and sacred Taos Mountain to the east.

Dan remarked that, in hindsight, he did not think to dig a hole before he bought the land to determine what the soil really looked like beneath, but he knew that he had found a place that he could work with, it would just mean some work. When he started really working the land, he discovered that while the soil was, in fact, fairly good, the topsoil was somewhat shallow and full of cobbles. Preparing the soil for cultivation started with working with a neighbor, who brought in 2 truckloads of compost and topsoil which they spread throughout what would become the roughly 1/4 of an acre of vegetable garden, and then they plowed and disked. He then planted a cover crop of winter rye on it for the winter, and the following spring he cultivated the rye into the earth, fortifying the soil with natural rich nutrients. He created paths, pulling the loose dirt out of them and putting it in the garden, which gave him slightly raised beds to enhance drainage in times of high water. By doing this, he turned his paths into micro swales, where in a good rain, they would collect the water and slowly allow it to distribute through the garden. The garden is planted with love and careful attention to the requirements of each plant – how much light they want, how well they want to be drained, how much water they want. The perimeter is planted with perennial crops including rhubarb, asparagus, strawberries, red and black raspberries, elderberry, aronia, currants, serviceberry and honeyberries.

Dan also has an orchard along the acequia with "every type of fruit that can possibly be grown in Taos." Dan's many fruit trees are planted into raised mounds 12-15 inches high, which allows the stone fruits especially, who do not like to be too wet, to be up and out of the high water table. He is successfully growing multiple varieties of cherries, apples, pears, peaches, apricots, nectarines, and plums.

The vegetable garden in the center of the property produces, in season: potatoes, tomatoes, brussel sprouts, broccoli, cauliflower, eggplant, carrots, peas, beans (string and drying), chard, kale, ground cherries, corn, parsnips, peppers, lettuce and many herbs.

Dan cycles his garden regularly, giving each area planted, especially those with tomatoes or potatoes, a three year rest to reduce disease transmission. In the parts of the land he allows to go fallow, Dan plants legumes for nitrogen fixation. This year, he is abandoning the idea of planting winter cover crops in his garden, because tilling them back into the soil in spring is too cumbersome to do by hand, and using a rototiller is just too much for his body any more. He offers that in many schools of thought now, rototilling is considered harmful to the soil structure. So this season, he has just added composted manures, some used potting soils, and composted wood chips to hold the soil down. Trying to find ways of working the land well, and in a less maintenance heavy way, is part of his strategy for long-term gardening.

Figure 12. Dan's Cold Frame

Building a 3 foot tall raised planting bed was also an important part of his strategy, allowing him to grow root crops which would otherwise be stunted by the hard ground and cobbles beneath his topsoil. That bed had 18 inches of junk fill dirt beneath for height and drainage, and was topped by another 18 inches of a superb mix of composted topsoil. D an also built a 25 foot long and 2-1/2 foot wide cold frame against the greenhouse. This serves the double duty of insulating the outside greenhouse wall.

One of the cornerstones of Dan's amazing garden is his "L"-shaped 25 foot long and 8 foot wide production greenhouse, which sits on the south and wraps to the west of his home for another 15 feet. Depending on the season, he can grow just about any vegetable. His only limitation is temperature fluctuations, which are typical of these types of simple greenhouses because of minimal automation to the heating and cooling systems. The greenhouse is a production-type, separated from the home by a thermal mass wall and exterior rated doors, with an automated ventilation system where chemical pistons open the upper vent windows once the temperature inside reaches 70 degrees. Dan hand-opens manual windows for ventilation at the base of the walls, which are raised above the external ground a couple of feet to accommodate the cold frame below. This does double-duty, ventilating as well as keeping his low windows up off the ground and operable even in the case of big snow. His greenhouse is heated from below by radiant tubes connected to his main house solar hot water radiant heating system, located 18" below the soil and in the concrete walkway.

Were there to be no heating, Dan's greenhouse would fail to produce in the winter. The radiant heat allows him to throw a frost blanket over the plants, creating a microclimate favorable enough for growing salad greens and cold-hardy plants during the coldest months of the year.

Dan uses a peat and perlite mix of soil in his greenhouse, because traditional soils do not really work in enclosed conditions, being susceptible to diseases and being too dense. He noted that these soils have to be amended constantly so they are fully capable of supporting all the plants, and that next year he is going to start using a coconut fiber-based soil in his greenhouse and potted plants, because coconut fibers are renewable resources and allow the roots to get good aeration.

Another critical component of Dan's successful greenhouse system is hose bibs at each end of the space, as well as a utility sink plumbed with hot and cold water. A floor drain and a misting system are the only items on his wish list. A swamp cooler would be an expensive addition, but another option for cooling and humidification, which is helpful in Taos' arid environment. Dan uses a shade cloth along the top and side of the west face of the greenhouse to prevent overheating from May through September. He does not need a shade cloth for the south because his home has a 5 foot overhang on the roof to prevent summer overheating of that thermal wall.

Because the acequia is on the downslope below Dan's garden, he cannot use the water in it without a pump, so uses well water for irrigation and supplements that with rainwater catchment. His recirculating rainwater catchment system is genius. He keeps captured water clean and constantly flowing by using a small pump to bring it to a high point near the front entrance of his home where there is a barrel with a running spigot for filling buckets for hand-watering. The water then flows through a manmade stream to the bottom part of his landscape. It is beautiful and functional. He decorates the front entrance of his home with annual water-thirsty flowering plants, which he hand-waters from the barrel nearby.

Dan made a special note that using solar hot water in a greenhouse (or for any other means, for that matter) is contingent on there being sunlight. Even yesterday, when there had been no sun during the day and the nighttime temperatures got down to well below freezing, there was a 60 degree difference in the water temperature he fed into the greenhouse from what he had available to use in summer. In worse weather, this detail can be critically important for the plants to survive. Dan's home's hot water system has the somewhat unique feature of a woodstove which is plumbed to heat hot water as a backup, so in cloudy weather he can still have ample hot water while the stove also sheds approximately 50% of its BTUs as heat for the house.

Dan notes that production greenhouses and tropical solarium style greenhouses like the ones used in the Earthships have different purposes and treatments. In a solarium greenhouse, or a conservatory in the old parlance, you can grow tropical plants and fruits year-round because you retain most of the heat.

One of the highlights of Dan's garden is an outdoor heated tub, which can be filled with solar hot water from a hose out of the greenhouse. It is simply an old cast iron claw foot tub set in a brick foundation, which is left hollow beneath the bottom of the tub. At the foot of the tub, there is a small fireplace, and at the head, a 4 foot chimney to draw the heated air under the tub and out the stack. This allows him to enjoy a heated bath even in freezing temperatures. He sets the fire about an hour before he wants to enjoy it, puts down a wooden board to sit on so his bum does not get burned, and he enjoys a good long soak. Dan noted that learning the nuances of how the fire bath works takes a bit of time and experimentation, but now he can soak for up to three hours with minimal disruption for stoking the fire. Like the greenhouse, learning the nature of the tub's inner workings is a bit of an art, and not for those who want instant satisfaction and no maintenance.

Dan says a successful garden is all about how much love, hard work, and dedication you put into it. He suggests starting with a small plot, finding out what you can manage easily and what grows, and then expanding a little more every year.

One of the best aspects of Dan's garden and now his CSA is that he is now making money on something he was doing anyway. The money he makes bringing his veggies to market will allow him to quickly pay off the investments he made in making his home more sustainable. His investment in his home and the investment of his time in the gardens are truly paying off for him, financially and spiritually. He is more comfortable, enjoying his garden more, and worrying less.

Another fabulous aspect of Dan's garden is that by creating so many microclimates and accommodating hot, arid/dry, warm, temperate, cool, and humid plants and planting areas… he has improved biodiversity on his land. That means better soil, and more diverse insects and birds for pollination, which means more diverse mammal visitors, the possibility of raising bees, and even a great opportunity to grow medicinal herbs as well as food. These are great ways to achieve both healthier ecosystems as well as true sustainability.

Check out Dan's professional work and get loads of inspiration at his website http://www.beyondwildflowers.com

Outdoor Living

One of the things we cannot help but notice on the Earthships is that they have put a lot of consideration into how to heat the space, but they have paid almost zero consideration to how to provide pleasant indoor/outdoor spaces during the hot summer months.

That is a shame, as having spaces that work for natural cooling and heating and for outdoor living are essential to increasing our time outdoors and giving us ways of being in nature even when we are at home.

ORIENTING TO THE OUTDOORS

Outdoor spaces tend to be used frequently in the late spring, summer, and early fall. South-facing buildings function best, which means the back yard will end up, most often, in the north. This is a great place for outdoor areas. Most outdoor entertaining and cooking happen after noon, so locating outdoors spaces with a shaded western focus allows us to really enjoy the warm afternoon and sunsets. If in a hot or temperate zone, or when days are warmer than 80°F, use deciduous trees or trellises on the south and west to block the hot sun.

Figure 12. My favorite house on Blueberry Hill Road features great outdoor living spaces on the roof

Another tip we gleaned from one of our favorite Taos houses is to make a flat roof a covered outdoor space for entertaining. To do this, you need to have a structural engineer design your roof framing because of the additional live loads. But this awesome space shades the roof as well as gives epic sunset views.

OUTDOOR COOKING

An outdoor grill is a great investment. Be sure to wire in some lighting above and around it, and provide some storage underneath and a countertop area if possible for those nights when you just cannot get away from the sunset to manage the food prep inside. Add a serving area for other picnic goodies, and you will find yourself outdoors up to 60% of the year. If you have natural gas or propane, be sure that it is extended outdoors for your grill!

We also love an outdoor fireplace. It allows us to enjoy the outdoors for a couple extra hours of nature-time at night.

BREAKFAST NOOK

I love an outdoor breakfast nook on the southeast side of the home. These spaces are perfect to use in the warming diffuse light of morning, which is great for reading, and it's just a lovely place to drink a cup of coffee and wake up! Put bird feeders and watering devices out on this little outdoor area and you will soon find you have created a little nature oasis for yourself!

OUTDOOR SHOWERS AND BATHS

In much of the vernacular architecture of hot climate areas, domestic activities including washing and bathing are completed outside behind low walled cubicles attached to the dwelling.

An outdoor shower is great for places that are historically hot, especially in humid areas where there is a lot of water to be had and a desire for multiple showers a day to rinse off.

Our friends Dan Jones and Carole Crews in Taos both have hand-made bathtubs in their gardens as well as inside. These spots are truly oases in the desert. Take an old iron tub, set it on an adobe or traditional brick foundation, add some adobe plaster to cover the foundation and fashion a small fireplace and chimney, and voila! Instant awesome outdoor bathing spot! Add a privacy fence if needed, and get ready to soak!

PATIOS AND PORCHES

Traditionally in warm climates, a great deal of activity takes place outside. The need to supply shade and outdoor spaces has spawned a wide variety of shades and sunscreens. Covered and screened patios and porches provide space to celebrate the great weather together while providing thermal comfort.

For the easiest-to-build outdoor space, build patios on grade, not raised decks or porches. Patios are less expensive to build and they cost less to maintain. Patios are not required to be engineered as they sit directly on the ground. They provide additional warmth in cold periods and allow water to pass from them without polluting it. Use tile, concrete, or better yet - flagstone, which can be placed in a sand bed and planted with thymes and other walking grasses that will provide you with fresh herbs and kitties with fresh greens!

DECKS

Most local building departments require engineering of exterior decks to meet Code. This can be cumbersome and requires the work of either an architect or structural engineer, and sometimes both.

DECKING TIPS

- Use preservatives recommended by the EPA, such as "quat". Chromated copper arsenate, which contains arsenic, has been banned and should not be available any longer. Do not use this if you find it in a "discounted" – it is toxic! If you have an existing deck that was once treated with copper arsenate, in lieu of removing it, which just transfers the poisons to another location, maintain it with a pigmented stain, which will block ultraviolet light and slow the release of harmful compounds.

- Do not cut corners in installing your deck. The metal plates required prevent termites from eating through your structure. Save a little now, or save a lot later.

- Use FSC-certified wood and certified installers if possible.

- Use salvaged solid wood if possible.

- In lieu of using screws and nails, use attachments like stirrups that happen under the decking. This minimizes the impact of water infiltration.

- Use corrosion-resistant nails, screws, and connectors when using treated wood, which is required in some locations.

- Flash the ledger! Make sure that the ledger that attaches the deck to the house has flashing that extends from UNDER the house siding OVER the ledger. This will maximize the shedding of water and minimize the damage from water collection in hidden places.

- Consider weather- and water-resistant premium wood such as redwood or cedar or even tropical teak if it is local to your climate. These woods are naturally preserving and require no treatment.

They also last longer. They are more expensive than treated lumber, but protect the environment, minimize the impact of toxins, and minimize maintenance.

- If maintenance is a consideration, if you will have lots of plants to water, or if you live in a humid area, consider synthetic lumber like TREX which is made of recycled plastic and wood waste products. It is lightweight and easy to install. Synthetic lumber does not need preservative treatment or staining/painting, does not release toxic substances, and keeps treated lumber out of landfills. Synthetic lumber is grey like bleached standard lumber. Even redwood decking will grey in time. TREX is more expensive than treated lumber.

- Wood should never be in contact with the soil. Use concrete pillars with metal caps instead. Cover these with stone if you desire a more rustic look.

- If you elect to use preserved wood, use a respirator mask to prevent inhaling carcinogens and toxins. Shower immediately after working with it, and wash your clothes separately so as not to contaminate the remainder of your clothing.

- Replace rotting or decaying wood immediately. If you wait, decay and its related organisms can infect your entire deck. When it comes time, replace only what you must to minimize the resources and preservatives used.

- Make sure treated wood goes to a lined landfill and never burn it.

STEPS AND STAIRS

In the landscape, a 2 foot deep tread at every riser is a good idea because humans tend to take larger steps outside. We can also use a slightly deeper step. We max ours out at 8 inches of rise because we find these are the easiest steps to use. Taller than that and the step is a bit more of a challenge, especially for older people and little ones to navigate.

Fire-Wise Design

by Rachel Preston Prinz and Asha Stout

Building within a forest or other area that has a propensity for wildfire? Use these tips and tricks to minimize the threat of fire damage to your structures.

WITHIN 150 FEET OF YOUR HOME

- Clear brush and dead trees.
- Trim trees of dead limbs at least up to 6feet high.
- Thin and separate trees by two times their height.
- Do not plants shrubs or vines beneath them.

AROUND THE HOUSE

- Keep trees 10-12feet away from the house.
- Keep plants well-watered and pruned.
- Use gravel or decomposed granite in lieu of bark mulch.
- Leave space between plantings to prevent "fire ladders".
- Use boulders and block walls to slow the spread of fire along the ground.
- Replace flammable plants, like Juniper which has resins that will ignite.
- Use fleshy-leaved plants like aloes, agaves, senecios, mimulus, lavenders, ice plants, mahonias, aeoniums, and bearberrys for gardens.
- Plant sparingly within 3-5 feet of the house.
- Cut back any trees overhanging the roof, or within 10 feet of the chimney.
- Keep grass mown to a max of 4 inches and keep shrubs and perennials below 18 inches.

ON YOUR HOME

- Replace shake roofs & wooden shutters with non-flammable ones.
- If you have a pond, pool or cistern, install a gas-powered fire hose so you can pump the water to save your home.
- Use fire-resistant laminated glass on the windward side of the home, or throughout if you can afford it.
- Use stucco instead of log or wood siding.
- Install interior sprinklers if possible.
- Use wildfire-rated foundation and roof vents or reinforce vents with metal screening.
- Clearly mark your house number so it can be seen from the street.
- Pay your fire department dues.
- If you replace your roof, or are starting new, use Class A cap sheet underlayment.
- Replace wood shingles with fire-resistant ones – i.e. tile, reclaimed metal. Be mindful of those made from plastics or cement as they may not meet your sustainability objectives.
- Clean pine needles and leaves off your roof and out of gutters every year.

IN YOUR CAR

- Keep: food, pet supplies, a flashlight, first aid kit, radio, glasses, face masks, gloves, and a map.
- Be ready to grab: phones (& chargers!), meds and important papers, photos.
- Be sure to close your windows and doors when you leave!
- KNOW AND PRACTICE YOUR EVACUATION ROUTES!

Vernacular Design Principals

"Through the course of history, indigenous architecture has been shaped primarily by three factors: environmental impacts – climate, geography, and wildlife, including pests and predators; available resources – building materials, as well as energy and skilled labor; human needs – the space required for specific uses. Unfortunately, in developing a more culture oriented view of architecture, we have often obscured the principle of pragmatism behind a veil of style. Elements are frequently appreciated more for appearance than for practicality or purpose. Efficiency is often sacrificed for the sake of an architectural "statement", leaving us with an ever-expanding need to rely upon technological interventions and the consumption of valuable resources."

- A Shelter Sketchbook by John S. Taylor

Before designing a building in any location, it is valuable to understand the traditional responses of historic structures in that environment. That is: the way that architecture has responded to its vernacular – its place and time. Vernacular architecture is part history, part culture, and part coming to understand local materials and methods.

To really "get" it, you have to look well into the local past: to buildings constructed before 1940, unless the building is high end (read: expensive). Because by the end of World War II, resources were depleted and the industrial revolution had encouraged a building society of "efficiently designed" boxes for easy construction. Before the wars, buildings were built without depending on mechanical heating and cooling. Most were designed without considering the use of electricity. They were designed to let in the maximum amount of natural light possible while minimizing the impacts of heat and cold on the building. Some were designed for fire protection. Some were designed to brace the building against high winds and deep snow. Or they were designed with minimal windows and doors and deep walls to maximize the coolness, as in the desert. They were all designed by a people from somewhere "else" who brought their own cultural building components with them. Over time, some of the cultural traditions fell away in favor of more environmentally-responsive solutions.

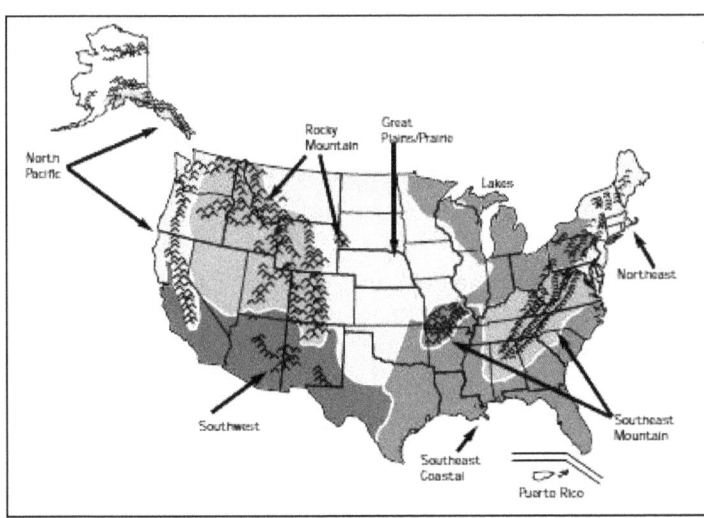

Figure 13. USDA Climate Zone Map

This is why we believe that the place to start is to minimize the loads on the home by using natural advantages, time-tested design solutions, and local materials. In doing so, we improve how our home performs without any technology whatsoever, which means the technology we need to make it work well and the energy required to power it all is minimized. We also help support local building practices, which gives local artisans work, preserves traditions that are worth saving, and helps us to create a space that is of our Place.

Refer to the map here for your zone for U.S. locations. We will talk about each zone's climate, architectural response, and heating and cooling needs in the sections that follow.

North Pacific Vernacular Zone

Climate

This zone encompasses parts of northern California, Oregon, Washington, much of the west part of Canada, and coastal Alaska. The environment here is in a relatively "active" state and is constantly being reshaped by tidal forces, glacial action, volcanoes, rivers that change their course, and earthquakes. 100 inches of rain is not uncommon in this region and some areas receive as much as 26 feet of snow per year. Storms tend to move from west to east as they move in from the Pacific. A very lush area replete with vegetation, some of the worlds' largest trees grow here.

Traditions

Since the beginning of human settlement here, structures have been designed to fit in with their setting. Native American structures tended to be of timber and designed to shed rain. Homes were often constructed of planks on driftwood or hooped branch houses, and community spaces were constructed of gable- or shed-roofed longhouses with vertical plank walls painted red, aqua, or black on exposed timber frames and with just a few windows. Totemic art is prevalent and today is it even used in unexpected places like porch posts (not in native societies).

Later Europeans utilized log resourced from clear-cutting for farming and its associated agricultural buildings. They often added unique details like punched shutters. Mainland European and British farmhouses, French trading posts, as well as Russian forts and onion-dome churches are common. Logs were typically fashioned in hewn square and rectilinear styles with dovetail joints.

An Asian influence can be seen in some locations, with low houses expressed though simplified post and beam structures and featuring wide expanses of windows.

The architectural style that predominates in the North Pacific has its own designation called Cascadian. Another architectural style predominant in northern California is much more Mediterranean, and is perfectly suited to that climate.

Response to Environment

Foundations tend to be battered stone. Wall-claddings are most often horizontal, sometimes vertical, but almost never both within one wall plane. Trusses and exposed timber frame structures are common. Details are not overly executed or overly detailed – this place exudes "natural". Windows are large and predominant on the south side, with divided panes. Windows on the north and west are minimized. South-facing gable-shaped open structure entryways are oversized to protect from driving rain and snow. Vestibules are essential for rain and cold weather gear removal as well as wood storage. These winter vestibules feature a 90° or 180° turn from the entrance to the interior door to minimize snow, rain, and wind infiltration to the house. Screens are necessary in many locations due to insects. Roofs are the predominant form in the building massing; in hipped, gable, or shed forms; and highly pitched with 6:12 to 12:12 slopes. In northern California where the Mediterranean climate prevails, roofs are much shallower in pitch. Roof rafter tails are most often enclosed in fascia and heavy bargeboard eaves, or cut back away from the roof edge. Landscape is often arranged to the north and west of structures to diminish winds, and structures often are placed in the north side of a clearing to maximize solar gain.

Calculations for sizing a heating and cooling system in this region

In the past five years, this region measured a rough average of:

- 5,000 Heating Degree Days (varying from between 5,500 in Oregon and 8,000 in Alaska), and
- 1,700 Cooling Degree Days

Thus, in designing your home for the north part of this area, you want to focus on HEATING, while providing lots of natural ventilation, and maybe some dehumidification, for the cooler, but humid, summers. In the south part, you want to focus on a combination of heating and cooling.

Rocky Mountain Vernacular Zone

Climate

The Rocky Mountain Vernacular Zone consists of the northern Rockies, the Black Hills, and the Wasatch Range. The Rocky Mountains are a beautiful and rugged landscape of rolling foothills, sharp mountains, valleys and canyons, and verdant high alpine meadows. Vegetation tends towards the huge, with deciduous and evergreen trees interspersed (where blights are not killing one or the other off). Winters can be quite harsh, with abundant snowfall typical.

Traditions

Some of the earliest settlers here were cliff- and pueblo-dwelling Native American peoples who massed their earth-constructed homes together to effectively heat and cool their spaces. Plains Indians also settled here, using tee-pees and wikiups to provide temporary shelter wherever they hunted and gathered.

Mexican and Spanish missionaries used Moorish inspired haciendas in conjunction with agricultural manipulation of the landscape to create engineered microclimates.

European and American settlers came much later, first seeking ores and pelts, and eventually settling into ranching and eventually modern lifestyles. Their homes were inspired from regional designs from their points of origination in most cases, and were oftentimes very simple and small.

Buildings are designed to withstand large snow-loads, high winds, and the hot summer sun, which was made hotter and more potent by the high elevation. Settlements were just that - small village-like habitations of often crudely-arranged impermanent buildings. As in the plains, vertical forms tend towards the structural, mimicking mining structures. When mining succeeded, stone and heavy timber was used to replace shoddily-built temporary structures with permanent ones.

Croatian carpenters constructed beautiful timber gothic–influenced structures in Crested Butte, Colorado. Vail was originally designed in the true Alpine style of Swiss chalets. Many others followed, using traditional-appearing Bavarian architecture as a model.

In the early part of the 20th century, the National Park Service invented a new style for the area, now called the Rustic Style. The style readily took hold and was massively successful from 1900 to1940. The style is characterized by a mixing of Swiss Chalet and American Adirondack influences, with distinctively massive log structures resting on stone or stone-clad bases for durability.

Response to Environment

Structures are often located on the edge of clearings here, to capture views and provide some degree of protection from the elements. Home shapes are simple, and massive at the bottom, often with boulder foundations that step down the slope. Roof pitches vary because of the dramatic changes in topography and are often steeper as you go up in elevation. Roofs are usually steeply pitched for snow shed of 8:12 to 12:12 in the high mountains; though they can be nearly flat (4:12 or less) in the highest elevations in order to use snow as an insulator. Roofs are moderately pitched from 6:12 to 10:12 in the foothills, and pitched from 4:12 to 9:12 in the valleys. Overhangs are modest and simple roof forms prevent ice damming and snowdrops, which can flatten a car. Interestingly, roofs are often more important here than walls, at least as far as the massing of the building is concerned.

Building corners are built up to appear massive, often with windows being more towards the center of the wall plane to emphasize this effect. Walls are often oversized so as to offer a sense of more mass. This also allows for more insulation, but requires more wood for window sills and headers. Large porches on the southwest part of the house are common. Avoid entrances or driveways on the north side of any structure in this zone. Vestibules are often added to create a more defined entry. The structure is almost always oversized and obvious. The ample sun in the Rocky Mountain vernacular zone makes it ideal for solar heating.

Calculations for sizing a heating and cooling system in this region

In the past five years, this region measured a rough average of:

    5,000   Heating Degree Days

    1,700   Cooling Degree Days

Thus, in designing your home for this area, you want to focus on HEATING, while providing natural ventilation for the cooler summers.

Southwest Vernacular Zone

Climate

The Southwest Vernacular Zone is composed of the southern Rockies, the Mohave and Sonoran deserts, and Southern California. The semi-arid to arid environment of the southwest makes for bitterly cold winters and hot dry summers. The earth forms include plateaus, mountains, valleys, plains, and canyons.

Traditions

The relative lack of timber and abundance of stone and natural clays has brought forth a regional architectural style that is so successful at responding to its environment that it has endured for over 800 years.

The more than 30 tribes of Native American peoples that call the southwest home have been able to maintain their cultural identity somewhat and have created enduring architectural styles of their own. Their earliest structures included pit-houses that were built into the earth and then covered with wood frames and sod roofs. Some elected to use gigantic rock overhangs in canyons to fashion their villages within, providing natural shade and weather protection. The forms of their more modern buildings are often both horizontal and vertical – creating a living "mountain" of stepped adobe mud brick that is cool in summer and warm in winter. Storage and utility functions are in the lowest sections of the structures, with access often by stairs or ladders to the upper living areas.

Mexican and Spanish-American families brought with them the hacienda concept with its ample cooling courtyards. The hacienda strategy continues to endure to this day, though many people are afraid of the relative size of these structures, even though they naturally outperform modern structures in energy efficiency.

In 1610, Governor Don Pedro de Peralta established the town of Santa Fe in New Mexico, under a town plan that followed a mandate called the Law of the Indies, which dictated that all Spanish colonial towns contain a central plaza with public, commercial, and church and government buildings facing the plaza, as had been done in Rome a millennia before. Homes were built along a grid of streets extending from the plaza.

The natives revolted in 1680, leading to the Spanish fleeing, and upon return, their buildings took on a more fortified shape, complete with turrets, lookout towers, and windowless exterior walls. In certain areas, this form has been retained. Missions came next, with their unique aisle-less naves, and many appear to be fortified - with small high windows and only one point of entrance and exit - because these sanctuaries were fortified to protect the villagers in case of attack.

After the Gold Rush in 1849, the first waves of European-Americans began arriving in the southwest, and with them brought their regional architectural styles, which they merged with the traditional architecture of the area – leading to the Territorial style, which has pitched roofs, milled woodwork, and often a Spanish-influenced layout.

In the early part of the 20th century, the Civil Conservation Corps created a unique architectural style for the area which has been termed CCC-Rustic, incorporating curvilinear earth forms in adobe, exposed log structural roof framing called vigas that are expressed both inside and outside, and stucco.

Areas in Texas and New Mexico also had suitable clay for brickmaking, and some parts of this region have a predominance of brick structures or brick coping at the parapet to make walls last longer.

The social nature of the dominant Hispanic culture has brought forth a need for large community spaces, and oftentimes you can see the Native American concept of kiva – a round community gathering space that is usually at least partially embedded in the earth - used for creating spaces of ceremony and gathering.

Response to Environment

Structures in these areas also tend to be designed to minimize the impacts of drought and fire, which are common. Only 4 percent of the region's available land has access to running surface water, and the land that does provide access is valuable beyond measure, as it is the only location capable of sustaining gardens and shade trees. In all cases, structures are usually expressed in vigas or trussing. Posts rest on stone bases and sometimes the house rests on a stone foundation. Walls are massive, monolithic and of the earth for maximum cooling and heating. They have soft rounded edges and corners.

Oftentimes, a vertical structural element will be dressed as a buttress. Wood details are common. Bright colors are not uncommon, in either detail or the mass of the building itself, depending on location. Windows are small, square or oriented vertically, located high in the wall, and deeply inset for shading, and most often larger and/or more plentiful on the north, east, and southeast sides. Often windows are double-hung for ventilation. Homes are often extended with *portals* (pronounced pore-talls) which are partially covered terraces constructed of *latillas* (pronounced lah-ti-yes) – a roughly straight young tree shed of its branches. Latillas are also used for "coyote" fencing, either alone or in conjunction with adobe walls. Roofs are often small, minimizing surface are exposed to the sun, and relatively flat - in pitches from 1:12 to 6:12. (Higher pitches are used for territorial style homes.) Landscapes are sparse – either xeriscaped or allowed to grow wild. It is extremely uncommon, and considered a flight of fancy of someone who is clearly non-local to have an ornate decorative flower garden, especially near the home, though home gardens and agriculture are very important aspects of design in this region.

Calculations for sizing a heating and cooling system in this region

In the past five years, this region measured a rough average of:

- 2,200 Heating Degree Days (closer to 6,000 in the north in places like Taos and 500 in coastal California)
- 2,490 Cooling Degree Days (closer to 5,000 down south in hot, dry places like Phoenix)

Thus, in designing your home for this area, you want to balance planning for some heating and some cooling, perhaps using evaporative cooling to help stabilize temperature and humidity in the hot dry summers.

Great Plains / Prairie Vernacular Zone

Climate

The Great Plains is a landscape composed of seasonal opposites: long summers of tornado activity, sometimes devastating flash floods in springs, and blizzards that melt nearly instantly to return back to icy cold sun-drenched days in winter. The wind always seems to blow. The land is flat to rolling, often with exposed rock strata, due to wind and glacial action.

The limited rainfall and low humidity make for perfectly clear blue sky days. Winters are bitterly cold when Canadian winds come through, and summers are hot and dry with storms coming in from the Gulf States. Trees are predominant only at the edges of wetlands, ditches, waterways, and lakes and are most often cottonwoods and other hardwoods. Introduced crops of wheat, corn, pasture grasses, and soybeans dominate the once grassland landscape.

Traditions

Native Americans in the area were nomadic and most used portable structures, though some used permanent structures of curved earth forms.

The earliest European settlers were homesteaders and ranchers. Their buildings are small and close to the ground and sprawled out to create tiny communities of buildings. The earliest settlers' cabin roofs were often of sod. Some pitch in only one direction to shed snow, rain, and redirect the wind.

It was here in the Great Plains that Frank Lloyd Wright was inspired to create low, horizontal buildings with large expanses of roofs (for capturing the abundant sun in the winter), lots of outdoor shaded spaces, and ample windows to take in views of the vast horizon. Central true-masonry fireplaces provided heat to the entire home.

Response to Environment

Many of the structures here seem to echo the horizontality of the horizon. Shading and shelter from the winds play critical roles in building design. Walls are thin and constructed of framed wood, thus the structures are hidden. Roofs are long and broad, with low pitches under 6:12 slope. Basements are advantageous in areas where there is low humidity. Trellises on the west side of structures provide outdoors shaded rooms. The buildings are more massive at the ground, appearing rooted. Vertical forms are usually structural, echoing windmills, silos, and barn structures. Windows are often horizontal in orientation or many squares arranged in a long horizontal line. Entries tend to be obvious. Tree windbreaks are common and landscapes are kept low near the house, mainly because large plants are exceedingly difficult to grow here due to thin soils. Rammed earth, strawbale, and solid masonry sandstone are alternative materials that are being used successfully in the plains today.

Calculations for sizing a heating and cooling system in this region

In the past five years, this region measured a rough average of:

　　5,000　　Heating Degree Days

　　1,700　　Cooling Degree Days

Thus, in designing your home for this area, you want to focus on HEATING, while providing natural ventilation for the cooler summers, perhaps using evaporative cooling in dry areas to help stabilize temperature and humidity in the hot summers, and introducing dehumidifiers in humid areas, to help your family stay less sticky inside.

Lakes Vernacular Zone

Climate

The Lakes Vernacular Zone includes the eastern prairies and the Great Lakes states. Once upon a time, the lakes region was one of forest and grasslands shaped by glacial action. That is no longer the case due to rapid (over)development. The growing season is quite short however, so certain portions, being abandoned by early farmers, have returned to their natural state of beauty. As one moves west, the plains unfold, with too little rainfall to support many trees. With a high groundwater table, basements are rare. Vegetation is plentiful, offering opportunities for creating intimate outdoor spaces in meadows rather than grand vistas.

Traditions

The earliest settlers here were Native Americans, who built dome shaped wigwams onto the earth of curved trees covered with bark, as well as longhouses and earthworks.

The first European settlers were French and British trappers and traders. They were interested in the protection of their goods and built fortified trade complexes, religious missions, and military compounds. The form of these structures was most often square, and surrounded by high walls of log or stone. As later settlers moved in from the East, they first built log cabins and then brought in the architectural styles of the east coasts' later periods, including Greek and Gothic Revivals. Lumber was plentiful in the forested areas, thus wood was the preferred building material, with horizontal siding on the main body of the structures and vertical siding in the gables. The structure was often celebrated with deep ornamental brackets, posts, and trussing. Craftsmanship was key, and the woodworking of the time was second to none. Arts and Crafts and Adirondack styles were highly prevalent here in the late 19th century.

Response to Environment

Protection of the wild landscapes (riparian zones) around the lakes and streams and rivers is critical to protecting the wildlife and plants that thrive here. Most winds come from the northwest, and evergreen plantings are used to deflect that wind away from the structures. Southwest winds are allowed in and turned into breezes with the use of deciduous trees. Most homes are no more than 2 stories. Windows are more vertical than horizontal and are usually double-hung. Shutters are common for keeping in the warmth on winter nights. Entry vestibules are usually projected out from the building in lieu of planned into the main body of the structure. The commonly hipped or gabled roof pitches are steep, often 7:12 or more, and have broad overhangs to minimize the impact of driving rain and snow.

Calculations for sizing a heating and cooling system in this region

In the past five years, this region measured a rough average of:

- 6,000   Heating Degree Days
- 1,200   Cooling Degree Days

Thus, in designing your home for this area, you want to focus on HEATING, while providing lots of natural ventilation, and maybe some dehumidification, for the cooler, but humid, summers.

Northeast Vernacular Zone

Climate

The northeast province encompasses the Middle Atlantic States and northern Appalachia into New England. The mountains here run north-south, allowing mostly east-west exposures. Winds are most often north-easterly. Vegetation is lush, with hardwoods in lower elevations and conifers in the upper. In some areas the treeline is as low as 1800 feet. Winters tend to be cold, wet, and overcast.

Traditions

Early builders here were concerned with two climatic aspects: how to stay warm and how to stay dry. They used masonry fireplaces within the body of the house to store and radiate heat from their fires. Farms and outlying buildings are often attached to the home for sharing warmth and ease of access. Placing farm structures close to the roads minimized the requirements of snow clearing and eased access to markets.

Wood frame and timber frame structures with clapboard, vertical board, or shingle siding are often the norm in the northern sections of this zone due to the predominance of British settlers, who were familiar with this building technique and style. Masonry structures in the north were considered cold and damp due to humidity. Farmers moved stones as they worked the fields towards the edges of the site, creating dry stack stone walls.

To the south, immigrants tended to be of Germanic descent. They built brick and masonry structures with elaborate brickwork designs.

Scandinavian settlers brought a passion for log buildings, first using rough logs then adapting to hewn logs with permanent chinking.

Response to Environment

Buildings are tucked into the vegetation at the edge of clearings or the areas around a house that is placed in an open field are planted to create a pleasant microclimate. Buildings tend to be tall and compact in plan, and to step down with grades rather than be placed on a flat site, which allows them to retain heat. Often, snow storage is considered, using a ravine or hollow to relocate the snow from the road. Gardens and plazas are favored over decks and balconies, due to their ability to retain warmth. The shapes of buildings are simple, and symmetrical double-hung windows are kept relatively small to keep in the warmth in winter and allow ventilation in summer. Visible foundations are most often of stone. Vestibules are normal at entrances. Gable roofs, with fascia and soffits in lieu of exposed rafters, are heavily pitched, with slopes of 6:12 –12:12, and small overhangs to minimize damage from ice. Cupolas allow attic venting.

In places like New Hampshire, salt-box style houses, with a roof pitching all the way down to the ground on the north side, were used to shed the wind and snow away from the home. First and second floor windows face south for heat gain.

Calculations for sizing a heating and cooling system in this region

In the past five years, this region measured a rough average of:

    5,000   Heating Degree Days (up to as many as 10,000 in northern snowy/ windy areas), and

    1,000   Cooling Degree Days

Thus, in designing your home for this area, you want to focus on HEATING, while providing for natural ventilation, and maybe some dehumidification, for the cooler, but humid, summers.

Southeast Mountain Vernacular Zone

Climate

The Southeast Mountain Vernacular Zone is made up of the southern Appalachian Mountains, the Ozarks, and the Ohio River Basin. This zone differs from the southeast coastal zone in several criteria, the most obvious of which is the lowered susceptibility to hurricanes, tornadoes, flooding, and humidity. This zone has warm and muggy summer, though not as stifling as the coastal zone, and has cool, wet winters. Winter days can easily have a 30 degree swing in temperature. The area is heavily forested on rocky soils, thus wood and stone are the preferred building materials.

Traditions

The earliest settlers here preferred settling in moist valleys, called hollows or "hollers", which boast rich soils and an abundance of hard- and softwood trees. These early pioneers were loggers, subsistence farmers, and frontiersmen of English, French, German, Scotch-Irish, and African-American descent. Early buildings here were raised on stone bases from stone found in the fields and were constructed of roughhewn timber or log, with lap siding, board and batten, or true-log finishes. By tradition, the forest is allowed to surround the building, but the lowest limbs are removed so the forest is "tamed".

Response to Environment

Wood structural supports are often massive, and corners of the buildings are built-up and substantial. Placing the structures within the vegetation at the edge of a forest or the crest of a hill also facilitated cooler summer interiors. There is not a great deal of flat land here, so buildings often step down grades. Buildings tend to be stretched out to be rectilinear on the East-West axis. Roofs are often gabled or hipped with a 6:12 –9:12 slope and deep overhangs. Porches are usually separate from the building, along the entire south side of the building, with a lower pitch than the main roof and used as an outdoor room. There is a welcoming obvious entrance attached to or at the porch. Windows are traditionally casement or double-hung and screened. Operable screened transoms over doors are common.

Calculations for sizing a heating and cooling system in this region

In the past five years, this region measured a rough average of:

2,800	Heating Degree Days
2,700	Cooling Degree Days

Thus, in designing your home for this area, you want to balance planning for some heating and some cooling as well as providing natural ventilation. Evaporative cooling may be required in dry areas to help stabilize temperature and humidity in the hot summers. Conversely, using dehumidifiers in humid areas can help your family stay less sticky while inside.

Southeast Coastal Vernacular Zone

Climate

The Southeast Coastal Vernacular Zone includes the coastal areas of the Southeast and Gulf States as well as Puerto Rico. This vernacular zone has been influenced by many cultures: Native American, French and British planters, African slaves, and even Spanish settlers in Florida. All were battling a unique set of climate concerns: high humidity, intense summer sun, seasonal flooding, hurricanes, tornadoes, and tidal effects on coasts and rivers. An abundance of water, insects, and heat made for challenging times and specialized architectural responses. Storms can be incredibly powerful and long-lasting. Hardwoods usually grow in drainages here and plants grow quickly.

Traditions

From the beginning, the creation of cool outdoor living spaces, capturing favorable winds, and creation of shade were of primary concern. Large wrap-around porches, sleeping porches, courtyards, and light-colored buildings all helped to achieve this. "Coolhouses" - dairies, cold storage, pantries, and springhouses - were burrowed into the earth to access the constant cool and humidity. Kitchens, smokehouses, blacksmitherys, and other functions which created additional heat or susceptibility to fire were contained in separate buildings. In some areas, wrought iron is common for architectural details.

Heritage is key in this region where the concepts of historic preservation first took hold in the US. The earliest buildings were constructed of wood, but brick and stone came in vogue as the planters and merchants acquired more wealth.

Response to Environment

Homes can be one, two, or three stories. They feature a small footprint in most cases and are simple in shape. Basements are rarely used because of high groundwater. Balconies, open breeze- and walk-ways, and floor-to-ceiling windows with louvers allow the infiltration of shaded light and air into the interiors. Entries are oversized and welcoming, with a single front door, often with sidelights. In many cases, homes are elevated to gain access to the cooler air in the trees as well as resist flood damage. Roofs are 7:12 or greater in pitch in hipped, gabled, or shed form. Gabled dormers on the roofline allow light and ventilation in attic spaces. Roofed porches are often huge - most are at least 8 feet deep. Structures are often exposed to accentuate the connection to piles raising the building above the ground, though the sizing of the structure is most often "small" in comparison to traditional timber frame. Trees are cleared 20 feet in all directions around the house.

Calculations for sizing a heating and cooling system in this region

In the past five years, this region measured a rough average of:

    2,000   Heating Degree Days (Closer to 0 in southern Florida)

    2,800   Cooling Degree Days (Closer to 6,000 in southern Florida)

Thus, in designing your home for this area, you want to balance: planning for some heating up north, and cooling everywhere, especially down south on the coast. Natural ventilation is critical for both the building and the undersides of buildings to prevent mold and fungi. Evaporative cooling may be required in dry areas to help stabilize temperature and humidity in the hot summers. Conversely, using dehumidifiers in humid areas can help your family stay less sticky while inside.

CHAPTER V

Designing for Thermal Comfort

by Rachel Preston Prinz, Pratik Zaveri, and Asha Stout

Thermal comfort has been one of the most difficult aspects of designing buildings since we started building them. Our earliest civilizations were more concerned about portability in regard to their buildings so they could move from hunting spot to gathering spot depending on the seasons. Once we started planting crops, we needed to build more permanent structures to keep our stores of agricultural products safe, at a temperature they could safely be stored at, and moist or dry depending on the product.

Using natural materials in their unworked forms makes achieving thermal comfort in cold climates more difficult, because natural forms are almost never perfectly square, which means they do not fit together in a way that can prevent air and thus cold from moving through the walls.

The stone buildings of our earliest major civilizations in Egypt, Mesopotamia, and Greece had sophisticated tools which allowed them to work stone. They also had slaves and mason/architects who could tell the slaves how to work the stone. They used stone, not only for its monumental qualities which we still get to enjoy to this day, but moreover because a massive stone building is a great insulator from the heat. The cliff dwellings at Mesa Verde similarly use their overhanging cave shelter to provide shade for the hot summer months, while allowing the low-angled winter sun to come in and warm the spaces naturally. The stone buildings there were able to be tightly fitted with minimal working because of the type of sedimentary rock that was used. It flaked off in linear chunks that were relatively easy to stack tall without mortar.

But stone was not always available, nor were the slaves that many civilizations used to get these buildings built. Pretty much everyone else, everywhere else, had to make do with less formalized massive structures made of natural, easily worked, materials. They just came up with simple solutions for filling in the gaps. In log cabins, they would add a chinking of mud between the logs to stop the biggest leaks. They would add lime if they had access to it. Then they would put blankets and animal skins over the insides of the walls to keep the heat in and act like insulation. Even the teepees of the Plains Indian are lined with skins and blankets to keep the heat in. Igloo builders would often build their entrance on a sloped ramp that accessed the inside space below the living level so the heat inside the space would rise and stay in the building instead of escaping out the access hallway. Using this technique, they could heat up a space with just body heat and the heat from a lantern or small fire.

Previous Page: Figure 14. Home exterior ideally designed with microclimates and shade devices for thermal performance in Des Montes, north of Taos.

Early farmhouses in the Midwest and Eastern U.S. had a double entry vestibule, which acted as a buffer to present the direct loss of heat.

Tropical buildings, like the amazing bamboo Green School by Ibuku in Bali, Indonesia, are often built in the treetops. Tropical architects design their buildings like this to get up into the areas that are shaded and have access to cool breezes. They want to stay away from the earth because in humid locations, being near the earth also means being near water. These raised buildings stay drier longer during seasonal and storm flooding, and they stay cooler in the heat too.

These are just a few of the many ways in which humans around the world have found a ways of achieving thermal comfort.

Some building scientists will build their research around the idea that comfortable temperature limits are around a low of 65°F (19°C) in winter and a high of 80°F (27°C) in summer. However, when people are asked what their idea of comfortable really is, they will say that it is 70°F (21°C) in winter and 75°F (24°C) in summer. Knowing what your own comfort limits are will help you to plan your home for what you really need.

To achieve temperatures in these ranges, we really need to understand what makes those temperatures comfortable, and why they might be different in the summer versus the winter. To get to that, we need to understand that human comfort is dependent on heat retention and heat loss, which is affected by:

CONVECTION – the circulation caused by temperature difference; when air temperature is lower than body temperature, we get cold. This can be exacerbated by air motion.

RADIATION – when heat transfers are caused by electromagnetic waves; we radiate heat to cooler surroundings and absorb heat from warmer surroundings. Glass in winter can be 25 degrees cooler than the inside temperature at windows. That is a form of radiation. This causes "cold spots".

EVAPORATION – changes liquid to vapor; this is another way we dissipate heat from our bodies: through the breath and perspiration. We can get hot or cold based on how much water we are evaporating from our systems.

We also need to understand a little bit about the physics of heat. Heat flows from the upper temperatures towards cooler temperatures. Like everything in nature, heat is trying to find balance or equilibrium. Because of this, the greater the temperature difference between two spaces, the more quickly heat will flow through them.

Building materials and insulation slow the movement of heat though them at a rate that depends on the properties of the material. No two materials work the same way exactly.

While it may be tempting to build as massive of a wall as possible, it is also important to note that resistance to heat flow (insulation) and heat storage (thermal) capacity are not the same. Concrete, brick, and stone are poor insulators, but work great as thermal collectors because they hold the heat for hours until the air outside them starts to cool down below the temperature of the warmth stored, and thus the heat starts radiating into the space.

One of the biggest ways we can improve thermal performance of the building is to minimize the air volume in the home. This allows us to use small systems to control airflow. Minimizing your footprint is the first step, and we will cover how to do that in later sections. The other important thing to consider is ceiling height, as this is what gives you your volume. The higher your ceilings, the more volume of air you need to heat, cool, humidify, or dehumidify. So soaring ceilings might not be the best idea throughout the house, unless you live in a hot/humid climate where getting that heat UP and out of the living space is a great idea for thermal comfort. When we have clients who want the beautiful effect of a large space but not the hassle of the larger systems, we suggest that they choose one room that is most important and make that space tall. Leaving the other spaces at normal heights will save you money.

Passive Solar Design

Passive solar design uses nature and good design, rather than mechanical systems, to heat and cool a building. It captures free and renewable resources like the sun and wind and uses them to your advantage. Using this method can provide up to 50% of your home's heating needs! The downside is... it can add to the cost of building... but not that much if you skip the long greenhouse design along the front of the typical Earthship.

Done incorrectly, passive solar design creates problems of a different sort, which we see often in Earthships – that is their propensity for overheating. This issue is not endemic to Earthships either, an oversized south-facing vertical window will cause a regular house to overheat in the summer in Taos also, which is why many of the sunrooms added in the 1970s-1990s have been abandoned or modified or use blackout curtains through the spring, summer, and fall when those rooms will overheat.

Good passive solar design is based on science and uses a time-tested ratio of floor area to window area to keep from overheating. It is easy to calculate the window area required to get the right solar gain and prevent overheating. It doesn't even require complicated math. It just takes a little effort and planning.

BUILDING SIZE AND SHAPE

The shape of the building plays a vital role in good passive solar design. In relatively warm places where there is not a huge heating or cooling load, a rectangular building with its long axis going east-west is best. This plan maximizes southern exposure and minimizes east and west exposures, allowing the house to more effectively heat and cool itself.

In cold climates, building a small, more square footprint on multiple levels is ideal, so you can minimize the surface area of the exterior walls and use the heat from below as it rises naturally to heat upper levels.

In hot-dry climates, you want to make the building more square so it has less southern exposure, maybe introduce a courtyard for cooling, provide fountains for humidification, and introduce lots of shade.

In hot-humid areas, you want to build up in the trees where the breezes are, go back to a rectangular building on an east-west axis, and use deep porches to get as much shade as you can all around the structure.

Tip: Orient the building (especially the window wall) to the Southeast if you are in a place with more cooling degree days than heating degree days and to the southwest if you are in a place with more heating degree days than cooling degree days.

SPATIAL ORIENTATION

In the northern hemisphere, we can harness the sun in our space by locating the major living areas on the sunny south side so they can always be warm, and locating storage and other less used spaces on the north, so they can benefit from the cooler temperatures there.

LANDSCAPING FOR PASSIVE SOLAR BENEFIT

You can also use deciduous trees on the east, south, and west to help shade your structure in summer, and when they lose their leaves in winter you will get maximum solar gain when you need it.

CAPTURING THE SUN

While the first step taken to ensure staying warm is to minimize the dwellings exposure to the cold, the second is to maximize the structure's ability to gain and hold heat from natural sources including the sun. Science, siting, orientation, materials, zoning, and placement of openings are all major considerations for achieving effective solar heat gain.

SKYLIGHTS

Skylights, while great in principle, are not always a good thing, as their size and location make them more susceptible to leaks and diminished thermal performance. Horizontal and sloped roof skylights add heat to a building in summer and leak heat from the building in winter. This often leads to condensation in humid climates and "hotspots" in most others.

One of the most documented issues in Earthship thermal performance is people forgetting to close the skylights, or choosing not to. The Earthship's design is intended for the ventilation to be closed and opened daily, at different times depending on the time of year and weather. Many people in Taos choose not to close their skylights because they help provide adequate ventilation so people do not feel as if the house is "stuffy".

Figure 15. Skylight Tower

Instead of the traditional Earthship's operable horizontal skylight, we recommend using a clerestory that faces south and has operable windows, or use a "skylight tower." These features punch the skylight above the roof like a chimney, locate operable windows vertically so they shed water and capture air more effectively, and uses a roof with an eave to protect from overheating. Variations of skylight towers have been used around the world for generations to create stack-effect - a natural ventilation draw through the space. The cupolas we see on historic homes are variations on this theme. Their louvered vents just allow heat out, rather than letting heat out and light in like a tower skylight does. All you need to do is open the windows on the leeward (where the wind is going) side of the tower from inside. No shoveling snow required! And they can be used effectively in summer or winter! A good rule of thumb here is making sure the window sill is a foot or more above the nearest horizontal surface, including roof ridges.

OVERHANGS

A true passively designed building will capture the sun in winter and shed the sun in summer. To shed the heat of the summer and prevent overheating, we suggest window overhangs of canopies, awnings, roof projections, or shade structures, preferably located vertically within 24 inches of the window head. In most cases, these are perfectly designed with an overhang of the wall between 16 inches and 24 inches deep. Less than that and your space will have more of a tendency to overheat. More than that and your space may tend to under-heat. If you want to get really anal and do the math, the depth of your overhang should equal the height from the bottom of the window to the overhang divided by 3.38.

A larger overhang can be secured by one of three methods: 1) cantilevering the roof framing by extending no more than 1/3 of the total rafter or viga span past the wall, 2) using posts or columns as supports, or 3) by adding diagonal brackets from the overhang to the wall.

Design tip: This might be the perfect way to store small solar panels!

Figure 15. Sculpted Shade Devices by Christina Sporrong

We love these floral and leaf design shade structures that metal sculptress Christina Sporrong made for a renowned Earthship build at the REACH community. These overhangs are an exquisite way to get the effect of shade trees without planting trees. This is not a small investment, but it is beautiful and functional. Do you have skills you can use to make something artfully beautiful and functional that serves this purpose?

DAYLIGHTING

The sun is an incredible resource - it provides light, heat, allows for photosynthesis, and can even be used to cook food. Buildings benefit from the heat of the sun by absorbing and releasing its heat and by using its light to brighten the space.

The level of illumination provided by the sun is finite, however, and changes with the seasons. There is more light available in summer and less in winter (this is reversed in the southern hemisphere). The amount of light diminishes as it enters a window and passes through a room. You can use the interior space for a depth twice the height of the window for any task that requires good lighting, like reading or sewing.

The ceiling and back wall (the one opposite the sun) are most effective for reflecting the light you have invited in. These walls should be light colored with a non-gloss finish to reduce glare. Glare can also be reduced by using windows on 2 adjacent walls, or having a window on a wall and a skylight in the ceiling. If your windows are right against a wall, paint the wall a light non-glossy color and it will reflect the light further into the room.

It frustrates me to turn on a light during the day to use a powder room, do laundry, or get things out of a closet. For a couple hundred dollars (U.S.), without the need for a contractor, you can add a tube skylight to just about any room in your house, and never need to turn on a light except at night. In our office, we use tube skylights to get light into dark spaces without the need for flipping a switch (and draining more resources).

Another option for daylighting is using interior windows like they do in the wall between the Earthships' greenhouse and the living spaces. We prefer to put ours in the wall between a bedroom and a closet or the kitchen and the pantry if we have high enough ceilings, to get natural light into these accessory rooms. We will also add a transom above a powder room, closet, laundry or pantry window if the adjoining room is bright.

To get light deeper into a room; simply use taller windows.

Another great way to harness more light with your windows is to use deeply-angled window jambs like the ones you see in the photo to the right. These throw more natural light onto the side walls and bounce better light back into the dark areas of your space.

North-facing windows allow in a soft, diffuse light that artists love.

Mirrors

Mirrors have been used since ancient Egypt to throw light further into a space. In the 19th century here in New Mexico, they used tin in much the same way to bounce natural light from openings or candle light into the space.

Mirrors work best when placed within 15 feet of an open (not curtained) window along a side wall. You can also use large mirrors along the top half of one wall in a small space to make it appear larger.

Figure 16.
Angled window jambs allow more light into a space

PASSIVE SOLAR DESIGN RULES OF THUMB

The simplest rule of thumb for good passive solar design is to use glazing equal to or less than 7% of the total floor area on the south façade, less than 2% of the total floor area on the west façade, and less than 4% of total floor area on east and north facades. Use skylights with shades and insulated wells in a space less than 2% of the total roof area. With these calculations, your house will most likely not overheat.

It is easy to have more glass on those walls than is laid out in this rule of thumb, too. Just add shading over the additional windows to balance heat gain. The more solid the shading device (i.e. a roof), the more glass you can have. The more transparent the shade device (i.e. a trellis) means additional shade devices like curtains or shutters are required to balance heat gain.

Then, under the south windowwall, provide 3-6 square feet of thermal mass flooring or wall for every 1 square foot of solar glass. For best passive solar design, we do not want to busy the thermal collector space with plants or cover it with carpets or the system will not work. We can help it to work better by painting the thermal mass dark colors and the nearby walls light colors.

Really. It IS that simple.

If you design to true passive solar principles your greenhouse might not work in the same way, but as designed, Earthship greenhouses do not really work for their intended purpose anyway so maybe a different type of greenhouse is called for. We love how our friends Dan's greenhouse works for him year-round. It shades the structure of his house and gives him free heat in the winter. The only difference between his greenhouse and a regular Earthship greenhouse is that his greenhouse is designed as a greenhouse, not a conservatory. This means he has a solid thermal storage wall between the greenhouse and the house, and the greenhouse and house are separated with exterior rated doors.

PASSIVE SOLAR DOESN'T WORK EVERYWHERE

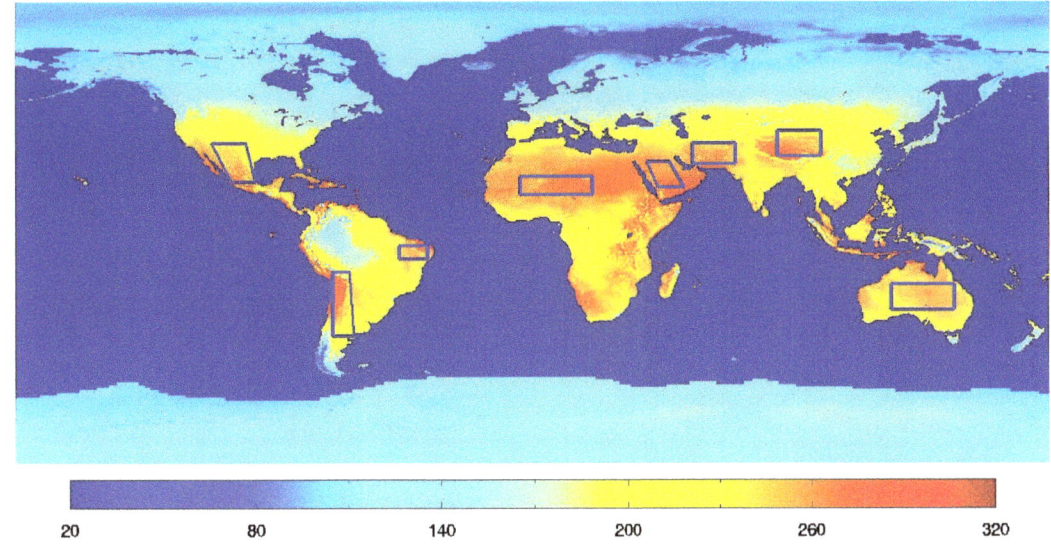

Figure 16. Solar Access map from RenewableEnergySt.org

One of the limitations of passive solar, and for any building that uses photovoltaics, is the accessibility of adequate sunlight. In the map above, you can see squares highlighting where the best solar gain is for commercial solar farms. That is great, but those locations are actually the second worst places for solar-designed homes. In these locations, you will overheat, so you want to build your home up off the ground if possible, or into the ground entirely, and eliminate as many windows as possible or provide as much shading overhang as possible to escape overheating. But this map is also telling in another way – you can see the regions where the yellow turns to blue? Well, in areas where there is blue, There is not enough solar gain constant through the year (many times because of the all-dark or all-light of the winter and summer seasons at these latitudes and/or a predominance of cloud cover) to justify building a house that depends on passive solar without backup systems. That includes in the UK, Sweden, and upper parts of France, Canada, and Germany, even! In these locations, you really want to play with bringing in, and shutting out, light... but focus on providing sources of heat, ventilation, and power that work even when there is no sun. Ideally, you need 300 days a year of sunlight to make passive solar work well.

You can check the viability for your area at this website: http://www.renewableenergyst.org/solar.htm

Ultra-Tight Construction

One of many common concerns we hear about Earthships is that the tight envelope and non-climatically designed natural ventilation system prevents enough air movement to manage dehumidification and thus, comfort. This is a characteristic that Earthships share with their PassivHaus counterparts, as they were both designed on some similar principles, including the tight envelope. The PassivHaus concept expanded upon this tight envelope, making the building ultra-tight. The issue with that design technique is that it is not physically possible for the PassivHaus to achieve occupant comfort or safety without technology. If the power goes out, you are going to have problems breathing in these houses because they do not use enough operable windows (which would sacrifice thermal performance) to provide enough airflow to be comfortable.

We know now that an Earthship will not work if air movement is inadequate. The fireplaces cannot work, natural ventilation cannot work, and air quality cannot work. Earthship designers have attempted to address this by adding operable skylights and air tubes, but those only work as long as they are open and their performance is not limited by current weather conditions. Furthermore, people suffering from allergies may not find constant unfiltered outdoor air helpful.

Other Ways of Staying Cool

The easiest way to naturally cool your home is to close it up during the day while you are away. This means closing all windows first thing in the morning while it is still cool outside, as well as putting out any operable shade devices. Close miniblinds and curtains if you have them. If there are only blinds, consider hanging a sheet or a lightweight blanket over each window during the day.

Functional exterior shutters keep the heat from entering the window and getting trapped behind the glazing, thereby making it easier to cool your spaces. Shutters can make your home up to 15 degrees cooler inside!

Interior shutters also function to shut out some of the heat, but they let the heat in the window before they stop it and you will have to work harder to get the heat you already gained out. By using exterior shutters, you have minimized the impact immediately by keeping the heat out in the first place. Choosing shutters you will use is key though. Exterior shutters may be the better solution to the overheating problem, but they only work better if you use them. If that means you have to get wet, or snowy, then do not use them. Use interior ones instead and just be sure to close them at night and in the morning depending on if you are using them to keep the summer out (open at night and closed during the day) or the warm in (closed at night and opened during the day). Add storm windows and/or insulated curtains to help hold in the heat in in cold climates.

If you will be at home during the day, use these techniques on the south and west sides of the house and keep your activities in the rooms on the north and east. The north side is far more shaded and will be cooler during the entire day. Use the eastern rooms—with shades open is fine—after noon, if possible.

If you have a basement, the pressure difference between a closed-up home and the outside may drive humidity into the lower parts of the house, where it will tend to collect and grow molds. If during the warmer times of the year you use the closed-house technique described above, try to open the house up at night to allow this moisture to dissipate and provide a cool breeze to eliminate these concerns. As always, close windows as soon as possible in the mornings, preferably before dawn.

It is important to design openings that admit cooling winds but not the heat of the sun. One way to address this is to recess your doors and windows towards the inside face of the wall so that the depth of the wall shades much of the opening. We see this often in Taos, and this trick works especially well on deep walls like adobe and strawbale.

Other Ways of Staying Warm

The easiest way to naturally heat the home is to open the shades on the south, east, and west sides in the morning, allow the sun to flow in all day, and an hour before the sun starts to go down, close them. This will help keep the heat in overnight. Use the south and west rooms during the day and through the night to stay warmer naturally. Also, be sure that all windows are closed and locked—this helps to make sure that air infiltration is minimized.

People, lights, equipment, appliances, and food prep all generate heat that must be harvested or removed. Yes, you read that right – people create heat. We remember this when we are cold and jump in bed with our beloved. The heat production of an average person seated is 110 Watts (375 BTUH); performing light work is 170 Watts (580BTUH), and doing heavy work is 440 Watts (1501 BTUH). For comparison, a typical incandescent light bulb produces approximately 100 Watts (341 BTUH) of heat. So we are putting off as much heat as a standard lamp when we are just sitting around! So yes, you can actually use body heat to warm up a space. In fact, in older societies, that is why everyone slept in one small room.

A standard residential kitchen's appliances creates 350 Watts (1200 BTUH) of heat when nothing is on. We can harness this heat to our advantage in cool times, or we have to move the heat out of the space in heated periods. My hubby and I like to bake when our terribly designed north-facing kitchen gets unbearably cold. It may not be a long term solution, but it works great for staying warm while we are using the space.

Heat that passes through a window can be calculated, but moreover it can be an interesting study in how to stay warm or cool more easily. Through single pane glass, we can collect up to 90% of the sun's heat. Through double panes, we can collect up to 85%. With dark blinds, which will absorb heat, we can capture 65-70% of the sun's heat, and with light colored blinds we can capture 50% because the light materials reflect some of the heat.

Thermal Mass versus Insulation

Thermal mass is a material's resistance to changes in temperature. Thermal mass works best in locations that have large swings of temperature from day to night, like here in the desert southwest. Thermal mass does not prevent heat or cold from passing between spaces. It just acts as a thermal regulator.

In contrast, insulation is like your puffy warm winter jacket - it holds all the heat in and keeps the cold out, in cold climates. In warm climates, insulation does the reverse - it keeps the cool in and the heat out.

Because surfaces of the mass will tend towards the average daily temperature, in climates that are consistently hot or cold, thermal mass effect can actually be detrimental. Thus, in tropical and equatorial climates, buildings are built in a manner that is open and lightweight. In extremely cold and sub-polar regions, we build buildings that are highly insulated, with as little exposed thermal mass as possible.

In some climates, you can get the same benefit that thermal mass might provide on the exterior by simply installing more and better insulation — and in many cases, the added insulation will cost less and require smaller foundations and thus, engineering, than adding equivalent thermal mass. Part of the challenge here is deciding what your values are and then building a system around your climate, value, and budget.

We will touch more on how this affects your exterior wall systems in the Enclosure chapter.

Thermal Mass for Heating

If you're familiar with the *hornos* (pronounced or-nose) or clay ovens in the southwest, you understand using thermal mass for heating. First a fire is built in a thick clay oven. Then after the fire has gotten good and hot, the embers and ashes are removed and the bread dough is brought in. The thermal mass of the oven bakes the bread with heat stored from the fire after the fire is out. To use thermal mass as a means of heating, we choose materials that have the capacity to absorb, store, and then slowly release heat energy from the sun. We locate those materials inside the building, away from the exterior walls, to protect them from the temperature extremes outside and to allow them to absorb as much radiant heat from the sun as possible during the day. Then when the air temperatures inside falls below that of the thermal mass, that mass will slowly re-radiate the heat into our homes throughout the night.

South-facing double pane insulated windows paired with thermal mass are the most common and effective means of capturing the sun. To use this technique most effectively, the home should be oriented within 10 degrees of due south. Even small derivations can cause significant heat gain in the winter months. In most cases, a more southeast orientation is a better option than more southwest orientation, as the building will not overheat as badly in the summer, because it is facing the cool morning sun rather than the blazing western sun.

The thermal mass aspect of passive solar is most often achieved with a darker-colored brick, stone, earth, or concrete floor inside under the south-facing windows, and/or with a masonry or adobe wall between the solar gain space and the body of the home. This "thermal battery" stores the heat of the sun captured from the light coming through the windows and allows it to re-radiate into the space through the evening when it starts to cool down outside.

On a clear day, the sun can radiate up to 100 Watts (350 BTUH) on each square foot of surface, but since the sun is relatively "moving" in relation to our buildings, that rate can change over the course of a day. So, we need to plan for enough surface area and depth of materials to store that heat until we need it. Many people erroneously believe that you can just use a thicker mass if you do not have the required surface area. That instinctual and seemingly logical response to the problem of thermal mass, unfortunately, does not prove out. The surface area of thermal mass, in this case, is more important than depth. If your thermal mass material is more than 4 inches deep, you start to lose thermal advantage.

It can take several years for an Earthship to feel comfortable to its inhabitants. It is said that it takes several years for the "thermal storage" of the berm to reach equilibrium. We are not certain that this is actually about an improvement in thermal mass performance over time. Rather, we wonder if this has to do with the occupants getting used to an Earthship's regular over- and under-heating periods.

Thermal Mass for Cooling

To use thermal mass as a means of cooling, we locate the thermal mass in the exterior walls.

> *"Researchers have found that hot-climate homes with high-mass exterior walls require less energy for air conditioning than low-mass wood-framed homes with similar levels of wall insulation. Nearly all areas with significant cooling loads can benefit from thermal mass in exterior walls... Greg Kallio, a professor of mechanical engineering at California State University in Chico who specializes in heat transfer, recently ... model[ed] 'the whole gamut' of wall systems, from stick-built to SIPs to insulated concrete, using industry standard energy analysis programs like EnergyPlus, as well as his own custom software. His conclusion? 'The effectiveness of thermal mass is very dependent on diurnal temperature variation. You want nighttime temperatures that get at least 10 degrees cooler than the thermostat set point.' In a study conducted at the Oak Ridge National Laboratory, researcher Jan Kosny said, "The most effective wall assemblies are those in which thermal mass remains in good contact with the interior of the building."*
>
> - Alex Wilson, editor of Environmental Building News

Remember, though, your exterior thermal mass walls will likely still need insulation!

Earth-Coupling and Earth-Sheltering 101

In the first part of this book, we mentioned that earth-sheltering is a 10,000 year old building practice that is well worth considering for our homes. Using nature to our advantage is not just smart design. It saves resources and reduces the number of building materials we need to use.

One of the great misunderstandings about Earthships is that earth-coupling is traditionally and best used as a passive cooling strategy for use in hot climates, where the earth temperature being cooler than the outside air is a benefit. Earth-coupling uses the regular temperature of the soil as a heat sink to cool the building through conduction. In other locations... in the tropics and humid equatorial regions, especially... we know that earth is not the right material. Here, we either want to use a seriously massive structure like solid stone with massively thick walls if we are in an arid region, or if we are in a humid region, we want to build high above the ground and of the lightest, most flexible building materials available, like trees and bamboo.

When it is used for thermal performance, earth-coupling works in one of two ways. The first is earth-sheltering, where the earth itself forms the backbone of some of our walls, thereby reducing air infiltration by the heated air outside, as well as mitigating the extremes of heat and cool within in the space. We see this type used extensively in ancient civilizations like Greece, Italy, Turkey, Egypt, and Mesopotamia. We see versions of this using stacked sod as a building material in Scandinavia and Iceland. Mesa Verde uses rock outcroppings to provide a permanent roof and shade for their earth-coupled structures, doubling down on using earth-sheltering for passive cooling and heating by harnessing the power of the southern sun for warming. There are entire villages in Africa that use earth-sheltering by carving livable spaces out of the earth. This same technique has been used in Native American pit-houses and kivas here in New Mexico for the past 1,000 years. Taos Pueblo, made of puddled and brick adobe and added to in layers to look like a mountain, takes earth-sheltering to an entirely new level - the stacked apartment block shares heat between spaces by stacking chimneys and rooms. The inner rooms and bottom parts of the block stay so cool that their food stores can last 7 years.

The second means of earth-coupling is to use earth-ducts, buried tubes meant to mitigate the temperature of the air before it is introduced into the building. This technique is quite ancient and can be seen in many Middle-Eastern environments where the tubes are paired with chimneys and even cooling pools to increase air cooling as well as humidity. To some degree, Earthships' cooling tubes do this. They just do not quite take it far enough.

Earth-coupling works, in the right climates and locations. We just have to be wise in the way we use it.

You can get ideas about traditional and modern uses of earth-coupling and earth-sheltering on the Archaeo-Architecture Pinterest Board we built for you.

DOING AN EARTH-SHELTERING BERM RIGHT

In principle, Earthships rely on a balance of solar heat gain at the south-facing window wall / greenhouse and the rammed earth walls and earthen berm "storing heat." Except, the berm is not really storing much heat, because it is not exposed to enough sunlight to gain any. It would be more accurate to state the Earthship's berm provides a kind of insulation that keeps the back spaces of the Earthship below frost line insulated to maintain something near the inner-earth temperature of 58 degrees (in Taos).

The Earthships were not the only more modern design to revisit the idea of earth-sheltering, either... in his co-op homestead plans in 1942, Frank Lloyd Wright proposed sheltering a house with an earth berm.

Now, an earth-sheltered berm is great in principle! But as we stated, earth-coupling is meant to be used for passive cooling. Therefore, this technique is really best suited to hot climates.

EARTH-SHELTERING BERM PROS

- It should shed the cold winter winds from the north over the roof of the house.
- It should allow your home to maintain the inner-earth 58 degree base temp.
- It provides a place for the cisterns and systems.
- It gives you a cold back wall perfect for food storage.

EARTH-SHELTERING BERM CHALLENGES

- The berm, being shaded the vast majority of the time, holds water against the northern back wall and creates issues of freeze-thaw. The solution to this is installing a French-drain system along the back wall. This is a necessary step if using cisterns, in case you get a leak, which could threaten the entire wall structure if left unchecked, which it will likely be unless you lose a lot of water at once. Else, if there is a leak in that back wall, you will have to excavate the entire berm to find it. To prepare the wall for a French drain, it is critical to have two layers of building paper or waterproof membrane applied to the wall from under the roof eave down the entire wall to the drain system. The outside layer should be trimmed 6-12 inches shorter than the one closest to the wall. The roof junction to the wall should be covered with a waterproof membrane that laps from under the roofing material and over the wall protection layer by at least 2 feet.

- Unlike it is asserted in *Comfort in Any Climate*, it appears that uninsulated ground-coupled thermal mass has a potential for substantial heat loss, especially in climates with more heating degree days than cooling degree days, and areas where there is not enough sunshine to justify the sole use of passive solar design techniques for heating. The extent of temperature fluctuations of the earth berm and foundation varies based on local prevailing weather patterns, and is further influenced by soil type and moisture content.

- Where in Taos, our inner-earth temperature can range from 56-58°F (roughly 14°C) based on elevation, the local inner-earth temperature of your area will most likely be different. In higher latitudes and altitudes, this temperature will likely be lower, and in lower latitudes and altitudes, it will likely be higher. The inner-earth temperature for your area can be roughly determined by taking the average annual temperature for your area and subtracting 5 degrees. So, in Taos, our average annual temperature is 63.4°F (17.4°C). That, minus 5 equals 58.8°F (14.9°C), so that should be our inner-earth temperature for design purposes. "Comfortable" is around 67°F (roughly 20°C). So, based on this, we can determine that insulation at the slab and additional heating will be required to achieve year-round comfort. In places like Belgium, the annual temperature average is about 10°C (48°F). That is 10°C (roughly 20°F) colder than Taos, which will require double the heating input plus additional insulation!

- Architects and designers versed in this design flaw, mainly in Europe, have added R-10 rigid board insulation beneath the tires and floors and along the inside of earth-sheltered walls. They have found that by doing this, the negative impact of the cooler inner-earth temperatures at these latitudes is minimized.

- Rodents burrowing into the berm will create little "gutters and downspouts" which will funnel water into the tire wall! One of the owners we interviewed had so many issues with rodents digging "water spouts" into in his Earthship's berm that he removed the berm and cement-stuccoed the back side of his tire walls!

Earlier I mentioned that part of my academic studies in architecture and some of what I speak on in my lectures is based on this idea Kenneth Frampton called Critical Regionalism. Critical Regionalism takes what has been built and perfected by regional vernacular designers (read: indigenous and early-settlers) and applies it to modern design, rendering architecture that is especially responsive to its culture and environment. So, when people ask me how I might use an earth-shelter, because I do not know their area, I always say, "I am not sure, exactly, but I would start with finding out what your ancient settlers did, and work from there." Our ancestral traditions had a way of building that worked for their place. We should not ignore the thousands of years of data supporting whatever techniques and materials they used successfully. All the materials should still be locally available. Want simple? This is where to start.

The issues with the Earthship's tire walls, combined with concerns about the cisterns and vent tubes limiting the berm's effectiveness, suggest that perhaps a double-wythe (double-wide) adobe, earthbag, or rammed earth wall is as good a solution as a berm for earth-sheltering for some climates. The time required for the continued maintenance of the berm and the cost of installation of French drains and an additional layer of insulation outside the building could easily be saved this way.

Natural Ventilation Strategies and Indoor Air Quality

We can use the wind to increase the airflow in our homes as well as to improve indoor air quality. It is pretty easy, actually. All we have to do is use the natural air movements caused by differences in air pressure and temperature to our advantage.

Remember how in the structural chapter, we talked about how wind creates a high pressure on the side of the house the wind is coming from (the windward side) and a low pressure on the side of the house in the direction the wind is going (the leeward side)? We can harness that natural action to improve ventilation. Ventilation should be a minimum of 5 cubic feet per minute (CFM) per person to provide enough oxygen to our bodies. 10 CFM is ideal but challenging to attain naturally. Ventilation in your kitchen, when you are working and cooking, should be 30 CFM or more to minimize overheating and humidification and maximize odor control.

A natural ventilation system designed without considering the specific climate of our building site cannot attain these levels of air movement. In order to get these airflow levels, we need to ask nature to work for us by coming to understand the movements of the air… and inviting it in.

The downside is that natural ventilation left unchecked can lead to moisture problems. What we learned from the thermal performance research on Earthships is that it is critical to design a system that addresses pressurization and de-humidification as well as air movement, especially if we use the attached greenhouse.

Using Windows for Ventilation

The first way we can invite natural ventilation in is one of the oldest methods of all - windows. We want to locate windows on opposite walls to facilitate natural cross-ventilation. We want to make sure that every room has a place for air to come in and a place across the room for air to move out. In climates with daytime breezes (and if you use the landscape techniques we offer here you will have those), open the bottom half of double-hung or awning windows on the side of the house that the breeze is coming from and then the high half of double hung or high awning windows on the opposite side of the home. This will encourage cross-ventilation.

If you have casement windows, which open vertically, you can use those to capture the wind in the evenings. Just open those that open toward the wind and also those that face in the direction the wind is traveling. If they do not open in the right directions, keep them closed, as they will invite warm air in and actually make it hotter inside!

One of the great things about living in a two-story or clerestory structure is that you can use the extra shade provided on the north side of your home and your basement and stairways to create a form of natural air movement called stack-effect, which can be effective for air circulation and cooling. This technique works by capturing the coolest, heaviest, air on the north side of the house and encouraging it to move through the house and take the overheated air with it. To use this technique, simply open the lowest floor's north windows, and if you have double-hung windows, open the bottom sash. Then, open the doors and head upstairs to open the windows on the highest story on the south side of the home, or in the direction the wind is traveling to. If you have double hung windows, open the top sash on the upper floor. You can also open your fireplace damper for a similar effect.

In all cases, the windows the air will escape from (preferably a high window on the side the wind is GOING) should be open as wide, or wider, than the window air is coming INTO.

If a room is overheating, open the high part of the windows to let out the hot air!

Make this work for you! In hot and temperate climates, with cooler nights than days, close and lock your windows during the day to keep the cooler night air IN, and then open your windows in the evenings to allow the cooler evening air in to cool down the house again. Locking your windows is not just secure – it seals leaks!

Other Means of Ventilation

A perk of using shade devices on your windows is that if you have a two foot deep or larger overhang at the window, you will be able to harness the wind by directing it into your home!

Comfort can be improved in hot/humid climates by simply ventilating your attic and crawl spaces.

In cold environments, high placed windows called transoms (usually located over doors) are opened to let heat in and closed to hold it in. Or, in hot/humid environments, transoms are opened to let the naturally rising heat out. A transom is always used for moving heated air, as heated air is lighter than cold air and will rise to the ceiling. This is part of why tropical homes often have a soaring ceiling leading to a tower skylight with openings instead of windows. The hot air escapes the house this way.

Ceiling fans decrease interior air temperature by approximately 4°F. Use them anywhere you need them, especially in tall rooms, living rooms, and bedrooms. Use floor fans to move air through the spaces and keep humidification even.

Earthship Ventilation Issues

In Earthships with kitchens and baths open at the ceiling or along the south wall, and in climates with high humidity, there are often considerable issues with over-humidification in the bio-cells. This can be addressed with adequate ventilation and de-humidification. A tried and true solution to this is to design a line of operable windows at the top and bottom of the south window wall to let out the humid, heated air. Small floor fans can improve the airflow in the greenhouse space when condensation is an issue. Be aware though, you need to buy a decent fan, as the moisture from the humidity may well have a negative impact on its performance over time.

Earthship Cooling Tubes and Alternatives

The Earthships' natural convection system design does not work for winter ventilation in most locations. Air just does not move the same way every day, or even in every season, and we need to work with what is actually happening instead of designing around the way we wish things worked.

To address lack of adequate ventilation, cooling tubes have been added to the northern berm. These are opened every day between 10AM and 2PM in order to bring in more fresh "cool" air. This is a decent idea in principle. In practice, the tubes do not perform as expected when it is humid outside or when it snows and the tubes get buried. In these locations, now you also have to get snow off those vents and pay attention to potential over-humidification, adding another checkmark to the already long list of daily maintenance activities.

When the outside air is not moving from north to south, the tube vents cannot bring in fresh air. Unlike windows, which can capture air that bounces off the side of the house, the vent tubes cannot capture air that is not moving in the direction the tubes are installed. As in the case of Taos in winter, when the storms blow in from the north, the cooling tubes can introduce bone-chilling air and potentially even snow into the house.

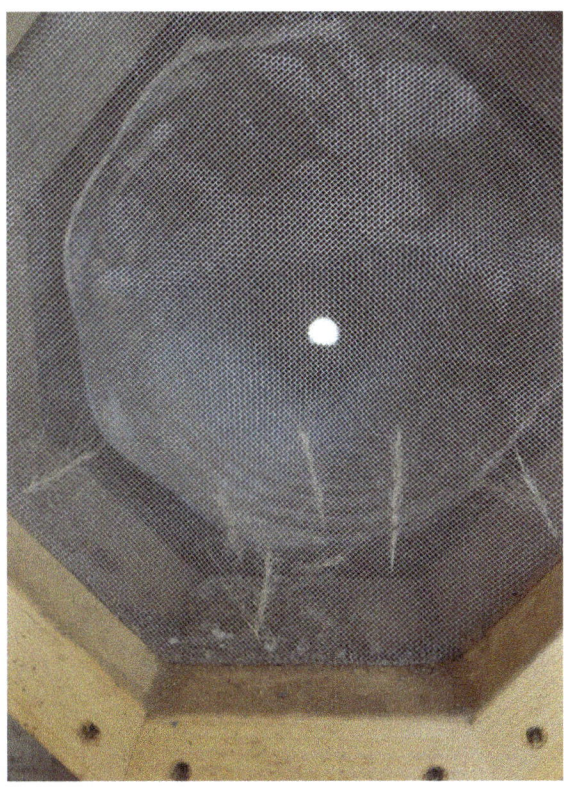

Figure 17. Air Tube Allergy Concerns

Our bodies prefer fresh, dry air, and when we live in regions where it snows or rains, we get fresh wet air. That corrodes the cooling tubes and it introduces yet more humidity into the house.

The cooling tubes also break up the berm's positive thermal impact and seem to capture dirt, critters, and tumbleweeds that are impossible to clean out. The impact on the berm's thermal performance is a complicated issue that may take some time and experimentation to figure out. The dust can be a maintenance issue, especially for those with allergies.

One of the best solutions to the cooling tube issue that we have seen was used recently in the modern granddaddy of Earthship-inspired design - the New Mexico International Spaceport. Here, Foster and Partners and their local architectural team SMPC Architects of Albuquerque used what is called a thermal labyrinth - a maze of concrete cooling tubes that fold back in on each other - in the earth berms on either side of the main body of the hangar. This allowed them to capture east and west winds (whichever way was blowing best) then cool those winds with thermal mass, and turn them into breezes by breaking them up in the maze before delivering the pre-cooled air to the terminal. This also captures dust and tumbleweeds rather than shooting them into the space at high velocity. It is an ingenious and maintainable solution that offers a place to start when rethinking the cooling tube idea.

Another great option for this is to use a Middle-Eastern inspired wind catcher or wind scoop if winds are common in your area. A wind catcher is a kind of reverse chimney that rises like a tower above your roof, with its opening facing into the prevailing wind and scooping the breeze down into the rooms below. A well-designed wind catcher can work in reverse when the air is still by drawing warm air upward and out of the house!

Indoor Air Quality

THE QUICKEST WAY TO MAXIMIZE INDOOR AIR QUALITY IS TO:

- Provide operable windows and know how to use them.
- Use Zero or Low VOC (Volatile Organic Compound) paints, stains, adhesives, and finishes.
- Provide natural light and operable windows from at least two directions in every room.
- Avoid using dirt- and mold-trapping finish materials like carpet.
- Use exterior grade plywood or formalehyde-free particle board on interior finishes to minimize off-gassing.
- Avoid vinyl or fabric wallcoverings.
- Provide radon and carbon monoxide detectors.
- If you use mechanical systems, design them to use higher levels of fresh air, and allow users to individually control their area or zone.
- Use a MERV-9 filter on your central air or ventilation system.
- For the best indoor air quality, ask for insulation that meets the air quality standards of GreenGuard, SCS, California 1350, or Berkeley Labs.

Humidification Matters

Cool dry air is necessary for human comfort. Maintaining relative humidity below 50% prevents dust mite infestations, inhibits mold and mildew growth, and inhibits bacteria. Lower humidity also reduces the off-gassing of VOCs. In colder climates, wintertime humidity levels must be even lower - generally 30-40% - to prevent condensation on windows and other surfaces.

So part of what we have to plan for is dehumidifying wet air, and/or cooling down and humidifying hot/dry air. This process can be easily accomplished using a mechanical system, but when we do not use a system to manage it, we need to get creative. Some people warm up a crock of water on their wood stove to increase humidity. Others use misters in their greenhouse (though that can wreak havoc on your structural system if that system is wood-based). Some use fountains and waterfalls to serve the dual purpose of cycling the water in the cistern to keep it fresh while creating humidity within the livable areas. You might even use water walls with plants to increase humidification and oxygenation. Whatever you do, if you work with water, you need to make a plan for maintenance too… interior ponds and waterfalls require filtration and algae control to work correctly.

Alternately, people in humid climates may need to utilize salt de-humidifiers, using calcium chloride in most cases, which is readily available at your local agricultural store. This technique has been used by farmers for generations to keep hay from molding. You can also use air-based heating and cooling like stoves and forced-air systems to remove humidity from the air.

Thermal and Moisture Protection

Keeping water and heated and cooled air where you want it is probably one of the hardest parts of building a home that maximizes performance and minimizes the need for mechanical systems. From the way window openings are flashed to the underlayment beneath the floor… these seemingly irrelevant details can determine the success or failure of a project.

We want to layer on waterproofing and insulation onto our homes in the same way we layer clothes on us when we go skiing or snowboarding… where there are openings, there will be issues because the snow and cold wind can get in. We can stuff the space between the open shoulder of our sweater and our neck with a scarf, but that will not be as warm as wearing a turtleneck that covers us up to our neck and then putting on a scarf. Without gaiters or wide enough pants to cover our boots, snow gets in. So we put on a layer that protects that gap. Or, if we were to wear our jacket open while we rode, our front may get cold before the rest of us, or we may even take on snow, so we zip it up. When all these layers are used as continuous systems, we stay warm and dry. The same is true for insulation and waterproofing. Putting insulation in a single location makes no more sense than having cold toes from wet boots and throwing in a hot pack. All that is going to do is make the boots hot and wet. It is not going to dry them. It may not be quite as miserable but it does not solve the problem.

Critical factors of good design include planning for water vapor, which is inherent in the building's interior because of plants, showers, and our own breath. When this humid air reaches a place where the temperature of the wall or roof becomes cooled by the outside air, condensation can occur. It may happen on an uninsulated pane of windows, or it can be tucked away in some crevice we do not even know is there. Where we put insulation and vapor barriers determines if that becomes a problem down the line.

R-VALUES

You have probably heard the term R-value in regard to thermal performance. R-value is a measure of thermal resistance of your building materials. We will not get into R-values too much here as it can be confusing. Instead, as is our goal for this book, we will just offer rules of thumb that we believe will help you make the most of your building system from the outset, no matter where or what you are building.

For the sake of information, however, if you are designing a home with more traditional materials, which are easier to determine an R-value for… the minimum recommended R-value for your major wall systems is an R-19 for the ceiling or roof and R-11 for walls and floors. That is really not going to get you a great design, though. In the south, we really want closer to an R-30 roof, and R-13 or better in the walls and floors. In the northern latitudes and higher altitudes, an R-40 roof and R-20 walls and floors are ideal.

Roof Thermal Performance Improvements

The roof requires the most insulation because the temperature difference between inside and out is most often highest here, because the heat from inside has risen up into the top of the house. For superior roof protection, use decking as discussed in the roofing section, then:

- A continuous vapor barrier sealed at all penetrations should be installed on the warm (heated) side of the system unless in a hot/humid area, where it goes to the outside.

- Radiant barrier (looks like aluminum foil) should be installed on the base of the roof decking if there is a mechanical system in the attic or ceiling structure.

- Two layers of staggered rigid insulation should be applied. The first one should be mechanically fastened to the roof to resist wind uplift, and the second glued down, unless the rigid insulation layer is made of polyurethane, polystyrene, or polyisocyanurate, which requires a second layer of gypsum board or perlite rather than another layer of rigid. Note: polyurethane and polyisocyanurate provide the highest R-values of the insulating materials for roofing.

- A layer of 36 inch wide #30 roofing felt with a minimum 4 inch lap should be applied to the entire roof.
- Rubber, galvanized metal, or aluminum flashing and vent seals are ideal. Stay away from lead. Another option is to use historic flashings: for instance... Early builders in Wales relied on projecting slates on the chimney to keep the rain away from the roof and wall junction. What local historic no-tech methods might you use to maximize your use of natural materials?
- Whatever base sheet is recommended for your roofing finish system for the drainage layer.

Roof insulation is far more important in hot climate zones than wall insulation!

Using R-50 ceiling insulation if you are not going to use exposed structure and live in a freezing climate is ideal.

If using a framed pitched roof, use a raised heel on roof trusses so insulation can cover the top plate. Provide insulation in the roof floor but be sure it does not block the airflow between roof eave vents and ridge vents.

Framing for Thermal Performance

If you frame any part of your home, use sill sealant below the sill plate and caulk the bottom plate at exterior walls to minimize air infiltration. We also recommend that you use termite-resistant materials and a termite barrier at the foundation in areas where these pests are a problem.

Remember: do not install caulks or sealants in temperatures lower than 40°F!

Thermal Bridging

Thermal bridging is when the structure - most often the framing - penetrates the insulated blanket around your home and provides a "bridge" for the hot or cold air outside to penetrate into the space. Because of mass and other related thermal properties of different materials, cold or heat can pass through them at different rates. For instance, the heat or cold will pass through the stud at a different rate than the insulation. This translates to alternating hot and cold spots on the wall, which you can often feel if you run your hand along the wall. Oftentimes, the result is condensation. Because water trapped in the air as humidity is naturally drawn into the space by air pressure, usually at an uninsulated place, the temperature difference makes it so that the vapor condenses into droplets.

The bigger issue in Earthships is that a lot of that moisture is coming from inside, which causes issues on the outside of the framing under your flashing. That is harder to notice. And to fix.

To accommodate this, the best solution is often to turn framing 90 degrees, to use structural insulated panels, or to add insulation along the exterior edge of the stud before applying the final finish material. Thermal bridging happens mostly in systems where there are lots of bits and pieces - a window, a stud wall, or the like. Paying special attention to the construction detailing as well as insulation and sealing of these areas is vital.

Choosing Insulation

While builders have been known to use 15 inches or more of cardboard as insulation in some builds, we do not advocate this practice. Cardboard is a fire hazard, encourages pests, and does not present a significant positive recycling impact.

The pink FIBERGLASS INSULATION of yore has been replaced a modern version which uses 30-40% post-consumer recycled glass content and still offers the highest R-value at the lowest price point of insulation products. This insulation is easily accessible to anyone within driving distance to a Lowes or Home Depot; however it can present health concerns because of the tendency for the glass fibers to break off and be inhaled. Because of this, and the fact that this insulation trends more towards the manufactured than the natural, most of our readers may find this a less than ideal option.

SPRAY FOAM INSULATION, with an R-value of between 3 and 7 per inch depending on the brand, starts as a liquid that is sprayed or poured into a wall cavity where it expands into a foam and then dries to a very stable material. A greener generation of vegetable-based spray foams available today uses oils from soy, sugarcane, corn fructose and other botanical sources, plus up to 10% recycled content for the foam spray. These insulation applications are blown in with water, carbon dioxide, or hydro-fluorocarbons (HFCs), which are less damaging to the ozone layer than older spray foam products. Concerns around foam include that it must be installed by a professional which can make it more expensive than other options; it only works in structures constructed with cavities in the roof, walls, and floors to blow it into; and it off-gasses during installation. When it is dry, it is inert.

CELLULOSE, which is made from up to 80% recycled newspaper, cardboard, and paperboard, is popular for home insulation because of its sustainability and low embodied energy. When removed from a building, it may be used again or disposed of safely without creating toxic waste. Cellulose insulation offers an R-value of R-3.5 per inch and is applied as a paste, sprayed in like foam insulation, or is used as loose fill. It is also limited in that it works best when installed in cavities. Cellulose is most often treated with Boric Acid as a fire retardant, pest repellant, and antifungal agent. Chemically-sensitive people may have difficulty with off-gassing - not from the insulation's foams or acid treatments but from the newspaper ink. Cellulose is particularly susceptible to moisture issues, so building a tight wall is essential. Cellulose costs only slightly more than fiberglass insulation.

GREEN POLYISO (polyisocyanurate) is a rigid insulation product that offers an R-value of approximately R-7 per inch and can be used on walls as well as on the roof. The newer versions of this insulation use cleaner hydrocarbons instead of the older HCFC's which were ozone-depleting. Other versions of foam insulation include polyurethane and polystyrene. When using rigid board insulation, one of the best insulators against heat and cold is expanded polystyrene (EPS). This plastic insulation is extracted from oil but it is 100% recyclable.

CEMENTITIOUS FOAM is another insulation product that is non-flammable and extremely stable, offering an R-value of 3.9 per inch. It is made from magnesium oxide derived from seawater. It is totally inert, which may make it an ideal option for people who are chemically-sensitive. It can be recycled or composted, and is non-flammable. It does need to be installed by a professional.

COTTON INSULATION, which is made from the by-products of denim and other clothing manufacturing, works extremely well as an insulator, providing an R-value of somewhere around R-3.5 per inch. It can also be prohibitively expensive, coming in at nearly double the cost of fiberglass batts. It can come in batt blankets or as loose fill and can be installed by the homeowner. Concerns about this product include that when it is not organic, cotton can create issues in the environment due to the use of chemicals and pesticides in production. Batt insulation can contain formaldehyde and/or Boric Acid, so pay attention to the small print on the packaging before you buy if this matters to you. Boric Acid is fairly non-toxic, so this is the better option of the two.

WOOL is a great alternative to cotton, and well-proven. However, unless you live on or next door to a sheep farm, it is a bit of a reach. We cannot help but ask, why use something with a high cash value for insulation when you could probably sell it for more money and better uses? That may be a consideration for you as well.

SECOND FLOORS AND LOFTS THERMAL PERFORMANCE IMPROVEMENTS

Air-seal joist cavities between floors by insulating and caulking them. If you want to go all-in and make your house as insulated as possible, install an inch of rigid insulation board over rim joists at the exterior finish material.

EXTERIOR WALL THERMAL PERFORMANCE IMPROVEMENTS

- Install a water protection membrane beneath exterior finishes.
- Install a drip cap above windows and doors.
- Make sure there is an air barrier behind showers and bathtubs on exterior walls.
- Block and seal knee-walls.
- Insulate and caulk window and door heads, jambs, and sills.
- Use rigid R-10 insulation on exterior door and window headers for additional thermal protection.

Another idea that may appeal to some readers: dampcourses, as used in England and other wet environments, are projecting courses of bricks or stone which keeps water from flowing down the plaster wall as well as preventing water from being "wicked" up from the earth due to capillary action and damaging the underlying structure. In humid locations, rainy locations, snowy locations, or those with high water tables, a dampcourse or a brick or stone base on the bottom 3 feet of the wall is a great thing to include on your exterior walls to help them last longer.

FOUNDATION THERMAL PERFORMANCE IMPROVEMENTS

Use foundation and slab waterproofing and rigid insulation in cold and climates where regular seasonal freezing occurs.

BASEMENT THERMAL PERFORMANCE IMPROVEMENTS

Use a secondary framed gypsum board wall on the interior side of your concrete or block basement walls, with R-13 or higher insulation between. This same technique can be used on the interior side of an Earthship's berm walls to improve thermal performance in cold climates.

CONCEALED SPACES AND UNHEATED SPACES

Concealed roof spaces, as well as walls, ceilings, and floors between heated and unheated spaces require insulation to control condensation.

OVERALL THERMAL AND MOISTURE PROTECTION IMPROVEMENTS

- Use caulk or foam to seal electrical, plumbing, and heating penetrations between floors and at the ceiling and exterior walls.
- Weather-strip attic hatches.
- Use rated Type IC recessed light fixtures.
- Use a gasketed door on your fireplace.
- Use insulating window shades.

Earthship-Specific Thermal and Moisture Protection Issues

Some Earthship owners have been installing insulation into the ground to frost line, especially at doors and windows, in hope that this insulation will diminish the poor thermal performance of their Earthships. This may seem like a good idea at first blush, but it is probably not effective at providing a full resolution of the thermal performance issues inherent in these designs at higher elevations and latitudes where the inner-earth temperature negatively impacts performance. Rigid insulation is not structural, nor does it have that high of R-value on its own. It provides some thermal advantage, but it is intended to be used as part of a continuous insulation system. Just burying it to frost line in the places we can easily reach (doors, exterior walls, etcetera...) does not promise any positive effect because the cold can creep into the spaces where the insulation does not go. That is kindof like making vertical cuts through your puffy down jacket and putting it on and letting the resulting flaps sway all around and then wondering why you are not staying warm anymore. It is not a solid blanket that is holding all the heat in anymore.

The layer of insulation that modern Earthships use at four feet out between the cisterns and back wall tries to reduce the negative impact of the cisterns on the berm's performance. This is yet another case of "wouldn't it be great if..." that we believe will ultimately prove out as not improving thermal performance. We believe the best approach is to either use the berm or lose the berm. We do not believe that adding more materials (and cost, installation, and headache) to make something that is dysfunctional only slightly better is a good design technique.

Good design can accommodate these issues. Spend the extra money on good windows and doors, well-designed structures that don't have a million thermal breaks, and insulation on your exterior walls, footings, and under your floors... and skip all the extra materials and connections that can and will fail.

Insulating the floor and foundation of your Earthship is critical if you live anywhere where the average yearly temperature is below 60°F. Otherwise you will have cold toes unless you have a radiant heat system. If you have a radiant heat system, it will work better on an insulated floor, thereby using less energy to heat the space.

Insulating the knee wall on the south will minimize freezing at the planters and plumbing. Other ideas for insulating this space would be to use earth-sheltering here, or use a cold frame on the exterior of the wall to grow your seedlings, which will act like a solar oven and capture and hold heat to keep that wall from freezing so quickly.

An additional heat source is almost always required in Earthships in cold climates. The can come from using a wood cook stove, radiant heat, a masonry heater, or various other heating methods which we will explain in more detail in the chapter on Mechanical Systems.

Acoustics - Sound Insulation

Sound Transmission is one of those areas that many designers and builders miss, even though it can make a huge difference in how we experience a space. Since even pros can under-plan for this, we thought we would offer just a few tips for making a home as silent and private as possible.

The way sound is rated in materials and assemblies is called Sound Transmission Class, or STC. With an STC of 45, we can hear the details of a heated discussion from the other side of a wall. With an STC of 50, we can hear that people are talking, and loudly, but the conversation is not intelligible. With an STC of 55, we will not even be able to hear the conversation. To address this, a designer will develop a sophisticated wall system that will get as close to an STC of 55 as possible. However, these systems are based on modern materials like gypsum board walls and resilient channels, which we most likely will not be using. So then what? Well, now that we know we need to pay attention to sound, we will try and share ways to reduce unwanted sound transmission that we know work no matter what the materials.

What does this sound thing matter for our homes, anyway? Because most people watch TV with the volume at least as high as a heated discussion, believe it or not. We want to design a home where mom and dad can read, and the kids can watch TV or practice their musical instruments, and everyone can have their space and do what they need to do without bothering everybody else. So, we want to either a) include an extra space that is quiet and away from all the noise, which increases our footprint and thus, cost... or, b) we want to create a "silent room" where whoever can do whatever without bothering anyone. And, we want to minimize noise overall for better occupant comfort.

Most exterior noise comes in through doors and windows. To combat this, we use the densest and heaviest doors and windows we can get. We also use the tips and tricks we talk about in the insulation and door and window sections to fill all the air-gaps in the framing to reduce sound transmission as well as thermal losses. We make sure weather-stripping is installed on our doors and windows, and that it stays in good repair, and that we lock our doors and windows when they are closed because an improperly sealed window or door opening can make the difference between drafty and loud and warm and quiet. Installing storm windows is not just good for warmer winters in cold locations either; they also cut down on noise!

Insulating framed walls with cellulose or rock /mineral batt helps us to achieve the needed sound reduction. Even more sound reduction results from using a double-thick frame wall with alternating studs that do not connect to both sides of the drywall. This is a great technique to use on plumbing walls which might want to be thicker than a traditional wall anyway. Adding another layer of drywall can help reduce the sound coming through a wall. We can pour sand into the cores and seal a block wall on both sides to achieve a higher STC as well.

We also want to minimize the number of hard surfaces in our space. Concrete or stone floors, gypsum board or window walls, hard ceilings... these all contribute to sound bouncing around and creating problems. Softening sounds with window coverings and natural carpets or other soft materials on frame floors can also have a dramatic effect on sound quality.

If sound is a real issue and you are building a loft or second floor, you may want to choose solid wood joists over the more sustainable TJIs, because the sound transmission in joists is more uniform. Using cellulose or 3 layers of rock /mineral batt insulation between floors can reduce the sound of footsteps dramatically. Adding another layer of ceiling material, or using a sound rated floor underlayment on the upstairs floor will reduce this even further.

Another item regarding acoustic privacy: Transom windows, or high window openings, are a good thing and a bad thing. They allow you to move heat out of the space if they are operable or open. I love these windows for that. However, if they are left open, you will find that you never have privacy. I lived in a loft designed by the renowned firm Architectonica when I lived in Charlottesville, Virginia for 3 years. That firm was known for its designs which left the upper walls open between rooms to encourage natural ventilation (which works great in Miami where they are from). When my roommate or friends were around, which was most of the time, I had to lock myself in the toilet room - the only room with full height walls - to make private phone calls. I do not recommend that. Further, when you do not want light in the space... like when you are taking a nap or editing a video... it is nearly impossible to get the darkness you long for with transoms or open windows because they do not really make curtains for that application.

Next Page: Figure 18. Elegant Structure at Nicolai Fechin Home in Taos

Chapter VI

The Structural System

by Rachel Preston Prinz and Michael Curry

The Roman architect Vitruvius taught that "firmness, commodity, and delight" were the foundations of great design. In his teaching, firmness isn't just structural soundness. A building's firmness also includes being designed for its place in an integrated landscape that works with the home, and being designed and built so that you can afford to maintain it. Basically firmness is all the things that make a home last and be loved for generations. This is the best kind of sustainable! But in this, a solid and sound structure is the core.

A building's structural systems are its bones. The connection of the elements of the structural system to each other (via bolts, screws, hardware, and even glue) are its joints: its elbows, knees, and ankles. The other systems of a building: the electrical, heating and ventilation, and plumbing… are analogous to a body's nervous, respiratory, and digestive systems. Those systems are able to do their jobs because the structure holds them in place.

The structural system includes the foundation, roof structure, floor structure(s), bearing walls, beams, columns, and the connection of all these elements to each other. The structure is oftentimes the place where the Building Code can be the most challenging. So let's walk through what matters so we all understand why we need to do what we do in regard to structure.

There are two types of loads we need to account for in our building design. These are static and dynamic loads.

A STATIC LOAD is constant. It might be what is called a dead load, which includes the weight of the structure itself as well as permanent features like an air conditioning unit. Or it might be a live load, which might include you as you lay in your bed, walk through the space, or sit in your chair… or the chair itself… or the load from snow pushing down on your roof. Live loads are transient, and are often the cause of collapses that hurt people. It may be a rare thing that your house and deck are full of people for a party, but it is during that party that the structure has to work the hardest, and the Code attempts to anticipate that to limit injuries. Live loads are prescribed in the Building Code; for example, the floor of a house must be able to support 40 pounds per square foot (PSF) live load in addition to the dead load of the floor itself.

A DYNAMIC LOAD is sudden and usually short-lived. Think of the jolt a building feels when an earthquake strikes or a gust of heavy wind hits your house. Wind is a great example of how complex a dynamic structural load can be. The wall the wind is actually hitting (the windward wall), feels a pressure toward the inside of the house - the wind tries to blow the doors and windows in. But that same gust of wind creates a negative pressure or suction on the opposite side (the leeward wall). The awesome thing about how this works is that we can also harness that pressure difference to move air through the space effectively!

So, by now you can probably see that designing the structural systems of a building can get pretty complicated. The static dead and live loads and dynamic loads must be determined for the building's location. Once those loads are known, the elements of the structural system (bearing walls, rafters, joists, connections, etcetera...) must be designed to resist those loads. But do not despair! The structural chapters of the Code have been developed over many years to allow non-engineers to design safe structural systems. For example, the size and spacing of wood exterior wall studs subjected to hurricane force winds can be chosen from tables in the Code. The catch is that the Code addresses 'conventional' buildings. While Earthships are anything but conventional, portions of an Earthship's structural systems may be considered conventional, and you can use the Code to design those elements.

Floors are good examples. Let's say you know you want the dimensions of your house to be 40 feet wide and 70 feet deep, and you want the floor joists to run from front to back (along the 70 foot dimension), and you plan on using 2x12 for the joists. You would obviously not expect the joists to span the full 70 foot distance. But by reviewing the Span Tables in the Code, you can figure out how far the 2x12 joist *can* span. If you find, for example, that the joists can span 16 feet for your particular situation, you will need to plan for supporting beams or bearing walls no further than 16 feet apart. This can end up establishing the basic floor plan of your house, because you will know that you will need walls or beams and posts every 16 feet (or less). One trick here that your designer can borrow from traditional New Mexican architecture: you will see in some of our historic churches and large residences that 1 foot to 3 foot long brackets are used at the edge of the wall to support the rectangular-cut beams of the roof structures. Using this additional member allows you to increase the span of the beam by up to 20%. The key here is getting this sized by a professional architect or engineer, who knows how to do the loading calculations to size the members correctly.

As we mentioned, only portions of an Earthship's structure would be considered conventional in the current Code. Even a professional architect or designer can get overwhelmed, especially when designing the unconventional portions of the structure. That is why we team with structural engineers to make our buildings work.

We will not cover other structural concerns like forces and moments and shear stresses and the like here. That is another BIG book worth of information. Everything we will share here is about getting in touch with what needs to happen, and offering some rules of thumb so you can make the best choices you can. We hope this section will help to prepare you so if the building official questions some or even all of your design, you will have better idea where he or she is coming from. We also hope this effort will help make your interaction with the building official less of a conflict and more of a collaboration.

The fundamental concept driving the structural design of a building is the creation of identifiable load paths for the various forces a building must withstand during its lifetime. Each load path extends from the point or area where the force is applied to the earth that ultimately supports the building. We like to think of the forces (dead loads, live loads, wind loads, etcetera...) as water, and the load paths as pipes directing the water (the force) to the foundations.

It can be helpful to structurally 'walk-through' your design from the top down; "Ok. The roof will be held up by the stud wall on the south side and a beam with posts on the north side. Now... what is underneath the stud wall and posts to hold *them* up?" Generally, it is safe to say that a structure has to be connected to all the other parts of the structure so the skeleton acts as a whole.

Most often, especially if there are heavy wind loads or earthquake loads in the area, we want to get the help from a structural engineer whether or not is it required. There are just so many ways this type of loading can lead to serious damage or even injury.

Generally, the simpler (and more conventional) the structure, the easier and less expensive it is to plan for. We can minimize cost and time to build, in most cases, by considering using a structural wall that serves as the building's skin too. An adobe wall, for instance, or true rammed earth... only has one material throughout. It serves as both the building's structure and skin. For the structural loading capacity of various wall systems, see the next chapter on The Enclosure System.

Foundations

Foundations in some form are necessary for all buildings today. The foundation is the element of the load path that transfers all the forces the building is resisting into the earth. The foundation may also be called upon to hold back the earth – as in a basement wall, for example. It must perform these functions with minimal settlement so that cracking and structural instability, as well as air and water penetration, are minimized.

How a foundation is configured is dependent on the design of the building and your area's geology and climate. The local building official may require the foundations be designed by a structural engineer. Most often, foundations for smaller residential buildings include a foundation wall of concrete or CMU (Concrete Masonry Units – commonly known as cinder block). Typically, foundation walls are supported on concrete spread footings. As you might expect, the width and thickness of the footings will increase with weaker supporting soils and heavier building loads. Think of a one story building versus a three story building – obviously the three story building will require a more substantial footing.

Spread footing foundations are essentially floating the building on the earth. If the soils near the earth surface are very soft, and the building is heavy, a spread footing foundation will begin to sink into the ground – not a good thing. In this case, drilled or driven pile foundations are often utilized. Pilings can be of wood, concrete, or steel, and they will pass through the softer surface soils to deeper and better supporting soils or even bedrock. If your soils are poor, or you suspect they may be, a geotechnical engineer can provide you with best-practice recommendations for your particular site.

A foundation wall that is buried in the ground like a typical Earthship or house with a basement supports all the static and dynamic loads from the building, but it also must resist the pressure of the earth outside the wall pushing inward.

You can hopefully see now why having a foundation wall or footing is a good idea, even though older Earthships have been built without them. Regular walls cannot support all these conditions, which is why footings have been added to the standard design.

On sloping sites, the foundation walls and footings have to be stepped down to track the slope of the ground and stay under the frost line or to bear on adequate soils. These foundations can be tricky to construct. In these cases, we recommend hiring a professional to build the foundation.

The Code can help you estimate the size of a one, two, or three story house's spread footing pretty easily. The footing, which extends beyond the inside and outside away from the foundation wall, will have a minimum horizontal dimension of 2x the thickness of the foundation wall. The minimum vertical dimension of the footing will be the same thickness of the foundation wall. Two continuous rebar will be placed approximately underneath where the foundation wall joins the footing, a few inches above where the footing where it rests on the ground, and rebar will be placed across the footing, on top of the continuous rebar, at regular intervals

Groundwater and rainfall that falls on the soil adjacent to the foundation can put pressure on the walls, especially if the walls go down below the water table, and that pressure can actually push water through the walls into your building! To combat this, we install a 6 mil polyethylene vapor barrier above a 6" deep granular base course when there is a slab at grade, then use a non-solvent-based dampproof or waterproofing around the outside of the foundation, install a 4"diameter French drain a foot or so out at the base of the wall, backfill with gravel along the wall, and then slope the ground away from the wall with a 3% grade when the backfill is complete.

Footings will need to be based a minimum of 12" below exterior grade. If you live in higher latitudes (or colder climates), footings need to be placed below the frost line to avoid freeze/thaw upheavals. Your local building department can provide the required frost depth in your area. Depending on your location, frost depths can be quite deep – 4 feet is not unusual in cold climates. The cool thing about this requirement is that you can often capture the space beneath for a basement and "free" square footage if you excavate the area inside the foundation to frost depth! You might also want to consider the use of what is called a Frost Protected Shallow Foundation

(FPSF), if you are building on a flat site. Instead of placing footings below the frost line, the FPSF uses insulation and drainage to raise the frost line to just below the surface. Even in the coldest climates, this technique permits footing depths as shallow as 12 inches. A National Association of Home Builders Research Center study showed a 15 to 21 percent cost savings with FPSF over conventional foundations. Use a minimum of R-10 insulation on a FPSF.

TIPS TO MAKE YOUR FOUNDATION WORK FROM THE OUTSET:

- Only excavate the earth absolutely necessary to get the foundation to the required depth.
- If a crawlspace results from a shallow foundation wall, you want to plan for it to have ventilation so it does not collect rot and mold and creepy crawlies. This is a Code requirement. If you are in a humid climate, a conditioned crawlspace will help eliminate mold and fungus growth.
- Untreated wood framing should not be closer than 6" to the grade of the earth after backfilling.
- In almost all cases, anchor bolts will be used to tie the wall to the foundation.
- In all but an arid climate, dampproof your foundation walls. Waterproofing is only required when in a submerged environment.
- If you are not averse to using board insulation, provide 2" deep rigid insulation on the exterior of your foundation and under your floor slabs in temperate and cold climates where freezing occurs.
- Never place concrete in freezing conditions or into frozen ground!

Rubble Trench Foundations

from Sigi Koko's Build Naturally Blog

Various forms of the rubble trench foundation have been used for thousands of years in construction. Earthen walls in the Middle East and Africa, for example, are built on top of shallow ditches filled with loose rock. Frank Lloyd Wright came across the rubble trench foundation system around the turn of the 20th Century. He observed the structures to be "perfectly static" with no signs of heaving, and thereafter built consistently with what he termed the "dry wall footing". Many time-tested structures stand as testimony to the longevity of the rubble trench.

A rubble trench, as its name reveals, is comprised of a continuous trench filled with crushed stone and topped with a grade beam. This type of foundation is unique in that it provides structural bearing as well as water drainage in one system. The result is a resource-efficient, high quality, low cost foundation system.

The trench is typically dug with a backhoe bucket several inches below frost depth, and sloped to daylight (or a dry well) for drainage. The trench should have straight sides and a minimum width of 16 inches. A wider trench provides additional bearing area if soils do not have adequate bearing capacity. The bottom of the trench is tamped flat and lined with several inches of gravel, on which a standard 4-inch perforated drainpipe is laid. The trench is then filled to grade with gravel, tamping every vertical foot to ensure compaction. The steel-reinforced grade beam is cast directly on the stone fill, and can either support a stem wall and crawl space (see illustration) or become the turned-down edge of a slab-on-grade. The "rubble" fill may be stone or crushed concrete, but in either case, it must be washed and should provide a variety of sizes with an average of 1-½ inches. Where silting-in is of concern, the trench may be lined with a geotextile filter fabric prior to being filled.

The compacted gravel acts both as a "French drain" system as well as a spread footer that provides bearing capacity for the grade beam. The required width of the trench is determined in the same way that a standard footing is: according to the building loads and the bearing capacity of the soil. The reinforced concrete grade beam distributes the building load evenly across the gravel footer. The size of the grade beam and placement of rebar depends on building loads and should be designed by an engineer. (For context, a typical single-story residential structure requires approximately a 16-inch wide by 8-inch high grade beam with three continuous lengths of ½-inch rebar.)

Because the footer itself is literally a drainage way, water cannot settle in or around the structure of the foundation. Without water there is no opportunity for freeze/thaw cycles to cause detrimental heaving of the grade beam.

STEPS TO BUILD A RUBBLE TRENCH FOUNDATION

1. Dig 16-inch wide (minimum) trench to frost depth plus 4 inches and slope to daylight or dry well (1/8 inch per foot minimum). Note: centerline of trench aligns with centerline of grade beam.
2. Tamp any disturbed earth in the bottom and line trench with filter fabric geotextile (highly recommended, but optional). Filter fabric helps prevent footer from silting-in over time.
3. Layer in 4 inches of stone and tamp. Ensure that surface of gravel fill maintains drainage slope and is at or below frost line.
4. Lay continuous 4-inch perforated drainage pipe and slope to daylight (as for a standard foundation footer).
5. Fill remainder of trench flush to grade with 1½-inch gravel, tamping after every vertical foot of fill. (Hand tampers work well for this.)
6. Coat formwork with biodegradable oil to ease release of wood for reuse. Any vegetable oil works well.
7. Set formwork for grade beam, adding steel reinforcing as required.
8. Pour grade beam and integral slab.

RUBBLE TRENCH FOUNDATION PROS

- Lower cost than a concrete footing.
- Uses much less concrete (production of concrete requires a great deal of energy and generates greenhouse gases).
- Can use recycled crushed concrete fill.
- Provides excellent drainage, and thus a "static" foundation system.

RUBBLE TRENCH FOUNDATION CHALLENGES

- Soils with low bearing capacity may require an extremely wide trench (or some other footing alternative) to achieve adequate bearing area.
- Not specifically addressed in Building Codes; requires additional dialog with permitting officials.

A rubble trench foundation meets the requirements and the intent of U.S. Building Codes. However, since this system is not specifically outlined in current Codes, acceptance is provided on a case-by-case basis. Since this puts permit approval at the discretion of individual building officials, it is recommended to initiate a dialog prior to submitting for a building permit. This provides an opportunity to inform and educate permitting staff and provide adequate information to satisfy their desire to ensure a safe structure. The article written by Elias Velonis for Fine Homebuilding (see "Additional Resources") provides excellent technical information to this end. It is recommended that stamped structural drawings be provided so the burden of proof is not purely conceptual.

My experiences with rubble trench foundations have been rather positive. I interact with the permitting office well ahead of time, and have not encountered rejection or delays. In one case the building inspector required that the structural engineer be present to verify tamping. I have needed to increase the trench width to 24 inches when a 16-inch backhoe bucket proved too difficult to find. The only impact was the need for additional gravel mix to fill the trench; even with additional gravel, the cost of the foundation was lower than a standard concrete footer would have been.

Floor Structures

by Rachel Preston Prinz and Michael Curry

Floors are part of both a building's structural and enclosure systems. A floor system may be constructed of joists, beams, and decking, or of a continuous solid material like concrete. The depth of the system required is directly proportional to the distance between supports and the strength of the materials used to make it.

The ground floor of many houses is often a concrete slab-on-grade. The slabs are usually a minimum of 4 inches thick with steel or fiber reinforcement to control cracking. To prevent water vapor and mineral deposits seeping up from below onto your slab-on-grade floors, use a layer of film (at least 6mm thick) under your floors and above the ground to prevent leeching and water vapor transmission. If you use a gravel basecourse (recommended as a capillary break to prevent soil moisture from migrating upward) under concrete or earthen floors, put the film above the gravel.

When a floor is also a ceiling, it often doubles as a chase for mechanical, electrical, and plumbing lines to pass through. A floor's acoustic characteristics can also have a detrimental effect on our comfort. It can act like a drum, making sound above or below reflect loudly in the space we are in. Designing a floor that 'feels good', limits sound transmission, and is not too thick can be a delicate balancing act.

There are lots of ways to build an elevated floor system. The two basic elements of a wood floor structure are the decking or sheathing and the joists. We recommend you consult with your local building department, lumber supplier, or structural engineer to give you a safe and serviceable floor or roof structure. Some of the most common materials, and their relative spans and spacings, are:

TIMBER DECKING
    Tongue and groove, 2" thick
    Span: Up to 8 feet

WOOD JOISTS:
    Depth: 6 to 12 inches
    Span: Up to 18 feet
    Spacing: 12 to 24 inches

PLYWOOD WEB JOISTS
    Commonly called TJI's
    Depth: 9 to 18 inches
    Span: Up to 30 feet
    Spacing: 12 to 24 inches

PRE-ENGINEERED TRUSSES
    Depth: 12 inches and up
    Span: Up to 40 feet with deeper trusses
    Spacing: Usually 24" floor

WOOD STRUCTURAL PANELS
    Includes plywood and oriented strand board (OSB)
    Span: Up to 24 inches standard, up to 48 inches with 1-1/8" thick material

VIGAS
    Span: Up to 20 feet
    Spacing: Depends on species and diameter. Usually 2 to 4 feet.

REINFORCED CONCRETE SLABS
    Supported by concrete or masonry walls or steel beams
    Depth: 4" to 12"
    Span: Up to 20 feet

Framing

by Rachel Preston Prinz and Michael Curry

Wood used for construction is classified as hard or soft, though those terms do not really denote strength or durability. Softwoods from evergreens (pines, spruces, firs) are usually used for general construction, and hardwoods from deciduous trees (oaks, hickory, poplars) are used for timber frames, flooring, stairs, panels, casework, and furniture. Wood is commonly available in 2 foot increments between 6 feet and 24 feet long.

One way you can be more sustainable in using woods is to use engineered lumber for floors, walls, and roofs.

EARTHSHIP FRAMING

Most Earthships in the southwest use vigas, or peeled logs, as roof rafters or floor joists. The building official may want to know the species of tree used and the minimum diameter of the peeled logs. Where peeled logs are not available, or if you want to use a recycled product that minimizes environmental impact, you can use TJIs instead, if the structure will be covered with a ceiling. If not, we prefer glu-lam beams.

If you use vigas, beams, or reclaimed timbers for your roof structure and are building without a contractor, you will need at least 8 people to get the roof members in place. And allow plenty of time. In the video *From the Ground Up*, it is said that it can take a half a day to place a single heavy roof framing member by hand, even with an experienced crew.

The front face (solar wall) requires excellent carpentry skills. Do yourself a favor and make sure that the people working on this part of your home are experienced.

SELECTING WOODS

Your choice of wood structural elements will depend on many variables; will it be visible in finished structure? What is available locally? What is the loading and span for the lumber?

New structures are often built with a mix of "sawn" and "engineered" lumber. Sawn lumber is cut full size from trees – 2x6's, 2x8's, 4x10's, etcetera… Engineered lumber is made from wood chips, veneers, even sawdust. Engineered lumber includes glue-laminated beams (glu-lams), laminated veneer lumber (LVL), and an extruded glue and oriented wood strand product usually called parallam lumber, or PSL lumber. Generally, a similar sized piece of engineered lumber is much stronger than sawn lumber. Reclaimed or antique lumber is a popular choice for exposed wood elements, but your local building official may want someone to identify the wood species and structural grade of the piece if it is being used as part of the structural system.

Woods can be air-dried, which is a lengthy process, or kiln-dried. Wood used in construction needs to have a moisture content of 19% or less, which helps limit shrinkage after the building is 'dried-in'. Also, wood destroying fungi require a relatively high moisture content to thrive. If the wood is dry, the fungus cannot eat it! Naturally decay-resistant woods include bald cypress, black locust, black walnut, cedar, and redwood. bald cypress, eastern red cedar, and redwood are also insect-resistant. Please, never use green (unseasoned) wood! To be more sustainable, use FSC-certified kiln dried wood or wood that was hand-cut, stored, aged, and turned properly for at least a year.

If the wood is going to be in contact with the ground, using a pressure-treated lumber with LP-22 water-borne preservative is ideal.

Also, you might want to check out the section titled "Correct Timing" in Chapter 10: Imbuing a Space with Spirit, which describes the traditional timing techniques used by old-timers for felling wood (and other projects around the home). The wood cut in these periods lasts.

PLYWOOD AND OSB WOOD PANELS

Wood Structural Panels include plywood, which is a panel of laminated wood veneers that are laid one layer over another, with each thin layer of wood laid perpendicular to the grain below.

Other types of Wood Structural Panels include particle board and oriented strand board (OSB). OSB is made from wood chips veneered and then overlaid in several layers, with each layer laid perpendicular to the previous layer so that maximum strength and stability is obtained. No mature trees are used in OSB production. Only thin stems from ecologically-managed forests are used. OSB is fully recyclable.

While they are recyclable and structurally sound, OSB or particle board products are not the ideal materials for building a home if you are aiming for a more natural and durable construction. We prefer longer-lasting low-emitting exterior grade plywood. We think the additional cost is worth the lowered maintenance, healthier materials, and increased durability.

SMART BLOCKING

We recommend providing blocking for your home's future changes when framing. These hidden framing materials allow you to securely fasten grab bars, large pictures, holiday wreaths, etcetera… with comfort knowing that they will not fall. You just need to plan where to hang things while you are framing! Use large 2 x 10 or 2 x 12 blocks to provide a large target area to hang large pictures. Tip: take photos before the drywall or other finishes go up to be able to locate the blocking.

Engaging with the Process: Part 3

What is your area's architectural language?

Did they use earth-sheltering back in the day?

What do buildings look like?

What shape are they? Round, square, or rectangular?

What was done to the landscape?

What is the pitch of the roof?

Is the floor above the ground or on the ground?

What materials were used?

What structural system are you leaning towards?

What passive heating and cooling strategies are you thinking of using?

Chapter VII

The Enclosure System

The enclosure system of a building includes it is exterior finish, insulation, the roof, walls, doors, windows, and flooring... basically everything that covers the structure, acts as the structure, and/or allows us to move through the structure. Designing the enclosure system well means we have a house that is warmer in winter, cooler in summer, quiet in the spots that matter, is easier to maintain, and is beautiful.

When I was attending Texas A&M for my Master's degree, I had the opportunity to travel around the country for several months with one of my professors, Dr. Charles Graham, who is considered one of the best forensic architects in the country. We were studying a particular type of stucco wall that had a tendency to fail quite spectacularly, and traveling to different locations to see how it failed in different climates. I learned from him two of the most important lessons I ever learned in design:

if something is going to fail, it will fail at the joints (either of planes or materials),

and

you have to understand the nature of the materials and the climate to design an appropriate architectural solution.

So, for me, the first rules of thumb regarding enclosure are: minimize the number of materials and corners you use and you will see fewer failures. Then, make sure you detail joints and wall planes so they shed water, wind, and weather. Then, design with materials and methods that work for your climate. That is where we start.

We often get to the point at the end of this section where we have to ask ourselves about our real values around Natural versus Traditional building. Here is the truth: Natural is easier to learn. It is more forgiving. It is easier to do yourself. It usually costs less, but it requires more time and effort to get built, in hand-crafting so much of the home and in maintenance. Natural homes are harder to get a permit for. But it can be done. Especially if you use a professional to design them.

As we have pointed out before, all buildings, but especially natural buildings are alive, in their way. Being alive means they need food (care), water (humidification), and shelter (good design/protection) to last. Going natural is SO worth the effort, to some. To others, the gravity of all this can be too overwhelming.

What works for you... has to work for you. So take your time and think on all this. It is worth the time and money investment you make to do it well.

Previous Page: Figure 19. Standard Earthship Wall Construction

When choosing the structural and enclosure methods you might want to use on your Earthship 2.0 home, consider this: A typical 3 bedroom Global Model Earthship uses thousands of board feet of lumber and around 35 vigas. Each tree can produce around 500 board feet of lumber, so that is at least 4 trees in lumber and 35 trees in vigas. Alternately, a rammed earth, earthbag, or adobe structure can use wood only for its roofing system. Combining a load-bearing wall type, a well-designed passive solar collection space in lieu of the greenhouse window wall and a smarter, smaller, footprint can reduce the wood required by half! There is no way around it... if true sustainability is your goal, all of the options should be considered.

Other options are available for interior walls than just those we cover here. Early Diné (Navaho) hogans used curved stick walls that were exposed on the inside and covered in earth or lime plaster for weather protection on the exterior. East Coasters know that their historic version of this system called WADDLE AND DAUB is a viable building material also, as it has been used successfully for hundreds of years. This is basically a wall made like a giant reed basket and then plastered on both sides. If you live in a wet place, you can borrow inspiration from the reed houses in Peru. Or use TABBY crushed shell walls like they use in the low-country of South Carolina. We invite you to check out all manner of building methods you might choose to use on the Archaeo-Architecture Pinterest Board we created for you. Really – the sky is the limit as to all your options for building, especially on non-load-bearing interior walls. Which is why we have not even begun to address all the options. There are too many to cover and we think we can help you more with planning for the main body of the home. Pay particular attention to the way it was once done in your area for the best and most viable sources of inspiration.

Secrets of Great Curb Appeal

by Rachel Preston Prinz and Shannon Matteson

Making a home that people are eager to buy is a good idea, if you think you may not live there forever, as well as to increase your property value. A house with great curb appeal helps to make a place that you love and that people want. Here are our best tips and tricks for getting it right from the outset.

Use period and location-appropriate paint schemes with non-boring colors. If you are building a house that is inspired by an earlier period, like a plantation style house in Louisiana, use slightly brighter than normal colors for the area. Or, alternately, if you are building in Taos, and do not want to use the boring old earth colors all your neighbors have, use lime to whitewash your building, or add some earth clays to your mix to give your house a bit more "pop." Just use colors that are a little bit unusual or have a little extra pigment, and you will give yourself great curb appeal by standing out from the crowd.

Make your windows stand out by using great details to accentuate them. Use appropriate trims for your region, and paint them in a lighter shade than the walls. This trick also helps you be able to replace windows when needed. Exterior shutters block out light, and keep heat in at night or out during the day. Flowerboxes are great in humid places like Savannah and Charleston - they are such an important design element here that they have whole books of photos of them for sale. A flowerbox is a great way to bring in nature in urban environments especially.

Use landscaping to emphasize and enhance an inviting covered porch at the entrance to your home. Trees provide shade and break up winds into breezes. Plantings below them prevent glare and bounce-back off the ground. If you have large trees and decorative boulders as part of your landscape, accentuate them with solar lighting. Lighting adds an inexpensive dramatic effect at night and helps us landmark how to move through the space in the dark. Plus, when we use mindful landscaping, we are creating microclimates around the house. Microclimates help our homes to perform more efficiently as well as invite nature in. And they make our spaces more beautiful and alive!

If the roof and eaves are visible, make them and their details beautiful. There is really nothing like an ugly roof to destroy the beauty of a building. When using a flat roof, we want to make beautiful canales (scuppers or drop downspouts) that fall in places that look like we wanted the water there. Pitched roofs want enough overhang to provide a little shade, and good details that show how well-built the building is.

Camouflage eyesores like electrical and sprinkler boxes by painting them the same color as the house or the background. Nothing can ruin the aesthetics of your home like unsightly piping and protective covers or boxes. Trash bins and air conditioner units also fall into the unsightly category. These can easily be hidden by a simple lattice fence or decorative paneling made up of local materials like latillas. Small bushes are also a great solution to unsightly issues and add to the creation of microclimates.

Do not forget your mailbox; it is the first impression of your home, and a small project that can make a huge impact. Dress it up with a flowerbed at the base, a cast stone post, and/or decorative hardware. Address numbers and an architectural finial on top of the post in a beautiful contrasting material like copper can make an excellent first impression.

Finally, curb appeal is all about the day-to-day care you put into your home. Maintain the exterior cladding material and keep your home in great shape. Fill holes and patch and touch-up paint on the inside and outside regularly.

With these tips and tricks, you are sure to be one step closer to a house you love to live in!

Walls

Walls are like a mother's arms. The hold you and protect you and keep you safe and warm. Exterior walls protect the home from the weather by controlling the passage of water vapor and moisture, air, sound, heat, and cold between the low pressures of the interior and the high pressures of outside. Well-designed walls also protect us from the weathering effects of the sun, wind, rain, and snow.

Walls may have an applied skin that lays over the structural skeleton beneath, or an integral skin that is part of the wall structure. The wall structure holds up the weight of the roof and floors above and passes that weight down into the foundation. The walls also protect the shape of the building in high winds and earthquakes, which can make the building move in unusual ways, and they offer fire protection. Because the joints between materials are the most likely places to fail, designing exterior wall details to carefully connect to the other planes of the building and around doors and windows is critical.

In our practice, we often borrow from the past when we want to maximize wall performance while minimizing maintenance. For instance, those brick caps on Territorial buildings around Santa Fe provide durable long-lasting protection for the parapet's exposed horizontal surfaces. Adding those cut down substantially the difficulty and time required for annual mudding repairs on these old buildings. Tricks like this make life easier and more enjoyable!

Waterproof membrane flashing should be used at exterior wall and floor intersections, where the building meets the ground, and at expansion joints.

Interior walls do not just subdivide a large space into smaller ones. They also provide acoustical separation for privacy, offer a place for mechanical, electrical, and plumbing runs to pass through the space, and they offer opportunities to surround oneself with beautiful materials and finishes that cannot or should not be accommodated in a load-bearing exterior wall. The glass bottle walls of an Earthship are a great example of this. Except in the rarest of circumstances – an extremely mild climate, for instance - they should not be used on the exterior walls because they do not provide adequate thermal protection. They do provide excellent opportunities to bring fabulous textures and light inside, though, so we use them there.

In this chapter, we called in expert help to discuss natural building materials, because we believe that these building blocks meet the ideals of our readers. We will also cover some basics of traditional building materials.

Natural versus Sustainable Materials

When our clients ask what materials they should use for their buildings, we often discuss the ideal of "natural" building versus the more achievable "more sustainable". Natural building is awesome for lots of reasons. But it takes more time and attention at planning, at design, and in construction to do right, and a certain degree of more maintenance in most cases. If these considerations are an issue, you may want to aim for something that is more sustainable and less totally natural. The more natural your building is, the more essential it is that you design for your climate, which is part of why we go into such depth about climate in earlier chapters.

Our friend Sigi Koko offers:

> *"The best way to dip your toes in to Natural Building... is to start with something small.*
> *An oven, a shed, a pavilion, an outdoor toilet, a playhouse, an outdoor oven or fireplace,*
> *a chicken coop... anything that lets you experiment. Understand your materials. Feel them.*
> *Single-handedly the BEST way to learn natural building... is to just do it."*

Insulating Versus Thermal Mass Building Materials

Finding the right enclosure system and building materials for your values, your climate and location, your skills and budget, and for thermal performance can be quite an adventure! Our friend Sigi Koko lays out a great example for us of choosing materials in the next section, using strawbale and cob as a means of illustrating the benefits of insulating versus thermal mass materials.

In the sections that follow, we discuss many of the available enclosure systems and materials. Each material is identified with its type of thermal performance - whether it is insulating or thermal mass (or neither); what it's ideal climate is; whether or not it can be used as structure or infill only; whether an architect or engineer is required to use the material; if it is suitable for a berm; if it is natural; its ease of learning and doing; and whether it is available as a kit.

You may notice that the can and glass bottle walls sections note that these walls are infill only and perform as neither thermal mass or insulating. These standard Earthship designs undermine thermal performance when used on exterior walls. This is why we are recommending these materials on the interior only.

Strawbale vs. Cob

from Sigi Koko's Build Naturally Blog

Which material works best for which application...

I often get asked this question: Which is better to use for my natural building, strawbale or cob?

The answer is simple: IT DEPENDS! (of course!)

To help sort out if strawbale or cob walls are better suited for your application, I'm going to describe the basic properties of each material, and then how to use those attributes to your greatest advantage.

STRAWBALES insulate. And they are thick, so they insulate really well. What this means is that a wall built of strawbales slows down heat energy traveling from one side of the wall to the other. A good insulator acts like a down jacket that keeps your body heat inside the jacket instead of getting disbursed to the cold winter air. A well-insulated house will use less energy to heat in winter than a poorly insulated house, because the insulation keeps the heat inside. If you use an air conditioner in summer, insulation will keep the heat outside, so again you need less energy to keep cool.

COB is a thermal mass because of its principal ingredients: clay & sand. Cob has limited insulating properties. Instead, a thermal mass is like a storage battery for heat (or cool) energy. This means cob is good at absorbing heat energy from the sun or a fire and storing that heat. When the air temperature around the cob is lower than the temperature of the cob itself, it releases its battery storage of heat into the air. In this way, cob can absorb a lot of heat energy and then release the heat over time, long after the heat source is gone. Conversely, a shaded thermal mass with no heat input will stay cool in the summer and absorb heat energy out of the warmer air around it (thus having a net cooling effect).

So how to best use these characteristics to your advantage?

The answer depends on your climate and what you are building. If you are using energy to change the inside temperature and keep it something different from the outside temperature, then you generally want a good insulator... i.e. strawbales. If you live in a mild climate where the temperature swings are day-to-night instead of seasonal, then a thermal mass exterior wall generally will help to average out those temperature swings...i.e., cob. Thermal mass can also provide a highly beneficial interior element in conjunction with passive solar design, to capture heat from the Southern sun in the winter (when the sun is low) but remain shaded when the summer sun is high in the sky.

STRAWBALES work best...

- As exterior walls anywhere you are trying to keep the inside temperature different from the exterior temperature; the insulating strawbales will help keep the temperature exchange to a minimum, so the energy used to change the inside temperature will be minimized.

COB works best...

- As thermal mass built around a masonry heater or rocket stove (or near a wood burning stove), where the cob can absorb heat from the fire, and store the heat energy even after the fire is out.
- For Trombe walls in passive solar design, with the cob thermal mass inside, where it is warmed by sun coming through south-facing glass.
- For any interior element when you are trying to keep the inside cool; this can be the same thermal mass used to keep warm in winter as long as there is no heat source warming it when you want to stay cool.

I use a combination of strawbale and cob. Because I design for a climate that requires several months of heat in the winter, I use the insulating strawbales for exterior walls. This ensures that only a minimum amount of energy is needed to heat the spaces and the heat stays inside. I then position some cob element to the interior. Either it surrounds a wood-burning heat source or it is positioned so that low winter sun shines on the wall from the South. That same cob element is shaded and cool in summer. This way the cob helps to regulate the interior temperature in both winter & summer.

Traditional Earthship Building Blocks

Some people really want to build an Earthship "the way it was intended". For those people, we offer these tips and tricks about using tire rammed earth walls as well as reused glass bottle and soda can walls.

Tire Walls

Wall Type:	Earth-sheltering
Appropriate Climate:	Non-humid regions. Regions with an average annual temp 60 degrees or below require slab and foundation insulation.
Structural Capability:	Load-bearing
Suitable for Berm:	Yes
Natural:	Earth is. Tires are not.
Learning:	Easy
Doing:	Difficult
Engineering Required:	Possibly, if permitted
Kit Available:	No

By tradition, Earthships are constructed of compacted earth-filled tire walls in order to maintain inner-earth temperature, be fireproof, and be termite proof. Earthship Biotecture has looked at alternatives, but they always come back to tires as their basic building block, though many Earthship building coalitions around the world have abandoned their use. Because the tires themselves are unnecessary, and potentially dangerous, we agree with the no tires philosophy, and favor the more natural investment in adobe, earthbags, rammed earth, or wood block concrete forms.

Each tire, when fully packed with soil, will weigh nearly 400 lbs. The walls are easy to put together, outside of the pounding of earth into the tires. Just place some earthbag material in the bottom of the tire (we do not recommend using cardboard as it will hold moisture), add 3 wheelbarrows full of dirt, and compact the tire brick with a sledgehammer right where you want it.

Tip: When excavating soil, use the front end loader to push the soil near the line of where the tire wall and buttressing will be. That way you minimize the number of wheelbarrow loads across the site. Many Earthship owners who have completed their builds say this would have saved them time, and their backs.

Figure 20. Tire Walls in the Phoenix

Tire walls are perceived to lack structural stiffness and your Code official may require vertical rebar, which is somewhat of a challenge to add to a single packed tire, let alone a stack of them. But if you need it, it is possible.

Many builders will leave rammed earth tire walls uncovered, or open at the top, in landscape applications. We strongly discourage ever leaving rammed earth walls open at the top, and rather, utilizing a concrete cap at any horizontally exposed earthen wall as per the Rammed Earth Building Code. By using best practices and following Code requirements, you get the peace of mind of knowing that you have a better build from the outset. Without it, well… in this example, dirt in a confined space that has water in it encourages plants. Plants have roots. That continue to grow in search of water. Guess where they find it? Against your wall. Guess what else they find? Cracks in that wall to grab on to. Then what? Cracks in wall grow as roots get large enough to create stress, the walls cracks, and bigger water moves in. This is a recipe for BIG repairs down the line.

TIRE WALL PROS

- A bricklike unit that is predictable to work with.
- "Simple" to build walls.

TIRE WALL CHALLENGES

- A typical Earthship build puts nearly 2,000 man hours into tire builds. As we understand it, the current record for the number of tires completed by one person in one day is 12. That means that person would have to work a minimum of 67 days at that pace to get the walls built by themselves. This is not a small job.

- Requires strength, dexterity, and stamina to build.

- Unnecessary to use tires to build a rammed earth wall.

- Another of the curious elements we had not considered in the design of the back tire wall before doing this study was to realize that, as we have discussed in other areas of this book, buildings fail at the joints, which means at the spaces between those tires. When you get a leak, it may well look like it is coming from one place on the wall, but in fact, the water may have travelled along a line of tires, or along the radials of the tire edge, and come out somewhere other than where it is penetrating the wall. So, you may well end up having to rip out several tires to find the actual source of infiltration. That can be a structural nightmare.

- Off-gassing. Once the Earthship settles, the breakdown of the rubber tires, which by nature was already in process, now happens in an enclosed environment. This means, the gas expelled by the tires as they disintegrate may be collecting in the walls, which then has the potential to release toxic vapors that no-one can smell but that could make the inhabitants sick. "They" will tell you that the walls are encased and that by adding vents, off-gassing is not a concern. But that is only viable as long as you re-plaster every surface every year and do not allow cracks anywhere on the tire wall, and as long as the gas does not find its way into any invisible pockets (which are unavoidable) not near a vent. If the gas builds up in a closed system... well, think of a balloon... if you blow it up past its surface area, it bursts. If you try and encase the gas, it might work, for a while... but then what? To combat the potential for off-gassing, please... re-mud your walls every year.

Figure 21. Typical Wall Leaks

Earthship Greenhouse

Wall Type:	Neither Thermal Mass nor Insulating
Appropriate Climate:	Non-humid regions. Non-freezing regions.
Structural Capability:	Load-bearing
Suitable for Berm:	No
Natural:	No
Learning:	Medium challenge to learn, difficult to manage changes to stop thermal bridging
Doing:	Challenging for the less than expert carpenter
Engineering Required:	No
Kit Available:	No

A typical Earthship uses a south-facing wall of combined windows that are 46 inches wide and 90 inches tall. In the old days, these windows were pitched at 60 degrees from horizontal or perpendicular to the winter sun. This design attempted to allow light into the darkest recess of the house. Reports suggest that this method does not provide adequate daylight for the better part of the year, and additional lighting is required to make these spaces functional. This additional lighting requirement means more power draw to plan for. Or more skylights to maintain.

Figure 20. Earthship Greenhouse

Issues with building and maintaining this slanted solar wall are common, as building anything at an angle is difficult and requires expert carpentry skills. The size of glass is a challenge to transport. The design of the framing and flashing leads to thermal bridging. The sloped glazing is nearly impossible to keep watertight. The Earthships that use the older double-pitched "teacup style" greenhouse roof to "block the heat in summer" do not actually perform in that way - they just complicate the issues of the roof collecting water, and thereby leaking.

OVERHEATING ISSUES

The sloped windowwall design causes Earthships to overheat due to excessive solar gain up to 8 months a year. Even on a windy day, it is not uncommon for the interior of the Earthship greenhouse to reach 95 degrees and 75% humidity. That is outside the range of comfort for most people. Additionally, in cold climates, because the window wall is not designed for thermal performance, supplemental heat made through other means (i.e. stoves and fireplaces) is often lost through the glass in winter.

Many Earthships use special interior shades called *tende plissettate* to minimize overheating once the heat has reached the interior of the building. The main issue regarding these custom shade devices is that they cost around $10,000. They also evidently tend to break easily, as they are designed for vertical applications. Owners note that getting in a physical position to install, remove, or repair the blinds can be a feat of dexterity worthy of a Cirque de Soleil performer, as can repairing or replacing the windows themselves. The blinds that many Earthship owners use can be found at the Velux Italy website at

http://www.velux.it/privati/prodotti/tende-persiane/tende/plissettate

However, using shade devices is not the ideal answer because we really want to stop the heat before it enters the home. This better design solution is most often addressed with greenhouse shade cloths placed over the windows on the outside of the home, which presents an interesting challenge of dexterity when it comes to installing and removing them - installing a very long sheet over pitched windows takes a certain amount of skill, and often, at least two people. Then, a means of securing that fabric for an entire season, regardless of the wind, and then raising and lowering it when needed, is required. None of this would be necessary if you just build a two foot deep roof overhang over the windowwall.

OVERLIGHTING ISSUES

Another of the issues with the windows in Earthships is they cannot be blacked out. It goes against the idea of the design to make it dark inside, so when there is a full moon, it will feel like trying to sleep in the daytime inside. Every month. For several days. The same goes for those months at high latitudes where there is 24 hour daylight.

NEGATIVE IMPACTS ON VENTILATION

A common discussion on the various builders' boards and in our research has been the negative effect of the greenhouse and ventilation strategy in winter. The premise that the Earthship model is built on is 1) bringing in air at the base of the greenhouse wall, 2) heating it in the greenhouse, and then 3) escaping the lighter, heated air above via the skylights. This presumes it is possible to maintain the three aspects year-round. This problem is... it isn't... not without a lot of work, in windy and especially snowy climates. Snow will block the low windows and it will cover the skylights. If it is not removed so these functions can work, the closed system renders the house super tight and makes it where there is not enough oxygen to breathe or to fuel fires. Builders have attempted to remedy the issue by adding vent shafts to the berm. Those present their own issues, as we have discussed previously.

One of the other concerns about the greenhouse is humidity. In humid regions, this problem seems to be exacerbated, with serious issues resulting from regular condensation, including rot and mold. Roof leaks often compound this issue.

In the Global Models, two separate ventilation strategies are utilized – one that works only in the greenhouse and one that attempts to encourage air movement between the greenhouse and the living spaces. But the air in the living spaces is not alive and active in the way that the greenhouse is, it is moving much more slowly, and the cool air is sinking slowly... where in the greenhouse the warmer air is rising... and the idea that the two different flows will "naturally" figure out a way to work together at openings at the top of the wall is questionable. In order for this idea to work, we would need low windows between the living and greenhouse, so that the cool air could seep from the living spaces into the floor of the greenhouse, be heated, and rise through the skylights. But then, where is the heated air we need for the living spaces going? It is supposed to move through high transoms to get into the living space, but without any draw at the bottom to create that flow, it really cannot perform that way. In order to get that dynamic to work, there needs to be an inflow and an outflow that works with the laws of physics. Otherwise, we just lose the heat we need for the living space, and keep the floor colder than necessary... which many people report makes them feel colder in the winter.

MAINTENANCE ISSUES

The secondary benefit of the new interior window wall in the Global Models is that is helps to keep humidity issues minimized that could negatively impact the furnishings. When there are no de-humidification efforts made to keep humidity in check, furnishings in the living spaces can start to rot and mold. Beyond the loss of valuables, this can be an allergy nightmare.

Another issue with the pitched windows is removing snow and ice accumulations when the weather turns, before the load from the snow cracks the glass, melts and leaks into the wall, and/or renders the passive solar design moot. Shoveling snow at a pitched angle for 70 feet of window when there is two feet of snow on the ground is no small task. It requires absolute dexterity and stamina. Because some Earthships are built into the ground, and the window sill at or near ground level, this is a place where water naturally comes into the house, thereby causing more serious humidity and water damage issues. Many have hoped that flashing can address this issue, but we have yet to see an adequately designed window that prevents thermal bridging, let alone flashes for vertical movement of water. What? Yes, water can and does move uphill. The process is called capillary action. There are videos about it on YouTube if you want to see capillary action at work. Try the experiment. It's cool. Unless you have melting snow against the windows. Then, not cool. Or, it is, very cool - when you are bundled up and shoveling. Sometimes three times a day. You will also have to remove a path of snow across the roof to get to the skylights to remove the snow to open them so the greenhouse does not overheat and ventilation can be maintained.

Some people use snow fencing to minimize snow on the window wall. This helps to reduce the amount of snow you have to move in each shoveling, but according to our research, it does not prevent snow removal from being required. Check out the Windbreaks and Snow fences section in the earlier Site Design section for tips on how to accomplish this.

GREENHOUSE SKYLIGHTS

In the *From the Ground Up* video, they state that the skylights are "detailed so they do not leak." You can see for yourself if this is accurate: just head to the Visitor's Center at Greater World, which was built 2 years ago, and look down into the open skylights in the greenhouse from the roof. You will see that water stains predominate the wood framing on the skylight. It is just a sucky design - it weeps humidity from the inside and collects rain from the outside when open. Are you planning to run outside and close the skylights when it rains? But, then ventilation will not work. This is a pesky design flaw. If using their skylight design, you might want to consider using a metal flashing that matches the design of the skylight and/or roofing to flash the exposed wood framing in order to keep the water off the wood. Or, buy a commercial-grade operable skylight designed for getting rid of water.

GREENHOUSE PLANTERS

In Earthship models that have planters above the floor area, the planters are constructed of can walls which are covered over with several coats of concrete stucco. What we see is only half of the planter. Another 2 feet or so of earth is removed from below the finished floor to allow for greywater filtering. The planter cells start shallow at the east and slope downwards to the west where the water is filtered and pumped to toilets, and then to the septic system.

The planter systems are problematic... people's kitties decided they are the best litter boxes ever, and these designs will not really grow edible plants because they get infected with pests, molds, and/or diseases and everything dies.

Most Earthships are using an in-ground at-grade planter now that is lined in EPDM and usually covered with river rocks or untreated cedar so it is less appealing to pets. This seems to be able to grow more food. Though pests remain an issue and some people have moved to tropical and air-filtration plants in lieu of food producers to manage that.

SOLVING OVERHEATING AND HUMIDITY ISSUES

We believe that the pitched window design is not a good one because it renders the home basically a solar oven.

After 30+ years of trying to work around this design issue without resolution, Earthship builders have quietly discontinued the double-pitched "teacup" roof as well as the more angled window design. But that does not help people who have existing Earthships, or those that use the old style plans and do not have the time to research what was going wrong so they do not make the same mistake.

The soil, water, heat, and humidity requirements for tropical and agricultural plants are different. That is why when you go to a nursery to buy your plants, they are almost always in different buildings. This is part of why the Earthships' standard tropical style greenhouses do not produce enough food.

If you have determined that a greenhouse is an essential element in your design, you will want to decide which type of greenhouse is preferred.

A tropical greenhouse like those used in the Earthships can be used to capture heat for thermal storage and to grow some plants, especially tropical types, but it cannot grow all your food and it is not suitable for plant starts. One design cost for the tropical greenhouse is bugs, and another is humidity, which can threaten the longevity of wood as well as furniture.

A production greenhouse will produce a variety of food you can live on most of the year and it is suitable for plant starts for outside as well. The design cost for a production greenhouse is that it really should not be considered part of the home, so using it as the major communication corridor is not viable. It can be attached, but should be separated from the home by a thermal wall and exterior doors, or detached entirely.

If using wood in a greenhouse, we recommend FSC-certified cedar which is naturally more moisture-friendly.

Veggies require between 12 and 16 hours of sunlight to grow effectively inside. The addition of UV lights might be required in the winter months, depending on latitude, to attain enough light to produce. Study how the sun works where you are over the winter and plan the power system accordingly if backup lighting is required.

ALTERNATE GREENHOUSE OPTION 1: ATTACHED

One of the best ways to guarantee that your attached greenhouse works well is to use the techniques our friend Dan Jones uses in his attached production-style greenhouse in Taos, which we talked about in Growing your Own: Dan's EPIC Garden in the Landscaping chapter. The production greenhouse method is proven.

When the greenhouse is part of or attached to the house, we do not want to build sloping window walls. We want to use regular, vertical windows on the solar wall, which are easier to install, detail, and maintain. Please do not use the window designs in the Earthship Books, as they are filled with thermal bridges! Use a well-designed homemade window, or preferably, use a professionally made window in the best grade you can afford! According to reports, a firm called Abundant Energy makes a good window for these applications. (Authors note: We have not tested the design.) Another great option would be to use a professional greenhouse design in lieu of the window wall. Better yet: reuse an old greenhouse!

Be sure to design the window wall with a 2 foot deep roof overhang or canopy. Overhanging eaves take pressure off the window drainage as well as providing solar shading. Roof overhangs can also be designed to provide soffit vents to vent the roof so that condensation does not occur within it.

For ideal ventilation, greenhouses really want operable windows down low and up high on the window wall, as well as to have skylights and/or venting at the high point of their ceiling/roof.

For thermal performance and comfort considerations, it is preferable not to open the greenhouse to the body of the house without a means of closing the space off, including weather-stripped windows and doors between the greenhouse and main body of the home.

Figure 21. Dan's Place, with greenhouse on right

Use exterior grade windows and doors for the interior window wall if you use this method. Be aware that an additional layer of window coverings will be required in order to offer privacy and darkness for bedrooms.

It is important to remember that if a solar wall is used as a functional part of the home, it should be designed so that good passive solar design principles are realized. The window area should be limited to less than 10% of the total floor area, and the amount of floor and/or wall for thermal storage should be 3 square feet per square foot of glass. The thermal storage material size may need to be doubled or tripled to account for shading from the plants and exterior shade cloths so that it can store enough heat in winter.

Fans are helpful for moving air between the greenhouse and interior spaces, but these present an additional power load and need to be planned for ahead of the build.

Provide connections to attach shade cloths on the roof if you are going to use them.

When the greenhouse is part of the house, be sure to prune back any interior trees in the winter to allow the sunlight to penetrate the house, and then allow them to grow wild in the summer to make shade.

Do not use Butyl caulk as specified in the Earthship books on windows! Use EPDM strips instead!

Do not build a greenhouse adjacent to the house if using any kind of bio-waste wall like strawbale between the greenhouse and home. We also do not want to use low thermal mass materials like strawbale if we want to effectively use passive solar design.

ALTERNATE GREENHOUSE OPTION 2: DETACHED

For those who wish to use a production-type greenhouse that is detached from the home, we recommend locating the detached greenhouse south of the vertical glass wall by at least 6-10 feet, so it can create a private garden courtyard in front of the home that is usable year-round.

When building a detached greenhouse, make sure not to place the greenhouse too close to outbuildings either as the shadows from the sun are longer in the winter than in the summer and the greenhouse might not get adequate sunlight if it is north of another building.

Choose tempered single-pane glass glazing in lieu of plastics for true greenhouses, though these are not hail or snow resistant. If plastic is an option that meets your values, polycarbonate has excellent light-emitting qualities. A viable "greener" alternative would be reused sliding glass doors.

RETROFITTING EXISTING EARTHSHIPS

A common "upgrade" to the overheating greenhouse that is challenged with humidity and mold issues is to add 4 inches of rigid insulation over the existing roof outside, and then to add another layer of roofing over that. That is not an inexpensive fix, as that also requires new flashings at the skylights and soffits, and covers 70+ feet of roof 10 feet wide or so – requiring about 7 squares worth, or 700 square feet, of new roof - but we understand it has helped people.

Of course, the best idea is to design your Earthship with a single pitched shed roof instead of the tea-cup roof. It is a much easier build if you do this from the outset.

INDOOR PLANTS

We were able to collect some tips in our research that might assist you in growing healthy plants indoors. The main factor to remember is to choose water-loving plants that do not mold easily. For best results, it is advisable to use a neutral or slightly acidic (between 7.4-6.0 pH) greenhouse-type soil like that discussed in the Dan's Epic Garden section. Maintain the pH of your indoor gardens with an inexpensive and easy-to-use pH test kit available at most garden supply stores. Any amendments needed to correct the pH can be found there as well. You can use sterilized soil if your soil becomes infested with soil-born harmful insects, blight, or powdery mildew, and when trying to germinate seeds or start young plants.

Experiment with your plants! Plant several in different conditions, with variations in the amount of sunlight/shade, soil quality, or the plants they are situated next to. Keep in mind that many perennials will not work indoors because they need to die back in the winter. Be willing to lose them or use tender perennials for decoration. Apparently butterfly bush grows extraordinarily well indoors – so much so that it must be heavily cut back regularly.

Remember: greenhouse plants grow best when they receive 16 hours of light, followed by eight hours of darkness each day.

PLANTS THAT GROW WELL INDOORS:

Veggies
- artichoke; broccoli/broccolo; cauliflower; celery; cucumber; eggplants; leeks; peas; peppers; purslane; rhubarb; silver beet; spinach; tomatoes; watercress (in the pond)
- lettuces / greens: arugula, black seeded simpson, chard, deer tongue red, frisee, kale, lolla rossa, royal oakleaf, mizuna, tango
- onions: green onions, garlic, standard onions
- squash: yellow crookneck, zucchini

Fruit
- bananas (dwarf); cantaloupe; coconut; figs; grapes; grapefruit; pineapple; strawberries; watermelon
- citrus: blood orange, lemon, lime, tangerine

Herbs
- basil; cilantro/coriander; mint; dill; marjoram; oregano; parsley; rosemary; thyme
- sage: pineapple sage; standard

Edible flowers
    fuchsia; geranium; hibiscus; honeysuckle; haskap berries; nasturtium; passion flower; rose; snapdragon; sunflower; viola; yucca

Avoid:
    cabbage; corn; carrots; berry bushes

Do not forget houseplants! Houseplants are adapted to tropical areas where they grow beneath dense tropical canopies and must survive in areas of low light. These plants are thus ultra-efficient at capturing light, which also means that they must be efficient in processing the gases necessary for photosynthesis. Because if this trait, plants can remove toxic chemicals from the air, including formaldehyde, benzene, and carbon monoxide. Use 12 medium-sized plants per 1,000 SF of floor area to recycle your entire home's air in 24 hours. The best plants include bamboo palm, chinese evergreen, english ivy, gerbera daisy, janet craig dracaena, dracaena marginata, dracaena massangeana/corn plant, mother-in-law's tongue, chrysantheiums, peace lily, and dracaena warneckii.

The most common pest issue in homes with indoor greenhouses is whitefly. If you do not want to introduce any beneficial insects into your home, there are number of ways to control a pest situation. Remove infested leaves and discard them outside, or some people choose to vacuum up or capture and release flying pests. Traps are effective for white flies, fungus gnats, and cabbage worms. Pests like mealy bugs and aphids can be removed from plants with a strong spray of water. Dusting the surface of dry soil with diatomaceous earth will dehydrate and subsequently kill any soft-bodied insect. A spray mixture of a couple of teaspoons of household soap to one gallon of water can help control aphids, mites, and white flies. Organic pyrethrin insecticidal sprays are also effective.

Weeds should not be a problem in your indoor greenhouse. Hand-pick any weeds that may pop up. Screen doors can help prevent seeds from entering the building and also help to keep any beneficial insects you may have inside.

It may be required that you hand-water your plants if you are not producing enough greywater or if over-heating of the greenhouse causes dehydration.

Glass Block and Bottle Walls

Wall Type:	Neither Thermal Mass nor Insulating
Appropriate Climate:	Warm regions for exterior walls. All regions for interior walls.
Structural Capability:	Infill only, frame required
Suitable for Berm:	No
Natural:	No
Learning:	Easy
Doing:	Easy
Engineering Required:	No
Kit Available:	No

Did you know that it is more difficult now to find the bottles you need in multiple colors? Recycling has made things better, unless you happen to be looking for cool materials for your glass bottle wall. Many Earthship builders spend months and sometimes even years scavenging for and collecting the "right" bottles. Wealthier builders just buy the bottles in the colors they want them in.

While beautiful, the glass bottle walls are poor insulators. So, many people now only use them on the south or west exterior walls if they are also leeward (the direction the wind normally GOES) and on the interiors of the home.

Do not use bottle walls on the north unless you live where winter is pretty much "summer-lite." Basically, you only want bottle walls where the need for insulation is minimized.

Figure 22. Bottle Wall

PROS AND CHALLENGES OF GLASS BOTTLE WALLS
ARE ESSENTIALLY THE SAME AS FOR CAN WALLS, SEE BELOW.

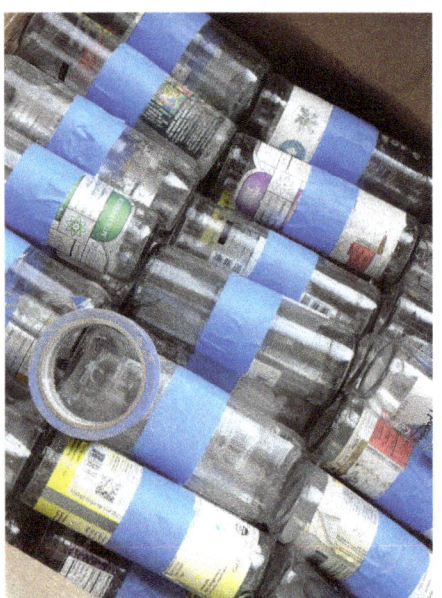

Figure 23. Bottle Bricks

Maintenance-wise, the glass bottles pose another concern: grossness. The open ones that were originally used in Earthships collect bugs and dust, they are ugly on the "cork" side, and they break easily.

Many people now take the bottoms of two bottles and to tape them together and make what is referred to as a "bottle brick". You will need about 2,000 bottles, a means of cutting them, and duct tape to make the standard 1,000 bottle bricks. You will want to remove the labels by soaking the bottle in water with dish soap and then using a putty knife to remove what remains. Using gloves to keep from getting cut, etch the bottle 4 inches above the base using a sharp glass cutter and dip the etched bottle into hot but not boiling water for 10-12 seconds, then dip it in an ice cold bath for a few seconds, and the hot again... until this cuts the glass through. Alternately, a high quality tile saw or a Kinkajou works well to do this quickly. Wash and dry the bottle bottoms completely. Using a clear glass bottle end and a colored glass end for the most light transmission, tape the bottles together with duct tape, painting tape, or two layers of packing tape, and then you have your bottle bricks!

Another trick for not using glass bricks but getting the same effect which many builders already know and are using: use pretty colored and shaped glass blocks. This moots the point of the walls "recycling benefit" but it works for the long-term. Maintenance is minimized, thermal performance is maximized, and privacy is maximized. Plus you can get exactly the look you want.

Glass blocks and bottle walls should not be used as load-bearing walls, and they should be laid in Type S mortar not more than 3/8 inch in thickness. For stability, especially if used on the exterior, these walls should not extend more than 15 feet in any direction and should be limited to an area less than 140 square feet overall. Curved wall sections are possible; they just need an expansion joint at each change of direction. The radius of the curve should be limited to no less than 4 feet.

Expansion joints - an expansion strip between the glass and the regular wall and sealed with a sealant either side - should be installed at the heads and sill of exterior glass block and bottle walls to allow for movement and settling. Recycled content expansion joint filler is available.

Can Walls

Wall Type:	Neither Thermal Mass nor Insulating
Appropriate Climate:	Warm regions for exterior walls. All regions for interior walls.
Structural Capability:	Infill, frame required
Suitable for Berm:	No
Natural:	No
Learning:	Easy
Doing:	Easy
Engineering Required:	No
Kit Available:	No

Oh the can walls. How we want to love them. We just can't. While they are cool looking, they have acoustical issues and frankly, they are gross. Here is a photo of a beehive shaped can constructed bathroom ceiling about 12 feet above the floor. Notice anything? How about the black mold at the ceiling? That is a serious danger in this children's bathroom.

Figure 24. Can Wall Dome with Mold

CAN WALL PROS

- Easy to build.
- Anyone can. (ha! punny!)

CAN WALL CHALLENGES

- While aluminum is a naturally-occurring element, once it is manufactured, it is far from natural.
- These walls should be infill only, and should not be used in a structural capacity. However, many Earthships use can walls in a structural manner despite the warnings. We strongly advocate not doing that.
- Can walls are extremely poor insulators.
- More joints = more potential for failures.
- May require plastering = another material connection to fail + more maintenance = more cost.
- Amount of cement used (up to half of the volume of the wall is concrete) which means higher carbon loads on the environment, and the wall is stealing oxygen from the air you breathe.
- Effect on breathability for those with allergies and lung issues due to dust collection in the bottom "dome" on the can.
- If used in a bathroom or kitchen, they can collect black mold at locations you are unlikely to see, and thus clean. This is not just unsightly. It is dangerous.
- Echo chamber effects in domed spaces.
- Susceptible to infestation of bugs and other creepy crawlies.

- When they are not painted, they are ugly. However, painting is a hassle due to the domed shape of the exposed can bottoms, which requires more paint than a normal wall.
- We have designed buildings for kids who have severe lung issues, and we err on the side of caution in suggesting materials for our clients. Aluminum is a poison. The impact of this on your Earthship will depend on the pH of the water you use in your concrete mix. If inhaled, people with a certain biological sensitivity can develop an allergy to aluminum, or asthma. According to the Agency for Toxic Substances and Disease Registry,

    "You may be exposed by breathing, eating, drinking, or by skin contact. It should be noted that aluminum is an abundant and widely distributed element and will be found in most rocks, soils, waters, air, and foods. You will always have some exposure to low levels of aluminum. Most aluminum-containing compounds do not dissolve to a large extent in water unless the water is acidic or very alkaline."

- Aluminum is also 100% recyclable, so instead of removing waste from the stream, in using it, you are removing a valuable commodity from the recycling stream. This means much of the initial embodied energy is wasted and it results in more aluminum being mined. The major expense of the beverage can is in the energy needed to produce the aluminum, though recycling can save up to 95% of the energy input into the fabrication. However, aluminum production uses so much energy that you would have to recycle the same piece of aluminum 20 times to just break even on the energy used to create it in the first place. Furthermore, to get 1 functional ton of virgin aluminum, they need to mine at least 8 tons of bauxite ore. That ore comes from places like Australia, China, Brazil, India, Guinea, Jamaica, Russia, Kazakhstan, Suriname, and Greece. This means it has to be transported overseas to be used. It takes 200 million BTUs of heat (provided from nuclear, coal, water, and gas powered plants) to make one ton of virgin aluminum. That is 7 times the amount of energy needed to make one ton of new steel. To put that into perspective, U.S. aluminum factories use on average about 2,600 Megawatts annually. That is enough energy to power over 2.5 million homes per year.
- As far as steel cans go, which some people use instead of aluminum drink cans, in 2010, 72% of steel was recycled in Europe. In theory, steel is 100% recyclable without any loss in quality. Its magnetic properties make it the easiest and most economical material to sort and recover.
- The embodied energy of your obtaining cans is another factor. Estimate 1 hour per person digging through the recycle center to get 300 suitable non-crushed cans.

If you want to eliminate many of the issues outlined above, you can plaster over the cans with cement stucco. Though that really begs the question of why use the cans. Earthbags can give you any shape wall you want just about and are easier to build and less damaging to the environment. We do not recommend using earth stucco as it will trap moisture in the cans, which will breathe out through the walls, carrying any mold or mildew with it and potentially causing delamination of the earth stucco.

The average number of uncrushed soda and beer cans used in Earthships is 10,000. To build a can wall, you will need approximately 14 cans per square foot of wall. That translates to 1400 cans per 100 SF (ex: 8 foot tall x 12.5 foot long) of wall. Can walls should only be used on the exterior of the building as landscape walls, or in mild climates where no insulation qualities are needed.

Earthship organizations in Europe have abandoned the use of steel and aluminum cans.

Other Types of Walls

As you may have figured out, we are not big fans of using walls the way traditional Earthships do. We just think that there are better solutions that are more beneficial to the environment and to you.

So here are some ideas for alternative wall materials. For bermed applications, we like earthbags, rammed earth, or wood block concrete forms. For regular wall applications, like the less-glazed front solar wall you should use for good passive solar design, we like adobe, rammed earth, earthbags, Durisol blocks, wood or log, and strawbale wall types. Of course, what you use should be dependent on location.

Soil Factors for Rammed Earth, Adobe, Cob, and Earthbag Construction

Soils have two parts: topsoil and subsoil. Subsoil is composed of a variable mixture of small particles such as sand, silt and/or clay, but it lacks the organic matter and humus of topsoil. As it is lacking in dark humus, subsoil is usually paler in color than the overlying topsoil.

Traditionally, for rammed earth walls that do not require cement stabilizer, the ratio of clay to sand has been established as 30% clay and 70% sand. When using cement as a stabilizer is required, clay content can be reduced as low as 8% to 10%, depending on numerous factors, such as uniformity of gradation, plasticity, particle shape, and parent rock. Adobe, cob, and earthbag construction use variants of this mix.

A geotechnical report of the underlying soil on the building site will yield valuable data: gradation, soil type, and in some cases, a plasticity index. Most site soils can be used in some proportion to create a usable formulation for whatever earth building technique you might want to use. Common terms in Geotechnical reports that may be useful:

- The gradation report, or *Sieve Analysis*, identifies how much of a given soil is fine particles, those passing a 200 mesh screen. This is especially relevant in rammed earth building: if the gradation indicates more than 25% of the soil passing through the 200 mesh screen, the addition of sand will likely be required.

- The *Plasticity Index* is an indicator of how much of those fine particles are "clayey". Clay particles help to bind together the soil matrix. High clay soils benefit from small gravel as supplemental amendments.

Unlike earlier times, when earth building materials were nearly always harvested on or near the construction site, today we have access to a wide range of importable mineral soils and admixtures to formulate a blend of soils capable of achieving optimum structural and aesthetic performance. Though, when any aspect of the soil mix is imported in, the measure of true sustainability is reduced as embodied energy rises. Benefits of using on-site soils include reduced cost of importing materials, increased LEED points, color continuity within the local geology, reduced hauling costs, and reduced carbon emissions from construction and transportation.

If site investigation and/or geotechnical reports indicate unsuitability, or if there is no excavation planned for the site, it is possible to source a portion of the wall building material in other ways. Excavating contractors, pool contractors, or other general contractors frequently have excess material they need to move off a site. Phone calls and scouting trips can be productive, as can the traditional "Clean Fill Wanted" sign.

The search for a suitable sand or gravel amendment can start at the local masonry or landscape supply yards. Coarse sands with a good distribution of particle sizes are usually better than fine or uniform sand. Cracked or crushed gravel is better than "pea" or river gravel because of its angularity.

Expansion and Control Joints

While most people tend to think of building materials being quite rigid, in fact many of them expand and contract with temperature and humidity fluctuations. For that reason, it is important to a) understand the nature of the materials and b) not put the materials together too tightly; else they will crash into each other or pull away and create an opening for air and water to get through.

Expansion joints, made of compressible filler and sealed with joint sealant, should be installed in masonry-based walls (any wall using mortar to hold pieces together) where the wall changes direction for form an L, T, or U shape.

Control joints are critical for concrete and rammed earth walls to account for shrinkage and also to reinforce joints at locations where the wall will be weak, including changes of wall height or thickness, at wall intersections, either side of a corner at a distance of ½ the wall height away from the corner, and on both sides of openings greater than 6 feet wide.

Adobe

Wall Type: Thermal Mass
Appropriate Climate: Warm regions
Structural Capability: Load-bearing
Suitable for Berm: No
Natural: Yes
Learning: Easy
Doing: Easy
Engineering Required: Possibly, if permitted
Kit Available: No

Figure 25. Taos Pueblo Adobe Buildings

In Taos, we have a thousand year history of using adobe to build our earth-sheltered buildings. Designers and architects here know that a 13 inch thick adobe wall or roof has a 12 hour thermal lag, which means, in the summer it takes 12 hours for the heat to get inside, and in the winter the heat collected from the sun during the day will warm the inside for 12 hours at night. This naturally keeps the home cool in hottest part of the day and supplements the heat in the house throughout the night.

Adobe, sun dried mud brick, or loam as it is called in Europe... is one of the most dependable natural building materials. It has been used all over the world since its earliest known use in Mesopotamia in approximately 3600 BCE. Adobe has a high thermal mass and can be easily built from on-site materials by inexperienced laymen. The bricks are stacked up much like traditional clay bricks, in alternating courses. Adobe is traditionally made with sand, clay, and water, and some natural binding material – jute, straw, bitumen, and/or dung are common. Historically, adobe was often made from earth removed from the building site. In some climates, the area where the earth was removed was used for a small basement or a root cellar.

ADOBE PROS

- Adobe has a moisturizing effect and is able to keep humidity at a constant level.
- Provides even heat distribution over the entire wall.
- Adobe can be used to create any desired form and its earth plaster counterpart can be applied on almost any surface.
- Adobe is an environmentally-friendly material when used without chemical additives.

ADOBE CHALLENGES

- Adobe homes can be cold because adobe is not insulating. Because of this, Code requires modern adobe to use rigid insulation on the exterior.

- Adobe must be maintained. It is not weatherproof. Being made of mud, it has a tendency to return to that state. A one inch thick application of earth stucco on the exterior is required at a minimum, and additional layers of earth stucco should be added annually. See the Earth Plasters section in the Finishes section to learn more.

- Adobe is prone to damage in earthquakes and is therefore not recommended for seismic zones. Minor seismic concerns can be addressed with additional structure and foundations.

- In some climates, adobe can be prone to developing molds. New Mexico has one third of the adobe houses in America – 60,000 of them – and old adobe buildings dot the landscape, left to decompose right where they are because they get a moldy "funk" in them that causes allergies and lung ailments. Just be aware that maintenance of the adobe home is a lifelong commitment, and that a lack of careful attention to this will almost guarantee that your home does not perform the way you want it to over time.

- Also see Rammed Earth Pros and Challenges for several similar issues and benefits.

Typical adobe bricks measure 4 inches x 10 inches x 14 inches and weigh approximately 30 pounds. These days, many adobe makers leave out the natural binders. A stabilizer is often added to make "improved" or "stabilized" adobe. Agave or prickly pear gel, Portland cement, asphalt emulsion, and lime are common stabilizers. Neither asphalt, a by-product of road construction, or Portland cement are ideal, if the other options are available to you and acceptable to your Code official. When used with lime in lieu of cement for stabilized blocks, adobe remains natural though does present some chemical changes which render it slightly more difficult to work with, requiring gloves as concrete does. An adobe wall is usually at least 14 inches thick for a single story structure and up to 3 feet thick for a 2-3 story structure. In most cases, if the walls are taller than 7 feet, it is best if the adobe is battered at the base of the wall to provide a slight incline up the exterior face of the wall.

Pre-made adobe blocks are manufactured here in New Mexico, which makes adobe an even more ideal material if you do not want to make the bricks yourself or if time is a consideration. With the right equipment and manpower, they can easily be made on-site if you have adequate soils. It is important if you make your own blocks to have or do a soil test to determine the soil content and its viability for use in your adobe. If you do not have the testing done professionally, it is possible that the permitting authority may find your home unfit for occupancy! See Soil Testing for Cob in the next section for how to self-test your soil, from our friend and expert Sigi Koko.

Moisture-impermeable finishes including cementitious stucco are avoided on adobe walls because they impair the wall's ability to desorb moisture, which is necessary to preserve its strength. We prefer earth plasters both inside and out. In arid climates, you can allow the adobe to remain exposed on some interior applications. Exposed adobe is quite pretty, but it will eventually decompose to some degree and leave dust to clean up.

Another benefit of adobe construction as well as uninsulated rammed earth construction… is that buildings constructed of earth are grounding for our emotional and spiritual well-being. Using earthen floors improves this quality.

Adobe construction starts at around $100 per square foot of floor area if contractor-built.

Recommended Reading: Adobe Homes for All Climates: Simple, Affordable, and Earthquake-resistant Natural Building Techniques, by Lisa Schroeder and Vince Ogletree.

Next up: Adobe's cousin, or maybe sibling, Cob. Cob is nearly the same material as what archaeologists call "puddled adobe" that was originally used to build Taos Pueblo.

Cob

from Sigi Koko's Build Naturally Blog

Wall Type:	Thermal Mass
Appropriate Climate:	All regions
Structural Capability:	Load-bearing
Suitable for Berm:	No
Natural:	Yes
Learning:	Easy
Doing:	Easy
Engineering Required:	No
Kit Available:	No

Clay soil provides a versatile building material used for thousands of years to create beautiful and durable structures. Clay can be formed into building blocks, such as adobe, or monolithic walls, such as rammed earth and cob. Cob walls combine the same ingredients as adobe sun-baked bricks – clay, water, sand, and straw – but cob is sculpted in place when wet, resulting in its nickname: "sculptural adobe". The ingredients for cob cost almost nothing, especially if clay can be dug from the building site.

Glass bottles or blocks imbed easily in the cob as the wall is constructed, and provide beautiful light glowing through the wall. Sculpted niches provide functional and aesthetic shelves. And benches, desks, and shelves are easily incorporated into the sculpted form.

Completed walls are plastered with clay or lime to obtain a fine surface finish. Tiles or stones can be installed into the finish plaster to create color and aesthetic details.

Course concrete sand and small stones serve as the aggregate in cob, similar to aggregate in concrete. The sand provides strength and shrinkage control. Maximizing the sand proportion in the cob mixture results in the strongest possible wall. Long pieces of straw help to knit together each successive addition of wet cob to the wall. Straw provides tensile strength for any pulling forces inside the cob wall, which provides additional resistance to cracking. Clay is the key ingredient that binds the sand and straw into a monolithic wall system. Screening the clayey soil through 1/2-inch wire mesh helps eliminate larger rocks and break up clay clumps for better mixing.

Tip: Do not use topsoil! Organic topsoil adds inert fill into the cob with no benefit. Topsoil shrinks over time, potentially creating voids in the finished wall. Dig below the topsoil to explore for clay below and keep the topsoil for gardening.

Mixing the cob ingredients together can utilize extremely low-tech tools: a tarp and foot stomping power. Mix dry sand & sifted clay together first, then add water and start stomping. Use the tarp to roll drier mix on top of the wetter mix, keep stomping, and continue adding water until the cob is sticky but stiff. It should look uniform and should roll into a "cob burrito" when the tarp is pulled. At this point begin adding straw. Use dry straw if the mixture got on the wet side; and use soaked straw if the moisture content remains low. Add as much straw as the cob will hold, and continue to flip the pile often with the tarp. Note that the dryer the cob mixture, the higher you can build in one day, since a wet mixture will slump under its own weight.

Machine-based mixing techniques include rototiller and tractor cob. Both methods create larger batches of cob, however the mixtures tend to be less uniform and less consistent.

Cob walls provide excellent thermal mass, which allow for absorption of heat energy. This means in the summer time, a shaded cob wall has the capacity to absorb excess heat. In a well-designed space, this can be used to great advantage, potentially eliminating the need for air conditioning without relinquishing comfort. In winter time, a cob wall positioned to absorb low-angled sunlight will warm up, and release heat through the cold night-time. The result is an equalization of temperature between day and night.

The high thermal mass properties of cob also make it ideal for use around a masonry heater or rocket stove. High temperatures generated by the wood-burning fires are absorbed into the thermal battery and released slowly over time, extending the benefit of a fire long after it has been extinguished.

Cob performs efficiently as a wood-burning pizza & bread oven, due to the high thermal mass properties. To construct, build a negative mold of the interior oven space using sand, then sculpt the cob oven mass over the sand in two layers: first a straw-free thermal mass layer followed by a high straw insulating layer. When the oven has dried for a few days, cut a door into the mass, pull out all of the sand, and plaster or finish as desired. A fabulous one-stop resource for building a cob oven is Kiko Denzer's book Build Your Own Earth Oven.

Cob can provide heated thermal mass around a wood-fired hot tub. Any water-holding basin can be used to form the tub container, such as an old claw-foot tub or a water trough. The basin is raised off the ground and surrounded with cob around the exterior. The wood fire burns below the tub to heat the water and the heated cob thermal mass keeps hot tub temperatures constant for a long time. I recommend reading Becky Bee's book You Can Make The Best Hot Tub Ever if you plan to build a cob hot tub.

COB PROS

- All of the ingredients used to make and finish cob are completely non-toxic. It wouldn't taste good, but technically you could eat them.

- Often the soil dug from foundation excavation contains sandy clay and can be used to build with. If you do not find clay soil locally, dry bagged clay works as well, however it should hydrate for several days to make the clay sticky enough.

- Cob walls have high thermal mass that can store the sun's heat energy in passive solar design and provide thermal storage for a masonry heater. Fully shaded cob provides free cooling in summer by storing cool energy and absorbing humidity.

- Techniques for mixing and building with cob are extremely easy to learn and fun. Tools needed are few and inexpensive: shovels, tarp, and buckets.

COB CHALLENGES

- Non-load-bearing cob walls meet current Building Codes, as long as their substantial weight is fully supported with an appropriate foundation. However, load-bearing cob built to support the roof structure above, is allowed only sparsely.

- Building with cob requires little skill but lots of patience. The process is time consuming and labor-intensive, and progress is usually limited to approximately 30-inches high in a day. (The cob then needs to dry overnight to be strong enough to support additional wall.) However, the reward becomes great opportunity for sweat equity construction & cost savings.

- The primary ingredients in cob, clay and sand, have no insulating properties. That is, they can absorb heat energy but they do not slow the flow of heat energy from one side of a wall to the other. The straw content is insulating, though it provides little insulating value when encapsulated in the clay wall. This means that the total energy to heat a cob building in a cold climate will be greater than if the walls had high insulating properties. In a temperate climate, however, cob's high thermal mass can be a heating & cooling advantage.

SOIL TESTING FOR COB

>see this post on Sigi's website for photos to walk you through this process
>
>http://www.buildnaturally.com/EDucate/Articles/Cob.htm#soiltesting

Worm Test

Making a worm with your soil provides a quick preliminary test to determine if any clay content exists in your soil. It works because clay is uniquely sticky when wet. Take a small handful of soil to test and remove any visible rocks. Mix in a small amount of water, just enough to make the soil malleable. Roll the soil in your hand into the shape of a worm. If the worm remains intact and provides resistance to pulling apart, the soil contains clay; if it crumbles apart, the soil likely contains little or no clay.

Shake Test

A simple shake test determines relative percentages of clay and sand contained in the soil. It works because clay remains suspended in water, whereas sand and silt sink in water. Fill approximately ¼ of a cylindrical-shaped glass jar with crumbled soil (free of visible stones). Fill to the top with water, close the lid, and shake well, until all of the clay is dispersed. Set the jar down on a level surface and watch for 10 seconds. All of the sandy solids will settle to the bottom. Draw a line on the jar at the top of the sand. The water remains cloudy with clay. When the water becomes completely clear, draw another line at the top of the settled clay. The ratio between the height of the sand and the height of the clay represents the ratio of sand to clay in the soil. Note: it is difficult to differentiate silt in this test, as silt is similar to sand, only smaller and spherical.

Test Bricks

Test bricks allow you to determine the strongest proportions of clay and sand for your soil. The strongest cob contains the maximum amount of sand, while still having enough clay to provide excellent binding. Not all clay is equally "sticky", so different clays allow more or less sand. Begin with a brick made with 100% clayey soil, then make bricks with increasing amounts of sand until it is clear that there is not enough clay in the mixture (you can no longer keep the cob intact). Write the proportions directly on each brick. Do not add straw to the test bricks. Once the bricks are completely dry, drop them from shoulder height, starting with the sandiest brick. The first brick that does not break is your ideal proportion of soil to sand.

Rammed Earth

by Chiara Riccardi and Rachel Preston Prinz

Wall Type:	Thermal Mass
Appropriate Climate:	Favored in regions where there is little wood and the climate is warm and dry.
Structural Capability:	Load-bearing
Suitable for Berm:	Yes
Natural:	Mostly
Learning:	Medium challenge
Doing:	Requires contractor in most cases
Engineering Required:	Yes
Kit Available:	No

Rammed earth, also known as *taipa* or *pisé de terre*, is a technique of building load-bearing walls using a combination of materials which may include earth, clay, chalk, lime, sand, and /or gravel.

Constructing rammed earth walls involves a process of compacting 4 to 10 inch layers of a damp mixture of earth that has suitable proportions of sand, gravel and clay with an added stabilizer into a frame structure called a form or formwork, which molds the shape of the wall section. Each layer of the soil mixture, called a lift, is compacted to approximately 50% of its original height to create a solid wall of earth. Historically, additives of lime or animal blood were used to stabilize the soil mix. Modern designers building to Code requirements based on concrete walls (since rammed earth structural research is a relatively new field) are often required to add Portland cement in a proportion between 5 and 10 percent of total volume.

Most professional rammed earth builders use pneumatic rammers to compact the earth within the forms. As each form is filled, another form is placed above it, and the process begins again. This is continued until the desired wall height is achieved. As soon as the last lift in the wall is complete, the frames are removed. The compressed earth walls are immediately self-supporting and if a surface texture is to be

Figure 25. Rammed Earth Wall

applied, it has to be done so immediately after the frames are removed since the walls become too hard to work after about an hour. The wall is allowed to dry over a period of many warm dry days. It can take as much as two years for complete curing. Here in New Mexico, a concrete cap and/or top plate is required for rammed earth walls. Check your local Building Code for additional requirements.

It is possible to add a water repellent admix to the soil to make a rammed earth home in a humid climate less susceptible to water damage. This waterproofs the walls throughout, not just on the surface, leaving a long-lasting and more dependable solution than applied waterproofing.

Rammed earth walls can be left smooth - an 'off-the-form' finish - or wire-brushed to provide texture. An off-the-form finish gives a smoother surface and formwork lines and textural changes are evident. A wire-brush finish removes the formwork lines, exposes the soil texture, and gives a softer finished look. Moisture-impermeable finishes including cementitious stucco are avoided on rammed earth walls because they impair the wall's ability to desorb moisture, which is necessary to preserve its strength. It is also possible to plaster, render, paint or otherwise treat the walls in the same way as other masonry products. Or even to embed rocks and other decorative elements into the wall to add character. Well-cured walls accept nails and screws easily, and can be effectively patched with the same material used to build them.

Rammed earth construction is best done in warm, not hot, weather so that the walls can dry and harden without extremes of temperature.

Rammed Earth walls start at around $35 per square foot of wall area.

COMPRESSED EARTH BLOCKS are made from rammed earth, often using a hydraulic machine that extrudes the blocks, which are often shaped to interlock so they can be assembled without the use of mortar.

RAMMED EARTH PROS:

- Protection from extremes in climate. The thickness and density of the wall means that heat (or cold) penetration is slow and the internal temperature of the building remains relatively stable. As with adobe, warmth takes nearly 11 hours to work its way through a wall 12 inches thick.

- Reduced noise infiltration. Even extreme noises, such as traffic, loud neighbors, or wild weather are much reduced. Internal rammed earth walls also provide sound insulation between areas with different sound requirements.

- Durable and weather resistant. There are numerous examples of rammed earth buildings that are hundreds of years old, including the Great Wall of China, parts of which are made using a historic method of rammed earth construction.

- Once rammed earth walls are sealed, they should not need further attention for 10-20 years. At that point they may need a second coat of sealer, which is an easy process.

- Earth does not burn. This is an ideal material for rural and prairie settings and leafy suburbs where fire is a regular concern. Testing performed by the Commonwealth Scientific and Industrial Research Organization, an Australian research group, showed that a 9 inch rammed earth wall achieved a 4-hour fire resistance rating. A 6 inch rammed earth wall achieved a rating of 3 hours and 41 minutes. Modern Codes require the walls to be much thicker than these.

- Non-toxic, non-polluting, and 'breathes'. This creates safer, more people-friendly buildings that are perfectly suited for those with lung ailments and allergies.

- Low in embodied energy.

- Comfortable to live in.

- Rammed earth walls can be load-bearing, and meet Code requirements of many different countries. The compressive strength of rammed earth can be up to 4.3 MPa (620 psi). This is less than that of concrete, but more than strong enough for use in domestic buildings. Rammed earth using rebar, wood or bamboo reinforcement can prevent failure caused by earthquakes or heavy storms.

- Rammed earth can effectively control humidity where unclad walls containing clay are exposed to an internal space. Humidity is held between 40% and 60%, the ideal range for asthma sufferers and for the storage of moisture-susceptible items like books. The mass and clay content of rammed earth allows the building to "breathe" more than concrete structures do, avoiding condensation issues without significant heat loss.

- Rammed earth is unappetizing and impenetrable to termites.

- Electrical conduits can be built into the walls during the construction process. Plumbing can also be included in this way. Building in these services requires some extra planning at the design stage.

- Historically, tamping was done by hand with a ramming pole. This was quite labor-intensive. Modern walls can be made by employing pneumatically-powered tampers. With a mechanical tamper and prefabricated formwork, it can take as little as two days to construct the walls for a 1,500 square foot house.

RAMMED EARTH CHALLENGES

- Rammed earth costs 30 to 50% more than a traditionally framed wall, which means the entire home might cost between 5-15% more. Cost is impacted by: how far the soil must be transported, how much wall area is required (economies of scale apply), how complicated the design is, and how high the walls are.

- Using soil from the site can create more work, as it needs to be screened to remove large stones, organic matter, and excessive clay lumps. It is often less expensive to select the soil mix from a quarry, where the heavy machinery at the quarry site makes light work of screening.

- Rammed earth must be designed according to its climate. An experienced architect, designer, or builder can advise you if the thermal mass of the walls can provide the sole means of heating and cooling, or if additional insulation or energy sources might be needed for thermal control. In rainy climates, for example, a home may need additional insulation and a larger roof.

- When cement is used in the earth mixture, sustainable benefits are reduced.

- Rammed earth construction might take more work to attain approval by building officials, bankers, and insurers. In the southwestern United States, there are several experienced builders and contractors and rammed earth is starting to appear in Building Codes. Outside of the Southwest, rammed earth is generally not mentioned and will require more research and persistence on the part of the person trying to get a construction loan, a mortgage, or home insurance.

RAMMED EARTH CODE REQUIREMENTS

When done to Code, modern rammed earth buildings require better structural design methods, the inclusion of dampcourses and concrete footings, mechanical compaction of the walls, and other regulatory controls as determined by your local authority. Confer with the local building authority prior to design. According to the NM Earthen Building Code, rammed earth buildings:

- Are limited to 2 stories in height. An architect or engineer must design and stamp 2 story portions.

- Exterior walls must be a minimum of 18 inches thick unless they are solar mass walls, where they want to be no less than 10 and no more than 12 inches thick. Buttressing is required every 24 feet unless the wall is 24 inches thick or more. Interior walls must be 12 inches thick.

- Soils used for rammed earth cannot contain rocks more than 1 ½ inches in diameter nor clay lumps more than ½ inch diameter. Soil should not contain more than 2% soluble salts and must be free of organic matter. Qualified soils must reach a 300PSI compression strength.

- Stabilized walls must be covered to prevent moisture infiltration.

- Minimum 6 inch deep wood or concrete bond beams are required at the top of exterior walls

- Keyways are required at wall/wall and wall/foundation intersections.

- Openings cannot be within 3 feet of a corner. Arched openings or wood or concrete lintels are required.

Earthbags

by Chiara Riccardi and Rachel Preston Prinz

Wall Type: Thermal Mass
Appropriate Climate: All regions
Structural Capability: Load-bearing
Suitable for Berm: Possibly
Natural: Mostly
Learning: Easy
Doing: Easy
Engineering Required: If bermed
Kit Available: No

Figure 26. Earthbag Dome

Earthbag construction is a natural building technique that evolved from military bunker construction and temporary flood-control methods. Rooms in earthbag structures often are circular in shape and have a dome roof, though square rooms are achievable with buttressing and/or interlocking of the bags at the corners.

Earthbag building usually begins by digging a trench down to undisturbed stable subsoil. The trench is then partially filled with cobbles or gravel to create a rubble trench foundation. On this foundation, several rows of doubled woven bags are filled with gravel and placed into the trench, and another two courses are stacked above grade to form a water-resistant foundation dampcourse. Then the actual earthbag wall starts.

The most popular type of bag is made of solid-weave polypropylene, like those used to transport rice or other grains. Polypropylene is very affordable and is resistant to water damage, rot, and insects. These bags can be purchased as mis-prints or bought used at agricultural warehouses and producers. Alternative bags include those made of hemp, burlap or other natural-fibers. Though, when exposed to air, water, and time, these natural options may deteriorate.

Moist subsoil that contains 5 - 50% clay, enough to become cohesive when tamped, or an angular gravel or crushed rock is used to fill the bags. Portland cement, lime, or bitumen stabilizers can be used to allow earths with high clay content to withstand flooding. The addition of stabilizers in a ratio of 5-10% may be required to meet Code. The thermal insulating value of the fill material is directly related to both the porosity of the material and the thickness of the wall. Crushed volcanic rock, pumice or rice hulls yield higher insulation value than clay or sand. However, thermal mass properties are also an important consideration, particularly for climates that experience temperature extremes. Materials like clay or sand have excellent heat retention characteristics.

Each successive layer of earth-filled bags is placed like bricks, with one or two strands of barbed wire placed on top to increase friction between each row of bags and improve tensile strength. Bags can be pre-filled with material and hoisted into position or filled in place. A light tamping and twisting of the bags serves to consolidate them and creates a wall with a strength between that of adobe and rammed earth. The same process continues layer upon layer, forming walls.

The completed structure is then quickly covered with earth plaster to prevent solar radiation from degrading the polypropylene. Natural earth stuccos allow the wall to breathe and natural mineral pigments can be added to provide beautiful color effects. A standard mix for earth plaster for covering earthbag superstructures is: 1 part clay, 3 parts earth, 1 part straw, and 1 part lime.

Windows and doors can be formed with a traditional masonry lintel or by using earthbags in traditional masonry corbeling or brick-arch techniques using temporary forms. Light may be brought in by skylights, glass-capped pipes, or bottle bricks placed between the rows of bags during construction.

A roof can be formed by gradually sloping the walls inward to construct a dome. This inherently limits the size of the space you can create and increases the size of the volume, because you want to use the minimum overlap on the bag that you possibly can: an inch or less of bag overhanging the bag below is best. Keeping the angle of the dome walls to no more than 60 degrees will usually work adequately. The trick with domes is waterproofing the roof; this can be difficult, and requires the use of commercial roof sealers. Using a traditional framed roof of panels or shingles is another option.

It is possible to combine earthbag building with earth-sheltering.

Self-built earthbag homes can start at $20 per square foot of floor space.

EARTHBAG PROS

- Heat (or cold) penetration of the wall is slow and the internal temperature of the building remains relatively stable.
- Allows the building to be constructed in culturally and regionally appropriate styles. This preserves the look and feel of the community.
- The tools needed to complete an earthbag build are limited to those that are readily available pretty much everywhere: gloves, picks, shovels, hoes, hammers, barbed wire, twine…
- Earthbag structures can easily be built solo or with just a few friends. The effort is much easier than that of traditional Earthships.
- Earthbag homes are the only way to get an Earthship in some European countries like Belgium who have outlawed the use of tires in architectural projects.
- Earthbag homes can range from cozy huts and domes to multi-story traditional homes.
- Earthbag construction uses the least energy of any durable construction method. With on-site soil being used, practically no energy is expended on transportation. The energy-intensive materials that are used — plastic (for bags & twine), steel wire, cement or lime, and perhaps the outer shell of plaster or stucco — are used in relatively small quantities compared to other types of construction, adding up to only 1-4% of the total construction materials.
- The buildings last a long time; however, when they are no longer useful they may simply erode with no serious threat to the environment, or even be recycled into new earthbag-constructed buildings.
- Earthbag buildings last many years with low maintenance. Earthbag structures do not rot or mold and they deter pests including termites, roaches and the like, because there is no wood to chew through.
- Building with earthbags means not contributing to the deforestation, air pollution, or build-up of landfill materials.
- Only 1-4% of earthbag construction uses manufactured resources. The main materials used are dirt, straw, and water.
- Earthbag structures can survive fire, flood, wind, tornado, hurricanes and earthquakes.

EARTHBAG CHALLENGES

- The process of filling earthbags and tamping them requires a fair amount of physical strength for the self-builder; United Earth Builders has developed a skid-steer operated earth home building machine. It fills earthbag tubes of many sizes at a rate as fast as 400 feet per hour. At production speed, a crew could fill about 30 feet per hour of earthbag by hand (depending on bag width). Another option is using a small concrete-mixer on-site to blend materials.

- Earth plasters are an acquired skill requiring practice to get the mix right. The difficulty is there is no list of definitive ingredients, and it all depends on your mud.

- Waterproofing earthbag buildings is a complex and sometimes expensive process for humid regions.

- Earthbag buildings might take more work to meet with approval by building officials, bankers and insurers.

- If an earthbag home gets damaged it is nearly impossible to fully repair. Large sections of the wall must be removed and replaced to complete a repair that could be considered more than a band-aid. Same with additions. They require a great deal of demolition if not planned for in advance.

- Polypropylene, which the bags are most often constructed of, is a toxic agent known to cause cancer, allergies/immunotoxicity, organ system toxicity, and neurotoxicity. Though, rats and bugs are not keen on eating this material and rot is rarely a concern. Like tires, this material is encased, and may present no threat. That has yet to be determined.

- Water Alert: earthbags cannot withstand prolonged soaking.

Since 2010, earthbags have been used moderate and high seismic risk areas with new reinforcement techniques. A reinforced concrete footing or grade beam may be recommended. Additionally, corner reinforcing is required, since corners are one of the most vulnerable parts of buildings in earthquakes, and can often be pulled apart. A typical and easy-to-build solution suggests barbed wire should be cut to extend 24" past each corner, and when the next course is laid and tamped, tightly pull this extra wire back up onto the upper course. Then lay the next set of bags and barbed wire, extending again out past the corners. However, the Build Simple Institute, an architectural research firm in Placitas, New Mexico, suggests using a 2 foot deep buttress, extending each wall beyond the intersection at corners in earthquake prone areas. They have several alternatives if buttressing is not preferred, just visit their website at http://buildsimple.org/earthbag.php for details.

Wood Block Concrete Forms

by Craig Schreiber

Wall Type:	Thermal Mass + Insulating
Appropriate Climate:	All regions
Structural Capability:	Load-bearing
Suitable for Berm:	Yes
Natural:	Not so much. Recycled wood + Concrete
Learning:	Easy
Doing:	Easy
Engineering Required:	Possibly, if bermed
Kit Available:	No

I love living in smart castles with massive walls. I call what I do Conscious Construction. It is a thoughtful design and building method that I have been practicing for 15 years. I designed and built with conventional construction materials previously, until I found Durisol blocks, or Wood Block Concrete Forms (WBCF). Codes would classify this building method as an ICF (insulated concrete form).

Figure 28. Durisol Block Home. Photo Courtesy Craig Schreiber

After working in architecture and landscape design for more than 35 years, I now know details, and like to customize and improvise them. These buildings allow me to do that. I travel to the Alps and Canada and see how they build in similar mountain climates to mine here in Leadville, Colorado. In my experiences of these projects around the world, I have come to believe that stick construction is archaic compared to a solid block wall and shell. I have built 5 homes and additions with WBCF.

Each block is $15 to $18, delivered on pallets. Blocks are perfectly 2 foot x1 foot x 1 foot. There are 3 standard building units: standard, corner, and ends. Typical 12 inch wall blocks come with 3 inch of rock wool in the cores to insulate the grout fill from the outside, giving it excellent thermal performance. 10 inch & 8 inch thick blocks are also available, and these come in 3 foot lengths. The wall voids are then filled with a concrete mix from a pump truck in order to stabilize the system.

The wall has an R-value of R-24, and has no thermal bridges. R-value, however, as has been covered here previously, is an incomplete assessment of a wall's performance... it does not measure a material's ability to sustain or remember its temperature. These walls use their thermal mass properties to stay cool when it is hot, and radiate collected heat when it gets cold.

Local permit approval is not an issue when you provide supporting fire rating and structural capacity tests. It can be significantly less expensive to build with WBCF, because so many layers of building materials and waste are eliminated. The only tool you need is a sledgehammer to adjust alignment. There is no cutting required. If a block is weakened or modified, a scrap piece of board or plywood just screws on until the cores are filled. Blocks can be ordered with half or without rock wool to increase the wall strength for retaining and earth-sheltering conditions. If a cut is needed for an electrical box or a bevel on a window sill, a skill saw, a hand saw, a sawzal, or any wood tool slices it easily. There is no grain direction. The walls and webs of the blocks are 2 inches thick. Each block weighs about 35 pounds, which makes them relatively easy to handle. It is not necessary to alternate the vertical seams with running bond as in masonry assemblies, only that the cores align.

WOOD BLOCK CONCRETE FORM PROS

- You can participate to save cost - kind of like Legos. If you draw an accurate model of your intentions, then ordering and pricing is easy.
- 30x more thermal mass than hollow stud walls - R24.
- Economical (70%-90% cost of conventional walls).
- Fire proof - masonry rate insurance.
- 800± year life vs. 200 ±.
- Breathable, quiet & humidity cache.
- Full shell above & below grade - footer to plate.
- Cuts with all wood tools.
- Screws holds everywhere - inside & out.
- Adhesives, stucco & concrete stick everywhere.
- Only has 10%± of the waste of stick construction.
- Superior structural capacity.
- Unlimited height potential – you can build a high-rise home with these blocks.
- Board, drywall & trim are not required.
- Antique finish, murals, faux, & rock finishes are possible.
- 1 foot dimensional architecture.
- Temporary steps and scaffolding.
- Climbing wall anywhere.
- Internal electrical with blue flexible conduit.
- Site grading can blend - no foundation top is visible.
- Blocks are insulated so concrete can be poured during cold weather with minimal protection.

WOOD BLOCK CONCRETE FORM CHALLENGES

- One must plan ahead, and make sure you have accurate drawings, because you cannot buy these at the local lumber yard.
- Mostly, owners are at the mercy of their contractor, who has likely never touched this product.
- Builder must be aware of electrical and plumbing sleeves and raceways as blocks get stacked. You can sink lines into the wood block later.
- If you cannot get a concrete truck to your site to fill the voids in the blocks, this is not the right option.
- House might be too warm in the winter.

The blocks are 80% shredded wood and about 20% pressure-molded concrete. No adhesives are required to stack them. Block ends interlock and layer seams have a wood biscuit to maintain horizontal alignment.

My recent home was $22,000± delivered to Colorado, for the shell and internal walls. That includes 3 to 4 courses below grade for frost walls, and a patio/garden/privacy wall of 8 inch block.

STACKING TRICKS

If blocks are not plumb because of an uneven footer, simple wood wedges will tip them until they are poured solid. I drive 2 inch to 3 inch deck screws into patches of lumber anywhere I need them. A paddle bit with a foot extension blows holes in these walls like a knife cutting through warm butter. An electric chainsaw for limbing is ideal to cut all the way across a block or scrape a surface flat, like the side of a window opening.

I build up faux rock and climbing holds with 2 inch thick scraps adhered with construction adhesive and a screw. Then, I add stucco expanded aluminum mesh to create relief.

CONCRETE & STEEL CORES

One concrete truck will fill wall cavities up to approximately 5-6 feet high. Steel is placed in horizontal openings in the block, along with electrical raceways. I usually cut a 20 foot #4 rebar into 3 equal pieces for vertical reinforcement in each core (1 foot on center). Fill walls 5.5 feet high with concrete, which leaves 14 inches of bar sticking out for overlap with the next lift and vertical steel.

The concrete mix is 3/8 inch diameter rock in a runny 6 inch slump so it flows into all voids. I fill lower layers with a belt truck until it gets 8 or more feet high, then I get a pump truck which is $500+ but worth it to me for ease of placement.

RADIANT WALLS & SAUNA

I have always enjoyed sauna here in the high country - the heat and humidity of the tropics. Building a sauna with Durisol is so easy! I run zones of hydronic tubes in each layer of block, on the internal side of the core. I dump solar, wood, or boiler heat into those for mass storage. I am presently wrapping tubes around my sauna room to distribute wood heat throughout the house. This does require that I thread the tube through a core of a block as it returns to the next course above or put it in the vertical seam of two blocks. All the floors are hydronic heated, set in concrete. I have 8 inches+ of gravel rock below the concrete floors and 2 inches of rigid insulation below that. Perlite bags are another great floor thermal barrier, though they are double the expense, they are also double the insulation.

I use to get rooms to 180° or more in conventional stick sheds. Now, with Durisol, I pre-heat the room longer and get the walls up to temperature, and the mass radiates like an oven, as does the stove. I have two doors in my new sauna so that I can dump any additional heat into the two rooms adjacent.

FINISHES

I buy nice wood windows and slide them in and screw them to the blocks. No drywall or plywood are required. You can screw tin, boards or adhere rock skin anywhere. My favorite finish is a smear of conventional stucco on either side. I use 3 equal parts of Portland cement, silica sand, and lime for the inside. I color the creamy spread with powder and water pigments. I leave the walls breathable, without a latex paint, so that they are a moisture mass, storing water vapor for when humidity is low.

Get more information, expert guidance, arrange home tours, and/or gain hands on experience by contacting Craig at 719-486-1856 or http://www.landart.info.

Wood and Log Construction

The Earthship literature says that using wood is bad for the forests, for our access to oxygen, and for durability sake. Yet, an Earthship uses a huge number of wood resources.

We do not really have an issue with using wood. Wood is a fabulous resource when used wisely. Because the forests in America are run by a vastly under-budgeted U.S. Forest Service, many of our forests are overgrown with small diameter trees and trees that have been ravaged by aspen blight and pine beetles. That means we have an abundant resource of natural products that, if left in place, are not only going to be wasted, but also threaten the fabric of our forests, reducing our ability to enjoy and protect them, as well as our ability to control wildfires. This is an American problem, but we understand that forests in many parts of the world are also undernourished by man's attention. For that reason, we advocate the responsible harvesting of wood products. Your local forest service office will even let you collect trees for a nominal fee in some areas. They have sections of forest they know need clearing of small diameter trees and fallen deadwood for the forest to sustain itself and grow. In some cases they are desperate to get that work done within their budget. It can be beneficial to collect the wood they need cleared, for both building and for your firewood needs. At Christmas, they sell permits for the cutting of small Christmas trees for this same reason. One of the best advantages of harvesting this wood, in certain locations, is that the beetles that kill the trees leave a trace amount of biomaterial inside that stains the wood. This can be incredibly beautiful. In my work in Vail, the blue and violet tones of beetle damaged wood were highly coveted.

Additionally, local woods can sometimes feature built-in pest and humidity controls that are perfect for your environment. Using local woods also minimizes the impact and costs of transportation. As we have noted previously, you can even use wood from right off your site, if you are so inclined. As contributor Sigi Koko notes,

"When you build with site-harvested trees, and have them milled in place, you have the option to use live-edge planks for trim, siding, even countertops. (Live-edge refers to wood that leaves the contour of the tree trunk intact, not squared off.) Live edge siding gives you 2 things: it saves the wood cut-offs from waste, and it gives you an organic element to enjoy in your home."

Small trees from on-site can also be stripped of their branches and used in the round, which is actually stronger than milled lumber, for pole trusses, posts, and beams. They can be used to create door and window bucks, studs, plates, rafters, cabinets and furniture by simply using a portable saw or an inexpensive chainsaw guide to trim the pieces.

If you use frame construction or logs to build with, be sure to install a metal sill plate with a flashing weep to the outside between the wood and the foundation. This will prevent moisture wicking up into the wood as well as pest infiltration.

In America, we use an organization called the Forest Stewardship Council (FSC) to rate the environmental responsibility of wood products and the manufacturers that produce them. Wood products not harvested from within your own land should carry the greenest FSC certification level possible.

WOOD ALTERNATES

Engineered wood should be FSC-certified and use natural or at least non-toxic binders. This product uses up wastes from wood and paper production and minimizes the use of virgin forest. Engineered wood is used for glulams, laminated veneer lumber, wood I-joists (TJIs), oriented strand board, parallel strand lumber, and other manufactured wood fiber structural materials.

The greenest thing you can do is to use salvaged wood for all your solid wood needs. Timber frames and structural brackets and details can often be found at salvage yards. You might even score an awesome deal with a timber frame manufacturer, when a client is not able to afford the house they designed and had milled.

Timber frame

Wall Type:	Depends on infill
Appropriate Climate:	All regions
Structural Capability:	Load-bearing
Suitable for Berm:	No
Natural:	Yes
Learning:	Medium challenge
Doing:	Medium challenge, easier with group
Engineering Required:	Possibly
Kit Available:	Yes

Timber frame homes are beautiful. They can look as complex as a wooden palace or as simple and elegant as a barn. They can function as load-bearing frames, with infill of cob, strawbale, or other building materials, or they can function as roof framing only, bearing on masonry or other high-mass walls that can withstand the structure's heavy loads. Timber frame is permitable in most cases.

Many people prefer the aesthetics of traditional timber framing. From our contributor Sigi Koko,

> *"Traditional timber framing uses mortise & tenon joinery, with tight pegs to keep the joints together. No nails needed. The roof construction includes a primary structure (frames that go across the whole space), a secondary structure (beams that run longways across the roof) and a tertiary structure (purlins that are small and close together and support the roof sheathing)."*

Figure 27. Traditional Timber Frame Style

In my previous work in Vail, our firm principal would design timber frame structures detailed so elegantly that a single wooden peg removed from the joint would cause the entire structure of the joint to fall into a 3-dimensional jigsaw puzzle of pieces. He would have the timber frame installer paint that peg red as a way of celebrating that delicate piece's importance. True timber framing of this type is delicate and detailed and requires a professional designer. It also costs at least $20,000 more than modern timber framing.

Modern timber framing, using exposed metal fasteners, is also beautiful, but is clearly more modern, as well as being more affordable. In lieu of the detailed wooden joinery, a cast iron or other structural metal plate is used on either side of a timber post or beam to through-bolt and connect members to one another. It is an efficient method of construction in both design and installation.

TIMBER FRAME PROS

- Prefabricated superstructures can be erected quickly
- Infill type can make for a wall excellent in thermal performance.
- Relatively easy to run mechanical systems through.
- Acoustical performance high.

- Ideal for open plan houses.
- Can be formed into unique shapes.
- Stunning architectural structures.
- Minimal milling equals more sustainable construction method.

TIMBER FRAME CHALLENGES

- Complex design tends to be done by specialists.
- Often lengthy lead times waiting for kits to be assembled at factory.
- Requires detailed foundation.
- Initial investment high - payment required upfront by many suppliers.
- Can be susceptible to fire, except really large timbers can burn on the outside only.
- Possibility of rot in poorly detailed conditions.
- Detailing to prevent condensation in humid climates is critical.

Timber frame does not need to look like a barn. Timber frame is also used in English cottages and manors, Germanic and Austrian design, and even in Africa, where round poles are bent into position and more natural shapes are used.

Like log homes, timber frame homes can be purchased as kits.

Using salvaged timbers for timber frame is ideal, especially in the mountains where timber frame is desirable (desirable = higher resale value). Salvaged wood uses a much higher quality of wood than you can even get today, and can be found easily in long spans in areas where old mills or barns have been torn down, though it may be a little more expensive. Call your local preservation contractors and see if you might find some! It needs a pretty stiff supporting structure though, because it is so heavy, and that requires a structural engineer. But if you long for high ceilings, this is definitely a good way to go.

Log Buildings

Wall Type:	Depends on construction
Appropriate Climate:	Ideal in mountainous regions
Structural Capability:	Load-bearing
Suitable for Berm:	No
Natural:	Yes
Learning:	Easy
Doing:	Medium challenge, easier with group
Engineering Required:	No
Kit Available:	Yes

We love the look and feel of the quintessential log cabin. But many designers these days shy away from log buildings because of their divergence from the energy Codes. Log has a low apparent R-value - the R-value for wood ranges between 1.41 per inch for most softwoods and 0.71 for most hardwoods. A standard construction frame wall has an R-value of R-14, but a 6 inch thick log wall only has an R-value of 8. That does not look good at first blush. As we have discussed before, what the R-value does not tell you is that the log also acts as a thermal battery, storing heat from the sun. So, in practice, an unshaded log wall acts similarly to a standard frame wall that is designed to shed the sun's heat. The general rule here is: the thicker the wall you can afford, the better off you are from a thermal and structural perspective. Maximize the amount of sun on the south wall by making porches here as small as possible and also keeping evergreen trees away from the building and you will have a well-functioning log building.

The look and performance of Swedish cope log walls is great for many environments, especially if you do not like the look of chinking – the white/grey cement plaster between the logs on standard log home designs. A small curve is cut into the base of each log and that sits on the log below, making for a tight log wall. These walls can by challenging in some ways, though, as the logs are rounded and therefore dust collects on the rounded parts and they are difficult to finish millwork around. Sometimes it is challenging to hang things on these walls as well. A type of coped log with a rounded exterior face and a flat interior face is available at an additional cost.

If you do not want a rounded log at all, we recommend chamfered rectangular logs in dovetail type joints. This gives you a solid surface that is easy to hang things on and reduces dust collection on the wall surface.

Figure 28. The Bavarian at Taos Ski Valley

LOG PROS

- These homes appear natural and low maintenance.
- They feel cozy, warm, and relaxing.
- Sound insulation is excellent.
- Super easy to build: just buy a kit and Lincoln Log it yourself or with a small group of friends. My parents built a Swedish Cope log home by themselves, literally. They only used contractors for the foundation, mechanical systems, roof, and to bring scaffolding and a crane in to place the logs at the roofline.

- Costs around 30% less than a new home of standard construction.
- Naturally cool in summer and warm in winter.

LOG CHALLENGES

- Log buildings are not allowed in every state because they are perceived as being inefficient in their energy use. Some states see the value of log homes and offer work-arounds to achieve energy quotas required by Code. Others do not. Before considering a log home, check the requirements of your state.
- Challenging to get creative on-site with the floor plan after the logs are cut.
- Pests, including woodpeckers!
- Requires re-staining and resealing of exterior wood every 3 years or so – a very time-consuming maintenance task. In high alpine environments, this might be required annually.
- Stain and sealants are expensive.
- Logs naturally will crack and pop as they dry.
- Electrical and plumbing installation in log walls is a consideration you should be prepared for. It is more complicated and messy than in some other systems. Time spent planning where switches, runs, and outlets will be before the build is a sound investment. See The Art and Science of Outlets and Switching in the Electrical chapter for more information.
- Requires mechanical systems to work effectively, if not a tiny house.
- Chinking repairs must be done annually.
- Log walls tend to fail at the foundation when not correctly designed. That can mean horrible issues in repair.
- Flexible walls that expand and contract with humidity mean doors and windows can shift and stick.
- Decorating can be somewhat difficult because of curved surfaces.
- Higher fire insurance rates.

To minimize air leakage, logs need to be seasoned, or dried in a protected space, for at least six months before construction begins. Cedar, Spruce, Pine, Fir, and Larch are the driest woods by nature and therefore easiest to use. Your contractor should know this and order accordingly, but you probably want to check to make sure he did not go for the "best deal" and get you a lessor wood. Requiring a proof of warehousing is your best tool for preventing contractors giving you a product that will ultimately cause you headaches later.

If you dream of a log house and want the look but not the nightmare of plumbing and electrifying, nor log interior walls, consider framed walls with log siding. This will look like a log home, but it will be easily insulated, and allow for the ease of installation of mechanical, lighting, and plumbing. Fill the space between the log veneers with insulation to prevent the walls acting like a drum and reflecting (and sometimes amplifying) sound between spaces.

The base price of a standard log home starts at around $125 per square foot of floor area.

Cordwood

by Richard Flatau and Rachel Preston Prinz

Wall Type:	Thermal Mass + Insulating
Appropriate Climate:	All regions
Structural Capability:	Infill, frame required
Suitable for Berm:	No
Natural:	Can be. Depends on mortar materials used
Learning:	Easy
Doing:	Easy
Engineering Required:	No
Kit Available:	No

Figure 31. Cordwood Home. Photo courtesy Richard Flatau.

In their most basic form, Cordwood walls are a combination, of dry, peeled firewood and mortar. Mortar types may include: papercrete, adobe, lime putty, cementitious, or earthen mortars like cob. Cordwood has been used in Nebraska, Wisconsin, Quebec, and Sweden since the 19th century. This building style became even more popular during the Great Depression, when people wanted to build homes and barns with inexpensive labor and use materials they had at hand. Cordwood is an especially good building material option if you have access to softwood (evergreens) in your region.

Cordwood plays well with other styles and can make an accent wall of beauty when combined with strawbale, cob, Earthship, stone or horizontal logs. Many energy efficient homes are being built in Canada using two walls of strawbale and two walls of double wall cordwood.

Cordwood walls are relatively inexpensive to construct and simple to build. Using a simple vertical post and beam framework allows the owner/builder to erect the roof. This gives ample storage space, a weather-protected building environment, and "sections" of walls to build. Just fill the spaces between the structure with peeled, dried and split softwood blocks of a uniform 16 inch length. Mortar them as if you were building a brick or stone wall.

The center cavity is filled with insulation (usually sawdust). The walls, if mortared with care, are basically finished, but one side could be plastered or stuccoed, if the owner so desires.

CORDWOOD PROS

- Made with locally available materials.
- DIY project - ease of construction (not time).
- Aesthetically pleasing.
- Energy Efficient.
- The wall breathes and transpires moisture; ergo, there is no rot or degradation.
- The thick, solid, breathable walls deter mildew/mold.
- Environmentally-friendly.
- Once the wall is up, it is finished both inside and out.
- Thermal mass.
- If Best Practices are used the home is easy to heat and cool.
- Code Compliant when using Cordwood and the Code: A Building Permit Guide.

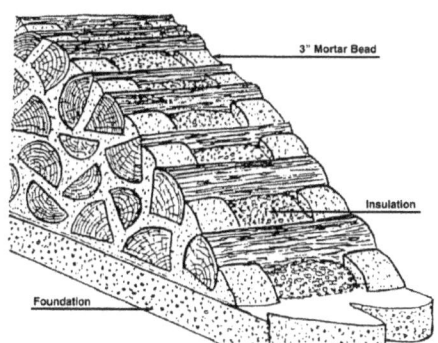

Figure 29. Cordwood Section.

Photo courtesy Richard Flatau.

CORDWOOD CHALLENGES

- Time consuming.
- Labor-intensive.
- No commercial builders.
- Wood and traditional mortar do not have a natural bond.
- Wood may expand & contract & darken.
- Resale may be for a niche market.
- Some people love the look, others do not.

CORDWOOD SOLUTIONS

- Permachink caulk, applied around any loosened log end takes care of shrinkage or log loosening.
- Primary checks can be easily filled with cellulosic material to stop air infiltration.
- Log end color changes can be remedied with a sander and breathable stain.

Suggested Reading: Cordwood Construction Best Practices by Richard Flatau. Also see Richard's website http://www.cordwoodconstruction.org, which has many other cordwood books in eBook and print format.

Strawbale

Wall Type:	Insulating
Appropriate Climate:	All regions
Structural Capability:	Load-bearing and Infill possibilities
Suitable for Berm:	No
Natural:	Mostly
Learning:	Easy
Doing:	Easy, with some building experience, when built under supervision of a skilled installer.
Engineering Required:	No
Kit Available:	No

Strawbale is one of the most ecologically efficient materials to build a home with. There are two installation types in strawbale construction: load-bearing walls and non-load-bearing, or infill, walls. Strawbales tend to be 18 inches wide east of the Mississippi, and 24 inches wide west.

Figure 33. One of Sigi Koko's Strawbale Homes. Photo courtesy Sigi Koko.

It is a commonly-held belief that you should not build with strawbale in humid climates. That, it turns out, is not really accurate. A well-built strawbale wall will be designed to endure humidity. Our friend and natural building expert Sigi Koko likes to say, *"If you can build with wood, you can build with straw."* The only difference in building with strawbale for various climates is dealing with details appropriate to your climate and seismic zone. For instance, in earthquake-prone areas, you may need to use a welded wire mesh as additional structural support for the bales. That is something of a trick, but nothing an experienced designer like Sigi cannot handle.

Super-insulating strawbale buildings are substantially more energy efficient than conventional wood-frame buildings. These homes are comfortable in hot or cold weather and help save money on utility bills. If you add passive and active solar design, the utility savings are even greater.

As a load-bearing structure, strawbales are stacked into walls and topped with a wooden beam or top plate for attachment, some structural framing for windows and doors, strapping for connecting the top plate to the strawbales, and then the weight of the roof rests directly on the bales. The first U.S. strawbale houses, built in Nebraska around the turn of the 20th century, were built in this manner, and many of them are still standing in good condition today. If done correctly, load-bearing strawbale does not settle. But it means you have to pay special attention to pre-compress the bales well & evenly.

Non-load-bearing strawbale uses a wood post-and-beam frame or traditional framing to support the roof, and the strawbales are then inserted as infill between the structural members for insulation and as a base for the wall surfacing material. This system is designed to meet structural and seismic Codes. The design for Code and the resulting ease of permitting is one of the main advantages of using strawbales as infill.

In a somewhat startling finding, our contributor Sigi Koko ran side-by-side accountings of strawbale infill projects versus load-bearing strawbale projects and found that strawbale infill buildings consistently use less wood than the same building with load-bearing strawbale walls. This is counter-intuitive, since load-bearing strawbale comes with the idea that it uses less wood. Evidently, after all the details and additional framing are done, load-bearing strawbale does in fact use more wood.

In both load-bearing and non-load-bearing strawbale, bales are compressed with wood atop the bales for levering, then wire strapping, then sometimes covered over with lath (Sigi says: NEVER USE CHICKEN WIRE!), plastered on the inside, and then either plastered or finished with a siding on the exterior. In hot and dry areas, almost anything can be used to cover the outside because there is no moisture to seep into the bales. In wet areas, using clay plasters inside and lime stucco or siding outside is the preferred finishing method. Integral plasters are a great choice, as they are made with natural earth clays for color and sustainability.

STRAWBALE PROS

- A completely renewable product.
- Affordable.
- Easily attain a wall insulation value of R-36 or more, (R-42 is not uncommon) providing superinsulation that performs twice as well as the energy Code requires.
- Owners, family, and friends can participate in building the home if an experienced installer leads the way.
- The thick walls allow for beautiful spaces and details like window seats or built-in furniture.
- Encourages sunlight reflection into the deepest parts of the room.
- Walls can be designed to be earthquake and hurricane resistant.
- Superior sound insulation.
- More fireproof than wood-frame buildings.
- Straw, having limited nutritional value, is often burned to prepare fields for the next planting, adding to air-pollution levels. Building with the straw clears the air.

STRAWBALE CHALLENGES

- Not a project for an inexperienced do-it-yourselfer. Research capabilities and building skills are required.
- The typical strawbale wall uses 4 times the plaster of conventional framing, which has both time and cost implications. Plastering is labor-intensive.
- You really need to know the size of the rooms you need and the size of the strawbales available to correctly design a strawbale home. Many people go for the bare minimum sizes on their foundation,

and then get the bales installed only to discover that the rooms are now too small to accommodate their furnishings.

- Strawbales are not practical if you live outside a hundred miles of a reliable supply source.

STRAWBALE QUALITIES OF WHICH TO BE AWARE

- Strawbales should be uniform in density, meaning if you raise it up by one string, it should stay in a bale shape and not deform.

- Heavy objects like cabinets must be planned for in advance of the build to ensure adequate support is installed.

- Electrical installation is sometimes problematic with inspectors. Sigi uses Romex to address these concerns. Installing flexible chases through the walls allows pulling additional wires later.

- Plumbing should never be installed in an exterior strawbale wall. Or any exterior wall for that matter. If plumbing absolutely must happen on an outside wall, install a large "sleeve" to accommodate the plumbing and send any leaking water out to the plaster surface and away from the strawbale infill.

Sigi offers this tip,

> *"For strawbale construction: trim your strawbale walls before you plaster them. It is much much much faster to shave the walls than it is to even them out with loads of plaster. I use a weed whacker to trim walls. Some people use a chain saw. You can also use the trimming to shape your corners, like at this window jamb. You can see here that the jamb has been trimmed to a gentle curve, while the remaining wall is still fuzzy and ready for trimming."*

Depending on your design and the number of amenities, building with strawbales can dramatically reduce the cost of your home, while increasing its energy efficiency and decreasing its environmental impact. Strawbale structures in the southwest cost somewhere around $30 per square foot if self-built, and $120 per square foot if contractor-built. This is on-par with conventional building.

Sigi has loads more tips and tricks for strawbale at her Facebook fan page's photo album here

https://www.facebook.com/media/set/?set=a.529230460434449.120245.171782289512603

Stone

Wall Type:	Thermal Mass
Appropriate Climate:	All regions
Structural Capability:	Load-bearing
Suitable for Berm:	Yes
Natural:	Yes, but high embodied energy if quarried
Learning:	Easy
Doing:	Medium challenge
Engineering Required:	Possibly
Kit Available:	No

Stone can be dry- or mortar-stacked to form retaining walls, mortared to create walls, used as a floor covering, or even ground up to create gravel walks and your road. Stone is an excellent choice for a covering for the foundation for an elevated home, it can be used to create a beautiful chimney, and it is an ideal form of passive solar thermal interior wall to capture and retain the abundant free heat from the sun.

Figure 30. 800+ year old remnants of stone wall at Chaco Cultural Center

STONE PROS

- Will last forever.
- Extremely durable.
- Beautiful when done well.
- Can easily be collected on-site in some locations, or salvaged.

STONE CHALLENGES

- Stone is prohibitively expensive for most building projects for use as more than decoration.
- Stone usually requires engineering by an architect or structural engineer.
- Complex Code requirements.
- Can be dangerous for bumps, bruises, and knocks if not done well and plumb.

For these reasons, we will not be covering stone as more than a decorative material.

Using stones in shower walls makes for a lovely grotto-like effect, and you can even add little ledges to support small humidity-loving plants if you desire. We embed river rocks in circles or spirals in concrete or even sand at the base of our chain downspouts and in evaporative cooling ponds. River rock details are also beautiful details for rooms that you want to be able to wash down with a hose into a floor drain.

As with all non-renewable materials, we advocate the salvage of stone before all other means of harvesting. Salvaged stone is widely available, though you will likely be limited in your color choices.

While marble and granite are mined deep out of the earth, other stones, including sandstone, slate, and soapstone can be locally quarried without the destructive effects on the environment.

Concrete

Wall Type:	Thermal Mass
Appropriate Climate:	All regions
Structural Capability:	Load-bearing
Suitable for Berm:	Yes
Natural:	No
Learning:	Easy
Doing:	Easy, requires contractor for foundations and hillside applications in most cases.
Engineering Required:	Probably
Kit Available:	No

Concrete is widely used in construction because it is easy to install, durable, the least expensive, and the most common structural building material. It is has been used in various form since it was first used in Rome over 2,000 years ago. Different regions use it in different ways, but the main components are the same: an aggregate to hold it together, plus Portland cement, sand, and water. Shake it up, pour it out, and let it harden. Voila!

Admixtures can be added to make concrete more workable, help it dry more quickly, slow down setting in hot conditions, add colors, or resist freezing. Variations use different aggregates and some even use waste fly ash from coal production. Ask your supplier to use fly ash if using a waste product meets your values of doing something for the environment. The waste has to go somewhere, after all.

Concrete's strength comes from its water to cement ratio. An ideal ratio mix uses a weight of water between 45% to 60% the weight of cement. This also means that if you are making your own concrete, you need to have a reliable water source.

CONCRETE PROS

- Permanence and ease of installation.
- Strong.
- Vermin-proof.
- Thermal mass.
- Non-combustible.

CONCRETE CHALLENGES

- Weight = 150 lbs per cubic foot.
- Concrete does not work well in tension, so rebar is most often required.
- Concrete cures over its entire life and it uses up oxygen in the process. Because of this, concrete is considered by some to be unhealthy. Studies indicate that respiration speeds up for those living in buildings largely constructed of concrete because they are being deprived of oxygen.
- The Portland cement used to make concrete accounts for between 5 and 10% of the entire world's carbon dioxide emissions. To put that into perspective, for every pound of concrete we use, almost a full pound of CO_2 greenhouse gas is created.
- Additives in concrete deteriorate over time. In some areas the additives are or become radioactive.
- Wildfires sprinkle heavy metals onto concrete, which can be absorbed and transpired into the building.

Despite these concerns, concrete is just not a reasonable thing to take off our inventory of usable materials. Handle it well, make the right mix, and keep it sealed with good maintenance, and it will be long-lasting, easy to get permitted, and easy to care for.

Do not ever pour your concrete in freezing temperatures. Pouring concrete in light rain is of benefit, which may seem counter-intuitive, but water helps to cure the concrete more quickly.

ALTERNATIVE CEMENTS

Calera has developed an innovative method to produce concrete cements and aggregates. For every ton of their cement produced, their methods remove 1/2 ton of CO^2 from the air.

Hycrete has reportedly developed a method to permanently waterproof concrete, eliminating the use of petroleum-based membranes to protect underground installations at foundations and basements from moisture in the soil.

While we have not tested these materials, you might want to check products like these out and see if they are worth a try.

OTHER CONSIDERATIONS

If you require gravel for use in concrete, as the base for a foundation, as backfill, in your French drain system, or even in the floor of your root cellar, request recycled or reused gravel. It has to be cleaned to be sold.

If you have a basement, you are most likely going to have to have it poured for you because of Code considerations. If a contractor is required, look for a contractor that uses reusable forms made of aluminum or other reusable materials. Using reusable forms prevents more wood and plywood from being put into landfills. Often, aluminum forms are recycled.

Also, if you have a basement, and are in an area with a lower than 60° F average annual temperature; install rigid insulation under your floor slab and around the perimeter of the foundation. It makes a remarkable difference in reducing the cold and damp.

Use environmentally-friendly sealers in lieu of asphalts when you can.

Roofing

by Rachel Preston Prinz and Michael Curry

The roof system is shelter from the weather, simultaneously protecting us from and allowing us to harness the power of the rain, the heat, and the cold. The roof is one of the most important parts of the home for heating and cooling. In the not so distant past, when our buildings were not dependent on mechanical systems, our ancestors designed and built their buildings in direct response to their environment. Thus, in hot/arid areas, roofs were relatively flat and as small as possible to minimize heat gain. In hot areas with lots of humidity and rain, the roof was placed on a high wall and had an open ceiling with vents to move the heat away from the living space, and it was pitched to shed dew and rain. In cold climates, roofs were steeply pitched and therefore very large - to collect as much sun as possible, and people lived up in those open roof spaces because the heat would naturally rise and make warm places for sleeping in. About a third of the unwanted heat that enters a home comes through the roof because of house designs that do not take these old understandings into consideration.

The pitch of the roof determines the style of the building, and has an impact on selecting what materials should be used to cover the roof, as well as the shape of the interior spaces below it.

The roof has to carry its own dead weight, any weight of mechanical units or solar panels installed on it, plus the live loads of rain and wind and snow, and sometimes… people. Sometimes the roof has to be fire-resistant as well.

GENERAL ROOFING CRITERIA

Overhanging roofs protect your walls by diverting the rain and sun. Shallower overhangs are better for hot and dry conditions, as they minimize heat gain from the roof itself, and large overhangs and wrap-around porches are better for hot/humid conditions where heat venting and shade are major thermal factors.

For best performance, install a medium to dark-toned roof for maximum solar gain in cold climates.

Use a solar-reflective or light colored roof in hot climates for as much heat dissipation as possible.

Be sure to install a drip edge at eaves and rakes in humid, rainy, and snowy climates especially. Install ice flashing at the roof's edge in icy climates.

Installing solar panels on south-facing roofs also provides roof shading and thus, cooling during heated periods, thereby reducing the thermal loading on the house.

VENTILATION

While it may seem intuitive to build the tightest roof possible, in fact, many roofs require some ventilation to keep moisture from building up in them, especially in hot/humid locations. Vent your roofs at the wall line and ridge if using a pitched roof.

GUTTERS AND DOWNSPOUTS

For the best roof design possible, install a gutter and drainage system that moves the water to a minimum distance of five feet away from the foundation if you are not harvesting your rainwater.

Gutters should be a minimum of 4 inches wide and 3 inches deep to make sure the water gets away from the roof and eaves. Gutter hangers should be spaced on 3 foot centers. To keep snow and ice from claiming your gutters, locate them so the front face of the gutter is 1/2" below the roofline. Gutters should be installed at a slope of 1/4 inch of rise to 10 feet of run.

If you live in an area with more than 60" of snowfall per year, use snow guards on the roof and heat tape in your gutters to prevent ice damming and it is potentially damaging structural impacts. Hint: Provide a switch for your heat tape to make turning it on and off easy!

Another interesting aspect of gutters is pest-proofing them. We learned from some of our interviews that evidently mice love to run up greywater collection gutters, and you can hear their little feet pitter-pattering all the way. Stuffing the openings at the ends of gutters and downspouts with a minimum of 2" of steel wool seems to help.

Another option for downspouts are rain chains. These beautiful Japanese-influenced features are beautiful and ideal details to use for directing water to a mindfully-designed landscape.

Figure 35. Rain Chain

When using rain chains or scuppers and *canales* that drop water directly onto the ground, that water can be harvested through a French drain system or can be allowed to recharge the area where it falls. Many people will use a small contained gravel bed on the ground to minimize erosion. The Puebloan people here in New Mexico have a unique means of protecting the side of the building where the water is allowed to fall. They take a large piece of flagstone, usually at least 2 feet wide and 2 feet tall, and lean it up against the building. This catches the water backsplash and prevents erosion of the earth plaster finish on the building. I love the look of this detail, and want to evolve the idea for my own home... I want to make a full-height decorative salvaged tile mosaic on the building at these locations for aesthetic effect as well as finish protection.

Interestingly, the Puebloans also believe that water is a living element/being, so they do not capture the water. They may encourage it to flow to ponds, so it has a home, but they believe the water should be allowed to flow freely, and they do not try and trap the water for themselves, and especially not in cisterns where it cannot "breathe". This approach encourages water to recharge the aquifer.

Earthship Roofing Considerations

The original Earthships utilized low-pitched and sometimes earth-sheltered roofs. Many used a double-pitched "teacup" roof with a break in the roof plane near the glazed windows so that more sunlight can come in. This roof style is a double failure of design that exacerbates overheating and leads to roof leaks. The problems inherent in the dual-pitch roof design can easily be remedied by a single-pitch roof, utilizing overhangs, and abandoning the angled glazing in favor of straight vertical glazing.

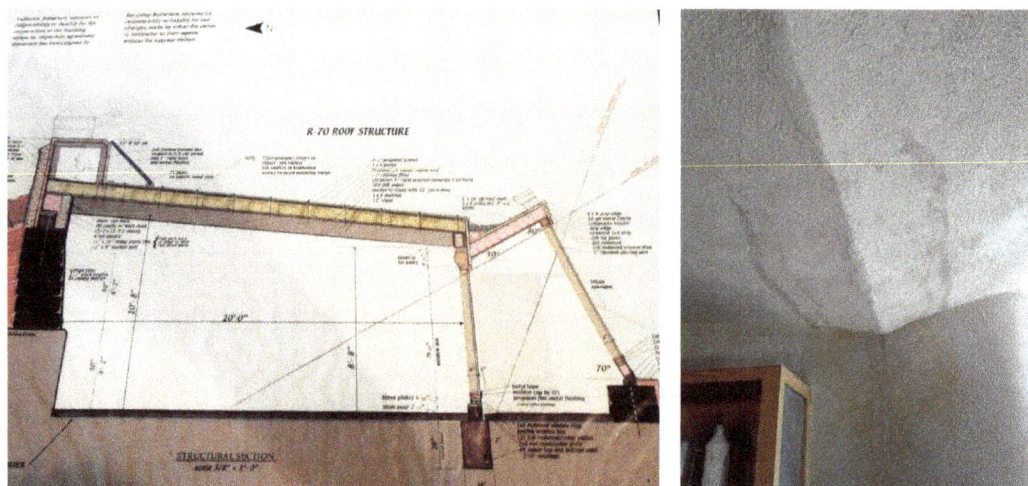

Figure 31. Earthship Teacup Roof Section and Leak Detail
Drawing on left publicly available at Greater World Visitor's Center.
(Details obscured to protect their work.)

Roof Structure

Roof structures support the weight of the roofing membrane, decking, ceiling, snow, and rain. If you are planning a green roof or a roof deck, you will need to account for the dead loads of the green roof system or walking surface, and the live load of people on the deck.

Pre-engineered roof trusses can be an economical roof, attic floor, and upper floor ceiling structure all in one. Roof trusses can span up to 100 feet.

The typical maximum spans for various roof structure materials are similar to those we offered in the floor framing chart, but we recommend that you consult with your local building department, lumber supplier, or structural engineer to give you a safe and serviceable floor or roof structure.

Flat Roofs

A flat roof is a bit of a misnomer. A flat roof actually pitches a minimum of 1/4" per foot, up to a pitch of 3:12 (3 inches down per 12 inches over). This shape can be achieved by pitching the actual roof members (the easiest way) or by tapering the insulation beneath the roof covering (the more expensive way, but you get flat ceilings inside). Flat roofs can be constructed of vigas (round beams), beams, joists, flat trusses, or concrete slabs.

The water collected from a flat roof needs to be held in place so that it can evaporate, or it needs to be moved elsewhere to prevent ice damming and water buildup. This means integral gutters, which are part of the roof/wall system, or *canales*/scuppers should be used.

One thing that many people do not realize… while you can use snow as insulation in places where there is lots of snow and the temperature does not freeze and then thaw so much, as in northern latitudes of the U.S. and Canada… if you live in a place where it snows, and melts and snows again, like the lower latitudes in New Mexico, you really want to shovel the snow off your flat roof so those freeze/thaw cycles do not cause the water to expand and contract into the seams and ruin your roof! A flat roof really wants to use continuous membrane roofing like EPDM to keep water from penetrating the roofing system. A flat roof does NOT want to utilize foam insulation in Taos. Those roofs fail here. Rigid insulation board is fine.

Flat roofs can be useful, too... field shelters in southern Italy use flat roofs for drying crops. The same is true here in New Mexico where some people dry herbs and chiles on their roofs. How can you use your roof to accentuate the performance of your home?

Pitched Roofs

Pitched roofs with a slope of 4:12 to 12:12 (a 45 degree angle) make rainwater collection easier. The amount of roofing material required increases with a higher pitch in order to cover the attic space beneath, so these roofs cost substantially more. In cold and hot/humid climates where these roofs perform superior to flat roofs, this is well worth the expense.

A pitched roof is most often formed from trusses, timber frame, or rafters and purlins.

Pitched roofs are suitable for any roofing material except membrane roofing, which will not look right.

Gutters and downspouts are essential in pitched roof design to get water away from walls.

Metal flashing is used at valleys, ridges, eaves (overhangs on a flat wall), rakes (overhangs at a gable), and around roof openings, including plumbing vents, skylights, and chimneys. Flashing should be sheet metal type if it is exposed, and it should have expansion joints. Not all metals are compatible with roofing materials, however, and it is critical to be sure that whatever flashing you use works chemically with the neighboring materials.

Roofing Types

While many people look to performance, appearance, and ease of installation when they choose their roofing material, the choice of material is especially critical if you intend to harvest your rainwater, and even more so if you intend to use that water for drinking.

Asphalt, tar, and some metals will leach toxins into the water, so be mindful if you intend to collect rainwater when choosing roofing systems. Also, all of these systems come from non-renewable resources.

When ordering roofing, you will need to order in what the industry calls "squares". It is a really simple calculation, just take the number of square feet you need, and divide by 100. So if your home is 2,000 square feet, your roof may be 2,400 square feet... so, you will want to order 24 squares.

BUILT-UP

Built-up tar and gravel, most often used on flat roofs, are not recommended. These roofs are toxic, full of VOCs, and use more non-renewable materials than you can count.

ASPHALT SHINGLES

Asphalt shingles, used on flat and shallow pitched roofs, consist of a fiberglass or paper mat coated with petroleum asphalt and topped with mineral granules that provide UV protection. While these are one of the least expensive roofing materials, they are less beautiful, require more maintenance, and they are not good for any roof that is used for rainwater collection. The shingles can also blow off from time to time, so an annual walk-around is recommended.

FIBER-CEMENT SHINGLES

Fiber-cement shingles are made with wood pulp and cement. The wood pulp used is a remnant from paper and other wood manufacturing processes, but increased demand has created a need for a vast supply, thereby exacerbating the draw on the non-rapidly renewable resources of wood. These shingles are durable and fireproof, but also brittle, and they can shatter in hail or lightning strikes. They can also blow off in the wind. Fiber-cement roofing is not a good resource for rainwater harvesting.

EPDM/TPO – RUBBER POLYMER ROOFING

EPDM is dark grey toned single-ply elastomeric membrane roofing specifically designed for flat roofs and pond liners. It is made up of a chemically derived rubber polymer made through the polymerization of ethylene and propylene in combination with ethylidene norbornene. EPDM mimics the best of natural rubber's performance, with a long-lasting, nearly waterproof finish that is made chemically, thereby reducing the use of natural rubber sources which are not rapidly renewable. EPDM is a suitable option for flat roofs in cold climates. EPDM is reportedly suitable material for rainwater collection as it is specifically designed for water retention and minimal chemical reaction. EPDM is rated for a 30 year life, though 40+ years performance is common.

TPO is a two-component single-ply white membrane roofing made of EPDM and a thermoplastic polyolefin such as polypropylene. TPO uses heat welding at its seams. TPO is a suitable material for flat roofs in warm and hot climates because of its heat reflection qualities. TPO may be suitable for rainwater harvesting. TPO is rated for a 20 year life.

EPDM and TPO can contain some recycled content, though they cannot be recycled themselves yet. They are reusable if they were originally mechanically fastened and/or ballasted with rounded gravels. They contain petrochemicals, encouraging continued dependence on these resources, and chemically derived rubber polymers, which support the chemical industry. While these systems are reportedly better performing in areas of acidic rains, ozones, and high UV radiation, we are skeptical of using rubber polymers on roofs used for rainwater harvesting due to chemical concerns, and due to their susceptibility to punctures.

WOOD SHINGLES

Wood shingles and shakes are a lovely and traditional roofing material. They are readily available and many installers are used to using them. The sleek shingles and rustic shakes are abundant, though the wood they use is a non-rapidly renewable resource. They are expensive and are not suitable (and often banned) in places where there are forest or wildfire hazards. Many permitting authorities require they be treated with fire-retardants. Wood shingles and shakes are not good for rainwater harvesting, as they can leach molds, algaes, fire retardants, and preservatives into the rainwater.

Choose FSC-approved shakes and shingles to minimize the impact on the environment.

Early Japanese builders often placed stones on wood shingles to prevent the wind from blowing them off. This technique was also used by the Puebloan people of New Mexico when tarpaper roofing was introduced. This is a cultural response to a real need - to stabilize roofing that wants to blow off. How does your local culture respond to architecture's less-than-ideal performance? What tips and tricks can you borrow to make your home work better for you, and seem of its place?

METAL ROOFING

Metal roofing comes in tiles, panels, and shingles. The most common metal roofing materials are steel, copper, and aluminum. These are lightweight, durable, and fire-resistant. Though, metal is a non-renewable resource, and mining and manufacture requires a huge amount of energy. Most metal roofing products are recycled and recyclable, though some coatings are not ideal for rainwater harvesting. A metal roof can easily last more than 40 years with minimal maintenance. Galvalume© is a common preferred brand of metal galvanized roofing which has a minimal chemical impact. Metal roofs that are painted should use a non-toxic paint process if rainwater collection is desired.

Standing seam metal roofs are an excellent choice for rainwater harvesting. A standing seam roof is constructed of interlocking panels that run vertically from the roof's ridge to the eave. The interlocking seam where two panels join together is raised above the roof's flat surface, allowing water to run off without seeping between panels.

SLATE ROOFING

Slate roofs can easily last a hundred years. When they are removed, they are entirely recyclable with minimal rework.

The roof support required for a heavy slate roof is substantial. Ideally it will be timber frame or heavy-duty framing, and most likely you will need a structural engineer or architect to design the structure.

Use local resources to minimize the transport costs.

Slate roofing tiles are mined from a non-renewable resource, and are quite expensive, costing upwards of $15 per square foot.

Using salvaged slate from restoration projects minimizes the environmental impact of using this incredibly durable and benign product. Slate is ideal for rainwater harvesting as long as it is kept clean. This roof is essentially maintenance-free.

CLAY TILES

Clay tiles come from an abundant though non-renewable resource, and they require some energy to fire and transport. Clay roofs are excellent for rainwater harvesting. Tile roofs are moderately expensive and can easily last 50 years or more. They are especially suited to hot climates.

One advantage of slate and clay tile roofs is that they do not deteriorate.

CONCRETE TILES

Fashioned to mimic clay, concrete tiles are less expensive by up to 30%. They contain up to 25% Portland cement, but are otherwise environmentally benign. A special clay and concrete ratio is required if you live in a cool climate in order to minimize freeze-thaw reactions. A concrete tile roof can easily last 50 years or more.

Both concrete and clay tiles are heavy, so look to local manufacturers to minimize the cost of transport. You will probably want to work with an architect or engineer to size your roof framing. Tiles are durable and fireproof, but are also brittle, and can shatter in hail or lightning strikes.

STONE ROOFS

In the Mediterranean, it is common to find buildings with roof structures built of drylaid stone, like those in the buildings called *trulli* found in the Itria Valley in Italy. These buildings' roofs are constructed similarly to an earthbag roof, with each layer of structure overhanging the one below until a conical roof shape is formed. In fact, the Italian word *trulli* derives from the Greek word for cupola, a building shape many here in the U.S. are familiar with from our Victorian tradition.

The roof formed by this method is called a drystone corbelled, or keystone, vault. The area these buildings are most often found is one in which the majority of the rain comes during the winter, and it is quickly wicked away by a dry soil into a limestone aquifer below. Local settlers must collect the water if they want to use it, else it will run off and not be accessible again without a deep well.

It is important to understand that a stone roof CAN work if done correctly, but it needs the right climate to work. That climate is warm and relatively dry, and soils should also be quick-wicking and not retain moisture. The walls of these structures are built in three layers, an inner and outer layer for aesthetics and structure, and an infill of rubble. The use of an inner and outer layer - the outer sloping slightly downward - is typical on roofs.

This building style prevents thermal overheating by breaking up the plane of the materials and preventing thermal bridges, as well as wicking any water which collects on the outside layer away from the innermost layers. An application of lime plaster on the interior of the walls and roof minimizes drafts. The arched design of the roofs makes these homes challenging to heat, as the heat is trapped in the ceiling. Because of over-humidification in winter, these homes are often left open even during the cold to try and wick out the moisture that forms on the wall surfaces.

Hopefully this explanation helps to illustrate that good design and design for climate are critical for a stone roofing structure.

ALTERNATIVE ROOFS

Recycled plastic and tire roofing shingles are available; however there are more questions than answers on the efficacy of as well as the polluting qualities of these products. They offer a 40-50 year warranty in many cases.

Other common alternative roofing types include bamboo, eelgrass, heather, palm leaf, and reed. These roofs can last anywhere from 30 (heather) to 200 years (eelgrass). Using these types of natural roofing systems is ideal in areas where the technique is common practice. Local custom and tradition should be followed to get the most lifespan for these materials.

Oliver Swann's Natural Homes blog has a great page of resources and videos about these and other natural roofing materials at http://naturalhomes.org/natural-building-roof.htm

THATCH ROOFING

As with strawbale, our advice for people considering thatch roofing is thus: if it grows where you are, it is a good thing to use, whether it be straw thatch in the British Isles, or palm or tiki thatch in the tropics. Your environment will support the use of local natural materials and the cost of transport will be minimized. However, there are not always good thatch installers in areas outside of England, Mexico, or the Islands… so just be aware and follow the industry best practices.

The three major types of reed used in European style hatching are: water reed, wheat, and straw. Water reed is imported from Eastern Europe in most cases and can last up to 50 years. Wheat lasts 25-30 years and straw lasts 15-25 years. Both wheat and straw are locally available in most locations. Importing, though providing a better product, requires both time and huge amounts of energy in transport.

Tiki thatch for tropical areas lasts 5-6 years.

THATCH ROOFING PROS

- Colors will fade after one year usually, making the house seem "of it is place".
- Minimal use of readily renewable natural resources, after the primary use has been fulfilled.
- After removal, thatch can be composted.
- Labor-intensive, and requires a lot of brute strength.
- When thatch is a traditional material in your area, using it supports the local economy.
- Superb temperature and sound insulation quality
- High roof pitches allow the capture of usable space beneath.
- Excellent for covering strangely shaped buildings, allowing for more creative freedom.

- Natural mosses will grow on the thatch and absorb water. This is not a bad thing, and it is pretty.
- Performs superbly in hot environments, providing ample shade.
- Integration – you can also use thatch to make rugs, umbrellas, and other decorations.
- Nearly hurricane-proof.

THATCH ROOFING CHALLENGES

- Challenging to install unless you know what you are doing.
- Cost and time up to 60% more than traditional roofing.
- Vulnerability to fire = higher insurance premiums. Plaster over the underside of the roof is common. Many modern thatch roofs, like on the Globe Theater in London, are for effect only, and just sit on top of a standard modern roof. Fire retardant is an option if you are inclined to use chemicals. Expensive fire alarms are required in thatch-roofed houses in most European locations.
- Repair cost can be extremely expensive.
- Maintenance: blown-on debris and fallen leaves must be removed from the roof every season, and the thatch itself will decay over time.
- The ridgeline must be re-ridged every 15 years, and the first several inches of the overall roofing replaced every 20-30 years, at a cost of approximately $40,000.
- Thatch should not be used in humid environments without ample wind to dry out the fronds.
- Pitch of roof must be 45 degrees minimum to promote water runoff.
- Trees should be kept away from the structure, without overhanging it, and absolutely must not brush against it.
- Critters.
- You might have to net over the thatch to prevent bird infiltration, depending on location.

GREEN ROOFS

Green, or sod, roofs are a multi-layered system of insulation, waterproofing, root barriers, drainage, lightweight soil or sod, and plants. Green roofs serve several purposes, including absorbing rainwater, creating a habitat for wildlife, and they help to lower air temperatures and combat the heat island effect in urban environments when they are kept irrigated.

There are several universally-accepted methods for constructing a green roof. One is built on top of a rubberized surface, another is built on top of a slate roof, and the last uses regional variations of the true earthen ceiling of *latillas* (decking) and *vigas* (beams) with 24 inches or more of soil atop that we find on Hispanic Period haciendas and the Native American pit-houses and kivas throughout New Mexico. The first two methods are ideal for humid environments, and the last method is ideally suited for an arid environment.

Green roofs require irrigation if you want to keep them green. That is okay unless you live in an area that freezes. A green roof is not a good insulator, so they are less "useful" as a roofing system in areas where it is very cold.

Pitched green roofs can be of nearly flat to slight pitch. Pitching allows for the use of simpler roof base materials due to water shedding.

Because green roofs are extremely heavy, structural engineering of the roofing structure is most likely going to be required. A local architect or structural engineer can design the perfect green roof for your needs.

INTENSIVE GREEN ROOFS, sometimes called roof gardens, require a 12 inch depth of soil as well as irrigation, feeding, and regular maintenance. Intensive roofs can grow anything from kitchen herbs to shrubs and small trees and may appear as if they are part of your lawn or garden.

EXTENSIVE GREEN ROOFS are virtually self-sustaining and require only a minimum of maintenance, perhaps a once-yearly weeding or an application of slow-release fertilizer. These roof types are not suited to constant walking or play. They can be established on a thin layer of specially formulated soil, and can easily support a planting of sedums and mosses.

GREEN ROOF PROS

- They can be beautiful - planted with fruits, vegetables, wildflowers, herbs, and grasses, and the final result can be a vibrant habitat for birds, butterflies, and other small animals.
- Reduce heating and cooling costs
- Provide usable outdoor space when installed correctly.
- If you happen to live in a city, green roofs will dramatically cool the area around your home!
- Adding rooftop ponds provides excellent option for greywater treatment. These require additional structure though so be sure to consult an engineer or architect to help you size the roof joists.
- Reduces stormwater run-off – capturing up to 74% of rainwater.
- Filters pollutants and carbon dioxide out of the air.
- Insulating for sound: soil helps block lower frequencies and plants block higher frequencies.
- Reduce heating loads by adding mass and thermal resistance.
- Reduce cooling loads by evaporative cooling.

GREEN ROOF CHALLENGES

- Green roofs are expensive – costing up to $24 per square foot, compared with $10 per square foot for conventional roofs.
- Required maintenance cost and time.
- Do not always work well in windy places, unless small wind-resistant plant species are used.
- Multi-layered = multiple resources, multiple trades, and multiple transportation costs.
- Green roofs work best on low slope applications – somewhat limiting the design.
- Are not ideal for rainwater harvesting because the plants need the water. This limits the amount of water directed to the cistern.
- Use of fertilizers is common.
- Require complex drainage systems.
- Differentiated growth – not all green roofs work well on north sides of pitched roofs (in northern hemisphere).
- Weight – these roofs are substantial and require larger structures (and therefore more structural design and installation cost) to support them. Not ideal in seismic regions.
- Green roofs have more moisture and a higher hydrostatic head than standard roofs, making it challenging to prevent water infiltration into the building and resulting condensation issues
- When you get a leak, it is going to cost a lot to locate and repair it.

TIPS FOR GREEN ROOFS:
- Borrow an idea from the north-eastern SaltBox style of building - slope the roof to the north and bury that in ground to shed cold northern winds.
- Plant a green roof with native species only to minimize water use and loss.
- Poor design = non-functioning roof. Be sure your architect or builder knows what they are doing. Check references! I learned this the hard way (by working for an architect that implied he knew what he was doing and did not) that you cannot "fake it until you make it" on green roof design. The client had to install nearly $50,000 in detailed modifications to get the *award winning green design's* roof to work correctly. The architect insisted it was not his fault as he was following "industry standard best practices," and the Owner was left with the burden of the cost and time lost for reinstallation.

GREEN ROOF PLANTS

For the best appearance, use super-tough and drought-tolerant plants, with both coarse and fine textures. Provide dramatic effect with color bursts interspersed throughout the greenery.

In the U.S. Southwest, you might try: echinocactus grusonii cactus (a friend told us these are available in bulk at egyptian-german agricultural company); nassella tenuissima grass; salvia clevelandii violet sage; sedum rupestre angelina groundcover; sedum spurium burgandy florets; sempervium hen and chicks; agastache rugosa violet hummy flowers; helictotrichon sempervirens bluegrass

THE EASIEST GREEN ROOF IN THE WORLD

In the Northwest U.S. and southern Canada, where epiphytes - plants that do not have roots, like moss - grow naturally, a traditional roof can be installed and made into a green roof. Simply collect a sampling of mosses from around the area and spread this "starter kit" on your roof. Lichens and more moss will follow!

Doors and Windows

Door and window openings in exterior walls serve a structural function: they transfer the load of the wall and roof above to the sides of the door or window so the door does not get squished and the glass does not break. Doors and windows directly impact daylighting and heat loss or gain.

Most window and door frames today are factory-built to a manufacturer's standard sizing. Knowing the rough opening size of your units before your build is critical for framing their openings correctly.

For framing door and window openings, a good rule of thumb for header spans is to use doubled members in a distance in feet less than the depth in inches of the wood framing member. So, use 2x6s to frame the head for up a 6 foot opening, doubled 2x8s for up to an 8 foot opening, doubled 2x10s for up to a 10 foot opening, and doubled 2x12s for up to a 12 foot opening.

Using insulating glass and weather-stripping controls heat and air transfer. Doors and windows must be carefully detailed to prevent thermal bridging. A precast concrete or stone sill offers the longest-lasting and easiest to install and maintain sill for exterior wall openings.

If your home is going to have a training or tour function or use volunteers for the build, consider commercial-grade doors and hardware on public spaces like a the main guest bath, front and back doors, and any workrooms or kitchens. These heavy-duty products can withstand being opened and closed repeatedly, are built to a higher performance standard with better materials, and will give you the best performance.

Visit our Doors and Windows into the World Pinterest Board for inspiration for awesome doors and windows!

Doors

Security, use, view, light, and ventilation requirements can determine the size and type of door used for an opening. Using 7 foot tall doors in lieu of the standard 6'-8" doors gives the feeling of more spaciousness.

The front door assembly at the Greater World Visitor's Center, while beautiful, exacerbates issues in design, construction, and upkeep for less-than-seasoned carpenters. Using a beautiful salvaged wood exterior door and a salvaged operable transom and sidelights may be a better option for unseasoned carpenters.

An R-5 or better rated insulated exterior door should be used at all exterior wall penetrations, including at the garage. Screens are a functional and welcome addition to exterior doors, especially in locations where doors and windows are opened up regularly for ventilation in good weather. Exterior doors should be weather-tight when closed, meaning they should be installed square and with full weather-stripping. Doors should be kept closed and locked to maintain the best thermal performance.

Figure 32. Visitor's Center Entry

Whatever doors you choose to go with, we strongly recommend not using rounded windows or doors, or homemade doors; unless you are an expert carpenter and can easily repair them.

One of the most important roles of interior doors is to provide sound privacy. Another important role may be in allowing light or air to penetrate an interior space. A frosted glass door is a great way to get light into a space while also ensuring privacy.

DOOR SWINGS AND OPERATIONS

A typical swing door, which can open from 45 degrees to 180 degrees depending on the hinge used, is often the most acoustically private and weatherproof door. They are also the easiest to operate.

Sliding doors provide a lot of light but they sacrifice insulation value and they are only are functional over half of their width. Half of the "door" is a giant leaky window, in most cases, unless you go with a higher end model that is ideally not made of aluminum or other metals. A clad-wood sliding door is a better option, as these use standard French doors as sliders, providing long term durability and better thermal performance as well as a more beautiful finish.

Folding and accordion doors open all the way to the edges of the opening, but are acoustically and thermally lacking, rendering them only really a good option for storage spaces.

Barn doors have the benefits of sliding doors except the entire opening can be utilized. They do not always provide great acoustic or thermal insulation value, but they are great for quiet space uses like closets and rooms without a need for privacy like dining rooms.

Pocket doors function in much the same way as barn doors, except the door slides into the wall rather than in front of it. The use of pocket doors may be limited by mechanical, electrical, or plumbing runs in the walls.

DOOR TYPES AND GRADES

Standard door types include flush, panel, French, full glass, sash (part glass), louvered, screen, and Dutch (two part).

The grade of the door panel determines how it can be finished. Premium finish doors can have a transparent or natural finish, Good doors can have a stained or painted finish, and Sound doors have to use two coats of paint.

Some doors can be pre-ordered pre-fitted and machined for hinges and locks.

Fire-rated doors usually have a mineral core and they can slow fires down for up to an hour and a half.

Acoustic doors, which offer unparalleled privacy, require additional thresholds, stops, and gaskets to make them super tight.

HARDWARE

Choosing door hardware can be more complex than one might expect. There is a difference between exterior door hardware, which is more sturdy, forgiving, and secure, and interior hardware, which is designed for ease of use and is not built for exposure to thermal variations.

When we choose hardware for our clients' homes, we always use lever-type handles, as knobs are harder to open when our hands are full, or for the little ones and older people who might not have a great sense of grasp.

When ordering a door or hardware, you will need to understand the idea of "handing". Doors are considered left-handed or right-handed. To determine the handing, face the door as if you are entering a room. If the hinge is on the left, the door is left-handed. If the hinge is on the right, the door is right-handed. If the door opens towards you, it is whatever hand it is, and "reversed". Some lever-type handles are positionable in either the left-hand or the right-hand configuration.

For exterior doors and garage doors, you will most likely want to choose a "keyed entry" function. This has a keyed entry on the exterior, and a thumb turn lock or a keyed lock on the interior. In most cases, you will want to add a deadbolt for added security. Many homeowners choose a "handle set" for their exterior doors, which has a more formal and beautiful appearance than a standard lever, and it is usually coordinated with a deadbolt.

Most homeowners find that for interior closet and hallway doors, they want what is called a "passage function". This means the handle you grab just opens the door, with no locks or function, per se. A "privacy lock" door handle has a push or turn button lock on the inside of the room, and is most often used for baths and bedrooms. For offices, you might want to consider what is called a "free entrance lockset" for better security, which allows you to exit the room at any time, and use a key to lock the door from the outside.

When locating hardware for a door, the bottom hinge wants to be no lower than 10 inches above the finished floor, and the top hinge no higher than 5 inches below the top of the door. The centerline of the lockset wants to be at 40 inches above the floor and the deadbolt at 48 inches or below. If you locate the backset hole for the door knob at 2-3/4 inches instead of the standard 2-3/8 inches, your knuckles will thank you!

Our designer Shannon Matteson reminds us, "Don't forget about forgotten hardware! Aged, tarnished, salvaged metal holds such wonder and it can be incorporated into bathrooms, kitchens, on doors, and in laundry areas."

Windows

Windows sizes and locations are subject to the Building Code, which may dictate the amount of area required for a window - especially if the window is an emergency exit from a bedroom - as well as how much natural light and ventilation is required, and how much wind resistance is required.

Windows can be fixed type (picture windows), casement (opening sideways), awning (transoms and greenhouses), sliding, pivoting, or, the ones most people know: double-hung. One thing that many people do not realize is that a true double-hung window opens at the bottom and at the top. The window opening is a critical component for naturally controlling air movement through a space.

Windows, in almost every circumstance, should be operable. Double-hung windows are the easiest to operate and to fit for blinds, but casement and awning windows are useful for capturing breezes if you know where to put them. On the South, East, and West sides, use low-emissivity or Low-E glass and shade the windows on the outside walls with 2' deep overhangs or shading devices, covered porches, awnings, trees, trellises, or pergolas, unless you live in a cold climate with temperatures that rarely reach above 75°F.

Always try to have windows on two walls of the room for effective ventilation. Ideally, the openings should be on opposite walls. If you only have one exterior wall in a space, put two windows in the exterior wall and one out to a hallway for improved lighting and natural ventilation. Beveled sashes on window frames allow a wider angle of sunlight to penetrate the space without an increase in the window size.

While wood is a precious commodity and its use should be carefully considered, cheap vinyl, aluminum, and fiberglass window frames are not sustainable. They use large numbers of resources, require additional inputs of energies in their preparation, are poor performers in thermal efficiency, and do not have great lifespans. I personally love old wooden windows and new versions of them when I can find them. However, that is my inner romantic preservationist talking. In our office, we almost always call for clad-wood windows, which have wood on the interior and a recycled content metal covering on the exterior. Clad-wood windows last 50 years or more with minimal maintenance and can be ordered in nearly any color you can dream of. They are amazing.

While many Earthships are designed with single-pane glass, presumably for heat gain, you really want to try and use insulated glass windows if at all possible, unless you are in a very mild climate that requires no heating or cooling. This will help to prevent the overheating caused by the long window wall's taking on too much sun. The air sealed between the two layers of glass in insulated windows acts in the same way as the insulation you put in the walls around your home. That pocket of air, which is sometimes infused with gasses like argon or krypton for better performance, acts as an insulating barrier and helps improve thermal comfort on the interior.

TIPS FOR GREAT WINDOW DESIGN AND AFFORDABILITY:

- Do not design for more windows than you actually need. They are expensive and make the mechanical system have to work harder. Refer to the Passive Solar Design section for limitations on window percentages in relation to floor area that may be helpful in planning.
- Do not skimp on quality windows. Cheap windows cost more in heating and cooling, and maintenance, and you will have to replace them twice as often.
- Use Low-E National Fenestration Rating Council (NFRC) rated windows with a U value of 0.35 or lower.
- Use EnergyStar rated windows and make sure windows are rated for your climate.

Buy a window at a price point and with a warranty that you can feel good about. I personally love Jeld-Wen© clad-wood windows because they are well-built, I have had great customer service, and many past clients love their windows. They are a bit more expensive, but I believe they are worth the investment. Serious© brand fiberglass windows are a high performance alternative window which uses no wood, no formaldehydes, and no metals. For super-tight assemblies (and super expensive windows), the window of choice for PassivHaus designer Joaquin Karcher of Taos is made by Indus©.

In New Mexico, we also use carved wooden or iron security bars on most of our windows. Part of this is cultural – building windows here have always been covered this way. The other benefit of this technique is that it provides security when home is opened up to achieve natural ventilation, which can be done for up to six months a year.

GLASS EMBODIED ENERGY

The glass industry has minimized virgin material use, however the glass manufacturing and coating process uses high levels of energy to heat and process the raw materials used in fabrication, which can include metals, heavy metals, and silica. Glass is relatively heavy to ship and requires significant amounts of packaging, increasing energy required for transportation. Toxins are produced from the distillation of heavy metals and chemicals used in the bonding process for some glass coatings. Mono- and di-organotins used in the manufacture of Low-E glass have been linked to some of the toxic issues related to pesticide and biocides. Films used on glazing are petroleum-based and generate air and water pollution in their production, and they often contain metals and chemicals. Argon gas, which is used for insulating between window panes, can escape over time but this does not significantly degrade window performance. Some insulating glass units remain sealed longer than others. Glass coatings make recycling more difficult, as coatings reduce the ability of glass to fuse into another usable product.

WINDOW FRAME EMBODIED ENERGY AND BEST PRACTICES

Wood frame materials use the least energy of the four major types of window framing materials (wood, aluminum, PVC, and vinyl-clad-wood), with aluminum windows and vinyl-clad-wood using the most resources. Wood products should be finished with low- or no-VOC finishes to prevent formaldehyde off-gassing. The extraction of aluminum-bearing ores and petroleum for PVC products, along with the processing for production, create air and water pollutants, some of which we are only now beginning to understand (i.e. dioxins produced during the PVC production process, as well as after disposal.) Vinyl-clad and PVC frames will off-gas over time, including small amounts of vinyl chloride, a known carcinogen in humans. Vinyl, especially when colored, tends to turn brittle and discolor over 5-10 years. PVC does not have a consistent recycling system in place anywhere in the country and, therefore, ends up in landfills 98% of the time. Because PVC products contain so many additives to enhance performance, they are generally difficult to recycle. Aluminum, if coated with high-grade finishes, will not discolor. Aluminum can be continually recycled, even if coated.

Chapter VIII

Rooms, Spaces, Colors, & Textures

by Rachel Preston Prinz and Shannon Matteson

"Do not keep anything in your home that you do not know to be useful or believe to be beautiful."
– William Morris

Create an Efficient Floorplan

Many of us who wish to live in a truly sustainable way know that the first thing to do to achieve that is to look at the idea of living smaller. Some of us even dream of moving into a "tiny house". The reality is though... that we can really only live as small as we, well... live. Moving from a 2,500 square foot home to a 200 square foot home sounds exciting, but many people who have attempted it have found that living "tiny" does not always end up being a realistic way to live for the long term.

On the other side of that, sometimes we have spaces in our homes that hardly ever get used – formal living and dining rooms are great examples. These are places where we can cut square footage relatively easily. By combining a living room, dining room, and kitchen into a "great room", we can easily shave up to 500 square feet from the size of the building we need.

When we walked through the visioning process in the earlier part of this book, the result was a personalized list of the places and spaces you want and need for your ideal home. Here is when we put those ideas into practice!

Most people, when they cull down to all the things they really want in a space as we did when we went through the From Vision to Reality assessment, will find that they would love to live in something between 500 and 1,500 square feet, depending on their specific values and ideals.

Previous Page: Figure 33. Beautiful Earth Plaster Detail at Carole Crews Workshop Site

Starting Small

Vitruvius celebrated the idea of places that were designed exactly as they needed to be to serve their purpose well. He called this idea "commodity".

Frank Lloyd Wright embraced this "less is more" philosophy in his Usonian Houses too. They had neither basements nor attics, and every inch of available space was used wisely, with built-in casework providing a great deal of storage in a small, finely detailed, urban footprint.

In the Hispanic period here in New Mexico, many homes started as only one or two rooms. When a child was born, or a daughter or son got married, another room could be added. This might be a way to start thinking about your build - maybe start really small with only a room or two, but plan to add more space later. Using the tips from Planning Ahead for Additions section may be of help in this.

Another option we would like to encourage is to look at our houses, especially Earthship-inspired ones, as ships. Maybe it is my bias showing, as I have always wanted to live in a houseboat, and I have sailed in some great ships that inspired me about getting creative with space... but for me, the lessons learned while being aboard have been instrumental about teaching me how I could live small. My folks upgrading their RV helped me to formulate even more of a plan for living with a small footprint. What do these modern "ships" do that we can harness in our designs? A ship or an RV will often use a built-in bench at a table or desk in lieu of chairs, in order to have a dependable seating space that minimizes space use. Where we need nearly 30 inches of space to move a chair around, with a bench, we only need to be able to get between it and the table. Ships and RVs are designed with storage in mind. Every available space, no matter how small, is used. Beds are often set up in berths, or bunks, in smaller than usual spaces in order to minimize space and share body heat. Kitchens are smaller, but open, and their work area is often part of the hallways accessing other spaces. (If this space is too small, though, it can create traffic jams.) Uses are stacked – a desk is a table is a bed, and appliances are minimized. True live-aboard models have baths with decent sized showers. Their portals and windows offer lots of natural light but can be easily sealed, as well as blacked out for privacy and darkness. There are hanging closets for work clothes. Plenty of drawer and cabinet space... All these techniques help ships and RVs to perform well for the long-term. We can borrow these techniques for our homes.

The most important tip we can offer about making an efficient floorplan is to remember that area (square footage) and volume are related. The more of each of those we have, the more... well, everything... required. Minimizing our footprint is great. Creating happy little hobbit homes instead of oversized soaring spaces is better. A "comfy" home space is psychologically-pleasing, uses less fuel to heat and cool, is easier to ventilate naturally, requires less time and effort in maintenance, and costs less to build.

Please feel free to peruse our Magic Cottages Pinterest Board for lots of Ideas of how to do small wonderfully.

Easy Spaces

Most Earthships are poorly designed from an ergonomic point of view. Some of the spaces are too large, some are way too small, some are awkward, strange places have steps, and the buildings can be... just... limiting.

We believe that freedom of movement is a right everyone should have. So we plan for everything to be on one level If at all possible... for a tub's edge to be no higher than someone could easily sit down on and turn around to get into, for instance. Our toilet areas are big enough to have grab bars added. We put the framing for grab bars in every bathroom we do, whether it is needed now or not. Because adding a few bolts and screws later is much easier than removing and replacing a wall. All of our doors are three feet wide. Because everyone will get sick or hurt sometime, and with an entire generation of aging boomers needing reliable housing, we want them to be as able and comfortable in their own homes as possible, for as long as possible. Just like when we put tube skylights into every closet so you do not have to flip a switch to get ready in the morning or find the clamp in the dark when a busted hose is pouring out water: we plan on minimizing how much we have to work (or pay the utilities) to be at home in our spaces. It is just good design. So we plan ahead, and make our homes ready for the worst case scenario, because you do not want to be paying thousands of dollars in doctor bills and then have to afford a major renovation to the place that was supposed to be your forever home. This idea is called Universal Design and we will talk much more about in an upcoming section.

Figure 34. This stair is too tight and using winders limits usability.

TIPS FOR MAXIMIZING SPACE USE:

- Halls or stairways can double as galleries and libraries!
- A landing can be a reading nook!
- A laundry can be a mudroom!
- Stairs make a great place to install drawers and bookcases!
- Remove formal spaces and merge rooms!
- Bring in the outdoors! Build lots of porches and decks! Use French doors, Nano© Doors, or Jeld-Wen's© new folding patio doors to open a living room or dining room to the outside.
- Reveal the structure!
- Use color to create drama!
- If you have a big family or like to share meals with friends, you might want to tie your kitchen and dining together with either a kitchen bar or a dividing wall (really awesome designs double as storage) with an extra wide top that can be used for a buffet. This is also a great way to have people help in the preparation of meals together.
- Use bookshelves along the northern interior walls of your interior. Books act as insulation. They help keep the cold from seeping into the space.
- Use benches! Make them 24 inches deep for a little extra space, put storage below, and you will love them!

One tip we have found helps people with imagining their space layout once the exterior walls are up: before you start building interior walls, use chalk on the floor to indicate where each piece of furniture is going to be, and adjust accordingly, so you can be comfortable!

What about All My Stuff?

Making the commitment and moving into a smaller home can be an exciting, as well as emotional challenge. Having a strategy and process in place for your stuff can help you to accomplish a peaceful, fulfilling transition.

You can create a beautiful interior with the things you love! Follow this simple, golden rule while making decisions about what to surround yourself with:

Seek out beauty and meaning in everything, then embrace and display it.

Don't be afraid to look in unusual places, to hunt, gather, reshuffle, and reuse. Open your eyes to your history, adventures, nature and dreams. Inspiration can come from the most peculiar and unexpected places!

Remember your home is not a showroom and your space moving forward will be well planned, but limited. As you go through the process of identifying what you love and find to be beautiful, you may find an enormous pile of stuff that you think has to move into your dwelling. At that point you most likely will feel overwhelmed and maybe a little discouraged. You just have to shake it off and start the elimination process by combining the first golden rule with these steps; carefully prepared by Peter Welsh, Professional Organizer and author of It's All Too Much:

1. THINK IT THROUGH. For each room, think about what's particular to that room in terms of the stuff that needs to be in it, the stuff that tends to accumulate in it, and how you're going to approach the task.

2. SET IT UP. Figure out the function for the room and establish zones for the different activities that take place in the room. Figure out what does not belong in the room and discard it.

3. MAKE IT HAPPEN. This is the action plan that will help you to make your vision for the space a reality.

For most people, outer order contributes to inner calm. It will take a bit of energy and discipline to accomplish the de-accumulation of stuff, but the results will be infinitely rewarding.

Living Simply with Less

by Rachel Preston Prinz and Maggie Schlarb

My friend Maggie Schlarb is an extraordinary woman who has spent the majority of the past three years camping while traveling around the world with her husband and raising their son Felix. I have been struck by how well they made their tiny-style life on the road work. I asked her if I could pick her brain on living light, so I could share her tips and tricks for making this lifestyle great with our readers, especially those who might be camping during the build, or considering a tiny house with limited or no mechanical, electrical, and plumbing. Here is that conversation.

How did you guys end up spending three years basically camping and living on the road?

When I first met my husband, he was in the Air Force and living a regimented lifestyle that lead us to become serious weekend warriors just so that we could feel as though we were really living life. I'd have the car packed and ready Friday afternoon so that as soon as my husband got home, we could drive 3-6 hours to go adventure, camp, and play in the mountains. It was fun, yet it brought us to think about what we wanted the rest of our lives together to look like. When my husband was deployed to Iraq 3 months after our son was born, we realized that that lifestyle wasn't going to work for us and we started to work towards saving up a stash of cash so we could go and travel for a year. That is how we came to our first adventure. Once we were done with our year of travelling North America and New Zealand, we landed in Montana for a short period of time, and before we knew it we were planning on getting rid of more stuff and taking another adventure together. I guess you can say we ended up spending so much time travelling and camping because it got to us…the sense of adventure, living with less, exploring more and enjoying rich experiences became addictive.

The majority of our readers are considering small and natural homes for their next homes. They intend to build these homes themselves which means living on-site in a camper or a tent in most cases during the build, and then living small and sometimes way off-grid (maybe not even having a potty or shower) when they do finally move in. What lessons did you learn that can help them be comfortable? How did you manage the day-to-day of eating, drinking water, clothing, living in a van, not having a place to pee? How'd you adapt? Did you figure out any "rules" you needed to live by?

I learned a lot to let go of expectations of how I thought life on the road was going to look like. The more I let go and let the adventure in, I was able to enjoy myself and the experience more. I also learned what it takes for me to feel 'home'. While most of the feeling of 'home' comes from within me, there were a few little things… a small laminated collage, a few pictures and some colorful flags… that came along on the journey to create a space of comfort and a sense of 'home'.

One of the things I became grateful for while travelling was, and still is, warm running water. I would often warm a small pot of water to have a washcloth bath and sometimes I would boil lots of water and pour it into a big tub mixed with freezing cold creek water so my son could have a bath. As for drinking water, we would make sure to fill up our bottles, especially if we knew we would not be near potable water for a few days.

As for eating, we still ate really well. We would go to the grocery store as a family and buy exactly what we needed to cook for our meals. This way of eating was more economical than how we shop due to having more space now.

For each adventure we would narrow down our clothing to what we thought we absolutely needed (and even then we brought more than enough). What I loved about only having a backpack of clothing was I never even considered I had 'nothing to wear'. I picked out clothing that all mingled well with each other, I didn't spend much time choosing what I would wear each day and I always was comfortable, and stylish too.

As for the toilet, I got over my stage fright of going to the bathroom in public places. Let's just say that I've gone pee in places that I never thought I would! When you've gotta go, you've gotta go!

The biggest 'rule' that kept the family happy was and still is keeping what my mother would call a 'tidy ship'. When everything is organized, a small space like a tent or a campervan doesn't feel so small after all. For 3 weeks of our

VW campervan tour we had 3 adults and 1 child sharing the space – surprisingly, as long as everything was organized, we didn't feel cramped.

What did living in small spaces and on the move teach you about living?

The four main things living in small spaces and on the move taught me:

- Life's about the journey… enjoy each moment. Life is way too short to worry about material things or even what people judge about you – because they will judge you. Good and bad judgments, just let them do that and not let it affect you.

- Having less is more… way more. Life is to be experienced through living and enjoying the beauty of our earth. Life is not about buying stuff and owning stuff – stuff in my opinion can really weigh you down – literally and figuratively.

- A tidy ship is a happy ship. As long as the 'stuff' is organized and tidy, it allows for more ease in the adventure of the unknown of living on the road, and living in small spaces.

- How to create community wherever I may be. I now consider myself to be great at meeting new people and creating fast and long-term friendships.

What aspects of living on the road have you imported into life now that you are back to having a home base?

Seeking the adventure in every moment. Taking the time to talk to strangers, hear their stories and their history. I now do a better job at checking in with myself when I want to buy something. I usually don't buy it right away, I wait, sleep on it and now I buy less stuff. It's ok to get dirty…and it can be fun too. Being open to whatever adventure arises. Creating community and long lasting friendships. AND… I REALLY enjoy my hot showers and washing dishes with warm water – more than I ever thought I would!

I love Maggie's attitude and hope her reflections and lessons from the road will help you to enjoy the time and space you have during and after your build!

Other Interior Considerations

ROOM SHAPES

The shape of a room will have an effect on the perceptions of as well as the use of that room.

Acute Angles and Triangle Shaped Rooms

We recommend not creating spaces that utilize acute angles. Those spaces squeeze people psychologically, in the most uncomfortable ways. In one build we visited in Taos, a designer used a hogan/octagonal/beehive shape for their home, which rendered every interior space a triangle shape. There is no room in this house where anything makes sense, and trying to use the space or find a way to fit something big – say a bed – into a trapezoid or triangle shape can be super frustrating. Plus, acute angles have been shown in psychology experiments to make people a little crazy. That is why Frank Gehry uses them - to titillate you and take you off balance a little so you will look around and up and down to see everything he is got to show you. It is also why it is said that maintenance teams hate these buildings – the buildings are a pain to keep clean. Vacuums do not fit into acute angled corners and all the weird shapes collect massive amounts of dirt and grime, so every cleaning task becomes a custom, tedious, job. When you are trying to use a space, acute angles leave you feeling crunched.

Issues with Round spaces and Domes

As people who built the earliest U-shaped room Earthships found out rather quickly that round spaces are awesome for giving you a cave-like feeling, but awkward to try to fit furnishings into. You either need to live with things falling into gaps, custom make everything, or aim for the straightest walls you can make happen.

Because of this, and the 15% additional cost of rounded walls, we save round rooms for one special room of the house that we can use as a sacred space of sorts - they make a good living room, a meditation room, or master bathroom. We might top the space with a rounded dome, or more often, a reciprocal roof, which is a self-supporting viga-framed pitched roof.

Contributor Sigi Koko points out that:

Figure 35. Reciprocal Roof

> *"The framing concept for this roof is simple...each rafter rests on its neighbor, which effectively locks all of the framing together into a kind of circular truss. The size of each rafter depends on the span and the weight of the roofing. The oculus at the peak can have a skylight or a cupola, or simply be roofed over."*

We prefer the reciprocal roof because domed roofs are almost impossible to cover with natural materials and make last. A reciprocal roof has many planes instead of a dome to cover, has an integral skylight opening that is easy to take advantage of, and can be much more easily covered with standard metal, tile, or slate roofing. Another option for a self-supporting round roof is a compression roof.

On that note, domed ceilings and round rooms tend to have acoustical issues. This is not an ideal space for privacy or loud-noise uses, as the sound will bounce around the space and be amplified. So consider the use of the space and subsequently the materials you use when building a round room. Aim for the most porous materials and softest fabrics possible in decorating these spaces.

VIEWS

Use natural lighting and views at the ends of corridors and in places you want to direct people to go, like installing a skylight in front of the bathroom door if there is no exterior wall there to offer a view from. As anyone who has driven at night knows, we will look into the oncoming headlights for no apparent reason. People are drawn towards light. Encourage guests to go where you want them to with strategic natural lighting and great views!

SIZE AND ROOM PLACEMENT

> *"Our beds are empty two-thirds of the time. Our living rooms are empty seven-eighths of the time. Our office buildings are empty one-half of the time. It's time we gave this some thought."*
>
> - Bucky Fuller

Deciding where we put our rooms and how big they should be is a challenging task. Different people have lots of different ideas about spaces. There are some great rules of thumb we can borrow from design around the world though, as the underlying patterns of great design seem to cross national, cultural, and emotional boundaries. For the most effective design, we take in the ideas of passive solar, and combine them with using the sun to accentuate our tasks, and derive a formula for room location that works for us.

BEST PRACTICES FOR ROOM LOCATIONS

	NW	N	NE	E	SE	S	SW	W
Bedrooms		Y	Y	Y	Y	Y	Y	
Living					Y	Y	Y	Y
Dining				Y	Y	Y	Y	Y
Kitchen				Y	Y	Y	Y	
Library	Y	Y	Y					
Laundry	Y	Y	Y					
Play					Y	Y	Y	Y
Laundry & Drying					Y	Y	Y	Y
Bathrooms	Y	Y	Y	Y	Y	Y	Y	Y
Utility	Y	Y	Y					
Garage	Y	Y	Y	Y			Y	Y
Workshop	Y	Y	Y					
Terraces				Y	Y	Y	Y	Y
Sun Porch					Y	Y	Y	Y

Entrance

The door, the place where life enters and becomes part of the space, is considered holy in almost every culture. What that means depends on the culture and time period, but there is almost always some attention paid to the qualities of being inviting, but secure, and providing a safe place to wait for the owner to get to the door. The front door will often bestow a silent message about the people who live there, as in the case of the Mezuzah on Jewish homes, and in the many layers of jamb details on a Buddhist stupa, which represent the path of the soul through the layers of reality. We can use careful attention to detail to make our front door a special place for us and our visitors too!

Builders years ago knew it was nearly impossible to stop wind-driven rain from getting past doors. That is one reason large covered porches and vestibules are common on old homes. Put covered porches over your exterior doors if you live in a rainy or snowy place and you will be happy you did! Do not locate the door on the north side of the house if you live in a climate where there is a tendency for ice or snow, as it will most likely be coming from this direction and pile up high. Also, when there is shade, there is cold, which means north porches are harder to keep cleared of snow. We also want to elevate the entrance in snowy climates, with the entry and steps up to it fully covered by a roof if we want to maximize solar gain and minimize maintenance, de-icing, and shovelling.

When designing a covered porch at the entrance of your home, do not slope the roof towards the sidewalk. If there is a long shed roof without a gutter at your entrance, for instance, either add a gutter or add a gable over the steps or sidewalk to keep rainwater from landing on you as well as minimize slipping on ice at these steps. Porches in hot/humid climates and anywhere you will be entertaining should always be extra deep - 10 feet deep is ideal.

The next entrance related idea we want to share starts with a common Feng Shui practice, but it is really just great design... we want to be sure not to have the front and back door facing each other on either side of the home without some sort of wall break between them, because the good energy and fresh air will shoot right through the house, and you will lose out on the healing benefits! While a long corridor with natural light on each end is great for views, it is not great for creating a space where air moves throughout the many spaces.

Back in the days of yore, in the deep South as well as in New Mexico, it was not uncommon to paint the ceiling of the covered entrance in a light blue, and either to paint clouds or stars on that in white. This whimsical paint scheme creates a lovely, welcoming, and playful effect at front entrances, and it also bounces more light into the covered space, so these areas are not so dark. We can borrow from that, and use a blue or lightly colored ceiling in exterior spaces that can benefit from a little more bounced light.

Figure 36. Dado and Window Trim

Another trick we can learn from our Hispanic heritage is to use what is called a *dado*, or double-color wall. The bottom half is medium earth toned or darker for wearability, and the top half of the wall is painted white with lime plaster. This also bounces light into the entrance where it can be useful for detailed tasks like unlocking doors. The earlier New Mexicans extended this idea to wrap the dado decoratively around windows and doors, creating a stunningly beautiful, simple, aesthetic affect.

When designing an entrance, be sure to have a large coat closet somewhere in your entrance space. For us, we try to have a mudroom near the garage or at the front door to store coats, hats, scarves, gloves, dog leashes... so we are always ready to pop outside but can do so without tracking our stuff, and mud, through the house!

Courtyards

A central courtyard has been a core component of great design in hot climates for many millennia, and this natural cooling technique is used everywhere from Nigeria to Rome to South America. Oftentimes, these courtyards are shaded by the buildings to the East, West, and South, and include a water feature – a pond or fountain – which acts like a swamp cooler, using the combination of shade, breezes caused by the shade, and evaporative cooling from the water source to provide natural cooling. The water does not just serve to cool the space, it also serves to cycle the water in the cistern which is usually included as part of the courtyard for security reasons. (An invader or controlling entity cannot cut off your water if they cannot get to it.) This keeps your stored water fresh and clean. In this case, this courtyard is called an *impluvium*.

Figure 37. Courtyard at Los Poblanos Culture Center
by Architect John Gaw Meem

A covered walkway around the courtyard can make accessing different spaces quite easy in warm climates, and will help to naturally control the amount of heat in and around your buildings. In cooler climates, it is not uncommon to enclose the exterior walkway with low knee-walls and large windows to capture the sun's radiation and maximize warmth in winter. If your walkway is open, you can use vines along the posts of the northern and eastern section of the covered walkway to shade the walk from summer sun.

Figure 42. Amazing Exterior Living Space by Edge Architects of Taos

One of the best courtyard arrangements we have ever seen is not really a courtyard at all. Edge Architects in Taos created a world-class exterior living area out on the mesa for a world-renown photographer whose home we covered in one of our magazine articles. Basically, they built a long and deep *portale,* or covered porch, that ran from north to south beside a modern home. This portale was closed to the west, only opening with a few small windows with shutters on them, and a heavy double wooden door that looks as if it once belonged to a temple in India. This puts the structure of the portale, that heavy wall, with its "back" facing west to shed to brutal hot summer winds. This wall becomes the main entrance of the home, and once entering the door, opens an entirely different world to our experience. The east wall is non-existent, but is implied by an arcade formed from columns that match the elaborately detailed door on the west. This non-wall frames the most extraordinary views of Taos Mountain. The covered space is deep enough for a dining table that could expand almost without limits, as well as lounge-type seating areas. It is as if Edge's design team wanted to create a wrap-around porch feel in the desert. The space is exquisite. We love using this deep porch, with its summer shading and wind-diminishing effect, as part of our extended indoor/outdoor living space, so we will locate ours off the main living space and perhaps enclose the end section like a sleeping porch.

Hallways & Hidden Hallways

The best home designs shorten or eliminate hallways, especially the invisible "hidden hallways." A hidden hallway is the path through a room to a closet, bath, desk, or other destination. This space is unusable for functions other than a walkway. When we are reviewing floorplans, we color directly on the plans to highlight the hidden hallways in a 3 foot wide swath through the house. That way we can make sure we have maximized usable space. Paying for space you cannot use is not in keeping with the ideals of sustainability. This can eat up your budget for the things that do serve you.

Living Room

What makes a great living room for you? For me, it is the ability to comfortably seat four adults, and squeeze in 6 for special occasions. In my home, I get that from either a combination of two couches, or a big sofa and several large, comfy chairs. My ideal living room has a central fireplace and a large coffee table so everyone who comes over can share food or make crafts together. People can easily come and go from anywhere they sit, without bothering other people to get around. They can even sit on the floor in front of a spot on a couch or chair if they want, or lay down in front of the fire. Currently, to achieve this, I have two sofas put together in the shape of an L. There is a dining room table converted to a coffee table in front of both couches, and I have two feet of walking space between the couches and the table. I love this arrangement. It takes up a space 14 feet by fourteen feet square. Thus, this is my base living room size.

One the most common examples of hidden hallways happens in the living room, when you pass through the main sitting area where the couch is to go to another room. This kind of setup may be more functional in certain applications where you have to work with what is built, but for our designs we believe we can do it better. There is no sense of destination in a living room set up like this because there is a constant flowing energy like a river running through it from all the passing through it that gets done. A living room intended for really living in wants to have 2 couches or a couch and two chairs that share equal access to the fire, either by having the couches set parallel to each other on either side of the fire or by being set perpendicular to each other. Ideally, this space becomes a "sitting area" rather than a pass-through area.

One of the most important tips we can offer in regard to living room design is not to locate a fireplace or stove in a corner of a room. A fire can be a place of destination and it should heat up as much space as possible. Locating a fireplace in the center of a wall rather than the corner allows the heat to be more evenly distributed. This also creates a larger space for more of the family to enjoy time together in front of the fire.

Dining Rooms

Dining rooms are one of the least often used rooms in a house these days. When they are used, they tend to be enjoyed most often in the evenings. Because of that, if you have a formal dining room, place it with an eye to the best views, and with a western view if possible so you can use the light from sunset as a paintbrush for your meal and time with family and friends.

A dining room might not want to be the most prominent room, and they can often be integrated into a family room or kitchen space to minimize the building footprint.

Great Room

A great room merges a living room, a kitchen, and a family room into one larger than normal space.

If the kitchen is attached to the living room, a great trick to use to separate those spaces more formally is to use a high-backed counter between them so the dishes can be "tucked away" and the bar space can be used for food prep, flowers, sculptures, and art.

The next evolution of this, which we borrow here from Frank Lloyd Wright, offers some sense of visual, sound, and room separation. Use a centrally-located masonry fireplace to break up the space. It is easy to combine or "stack" uses in this feature, as well… locate the kitchen oven on one side of the mass, the fireplace opposite towards the living and/or dining space, locate a bar on floor cabinets between the kitchen and living space for serving, and utilize the mass of the fireplace as your passive solar thermal battery. One slightly longer line of masonry and you have handled four needs while offering a grounding and aesthetic feature for the space.

Kitchens and Baths

Kitchens and baths are probably the most important spaces in most people's homes. The kitchen plays a vital role in the social structure of a family - it is where we meet, talk, make plans, prepare foods, study, hang out, and get loud. It is often where we play, celebrate, and enjoy time with friends.

The bath is just as critical of a feature, but we expect it to offer the opposite benefits… this is where we want to find solace, sanctuary, and privacy. The bath is where we wash away the day and start anew.

There is a reason why the most renovated spaces in homes are kitchens and baths. They are the most expensive parts of a home to change, but when they do not work, you may find yourself making a big investment in trying to get them to. So great design in these spaces is where we aim. Both spaces require careful integration of mechanical, electrical, and plumbing systems and should be finished with materials that are durable, easy to clean, and sanitary.

In our research, the number one complaint people had regarding space use in their Earthship homes was feeling that they did not have enough kitchen or bathroom. The Earthships with half baths and half kitchens were disasters of organization and usefulness. We have a psychological need to feel safe in these spaces and to take our time doing what we need to do. For some, the moments of alone time in the bath are the only ones they get. For others, preparing food is a form of meditation or prayer. We cannot take time and enjoy the process of what we are doing when we are too crunched to function well. Or when there is not enough room to put our little one up on a step stool at the counter and show them how to knead the bread by doing it alongside them. So we plan for spaces that are reasonably sized. Borrowing from the ship model we offered earlier, reasonable size equates to a 30 square foot area for a kitchen. That would be considered a "tiny kitchen" to many people. That is okay. This is a just place to start.

We want to locate bathrooms, kitchens, and utility rooms in the same part of the house and against shared walls if possible. Stack them over each other if you have got multiple floors. Locate them near the mechanical room to minimize the length of plumbing runs, pump size, and the fuel required, or near the greenhouse if you straight-dump your greywater into planters. Locate your kitchen and utility room away from bedrooms to minimize noise impacts from appliances like dishwashers, washers, and dryers while sleeping.

Kitchens

The best designs for homes these days consider the kitchen as the heart of the home. Creating a central space to gather the family and share ideas, meals, and time together is awesome... and capturing the heat from appliances is a means of staying warmer with no additional energetic inputs is just good design.

One of the most effective ways to plan a kitchen is to locate the refrigerator, sink, and range in a triangle pattern, with two functions on one side of the aisle and another function opposite, so that you have one central space for doing most of the work of preparing food. This minimizes the size of the space you need as well as the amount of time you spend moving between these tasks. If you add the distances between each of these task centers, the total distance travelled between the three to prepare a meal should be less than 22 feet. Many people make the mistake of using a corner for this purpose. But the corner cuts the space you use in half. That sounds good at first, until you try to use the space and find yourself crunched. This is exacerbated when someone else comes into the space. By using the cross-aisle arrangement, comfort and ease are maximized, as is efficiency.

We recommend making the kitchen aisle a minimum of 42 inches wide to accommodate more than one person most comfortably.

One of our favorite tricks in kitchens is to use breakfast nooks (that do not project from the walls on the exterior if money is an issue) as study and/or office spaces. We just plan for benches on two sides of the space with storage underneath. Add a big table, some electrical outlets in the benches for laptops and speakers, and voila! We have created an instant home-base and homework station where we can keep an eye on the little ones and have conversations as a family while we make dinner. We love nooks that take the place of a dining room table and can seat 8 with additional chairs.

Figure 38. Inset dining nook by contributor Shannon Matteson

COUNTERS

Always leave yourself a little bit of open counter without wall cabinets above. That way you can access your mixer, a nice big pot of stew, or your coffeemaker without having to move them away from the wall cabinets. This also prevents the deterioration that commonly occurs at the wall cabinets caused by steam delaminating the paint or sealants. Using a heat-resistant surface on either side of the stove or range is ideal. The easiest-to-clean backsplash is one the goes up full height to the base of wall cabinets. Make sure to plan any window sills to be at least 4 inches above your counters to prevent back-splashing and minimize clean-up.

The countertop material you choose has a direct correlation to how much work it is to clean and maintain them.

TILE counters are cheap and easy to install. They are heat and cut-resistant and resist staining. Their porous grouts collect germs, however, and because of that, the grout is more difficult to keep clean. Tiles can often be had at a deep discount if you are willing to mix and match colors at salvage yards and places like Habitat ReStore. Reused tile options are also available from manufactures like Crossville and Fireclay. Reused or recycled tiles can cost $20 or more per square foot (PSF).

BUTCHER BLOCK counters are oftentimes made from reclaimed or recycled lumber. Others are harvested from beautiful lesser-known tree species that have been sustainably harvested. Butcher blocks can be made from slender lengths or end-grain blocks. Block is not heat-resistant and needs to be oiled regularly, and you really should not put hot things on it, so you only really want to use that in work areas. Maple cutting boards and countertops are naturally germ-resistant. These can cost $50 PSF.

STONE AND SYNTHETIC STONE counters are beautiful and last forever. They are more expensive, but well worth it for many homeowners. Many times, these counters can be had at a discount by using salvaged materials or cut-offs from big projects at stone yards. Seal stone counters for maximum durability. Granite can cost $35-$100 PSF.

STAINLESS counters, which some chefs and people who want to make products for sale will love, are oftentimes available used from restaurant supply stores! Stainless steel, a combination alloy of steel, chromium, and nickel designed to resist rust, is attractive for aesthetic and cleanliness reasons. Stainless can be easily cleaned with a stainless cleaner used once a week. Stainless counters can cost $40 PSF, and as much as $90 PSF.

SOLID SURFACE countertops like Corian brand are effective at resisting cuts and some stains. Corian is a solid surface material made from bauxite, an aluminum ore by-product, as well as oil by-products. It is easy to clean, and is mold- and bacteria-resistant, but its impact on the environment causes us to favor other alternatives. There is also a limited potential to contact with aluminum, which some believe is the cause of Alzheimer's disease. Solid surface countertops can cost $35-$100 PSF.

RICHLITE, PAPERSTONE, and similar products are made of postconsumer recycled cardboard, paper, cash money, and natural, non-petroleum, formaldehyde-free resins. They can be cut and shaped with standard woodworking tools. We recommend that you not use counters with aluminum, fly ash (a derivative of coal production), or Portland cement by-products if possible. Usually the only maintenance requirement for recycled composite countertops is a regular application of mineral oil. These countertops start at around $50 PSF.

RECYCLED GLASS countertops are made in much the same way as terrazzo and mosaics, and they offer great durability. Shards of recycled glass are set into a cement or resin base. These countertops can be integrally-colored or stained for more color. The downside of these is they can cost $50 PSF or more.

CABINETS

The amount of cabinet to design for is directly proportional to the amount of storage needed. A list of what needs to be stored can be a great asset here. Most cabinets are designed in standard factory dimensions based on 3 inch modules. For preliminary planning purposes, plan for a 32 inch wide sink, a 24 inch wide dishwasher, a 33 inch or 36 inch wide range, and a 32 inch wide refrigerator if you plan to use affordable, easily available options.

Designing the inside corners of cabinet intersections is critical, as we want to make sure that there is enough room for the door or drawer hardware on one side not to bang into the cabinet beside it. One great modern option for kitchen cabinets is to pull-out drawers with heavy-duty full-extension hardware so you can eliminate back-breaking searches for the top to that whatchamacallit.

In our experience, the easiest and most affordable coordinated kitchens are made by Ikea. These kitchen systems are designed to an extremely high standard for sustainability and durability which are far more comprehensive than that of U.S. warehouse and building stores. They have lots of style options and finishes as well. While their products are notoriously challenging to put together, we have found that even a semi-skilled installer can make quick work of putting together these beautiful kitchens.

Use exterior-grade plywood for hand-made custom cabinets and shelving. Exterior plywood uses phenolic waterproof resins that off-gas one-tenth as much as interior plywood, which typically uses urea-formaldehyde glue.

APPLIANCES

We will go into great detail about choosing household appliances in the Electrical section of the Mechanical Systems chapter a bit later. Household appliances can be major sources of unintentional heat gain. Can you put your refrigerator, clothes dryer, dishwasher, water heater, and oven in the coolest part of your home? That usually is in the north or along a west wall. Use appliances like a dishwasher and laundry in the morning or late evening to minimize the impact of heat during the summer, and make more warmth when you need it in the winter. Now is a great time to lose your crockpot and invest in a pressure cooker, if you really want to cut down on your fuel use!

FLOORING

Kitchen flooring should be non-slip, durable, resistant to water and grease, and be easy to care for. We will get into available flooring options in the Finishes section in the next chapter.

PLUMBING

At the sink, a water supply line, a waste line for the sink and waste disposal, and supply and waste lines for a dishwasher (if used) are required. Skip including your kitchen sink in your greywater plan unless you plan to use and maintain a grease trap. (Ew!)

Low-flow kitchen faucets

A simple aerator can reduce the kitchen faucet flow rate from 4 gallons or more per minute to as low as 0.5 gallons per minute. However, you might want a bit more power for dishwashing and rinsing, so we recommend a 1 gallon per minute setting.

Recycled sinks

100% recycled steel sinks are available, though not as commonly as 60% recycled steel. They can also be prohibitively expensive. Cobre sells 100% recycled copper sinks, which are naturally anti-microbial! EnviroSLAB offers countertops with inline sinks made from 100% recycled glass and porcelain. These options are offered as a place to start in your search for the perfect sink.

LIGHTING AND ELECTRICAL

Provide ample daylighting on two sides of the kitchen if possible. Add a tube skylight if only one widow is provided, and you will love the effect of less glare and more even light distribution in the space.

Plan for area lighting for the overall kitchen space and plan for task lighting over each work area and above the sink.

A minimum of two grounded outlets for small appliances (at four feet apart except when the space is broken by a range or sink) should be provided. These should be located at least 6 inches above the countertop.

UNIVERSAL DESIGN FOR KITCHENS

To accommodate wheelchair-bound friends and family, we use cabinets that are 30 to 33 inches tall, make sure the sink is at least 26 inches high at the bottom, make the kitchen aisle a minimum of 5 feet wide, add front or front/side controls for the knobs and faucets, design the bottom of cabinets no less than 10 inches above the floor and with a 7 inch deep space beneath them for toes.

HERBS!

Another part of a great kitchen that we include in our designs is an exterior herb garden. We make this accessible through the kitchen itself, either by reaching through an opened low window or by walking out onto a patio.

Bathrooms

Bathrooms are one of the most important rooms of a home, because we spend so much time there. Most people's baths are more like afterthoughts than planned spaces, and we think that we can do better than that.

A bathroom wants to be a private, ample space. We do not open our baths at the ceiling. While this may be some means of getting the humidity of the bath into the greenhouse in old fashioned Earthship designs, we are far too concerned about privacy, especially for guests, than to do something where everyone knows exactly what you did while in there.

Staying on the topic of privacy, most people prefer to feel as if their heading to the loo is a private affair. So locating the guest bathroom off a hallway or off the kitchen instead of directly off the main living space is preferable. There are several reasons this works better... a bathroom door tends to be undercut so sound bounces out from under it on a hard floor. Locating the bath out of the main space reduces unwanted noise-induced knowledge of what people do in there. We also tend to like to "sneak off" to the bathroom, and it is more fun to "go refill my water" (or wine) while also popping in to the loo for a quick visit. Good design makes people feel more comfortable and less exposed, and thus... more happy and safe.

In Japan, the toilet and bath are sometimes separated on opposite corners of the home. This is not such a bad idea, because you can take a bath without being bothered by someone needing to use the one potty you have, if you only choose to have one. This idea is especially useful if you want to use a composting toilet or outhouse but still desire a fabulous bathtub space.

BATHROOM FINISHES

Finishes should be easy to clean, durable, and sanitary. We use non-slip tile or stone on our bathroom floors. We recommend a tile wainscot on the walls to a height of four or five feet above the floor for ease of cleaning and durability. I personally prefer non-glossy finishes like faux stone for my bathrooms... I like the rich color and texture and I think they show fewer small stains like waterspots. This means the house is easier to manage (and it helps me not freak out when I don't have time for a deep clean before guests arrive). I also try and stay away from unfinished stone and irregular rough surfaces with hard edges in the bathroom, and really throughout the home... I have really tender skin and am partially blind so my depth perception is really affected. If there is something I can brush against and hurt myself on, I will! For homes with little ones, aging adults, or grandparents around, thinking about this as you design is a really kind thing to do.

CABINETS

The typical base unit for a bathroom vanity is 30 inches high and 21 inches deep. For comfort and ease of use, the centerline of the sink wants to be 22 inches away from the closest vertical surface (wall). The toilet bowl and sink should be at least 26 inches apart at their centerlines.

Who says you have to use low cabinets in a bathroom? Are you tall and tired of bending over to brush your teeth? Use kitchen cabinets in a bath or see if your cabinet company makes a 34.5 inch high cabinet instead of the usual 30 inch high bath cabinet and make life a little easier on yourself!

The minimum width of bathroom vanity cabinets for daily use should be 36 inches. Bigger is better here. Add 6 inches for every male who shares the space and 12 inches for girls.

One of our favorite tricks for baths is used when toilets are included in the main body of the space. We locate a drawer cabinet unit within arm's reach of the toilet. This unit has three drawers – one regular vanity drawer at the top, and one drawer that is 16 inches wide by 10 inches tall over another drawer of the same size below. The upper (center) drawer holds 12 rolls of standard toilet paper and is always within reach of the person using the toilet. The drawer below keeps wipes, ointments, and girly products with easy reach.

SHOWERS AND BATHTUBS

One of the biggest mistakes we see in bathroom design is showers that are too small. One friend in particular designed himself a simple solar-heated shower using oversized blue water jugs propped on top of a framed shower enclosure right smack dab in the front greenhouse window of his tiny house Earthship. That was all he had for a bath. It might not have been so bad for privacy, since he lives way out there... but his girlfriend did not enjoy having to pee and poop in a bucket in front of him. So let's just decide from the outset that a private place to pee and poop is essential, even if it is no more than a half wall to squat behind.

But it was the 2 foot by 2 foot shower that caught my attention. I asked him if it was a plant watering station, because I did not "get" that it was a shower. It was SO small! Even though you can get small shower trays, they are not legal, or practical. Code requires shower stalls have a minimum inside dimension of 30 inches square. We prefer a shower 36 inches square or larger. One way you can decide the exact size for your shower is to design it based on the size of tiles you use, in order to minimize cutting.

Figure 39. Fabulous shower with river rock detail by architect Levi Romeo

If you use a standard tub dimension for your shower, and leave the one half of the side wall or glass open, and utilize a shower head on the opposite end from the opening, most likely you will not need a shower curtain or door on the shower.

Shower seats are luxurious and useful for shaving legs as well as washing critters and little ones! If you would like to use one, make sure your shower bench is the width of the shower, at least 16 inches deep and anywhere from 14 to 17 inches tall.

Forget about all those fancy shower devices! If you want dual shower heads, just install two faucets on opposite walls! The shower heads hit you from opposite directions. You may need an extra-large water heater if using double heads, so plan ahead! If you want one of those fancy rain-type shower heads but do not want to spend the money, just hang a galvanized steel bucket with the bottom pierced with holes under a highly placed shower head pipe. No need for a showerhead at all, and you will get an instant rain effect! One last item on showerheads: we bet that you will love a handheld shower head if you give it a try.

The backsplash for wall-mounted tubs and showers should be at least 6 feet tall and finished with a easily-cleaned, non-porous moisture-resistant material.

If you want to sculpt a tub like those you will find in many Earthships, be sure to finish the backrest and bottom of the tub with tile or river rocks, as the concrete tubs of yore "will rip your skin off" as one of our sources noted. Also, if you have an organic or undulating hand-built tub design, or have the access point high off the floor, consider adding handholds and footholds to make it easier to get in and out of.

My personal favorite bathtub is an old reused and restored cast iron clawfoot tub set on the floor. A tub should have 34 inches of clear space in front of it for easy access.

If steps are used in the bath, be sure they are slip-resistant, at least 3 feet wide, and more than a foot deep at the tread, so people with arm-fulls of kiddos or pets can easily navigate them. This is also a great technique to use for any single step in the home.

PLUMBING

Plumbing walls may need to be deeper in bathrooms to accommodate vents and plumbing lines. If space is an issue, look for fixtures that have one handle instead of separate hot and cold taps. A pedestal sink has a beautiful form but limited function. Everyone has stuff to store. Make a plan.

LIGHTING, ELECTRICAL, AND VENTILATION

Bathrooms require natural or mechanical ventilation by Code. That can be achieved through an operable window or skylight, or an exhaust fan, which should be located near the shower and on the opposite side of the space from the bathroom door. Be sure to add this device to your electrical loading plan, if you do not choose a solar powered one.

Lights are required in the bathroom, and not just one light will do for Code. If the toilet compartment is separate, it needs a light. The sink needs its own light, and the shower or tub requires a light. The light fixture over the tub should be bathroom-rated to prevent water vapor getting into the fixture. Outlets in bathrooms must be located outside of reach of the shower or tub, and they must be GFCI type per Code.

OTHER TIPS FOR A MORE SUSTAINABLE & MAINTAINABLE BATHROOM

- Say no to textures on finishes in this room. Simpler finishes are easier to clean.
- Use nylon shower curtains in lieu of vinyl.
- Use baking soda and hydrogen peroxide grout cleaner. Just let it set for 30 minutes before scrubbing and rinsing.
- Open windows or turn on the fan to vent baths for 20 minutes after a bath or shower.

UNIVERSAL DESIGN AND PUBLIC UNISEX BATHROOMS

To make a bathroom that is accommodating for everyone (and doubly so if the space will ever house a public function like parties, tours, or workshops...), use a 3 foot door, so people with crutches or in a wheelchair can use the space. Include a minimum 5 foot round empty space (5 foot is the spinning diameter of a wheelchair) and place the sink, toilet, and bathtub around the outside of that. Use a wall-mounted sink and make sure there is a 26 inch high clear space under it so wheelchair users can wheel up to the sink and use it. Add ADA-compliant hardware and include a floor drain in the center of the space with a beautiful cover on it. You may find that you will thank the Code for this requirement someday when you need to wash the skunked dog or dump buckets of mop water from some minor disaster and can hose the place down when you are finished. There may be other details you want to include in the bathroom and the rest of the house from the Universal Design section of this book.

EARTHSHIP-SPECIFIC BATHROOMS

In older Earthships, the shower/bath and toilets are elevated off the floor on steps to account for drainage. This creates a toe-stubbing and tripping hazard that is best avoided. The simple solution for this dilemma is to put a foundation around the bathroom as they have in the newest Global Model designs, and then have everything on one level on an inset tiled wood floor on framing. The key here is in getting the floors to meet up with less than a half-inch change in height between them.

The issues of bathrooms in Earthships can be further exacerbated when the bath is located along the south window wall. This appears to have been done to put the humidity where it might be needed - by the planters - but in practice it creates damaging conditions that erodes the materials on the window wall. This design exacerbates overheating and humidity issues. To solve this issue, locate baths in the main body of the house, preferably next to the kitchen to minimize plumbing, and vent them properly to meet Code.

Many of the bathrooms in Earthships are open at the top. That may offer cool plants hanging into the space but it also dramatically diminishes privacy in the one spot you are most likely to want it.

Bedrooms

We spend a great deal of our time in bedrooms when we want to find privacy in a space-minimized home, so the design of these spaces becomes more critical than if we are just sleeping there.

In our research, we often heard complaints of Earthship bedrooms being awkwardly designed, being either too large and seeming more like a living room, or being too small, and the walls of the built-in headboard too close to the storage/work wall behind it to use the space well. Other people commented on the inability to black out the natural light of the sun, as well as the moon. Still others found the bedrooms lacked adequate privacy.

BEDROOM SIZING

In guest and children's bedrooms, we recommend sizing for a queen bed as the baseline, plus 4 feet on two sides and 6 feet on one side so you can have a chair or desk in this space, presuming that the head of the bed is against a wall. If you do not have or want that kind of space (which allows the room to grow into other uses later), size the room for a twin bunk bed or full bed. Finally, place bedrooms, especially for children, where they can have access to natural light from the east, as the morning light can help them to start their day.

Designing the Master bedroom for a king bed plus 4 feet on two sides and 6 feet on one side allows enough room to have a chair or desk in this space. Make one side of the space have 6-8 feet between the bed and the wall if you plan to have a crib in the room.

BEDROOM WINDOW PLACEMENT

Locate bedroom window sills 30 inches above the floor so that desks or tables in front of them do not block their light or spill things into the window sill. Space windows 24 inches wider each side than the bed is wide to allow for end tables, and 12 inches or more away from the corners on the outside walls.

OTHER TIPS FOR BEDROOMS:

For the most acoustical privacy, we want to make sure that bedrooms do not open directly onto a great room or other public space, but off a hallway. We also want to be sure that bedrooms do not share mechanical vents with other public rooms or each other without sound dampers between them.

Avoid using computers, copiers, and printers in the bedroom as they produce lung irritants.

In cold climates, locate bedrooms along the south window wall so the room is naturally heated. Put the bed along this wall under a window and you have instant bed-warming!

Once upon a time, in pit-houses, at Chaco Canyon, and even the early Hispanic Period homes here in New Mexico, they would build spaces with quite short doors. Sometimes these spaces featured a hearth above the fireplace that acted as a storage space during the day while the food was cooking, and that was used as a raised and heated bed platform at night. Legends assert that our low doors were to keep marauding invaders at bay, but this design really did nothing to deter invaders. There were most likely functional aspects at play. Three potential explanations include: 1) some native people say the doors are short because their ancestors were short, 2) they were covering the openings with skins rather than doors, and 3) that they were using physics to keep the space warmer. Heat rises. We can see an example of the third explanation in hot air balloons - add hot air and off they go. Well, if you add hot air to a space and there is nowhere for it to escape, the hot air will slowly cool down over many hours and sink back to the ground. Coupled with the bed-warming fire heating up the massive thermal storage battery at the raised hearth, this design trick served the ancient people of New Mexico, and elsewhere, for centuries when they had no mechanical heating systems. We offer this here because it seems like a way we can start to think about using heat in alternative ways for our builds. If you have radiant floors already, why not we use them through the bed platform if it is built-in? Why not run a masonry heater or rocket stove flue underneath the bed platform? Or use beds on lofts in smaller spaces to maximize thermal comfort? Or place the bedrooms along the south wall so they are naturally heated through the day by the sun? And, we can use this same principle to naturally heat loft spaces. Just some food for thought...

Second Floors and Lofts

It is super easy to capture naturally-rising heat and use lofted spaces for warm libraries, tucked away bedrooms, and private "hideaways".

If you are building an upper story, remember to keep the shortest walls 4'-6" or taller above the floor if there is a slope on the ceiling, and verify that the minimum wall height in your area's Building Code is not even higher than that. If you are using the second floor with a pitched roof and ceiling, you might want to add shed dormers to make more standing room and bring light into the space. If you have knee walls in these spaces, (short walls at the roofline with space behind) use them for storage. Build a cupboard, shelves, bookcases, or drawers into this otherwise wasted space.

Storage

One of the biggest complaints we hear about Earthships is that there is no storage, or what is there is poorly planned and lit.

So, catalog what you own, identify where you want it to go, and figure out how much space is required to put it away. Then, design and provide ample storage and use task-lighting for places where you know you will need light.

Build cabinets, bookcases, and benches into rooms! A window with cabinets on each side makes a great space for a window seat! Make these at least 24 inches deep and put drawers beneath them!

Locate storage and pantries on the north side of the home where it will always be cool.

Laundry Room

TIPS FOR A SUCCESSFUL LAUNDRY ROOM:

- Do not skimp on appliances. A new model washer and dryer will outperform an old model, and save you electricity and/or gas in the process.
- Plan lots of storage.
- Plan for more than one light. Multiple locations of bright light can take a laundry room from blah to wow.
- Plan for at least a tube skylight and/or an operable window so you do not have to flip a switch to use the space and so you can vent out humidity and odors if needed.
- A tile floor stands up to high traffic and is easy to clean.
- Do not be afraid of color in your laundry room. A place that feels more like a space and less like an afterthought is psychologically easier to keep clean and organized.

- Do not be afraid to use a sheet of shiny new corrugated aluminum around the front of your water heater if it is exposed. Leave room for venting at the back, but this little trick will bounce light throughout the space and make it look more modern.

- Install a hideaway wall-mounted ironing board and outlet next to it to maximize usable space.

- Paint unfinished concrete or CMU walls to make them easier to dust. Just seal the wall first.

- Make a movable folding table out of a vanity cabinet, a piece of extra countertop, and casters.

- Trim your windows and door, even in utility and mechanical spaces. This is less about aesthetics than it is about good insulation from air and sound. This also helps prevent over-humidification by isolating the humidity from the washer and the heat from the dryer from the main living space.

- Use your washer and dryer in the evening to make the best use of their creation of heat and humidity when it is least likely to cause a negative effect. Open the utility room door if you want to capture the heat and humidity.

- If a lack of humidity is common in your climate, one way you can introduce humidity into the home is to place the washer in the main body of the home. Many people choose to install an under-counter unit in their kitchen for this purpose.

Garage

The garage can act as the storage spot for your car, your stuff, and your workroom. It can be a totally passive place where things get put, or an active place where things get done. Knowing which of those you prefer is a key to designing it well for the long term.

In almost every environment, the garage is best placed on the west, so that it can buffer the heat from the house during the hottest part of the day. If you live in a snowy area, it is often best to face the driveway and doors to the south for maximum solar heating and melting. Using a commercial glass garage door will allow you to use passive solar gain to heat the space in temperate areas where insulation is less of a requirement. You will want to slope the driveway away from the garage at a 1% slope to keep water and snow out.

Use operable windows on opposite sides of the garage to get good cross-ventilation so that the room is not hot or stale, especially in hot/humid climates. This also provides light for this typically dark room.

A garage wants to be at least 22 feet deep (in the direction the cars go in). It should be at least 16 feet wide with a 10 foot door for a single car, and at least 22 feet wide with a minimum 18 foot wide door for two cars. That gives you enough room to walk around and have some stuff, but no room for cabinets or a workspace. If you want cabinets or a workspace, add another 4 feet to whichever side you want to storage to go. (2 feet for the cabinets and 2 feet for you). If you would like to install cabinets along one side of your garage, locate the window sill no lower than 40 inches above the finished floor so the cabinets and backsplash do not interfere with them.

Also, you might want to slope your garage floor at 1/4 inch per foot towards the door or towards a centrally-located floor drain that daylights (comes out at grade) outside. An area floor drain in the garage and utility/mechanical room(s) is a great idea, as it allows you to wash the dog, allow the car to dry, deal with a leak, or wash mop buckets out with minimal impact and mess in the house.

The EPA has determined that more than 30% of toxic air particles in the home originate in the garage. Much of the home's heating and cooling capacity is lost to inattentive detailing between the home and garage. To address this, the wall between the garage and house should be fully insulated, all penetrations between the spaces should be sealed, a continuous air barrier should be installed, and the doors into the home should be exterior rated doors with good weather-stripping. The garage should also be separately vented from the house. Careful attention to this will minimize dangerous fumes and temperature differences affecting the main body of the living space.

One last note: many builders use a means of building that equates to a step between the garage and the house. Older people, and especially people with temporary or permanent handicaps, find that an easy ramp from the garage into the home is useful.

Root Cellar

The cultivation of crops began at least 10,000 years ago and since that time, we have needed to plan for what to do with those crops to store them for long-term use. As society moved towards a more instant-satisfaction model, we minimized the amount of space we used for storing foods, and started getting our food from THE store, rather than OUR stores.

To minimize our energy dependence, and since refrigerators (even the most energy efficient ones) are big energy suckers, we have to come up with better solutions for storing our food. That is yet another reason why we believe that one of the best ways to achieve true sustainability is to study vernacular architecture models! Our grandmothers knew how to deal with the need for food storage. They simply built a cellar into the earth. Fast-forward to today. Many people live in areas where root cellars have been for a hundred years, and are still using this free and natural means of protecting and preserving their crops. Thus, the design of root cellars has been finessed and a clear set of building criteria developed.

From raised granaries to stream-, well-, or spring-fed pools that can be used to keep milk cool inside stone springhouses... There is almost no storage need that cannot be met naturally by just doing a little research and getting creative with our designs.

Root cellars, which maintain a constant cold temperature for storing tomatoes, beets, turnips, and other veggies, are built into the earth, or surrounded with earth once they are built above the ground to stay dry and away from the water table, and are located on the north or east side of a house. There are three styles of root cellar – hatch type, hillside type, and above-ground type. All three have slightly outward-battered walls to prevent collapse.

The HATCH CELLAR type is the simplest, being a hole dug into the ground and walled in with mortared stone. It has a dirt floor. Wood beams and plywood sheets or wood decking are installed as a roof foundation, with a hatch in the ceiling and a ladder for access. A shed is then built over the entire cellar, with walls extending past the cellar on all sides by no more than 3 feet, so that moisture can still penetrate the cellar.

The HILLSIDE CELLAR type is partially dug out of a hill, lined and walled with mortared stone to create a square room or rooms. Wood beams and plywood sheets or wood decking are installed for the roof foundation, an underlayment applied, and a traditional roof installed above. The access to this cellar is through a framed insulated door at the floor level. Sometimes this cellar is accessed through a few or several stairs, though we do not recommend this as it creates a falling danger in ice and snow. Especially for little ones, who have a tendency to use the cellar as a secret fort.

The ABOVE-GROUND CELLAR type is either framed traditionally then covered in building paper and felt and a finish cladding, has a thick sod wall applied to the exterior, is lined inside with dry-stack or mortared rock, or is built of stone. This cellar is accessed at ground level with a framed insulated door.

The best cellars in cool climates have four different rooms: The first - for fresh foods that must not freeze - with insulated walls and soil floor; the second - for fresh foods that may freeze and require high humidity - has soil floors and no wall insulation; the third - for fresh and dry goods in sealed containers - has sealed concrete floors and walls and no insulation; and last - for fresh foods requiring some humidity - has a concrete floor. The next best cellars have two rooms – one with a concrete or stone floor and one without. The smallest cellars are a single room, with humidity of 80-90%, and dirt floors.

Shelves in all cellar types are self-supporting, not attached to the walls in any way, and are kept away from the walls by 3 inches to allow ventilation, deter the growth of molds, and deter access by pests. In the best designs the shelves are placed on concrete blocks or stone bases to keep them off the floor as well.

A 6 inch minimum diameter exhaust pipe is installed in the ceiling to allow hot air to escape the cellar. If the roof is pitched, this pipe should be located in the crest of the pitch. If the cellar is installed in a basement or under a shed, run the pipe outside as quickly as possible as it is critical that it have access to fresh blowing breezes to function correctly. Include a 90 degree elbow bend at the end to face the pipe north and put a covering over it so that wind and other dropping things like leaves and bird poop do not plug the opening. A supply pipe should also be included near the floor and up through the outside of the cellar walls to the fresh air, in the north side of the cellar. It should have a 90 degree elbow inlet pointing north or northwest, but not permanently attached for adjusting during those periods when the prevailing wind direction changes. Vents should be sealed around the pipe as they enter the structure with packed cloth, expanding foam or tight rubber gaskets. The vents themselves need to be equipped with closing and opening valves, and it is usually most convenient to make these valves operable from outside the cellar. Closing vents in freezing weather and during summer heat spells will help keep the temperature inside the cellar more uniform. Stuff the first little bit of the vent's outside opening (2 inches, not enough to block flow) with steel wool, and cover with netting to keep pests out.

Humidity is key in successful cellar design, and in arid regions, you might need to bring water into the cellar to achieve the desired humidity. This can be done by pouring water directly into the cellar floor if you have a 6" gravel base installed, or you can just bring in a large pan full of water and put damp towels over your bushel baskets and allow the humidity to self-regulate. Also in arid regions which are ideal for sun-drying foods, you might have a larger area in your root cellar for dried foods in sealed containers. In humid environments, especially tropical ones, you might need to use a deeply-planted hatch cellar that is highly insulated and with a minimal sized access door in order to minimize the area exposed to the hot air and humidity.

The ceiling of the cellar should be sloped slightly to encourage dripping to occur where you want it, and the finish should be as smooth as possible. Do not allow the structural elements to be exposed as this will quicken their deterioration. Plywood can easily be attached to the underside of your rafters, or a humidity-friendly wood decking installed.

Stairs and Towers

Stairs provide a vertical means of moving through a space and are critically important to circulation for buildings with multiple floors. The design of stairs is so important because you need to get two things up and down them: your self/family/visitors, and… your furniture!

Towers have traditionally been used as communication spaces. They provide an easy place to locate stairs and even elevators for those that need this. Also, if you include operable windows at the top floor of your stair tower and open the windows on the side the wind is heading, the tower will act like a chimney, and will draw the warm air up from the lower floors, where it can be used to warm the space or allowed to exit through vents and create a fresh air flow through the entire house. Stair tower "chimneys" are especially useful tools in hot climates when we want to get that hot air out fast and naturally.

STAIR DESIGN

The Building Code generally limits the distance between floors to 12 feet, and the final floor-to-floor height has a direct impact on the design of stairs because we want to make treads and risers all the same height and depth so they are easy to navigate. The best stairs are designed with a maximum of 7 inches of rise for every 11 inches of run. When we can, in our office, we do that one better and make it 7:12. It makes it easier for my big size 9 foot to fit the tread. It also makes the math easier. But, it does mean a longer set of stairs. We use that to our advantage though, and build in drawers, cabinets, closets, bookcases, and other storage into the space below.

The easiest stairs to build are straight-run type, but sometimes these stairs can be a little "long" and a landing at the halfway point is useful. These stairs can also take up a large amount of space. Another option is to use a U-shaped stair, which uses the least amount of space. When landings are used, they should be at least as deep as the stairs are wide. Landings at eye level or below are the easiest to use.

Winders are the angled steps used in some places in lieu of landings. These are difficult for children, parents with armloads full of anything (especially squirmy kiddos), and older people to navigate, so we recommend using a landing instead. Rails should be 2 inches wide, located a minimum of 1 ½ inches away from the wall, should be placed at 2'-6" to 2'-10" above the top joint of the riser/tread, and headroom above the treads should be 6'-8" or greater.

Figure 40. L-Shaped Winder Stair

While many people use found stones to build short stair sections in Earthships, we have found that these are troublesome. They often have different riser heights, which messes with people's equilibrium, and their rugged and uneven surfaces encourage tripping. A "dressed and finished" stone step is cut level. This much safer option can be well worth the expense, if it helps you to avoid having to call an ambulance when someone takes a bad spill.

DUAL STAIRCASES

Old homes often had a main and rear staircase, with the rear staircase being smaller in most cases, as it was mostly for emergencies and household staff (and teenagers sneaking in and out). These days, even though most of us do not have household staff anymore, everyone needs to get around equally easily, and Codes want you to have two ways out of the upstairs. Dual staircases might be a good way to go, just make sure that the tread width meets Code.

SPIRAL STAIRS

Spiral stairs use the least amount of space in plan, but they are often not allowed by Code because they are quite dangerous. They are also difficult to manage for long term regular use. If they are allowed, it is usually only as a secondary access to a loft space. Per Code, the spiral stair option only applies if the lofted space is 400 square feet or less.

SINGLE STEPS

We always try and avoid putting a single step anywhere in our designs, whether in the landscape, along a corridor, up to a room, or even out into the garage. Our minds just do not process spatial information in singularities - we do much better if there are two steps instead of one. How many times have you launched off a single tread step that you have used a hundred times before? Probably at least a few. Good design practice for small stairs is 2 risers minimum, with a 7:12 ratio of rise to run or riser to tread. In cases where only one stair is needed, you might consider using a ramp, with a 1:12 maximum rise to run and a non-slip surface.

BANNISTERS AND BALLUSTERS

We love the creative railings used in Earthship designs. Just be aware that balusters and bannisters on stair rails should be spaced such that a 6" ball cannot pass between any two members in order to meet Code. This keeps your kiddos' heads from getting caught when they are playing around railings.

STAIRS AND FURNISHINGS

For furniture, I offer the chart on the next page, which I scanned into my computer several years back. I am not sure anymore where it is from, but it is a great design tool if you want to get that bed or sofa up to the loft or second floor:

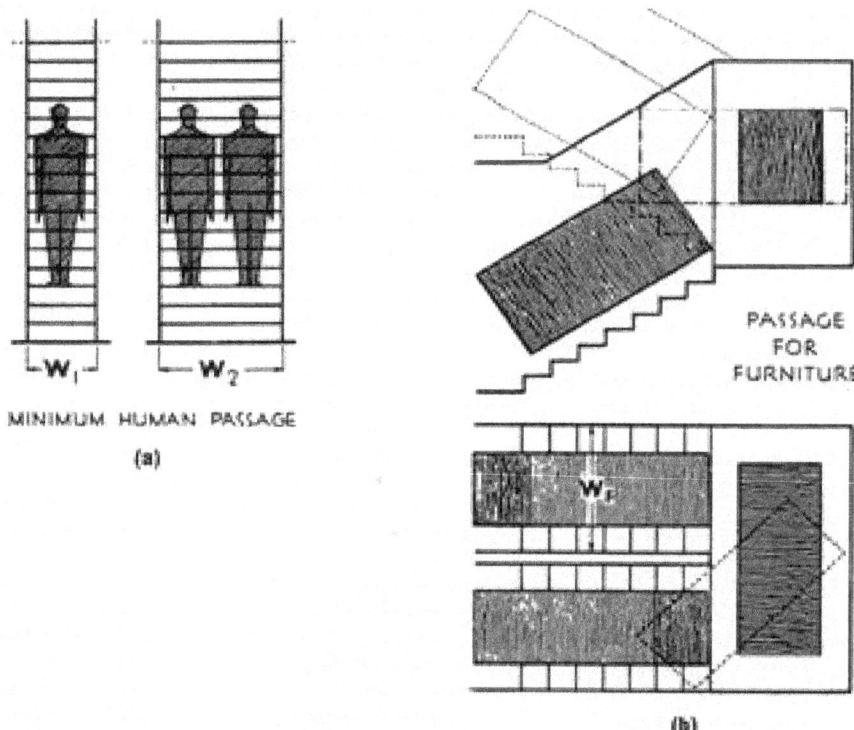

Fig. 2 Minimum stair widths. (a) Stairs designed for comfortable human passage only may be relatively narrow. W_1 may be 2'0" but 2'6" is better. W_2 should be at least 3'6". (b) Furniture passage demands greater width. If stair landing is increased or headroom unlimited, W_F may be decreased. See Table 2.

TABLE 2 Recommended Minimum Clear Widths of Stairs (W_F) for Furniture Movement*

Furniture		Min. Headroom ▲		Unlimited Headroom		
Article	Size	Wide U Type	Narrow U Type	Wide and Narrow U	Narrow U only ●	
					Stair	Landing
Double Bed Box Spring	4'-6" x 6'-6" x 8"	3'- 2"	3'- 2"	2'- 3"		
Dressing Table	1'-10" x 4'-0" x 2'-6"	2'- 5"	2'- 5"	2'- 5"		
Bureau	2'-0" x 4'-0" x 3'-0"	2'- 8"	2'- 8"	2'- 8"		
Chiffonier	1'-8" x 3'-4" x 4'-8"	2'- 6"	2'- 6"	2'- 6"		
Chest of Drawers	1'-9" x 3'-4" x 4'-8"	2'- 7"	2'- 7"	2'- 7"		
Divan - Club	3'-6" x 7'-2" x 2'-9"	4'- 8"	4'- 8"	3'- 4"	3'-0"	3'-8"
Divan - Average	3'-0" x 6'-8" x 2'-6"	4'- 4"	4'- 4"	2'-11"		
Piano - Concert Grand	9'-0" x 5'-4" x 1'-8"	4'- 8"	4'- 8"	3'- 2" ■	3'-0" ■	3'-4" ■
Piano - Music Room Grand	7'-3" x 5'-2" x 1'-6"	3'-10"	3'-10"	3'- 0"		
Piano - Drawing Room Grand	6'-9" x 5'-0" x 1'-4"	3'- 6"	3'- 6"	2'-10"		
Piano - Baby Grand	5'-8" x 4'-10" x 1'-2"	3'- 0"	3'- 0"	2'- 8"		
Piano - Standard Upright	2'-2" x 5'-10" x 4'-6"	4'- 0"	3'- 9"	3'- 3"	3'-0"	3'-6"
Highboy - Large	2'-0" x 3'-6" x 7'-6"	4'- 4"	4'- 4"	2'-10"		
Highboy - Average	1'-8" x 3'-4" x 6'-0"	3'- 6"	3'- 6"	2'- 6"		
Secretary - Large	1'-10" x 3'-8" x 7'-2"	4'- 0"	4'- 0"	2'-10"		
Secretary - Average	1'-10" x 3'-0" x 6'-10"	3'-10"	3'-10"	2'- 6"		
Sideboard	1'-9" x 5'-0" x 3'-2"	2'- 6"	2'- 6"	2'- 6"		
Buffet	2'-1" x 3'-3" x 6'-6"	4'- 0"	4'- 0"	2'-10"		
Dresser	1'-9" x 6'-0" x 5'-6"	4'- 4"	3'- 6"	3'- 4"	3'-0"	3'-8"
Table (6 People)	3'-6" x 5'-0" x 2'-6"	3'- 2"	3'- 2"	3'- 2"	3'-0"	3'-4"
Table (8 People)	3'-6" x 7'-0" x 2'-6"	4'- 4"	4'- 4"	3'- 2"	3'-0"	3'-4"
Table (10 People) Rd.	6'-4" Diam.	4'- 8"	4'- 8"	3'- 0"		
Desk - Slope Top	2'-6" x 3'-8" x 3'-4"	3'- 3"	3'- 2"	3'- 2"	5'-0"	3'-4"
Desk - Flat Top	3'-0" x 5'-6" x 2'-6"	3'- 2"	3'- 0"	3'- 0"		
Desk - Executive's	3'-2" x 6'-0" x 2'-6"	4'- 2"	4'- 2"	3'- 1"	3'-0"	3'-2"
Trunk - Wardrobe	1'-11" x 2'-6" x 3'-7"	2'- 5"	2'- 5"	2'- 5"		

*Clear width between faces of rails, newels, etc., or between rail or newel and finish wall.
Notes: ▲ Headroom limited to minimum for comfortable human passage (see Table 1 and text).
● Narrow stairs and wide landings.
■ Absolute minimum not recommended (see text).

Standard Furniture Dimensions

While we are talking about getting furniture up to a second floor, here are standard dimensions of furniture, so you have an easy tool to use for designing your home. All of these measurements are in inches.

TABLES	Height	Width	Length
Bedside	26	15	19
Buffet	34-38	24	60
Card	30	36	36
Coffee	19	18	36-48
Conference	30	36	96
Dining	29	40	64
End	20	17	28
Hall	27	15	55
Kitchen	29	36	60
Picnic	28	36	72
Poker	29	48	48
Printer	26	22	26
Sofa	26	14	72
Typewriter	25	18	30
Workstation	26	30	48

MATTRESSES	Height	Width	Length
Twin (Regular)	6	39	75
Twin (Long)	6	39	80
Double/Full	8	54	75
Queen	8	60	80
King	10	80	80
King (Calif.)	10	72	84

CHESTS	Height	Width	Depth
Lowboy (7" leg)	36	36	18
Tall Chest (6" leg)	54	36	18
Bookcase (Paperbacks)	38	36	7
Bookcase (Hardbound)	50	36	10
Blanket	24	36	19
Cedar	20	40	19
Buffet	34	50	20

CHAIRS	Width	Depth	Seat/Back Height
Barstool	17	17	30/42
Dining, Side	19	19	18/36
Dining, Arm	24	18	18/36
Easy	25	26	17/31
Kitchen	19	19	19/34
Kitchen Stool	12	12	27
Rocker	20	26	16/42
Upholstered	30	26	16/42

SOFAS	Width	Depth	Seat/Back Height
3 seat	84	35	18/30
Loveseat	60	35	18/30
Armchair	35	35	18/42

Details of Design

"It's all in the details" is a well-known saying because it is true!

One of the things the Earthships do quite well is in the way they celebrate the tiny details of design. I think this is a lot of why people are so drawn to these structures. Some of the details are just so pretty.

Figure 41. Details of Design at The Phoenix

People often ask me what I love the most about architecture in the Southwest, and the answer is closely related to why I also love the ideas of the Arts and Crafts movement, and of Frank Lloyd Wright in particular. The spaces in all three are designed and built to serve a larger purpose – to bring people together and inspire them while doing so. They all use built-in furnishings and details to encourage people to use the spaces for reflection, work, or building community. They are often so inviting, it's almost like you cannot not use them.

In New Mexico, we have a long history of using our basic building materials - like adobe and earth-plasters - and the qualities of those materials - like the depths of our walls - to add built-in features to our homes. You can always tell a home designed by someone who is really from here because it has combinations of these features in the various rooms.

BENCHES AND BANCOS

Benches, which we call *bancos* here in New Mexico, are extremely common built-in accessories in New Mexico homes. From sleeping bunks over fireplaces to sitting areas at fireplaces... we love built-in design! And we want it to be curvy and undulating! We find that the typically 18 inch deep bancos just are not all that comfortable for longer than a few minutes. That idea is supported by standard furniture dimensions, where chairs are typically 19 inches deep. We like our bancos slightly deeper than average, at 20-24 inches deep, for comfort and ease of use. Either way, you will almost always need to make custom bench cushions on your benches if you design them with a fluid shape, unless you pick a standard size that can be found at World Market or somewhere like that that always has bench cushions available, and design around that.

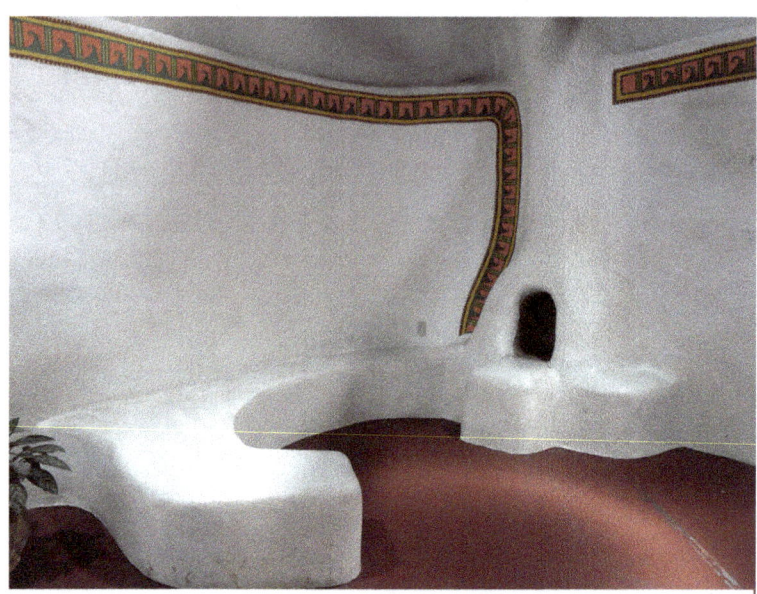

Figure 42. Built-in Banco and Fireplace in Taos

NICHES AND NICHOS

We love our deep walls here in New Mexico, and if you have deep walls from using strawbale or adobe construction, you might also want to use deep-set bookcases and *nichos* for special and sacred items. We recommend nichos only on interior walls so thermal performance is not jeopardized.

Figure 43. Niches and Nichos

NOOKS

Nooks are getaway spaces, too small to be a room and too large to be a bench. Most often, they use a bench-like form; only the bench goes the entire way across the opening and the space. Most often, they have bed-like qualities, and are designed alongside a window, or tucked into some little-used space like under a gable or stairs.

What makes a sculpted nook cozy and inviting? According to our contributor Sigi Koko,

> "1) it has enclosure on 3 sides, 2) it has windows and an open 4th side that connect you to the spaces beyond (so you do not feel trapped), 3) the size of the space (including ceiling height) is scaled to our bodies... it is not a vast space, it is a length-of-your-body sized space, add a fluffy rug and warm pillows..."

Figure 44. Nook at Lama Foundation and Bed Nook at Private Residence

BED NOOKS

When I worked in Colorado, architects in the area would often design built-in bunk-beds for the kids' wings of the multi-million dollar homes we designed. These were not just any beds, either... They were wooden bunk palaces with built-in wardrobes and shelves and the same qualities of bright colors and ornate wooden detailing you see in gypsy carts and wagons. I fell totally in love with these bunk bed pods, and I think more people should be using them now, even without the bunk bed aspect. With a south-facing window for solar heat gain (natural bed warming!), a view, and some decent lighting... a bed pod takes the idea of nook up a notch, and makes the space personal. It takes the old idea of a four-poster bed and improves on it. The four-poster bed was not designed just to be pretty. In old estates, the stone walls and soaring spaces made for cold bedrooms. Using a four-poster bed with velvet curtains allowed you to create a "room within a room" when you closed the curtains. A person's body heat was enough to warm that space up to a more comfortable level overnight. Bed pods use this thermal performance idea and minimize space use.

The raised beds on a dais you see in many Earthships seems to want to raise the bed into the warm zone midway up the wall, to make sleeping in a cold climate more comfortable. This concept could be combined with a masonry heater to provide a nice warm bed in areas that do not receive adequate sun warming.

Figure 49. Bedroom in The Phoenix

One lesson we learned about bed nooks from one of our friends in Taos who used built-in beds in her modern round pit-house with reciprocal roof, was that using a standard bed size makes maintenance, and day-to-day upkeep and cleaning infinitely easier. A standard twin bed using standard sheets is a better option than using some off size and having to custom-make everything.

BUT YOU ARE NOT IN NEW MEXICO. NOW WHAT?

In places other than New Mexico, they also use their building materials and qualities of those materials to make built-in features, but they are usually very different features. For instance, in the American South, you might find screened-in porches with built-in furnishings constructed of wood, houses with much taller ceilings and windows and doors covered with full-height louvered shutters to let out the heat, or people using porch swings to create a breeze for themselves. What you might want to build depends on your climate and building materials.

One thing of particular note here: in the Deep South, and parts of the country where humidity and heat are high, as on trees, the north side of the home and any area in the shade will have a higher tendency for mosses and molds due to less sunshine. Drainage and ventilation on this side of the structure is critical. So is access to sun in the summer. So do not locate raised porches here unless they are well-ventilated, kept high above the ground, and ventilated beneath too.

WOOD TIPS FOR BUILT-IN FURNITURE

If you are planning on built-in furniture with any parts that have exposed wood, you might want to consider using furniture grade woods on the build-out. Plain-sawn lumber is cut in rectangular forms along a grid super-imposed on the cut end of the tree. This lumber has a higher tendency to twist and warp, as it is cut along the grain. Plain-sawn lumber is less expensive and more available in most locations.

Though it is more expensive and results in slightly more waste, quarter-sawn wood is preferred for furniture applications, as it is cut at a 45 degree angle into the center of the tree. This cut will have more even grain pattern and will wear more evenly. The waste materials from the lumber-making process can now be recycled into wood pulp products.

Planning for the Long Game

Planning for the long game addresses the reality of trying to make your self-built home work for you in the long term. It may mean adding to the home later, and it may well mean evolving the home into more than just a home.

ADDITIONS

One of the many complaints we hear about Earthships in particular, but that also applies to strawbale, earth-sheltered, earthbag, and rammed earth structures... is that they cannot be easily added to. The family outgrows it, or we want a studio, or an office added on, and what do we do?

The easiest solution is to plan these spaces, or at least connections to these spaces, into the design from the outset. Leave one side of the berm open, without any piping or cisterns in it, in order to add space. Plan ahead for new openings by framing in the openings you may want later at the outset of construction, and then infill them or use a window in opening if it is an exterior wall. Just set the head height of the window at the same head height as your future door. Plan for a location and piping connections for another cistern, if one might be needed. Really, it's about being proactive instead of reactive. If we have gone about the exercises in the From Vision to Reality section, we may well know exactly what we have on our wish list "for someday". So plan for it!

ASSEMBLY OCCUPANCIES

The other part of the long game that we want to address is if you open your home to the public. It does not matter if you design your space to be a home and then decide later to host tours or building workshops. Once you open it to the public, it will no longer be considered just a residence and you will need to acquire adequate permissions and permits in order to continue using the space for public use.

An Assembly Occupancy is what the Building Code considers a space for public accommodation that is not a business, school, or industrial site. Usually the space will be deemed an A-3 occupancy, which is for public spaces other than restaurants without fixed seating. So, if you want to avoid having your classes shut down and avoid having to do a lot of expensive upgrades to the space later to make it meet Code, plan now for it to be considered an Assembly Occupancy (minus the expensive fire sprinklers). It will cost a little more. It may take a little longer in design. It may not look exactly the way you hoped. But, you may find that these accommodations will make your home perform better for day-to-day use anyway.

Plan ahead. Spend some money now. It will cost much less now than later.

You will likely have to design the structure according to stringent rules for occupant safety and accessibility. Use the large unisex bathroom we described in the bath chapter. Put a sign on the bath noting that is a handicapped unisex bathroom. There will likely be maximum hall lengths and maximum distances between the furthest corner in a usable space and an exterior door (usually 75 feet). Sometimes they will make you install mechanical ventilation and electrical outlets every 7 feet. There will likely be sewage/septic requirements and you will want to have a drinking fountain or a filtered water bottle available. The publicly-accessible parts of the building will have to be handicapped accessible. This is easier if you just plan a minimum of 3 feet clear floor space around every obstacle (like a curve in the planter), plan 4 foot wide hallways on the public corridor, and make all stairs at least 36 inches wide *at the inside of the railing* (That is about a 40 inch wide stair tread in most cases). The area on the handle side of a door will have to be open (without projections or walls in it) a foot or so beyond the door is wide. There will not be able to be steps between the public parts of the space and the exterior or they will require rails. If you plan on cooking greasy foods and not just bringing cold foods and using crockpots for your guests, that means big grease traps and expensive ventilation. (If you use crockpots you will want to have lots of counter space and extra plugs.) Smoke detectors will be required and possibly a fire alarm. You may have to install a fire sprinkler later. (It can be fed by the pond in some cases.) There will likely have to be a phone in case of fire so you can call the fire department. You will need a mop or service sink in the mechanical room, which you should have anyway if you really want the space to work as well as possible. Install exit signs to guide people back outside.

The key ingredient here is to make sure you use the services of a licensed architect either now or later to make sure you have all the things you need to meet the Assembly Occupancy requirements. We are not attempting to serve as architects here and do not claim to have knowledge of your local Code considerations or what your permitting authority will and will not accept. However, this area deserves some careful consideration and we are offering some guidance to make it as painless as possible for when you hire a local architect to help navigate the process. For more help choosing an architect, see the Overwhelmed? Need Help? section at the end of this book.

There is a great mounting height diagram to help you make your bathroom ADA compliant from the outset at http://img.docstoccdn.com/thumb/orig/159038643.png

Universal Design

Most home designers these days fail their clients in regard to the long-term livability of their homes. We build things that cannot easily be modified when someone becomes disabled or ill, or when our child is born with special needs. Universal Design makes architecture that works for everybody, whether they be in a wheelchair permanently, on crutches for a couple of weeks, just having a little issue with "a hitch in their giddyup", or even are just too little to manage bunches of steps and tight pathways. We find that our clients love the ease of getting around in spaces designed on Universal Design principles, and believe it or not, it also reduces the efforts required in mundane tasks like cleaning, which can be a bear when hoisting a vacuum and cleaning supplies up and around steps and landings. What is awesome about this, for us, is that many users of Universal Design in their home designs are finding that they are ready-made for the market for Baby Boomers who want something a little more manageable to buy for a home. So, they are selling their homes for a premium.

Here are the ways we can tweak the home's design to make it work for everyone:

FLOORS AND LANDSCAPE

- Use 1:12 slope ramps instead of single steps.
- Use a 3 foot door with a threshold less than ½" high.
- Make a lightly textured non-slip path 36 inches wide and without steps from the street curb and driveway to the home entrance. Use 1:12 slope ramps as needed and place 36" long landings at top and bottom of any ramps. Use handrails at locations where the path has a drop off of 12 inches or more at the side.
- Place trees so they do not drop berries or leaves onto the path.
- Provide path lighting on the major access to the house.
- Provide a handrails and good lighting at steps.

DESIGN

- Have a ground floor bedroom and complete bath.
- Place the washer and dryer on the main floor and use front-loading machines.
- Design halls and stair treads at least 36 inches wide.
- Use one landing for every 10 steps in a staircase.
- Provide a light switch at the top and bottom of stairways.

ENTRY

- Have a 5 foot square space available inside and outside at the front door.
- Cover the front entry so it is weather protected.
- Provide exterior lighting at the front door.
- Have a wipe off mat on both sides of the door to keep dirt and pollen minimized.

KITCHEN AND BATH

- Use sinks that can be "pulled in to", without casework below, and install them 34" above the floor.
- Vary the height of countertops so little ones and big people can use them too. For instance, really tall people might want to use a kitchen cabinet in the bath. Those extra inches of height can keep a back from going out!
- Provide extra-long hoses for spray attachments.
- Use lever handles, not knobs, on sinks, baths, and tubs and use one handle to control both hot and cold water if at all possible. Locate the handles and faucet at the side of the sink instead of the back if possible.

KITCHEN

- Locate the kitchen close to the entrance where you bring groceries in.
- Have a fire extinguisher located within easy reach between 27 and 48 inches above the floor.
- Use a sink 6 ½ inches deep.
- Use a dishwasher, and any other appliance, with button or push controls instead of knobs.
- Use heat resistant countertops.
- Use a side-by-side type refrigerator with sliding shelves and a water and ice dispenser in the door.
- Store heavy pots and pans in bottom shelves and drawers.
- Mount the oven with the top pull less than 48 inches above the floor.
- Use a range with push button controls at the front instead of sides.

BATHS

- Provide a shower bench in a walk-in shower with a 36 wide opening at the entrance.
- Have a shelf for shampoo and soap in the shower at 48 inches above the floor or below.
- Provide a hand-held shower sprayer with extra-long hose (these are great for washing dogs and little ones too!).
- Add 1 ½" textured grip grab bars to the bath, toilet, and shower or install blocking for them, when framing the walls.
- Use a raised toilet seat.
- Use a door that opens out instead of in.
- Have a 5 foot wide circle open between all the fixtures and cabinets.
- Have a sitting bench on the edge of the tub.
- Have a non-slip bathtub and shower floor.
- Make the top shelf of the medicine cabinet less than 50 inches above the floor.
- Use a tilting mirror.
- For wheelchair users, leave 42 inches of open floor space on one side of the toilet.
- Locate the TP holder at 27 inches above the floor.

CABINETS, COUNTERS, AND CLOSETS

- Use shelves less than 12 inches deep throughout.
- Use lazy-susan corner cabinets.
- Use rolling carts under counters.
- Use pull-out shelves.
- Use height-adjustable cabinets and closet shelves.
- Use loop or lever shaped drawer pulls and handles.
- Use easy-gliding hardware.
- Locate some wall cabinets at 48 inches above the floor or lower.
- Use cabinets on 6 or 8 inch tall toe kicks (spaces under the bottom shelf for toes to go underneath).
- Use clothing rods 22 inches to 44 inches above the floor.
- Use drawers 40 inches or less above the floor.
- Use 18 inch deep or less shelves in closets and pantries.
- Locate the light switch in pantries and closets close to the entrance.

WINDOWS AND DOORS

- Use 3 foot wide doors throughout, with 18 inches minimum of clear floor space on the handle side of the door.
- Use 5inch long lever type handles that curve towards the door and hinges with the tension reduced on them. Set them at no higher than 44 inches above the floor.
- Use swing-clear door hinges.

ELECTRICAL

- Locate switches and thermostats less than 48 inches above the floor.
- Locate outlets 27 inches or higher above the floor.
- Provide direct and indirect lighting in every room.
- Switch lamps at the door of the room they are in.
- Use nightlights in night-visited rooms like baths and kitchens, as well as the halls between them.

FINISHES

- Use non-slip flooring.
- Use low pile carpets with a firm pad.
- Secure the corners and edges of rugs.

Of course, some of this costs more. We are offering all the suggestions we know of, because we have a wide range of clients to serve. Some people will want all of this and will be happy to pay for it. Others maybe not so much. Just know that you do have a choice!

Finishes

by Rachel Preston Prinz and Shannon Matteson, with input from Sigi Koko

The materials that we use to cover and decorate our ceilings, walls, built-ins, trim, and floors have implications for the use of the space because of the impact of colors and textures on our psyche. The materials used also impact sound transmission, as well as durability and maintenance requirements.

The easiest way to finish ceilings, walls, and trim is to buy pre-made paints, stains, and coatings. The more affordable, though more challenging, way is to make your own coatings with a few base ingredients. There are manufactured as well as home-made ways to go for almost every option. Figuring out which finish will give you the performance you want and the durability you need can be time-consuming and frustrating. It takes patience, perseverance, and working to understand what you really want for the long term.

Some finishes require skilled applicators to install. Others are easy to install yourself, even if you are brand new to finishing. To get the most bang for your finish buck, especially if you are feeling underqualified or using volunteer labor that might be, we offer the following ideas for finishes that are as fool-proof and good looking in imperfection as possible: For floors, flagstone or brick are relatively easy to install, though choosing someone to lead the project that is detail oriented and/or geometrically gifted might be wise, so they can put those shapes together in a way that maximizes the tightness of the joint and minimizes the width of joints. For wall decorations, consider earth plaster with integral tinting, sculpting, and hand-painted details using stencils. For bathrooms, mosaics of broken tiles, plates, mirrors, river rocks, and glass pebbles are easier to install than straight tiles and offer creative types an opportunity to shine.

Where possible, use recycled content and/or renewable materials, water-based finishes, and use building materials like cabinets that come pre-finished. Pre-finished pieces minimize the negative impact on the environment, indoor air quality, and installation time.

Glues

For the most health and environmental benefit, use solvent-free products for interior applications including the installation of flooring, countertops, wall coverings, panelling, and tub/shower enclosures.

Paints and stains

Paint consists of a basic formula: a "thinner", a "binder", and a "load" which gives the paint its pigment and finish. Other ingredients may be added to accelerate drying or to act as a preservative.

Self-priming paints are the best performers. Two coats will give you the best look and performance. Brightly-colored paints will tend to fade more quickly. We recommend skipping economy grade paints, which cannot withstand the weather and require re-painting more often, as well as skipping top-of-the-line paints because there just is not enough value in the features they offer to justify the cost.

If regular paints (which might include new greener alternative blends) are acceptable for your build. For both interior and exterior applications, Home Depot's Behr brand and Lowe's Valspar brand paints are the best performers in paints available from big-box suppliers. Sherwin-Williams and Benjamin Moore top the independents' list. Glidden also makes one of the better satin paints. A good exterior paint will cost between $25 and $40 per gallon. A good interior paint cost between $20 and $70 per gallon.

One word of advice here: if someone offers you paint or stain that is over a year old, and that you are not sure they kept from freezing, (or, for that matter, if you are given anything free that you do not really want to use) please just do not take it. It is not worth the time and effort only to discover you have to redo everything because the paint starts flaking off.

NATURAL PAINTS

Natural paints describe a variety of paints for a range of applications, all of which are made from natural, low-energy, non-toxic, non-petrochemical, non-off-gassing ingredients. Natural paints start with a mineral- or plant-based binder, such as clay, casein (the protein found in milk), egg, beeswax, or lime. The binder provides the glue that allows the pigment or color to stick to the surface you are painting. The load or pigment is generally mineral- or plant-based, so they are also natural and non-toxic. A load may include such unique ingredients as onion skins, chalk, or iron oxide. The final ingredient in a natural paint is the solvent, which thins the paint to a usable texture. The solvent can be as simple as water or oil. You might add clove oil for preservation.

You can make your own paint, buying all the ingredients you need from a supplier like EarthPigments or UnEarthed. This is a great option for those people who love tinkering with recipes and making things. When handcrafting paint, every recipe is different and responds to its climate differently, so it has to be tweaked. The paint can also come pre-made from a manufacturer like Bioshield, Auro Paints, or Safecoat. Some natural paints are better than others for different applications. For example, clay paints need absorbent surfaces (like unpainted drywall or clay walls), lime paints & washes can be used outside where weather resistance is important, and egg yolk paints work on furniture. The trick with natural finishes is that they can be challenging to re-touch. Handmade batches and measuring techniques mean matching colors can be a bit of an art. Another downside of using biodegradable paints is that they are... biodegradable, which can mean more frequent re-application. Natural building guru Sigi Koko suggests The Natural Paint Book as a great resource, and she has milk, egg, and clay paint recipes on her blog at: http://buildnaturally.blogspot.com.

STAINS

The best performing exterior stains can last three years. They resist cracking, dirt, and mildew. It is well worth the additional cost for good stain to minimize having to make time for this huge maintenance effort. Opaque stains last longest and cover the best from the outset. While less expensive, clear stains emphasize the natural finish of woods, but require yearly re-application.

Natural stain options you can make include stains made from coffee, tea, hot chocolate, and wine. Recipes vary widely and are available online.

A gallon of good manufactured stain will cost around $35. Two coats are required for the first application on fresh wood. Benjamin Moore, Behr, Cabot, and Thompsons are all respected and dependable brands.

CLEAR AND NATURAL FINISHES

Clear and natural finishing products can be grouped into categories based on the degrees of protection they offer: lacquers, oils, shellacs, varnishes, water-based finishes, and waxes. The different finishes offer varying degrees of protection, durability, ease of application, reparability, and aesthetics. No single finish appears to be a clear winner - a finish that excels in one criteria may fail in another - so in choosing a finish, you must first determine what trade-offs you are willing to make.

Lacquers, shellacs, and water-based finishes are evaporative finishes that dry to a hard film once their solvents evaporate. Because they can dissolve when exposed to their original solvents, they are considered less durable as final finishes.

Reactive finishes, including oils, catalyzed lacquers, and varnishes also have solvents that evaporate, but they cure by reacting chemically with the air or a chemical component added prior to application. Because they undergo a chemical process to cure, they are forever changed and cannot re-dissolve when exposed to their original solvents so they are more durable. Excepting the pure oils, these finishes hold up better to heat, UV exposure, and chemicals.

OILS

Linseed and Tung oils are the preferred oil applications for finishes because they cure chemically through a process called polymerization, which renders a lasting, durable finish. Soybean oil, a common request, does not dry or cure and therefore is not recommended. Raw Linseed oils take an incredibly long time to dry. Boiled Linseed oil has changed chemically to become polymerized and will dry much more quickly and with a more durable and lasting finish than raw oil. For wood especially, boiled Linseed oil is the most durable choice. Non-heat-treated Tung oil can frost to a white matte finish and is best avoided. Heat treated Tung oil performs in much the same way as boiled Linseed oil. Though a Tung oil finish appears somewhat lighter, it has a more moisture-resistant finish. Application of oils is easy… wipe some on, let it soak in, and wipe the excess off. The film that results will be very fine, not like a "finish" you would see with varnish or lacquer. This is a suitable task for an attentive novice.

VARNISHES

Varnishes are made up of synthetic resins and drying oils, including Linseed and Tung oils. Varnishes also are polymerized chemically, but the added resins render a longer-lasting finish than a straight oil application. Long, medium, and short oil varnishes are differentiated by the drying temperature and oil percentage. The one you want to use (and is easiest to get) is a medium oil finish. Alkyd varnishes are used inside, phenolic varnish is used outside, and polymer varnish is the most durable. Varnish is resistant to water, heat, solvents, and other chemicals. Varnishes are the most durable finish that can be easily applied by non-experienced finishers. Varnish is typically applied with a brush, though a "wiping varnish" might be a better option if it is available. If you love the qualities of oil finishes but want more durability, an oil-varnish blend might be the way to go.

WAXES

Carnauba and Beeswax are not actually finishes, but are suitable as *polishes* for application over lacquer or shellac.

LACQUERS

Lacquer is considered one of the best all-around finishes for professional and skilled applicators. It dries fast, has a rich finish, is durable, and finishes beautifully. Standard lacquer finishes are usually made of nitrocellulose, which gives it a tendency to yellow as it ages and makes the finish sensitive to heat and solvents. Acrylic-modified lacquers do not turn yellow, and are better for light to white finish applications. Catalyzed lacquer is by far the most durable lacquer finish type, but it must be custom mixed and professionally applied.

SHELLACS

What do you get when you mix bug cocoons and denatured alcohol? A waxy finish material called shellac! You can get it pre-mixed or dry and add the alcohol yourself. Shellac is not the best at protecting from water, so it is probably not the way to go for most durability-minded applications.

WATER-BASED FINISHES

Water-based finishes contain some of the same ingredients - urethane, alkyd and acrylic - as varnish and lacquer, but the most flammable and polluting ingredients have been replaced with water. Resins do not have a natural affinity to water, so often they are chemically "forced" to work in this application. Most finishes of this type are acrylic-based, with either a resin binder to create a lacquer-type finish or a polyurethane binder for a less durable more varnish-like appearance.

LAST TIPS FOR CHOOSING A CLEAR OR NATURAL FINISH

Solvent-based finishes including varnish and lacquer contain organic solvents, which can affect the environment as well as your health. They are also highly flammable. If this is of concern, use a water-based finish, shellac, or pure oil. Pure oil contains no solvents and comes from renewable resources. Oil-soaked rags need to be disposed of carefully. Denatured alcohol, use as the solvent for shellac, is distilled from corn and most people do not find the odor objectionable. Despite common beliefs otherwise, all of these finishes are non-toxic when fully cured and the solvents have evaporated.

Shellacs and lacquers may be the best clear finishes for dusty and cold areas, as they are not as affected by dust or temperature in their application. Oil-based finishes dry slowly and are more temperamental for cold and humid applications, and they are more susceptible to dust infiltration affecting the final appearance.

WHAT PAINTS AND STAINS TO USE WHERE

For ease of calculating how much paint or stain you need, a gallon of paint or stain will usually cover an area of about 400SF. So, take the length times the height of your wall(s) to get the total area, and divide by 400 to get the number of cans you need.

HERE IS WHAT TO USE WHERE:

- Flat finishes hide flaws more effectively than semi- or glossy finishes which accentuate them. A flat finish is the perfect finish for a less-than-perfect wall.

- Use flat paints for formal living and dining rooms, because they tend to be used less and require less maintenance.

- Use eggshell or satin paints, which are easier to clean, for high-use areas like bedrooms, family rooms or great rooms, kitchens, and baths.

- Use flat or satin exterior finishes for siding.

- Use semi-gloss in lighter colors on interior and exterior doors, windows, trim, and shutters to increase contrast, bounce more light back into the space, for ease of cleaning, and to improve curb-appeal.

- Paint the inside and back of closets, cabinets, and shelves white or cream to bounce as much light as possible into these spaces.

- Use mildew-resistant exterior paints and stains for the north side of the home and shady locations, if you live in a humid climate.

- Fade-resistant finishes are ideal for the east, west, and south facades in sunny locations and hot climates.

- Integral stains on grouts, concrete stains, and plasters will give you a life-long finish that is easier to maintain.

- Color plays an important role in our psychological perceptions of comfort. Blue makes hot spaces feel cooler. Golds and reds make us feel warmer. Fire engine red makes your heart rate speed up! Green is a relaxing color. Purple is soothing and relaxing.

- Light colors reflect light and dark colors absorb it. Using light colors on your roof, floors, and walls in hot climates and dark colors on your roof, floors, and walls in cold climates allows nature to start the work of cooling or heating for you.

COST SAVING TIPS:

- To save the most on finishes and textures, pick a few simple to repair finishes and use just a few colors. The more finishes you use, the greater the cost and more complicated the maintenance.
- If you can use only a few colors and finishes, you can realize cost savings by buying 5 gallon buckets instead of gallons.
- When buying at big retailers, you can often save 20% or more by shopping holiday sales.

SURFACE PREPARATION FOR PAINTS AND COATINGS

Brick and concrete should cure for 30 days or more and then should be dusted before coating with any material. A block-filler or grout primer may be required before painting highly-porous concrete. Clear silicone water repellent can be used as a concrete sealant. Concrete floor surfaces should be etched with a muriatic acid solution to improve adhesion of coatings. Concrete floors may require an alkali-resistant primer.

Gypsum board (drywall) should be primed with a primer/sealer prior to finishing or the finish used should be self-priming.

Pre-painted surfaces that you want to refinish or paint over should be roughened by sanding or washing with a detergent solution.

Seal any cuts or ends on particleboard or OSB prior to painting.

Wall Coverings

PLASTER AND STUCCO

Plaster and stucco should ideally be allowed to cure for 30 days prior to finishing. Fresh plaster should be primed with an alkali-resistant coating prior to painting.

EARTH PLASTERS

A mixture of adobe, white glue, and straw can provide a great, long-lasting plaster for your walls. Finishes in earth tones can often be used from natural, local materials. What is available in your area? Many people use natural clay pigments like those available from American Clay. These pigments are natural, non-toxic, and made from local materials. They allow the wall to breathe and self-regulate humidity which keeps the home comfortable. Clay plasters, as our friend Sigi Koko says, "beg to be sculpted." Sigi teaches workshops on these techniques. She notes that,

> *"One of my favorite techniques for shaping clay plaster and preventing cracks in vulnerable spots, is to embed burlap into the surface of the plaster. I use the burlap on window sills, at joints between dissimilar materials, or where I want to apply clay plaster over wood. The tricks are :1) be sure that the burlap is installed while the plaster is still wet, otherwise it will be tough to embed the burlap fully; it also helps to dip the burlap in water or very runny clay slip; 2) start at one end and work your way to the other...and do not pull on the burlap as you go (or it will pull itself out of the clay plaster surface); 3) install the burlap so that it is fully embedded into the layer of plaster below; it should look like one surface; 4) make especially sure that the edges of the burlap are embedded well...if the finish plaster floats have a thread to get caught on, it can rip the whole piece of burlap out5) do not apply any plaster over the burlap unless the wall has dried out completely."*

Sigi also offers another natural building tip:

> *"You can save the painting step if your final coat of plaster is pigmented the color you want your finished walls to be. If you pigment your plaster, be sure to do test areas with different colors, let them dry completely, and then seal them however you plan to...this will give you the clearest test of what your finished plaster color will look."*

Figure 45. Tierra Blanca Finish at Hanuman Ashram in Taos

One of our favorite traditional finishes from New Mexico is an earth plaster called *Tierra Blanca,* or white earth. It is really more of a cream color than white, but it has flecks of mica that are applied as a finish coat. This amazing finish uses the light color as well as the shiny qualities of the mica to reflect daylight as well as electric and candle light throughout the space, making the spaces brighter, and best of all... it makes walls seem to "twinkle". It is an extraordinarily beautiful effect achieved with just a small investment in materials and application time.

Contributor Sigi Koko shared on her Facebook fan page a fabulous natural finish that we have totally fallen in love with. *Tadelakt,* a Moroccan earth plaster technique uses lime plaster, pigment, olive oil soap, and a lot of elbow grease to make a finish that is exquisitely beautiful and rich.

Check out her pics of the entire process at
http://www.facebook.com/media/set/?set=a.841172532573572

Earth plaster should be re-touched every year, especially on the building exterior. It is even more critical to re-mud each year on the interior when tire walls are used in order to make sure off-gassing is not an issue. In New Mexico, the annual re-mudding of our adobe buildings is called an *enjarre*. We just scruff the surface of the plaster to help new layers adhere, removing any damaged earth plaster, and then we put on a new coat over the entire building. This is a great time to bring back your community of builders and friends to have a reunion!

If you would like to visit a world-class earth plaster workshop, we recommend taking one from legendary Taos icon Carole Crews. She literally wrote the book on earth plasters. Her workshops are part work and part opportunity to find and express yourself. As with the traditional enjarre of New Mexico culture, which used to be done completely by women, her workshops tend to be mostly women. But this by no means excludes men.

A little story: When I was working on the enjarre a couple of years ago at the San Francisco de Asis church in Ranchos de Taos, I was asked to remove some damaged plaster from a landscape wall. I came upon a layer where I could see the fingerprints from the *golondrinas* (Spanish for swallows - what they called the women who did the enjarre in the old days). I stopped tearing at the damaged plaster and just knelt down and stared at those fingerprints. Finally, I put my hand up to one and placed my finger on the fingerprint. It was as if I was reaching back into history and connecting with that person. There was something so powerful and moving about this experience that I have carried it with me ever since. I think about the ideal of community that Earthships want to create, and I cannot help but to believe that an enjarre is the perfect opportunity to bring people together annually to sow intentions and love into and around the space.

GLASS AND CERAMIC TILES

We love the use of salvaged glass and ceramic tiles. Tiles can be used almost anywhere, and they are beautiful and colorful additions to any artfully-created home, whether they are used as tiles or broken apart and used for mosaics.

While using the standard 4 inch tiles is the most common way of tiling a space, you can also use 12 inch or 15 inch tall (not necessarily square) tiles in your bathrooms and showers to make the spaces, especially small showers, seem larger. If you design the size of your shower based on the size of tiles you use, you can also minimize cutting, and thus… waste. Though, these waste tiles are great for making mosaic borders and details!

Saltillo tile is nature at its finest. These tiles can be purchased or hand-made from clay. If you elect to go the hand-made route, you can capture the sweet details in life… like a little one's handprint, a fast-growing puppy's paw print, or a whimsical chicken footprint… before the tile is sun-dried and then fired in a kiln.

River rock pebbles make for an interesting mosaic-like finish for bathrooms especially, and can be installed similarly to glass and ceramic tiles on counters, walls, in showers, and on floors.

Tile tips: Use cement backer board under tiles rather than standard gypsum board. Glass or ceramic tile can with 50% or more recycled content is available. Use low-toxic adhesives and plasticizer-free grout. Be aware that any smooth surface can cause someone to slip, so using a slightly rougher surface on floors is desirable.

If you'd like to find inspiration for mosaic-type glass and ceramic designs, check out our Tiles of Bright Pinterest board!

OTHER FINISH IDEAS

The traditional Japanese technique of charred or burned wood, first discovered by Terunobo Fujimori, creates a gorgeous facade. This is a natural way to preserve timber and (paradoxically) makes it fire-resistant. It is a distinct and beautiful application for outdoor siding, ceilings and accent walls. The best part is, chemical preservatives, paints, and retardants are completely unnecessary and the silvery finish is rich and unique.

Salvaged slate chalkboards are a fun and interactive wall finish!

Floor Coverings

Feeling warm and cozy is one of the essential elements of a comfortable home. Achieving this feeling is much easier with well-planned flooring. Our favorite floors offer thermal mass or radiant heat, and wonderful, rich, textures and finishes whose joints do not eat away at our tender feet.

EARTHSHIP FLOORING

Except in the case of decks and porches, an on-ground floor system rarely has to deal with weathering. This is not always true in the case of Earthships, because the floor is acting as a heat collector and it is exposed to humidity from the greenhouse plants. So the flooring, especially in an Earthship's greenhouse space should be stone, brick, earth, or tile.

We recommend using spacers on regular shaped materials like tiles and bricks. For masonry, stone, and tile applications, grout up to the top edge of the flooring material in order to prevent toe-shredding from the raw edge of the flooring material.

EARTH FLOORS

Earth floors have been used since the dawn of homebuilding. The earth floors in Taos Pueblo have lasted for somewhere around 1,000 years. They never need replacement, and they do not require framing, off-gas toxic chemicals, or add to landfills. The main drawback to earthen floors is they are very slow-drying. Tamped earth floors are much faster-drying than poured earth floors and are more practical for some applications. They have a similar texture to leather, can be maintained as easily as traditional flooring, and cause no dust when properly sealed. Earth floors are constructed of local earth plus clay additives when required. They are bound together with straw or other natural fibers and stabilized with natural oils. Stabilizers, like the historic oxblood we occasionally see here in New Mexico, can be added for harder floors. Modern alternatives to blood include starch paste, glues, and/or casein. For those who might want to go see them, traditional oxblood earth floors can be seen at the Martinez Hacienda in Ranchitos as well as at Robert Cafazzo's Two Graces Plaza Gallery in Ranchos de Taos.

Be prepared. Earth floors require big investments of time and labor to install. In most cases, it is easier to have a good contractor involved with lots of experience in this flooring type to manage the installation. High-traffic areas might need to have a durable surface like flagstone applied for longevity and water-resistance, especially at entrances and rooms with high humidity like kitchens, mudrooms, and laundries. Earth floors virtually eliminate the pollution, waste, and energy required to manufacture a floor. They are 90% more efficient than concrete. They are low-maintenance and can be swept or mopped for regular care.

A tip from natural building goddess Sigi Koko:

> *"Trying to walk on a wet earthen floor can be tricky...and the floor stays damp for weeks. To solve that problem, I usually take squares of spare rigid insulation and make a path. The insulation distributes your weight so you do not leave footprints. But I cannot wait to try this clever innovation on that theme... taping the insulation to your shoes...like snow shoes, but for clay floors."*

NATURAL FLOORING ALTERNATES FOR FRAMED SPACES

Alternate natural flooring materials for loft spaces and second floors on framing include reclaimed wood flooring, natural wool carpet, jute, sea grass, cork, true linoleum, and river pebble. You really do not want to put these directly on the ground or on concrete floors without gravel courses and moisture barriers beneath due to the tendency of these floors to retain moisture.

WOOD

Beautiful and durable hardwood flooring is a great traditional flooring option. Wood flooring can be laid on most substrates. You just want to make sure that the subfloor is clean, level, smooth, and dry with no holes and bumps of more than 1/8 inch. Wood flooring must have a moisture-protective underlayment when installed on concrete. Also make sure that the moisture content does not exceed 4% on concrete and 12% on wood subfloors prior to installation.

Wood floors should be one of the last things installed in your build, as it takes a while to do and installing it last gives all the other materials time to dry out to a workable moisture content. Plumbing and plastering or drywalls should be fully dried-in prior to installation of wood flooring.

Wood will shrink and swell with humidity and temperature extremes, so it is best to install it in a period of good weather. Wood flooring boards need to be allowed to adjust to the space's inherent temperature and humidity for two weeks or more for ease of installation. Also, door frames must be undercut to allow the flooring to be placed under them. Wood should be sanded and sealed at knots, primed and sealed on all surfaces, and all holes should be filled after the first finish coating.

Reclaimed wood flooring is a great sustainable option. Salvaged floors from farm buildings, bowling alleys, and historic buildings can provide beautiful reclaimed wood material.

As alternates, use cork or bamboo rather than hardwood floors. All three of these floorings – cork, bamboo, and wood - need to be installed in climates where humidity is at or above 30%. In arid locations, humidity requirements should be addressed mechanically to help these floors last.

NATURAL CARPET

Wool, sisal, and coir are some of the most common natural carpet options available today. Consider carpet tiles for easy replacement if these are available. Use 100% recycled content underlayment and make sure carpets, pads, and floor coverings have a "green label" from the Carpet and Rug Institute if possible.

WOOL

Wool is strong, resistant to stains, pilling, and fire, and is water-resistant to small spills. Wool is insulating because its individual fibers catch and hold air. This means that it has both sound and heat insulating properties. A wool and hemp blend may be more desirable in some locations because of hemp's added durability in humid environments. Wool carpets are far more expensive than their synthetic counterparts but their durability and other benefits make them well worth considering.

SISAL

Sisal comes in a wide variety of colors due to its ease of being stained. Because of this staining tendency, sisal should not be used in water or mud heavy areas. Sisal requires chemical treatment to make it spill and dirt resistant. Sisal's price falls between wool and coir.

COIR

Coir carpeting is made from the fibers of coconut shells. Its appearance is coarse, dark, and natural. Coir is perfect for cabin-type settings and areas of high traffic where its rough texture is of benefit. We recommend avoiding coir anywhere people will be barefoot as it is anything but soft. Coir should not be used on stairs, and it is susceptible to humidity and water so it should be avoided in areas where it might get wet.

JUTE

Natural Jute, or Hessian, is the fibrous inner stalk of a tropical herb in the Linden family and it is a cousin to hemp. Jute is grown in India and other hot/humid Asian countries. Jute is the ultra-inexpensive fiber used in burlap sacks, though it can also be used in a variety of materials and finish levels. It is one of the most environmentally-friendly materials there is, as it is rapidly renewable, recyclable, reusable, and 100% biodegradable, which is why it is used to wrap baby trees that you plant in their container. Cotton bales are wrapped in jute for shipping and you might be able to acquire this material for minimal cost if this type of farming occurs in your area. Jute is finely-fibered and is used to make a yarn which is woven into a fine carpet. It is best suited to light-traffic areas because of its delicate nature and tendency to tear. Jute is low-static, resistant to fading, and acoustically insulating. Jute should not be used in humid climates or wet areas as water will degrade it.

SEAGRASS

Seagrass is made from the fibers of a plant that is grown similarly to rice. Seagrass is woven similarly to a basket, and its fibers are naturally stain, dirt, and fade-resistant. Because of this, it cannot be colored and it is only available in a natural creamy hue. Like most natural flooring options, seagrass does not want to be installed in humid areas or wet locations like the kitchen and bath. When placed on stairs, seagrass should be laid with the grain facing parallel to the tread.

CORK

Cork flooring is made from harvesting the bark of the Cork Oak tree that grows in the Mediterranean. Cork is considered one of the most sustainable, non-toxic, and healthy flooring choices available today. Cork is a renewable resource - every nine 9 years, the bark of the tree will be removed again. The manufacturing process breaks the cork bark down into small chunks, mixes it with cut-offs from other cork manufacturing processes, and the paste is formed into flooring. Cork is insulating, hypo-allergenic, and not susceptible to static, dust, mold, mildew, fire, or pests.

One of the issues with cork flooring is that cork can sometimes be easily crushed and does not always regain its original form. Cork can also be challenging to clean. Cork needs to be sealed and then re-sealed every couple of years. Cork cannot sustain large water spills or penetrating dirt without damage and cannot be cleaned with typical cleaning agents, and therefore requires a higher degree of attention in the day-to-day and for long-term maintenance.

BAMBOO

The best bamboo flooring is made of the stalks of renewable bamboo grass that is harvested at most every 5 years. When well-selected, bamboo floors are beautiful, strong, and durable. Bamboo is usually found in a light straw or caramel color, though it can be stained. Bamboo floors take as long as wood floors to install, however that time can be reduced on both flooring types (and cost savings realized in the process) by using engineered floors that lay on the subfloor like tiles. Bamboo flooring is suitable for all applications including kitchens and baths. Bamboo requires minimal cleaning. Bamboo is grown in China, and therefore is not as sustainable as other products made locally or at least on our own continents. But the benefits may outweigh that issue. The only real performance negative on bamboo flooring is that it is not sunlight or UV-resistant without additional finish treatment.

Be careful when choosing bamboo. Make sure it has been certified by the FSC-certified as non-certified bamboo is often harvested earlier than it should be, rendering it not strong enough to last. Bamboo that is not certified is often also harvested in ways that are harmful for the environment. Also, select flooring that is low in VOCs, as many manufacturers seem to use high-VOC binders and stains in these floors.

VINYL FLOORS

We recommend avoiding vinyl products, which are synthetic products made of chlorinated petrochemicals. We prefer natural linoleum instead.

LINOLEUM

Linoleum, which is made today very nearly in the same way it was in 1863 when it was first invented, is a sheet flooring surface made of all-natural ingredients including linseed oil, cork bits, wood flour, resins, lime, and pigments pressed onto a jute backing. It is heat-resistant, durable, and can be beautiful. Linoleum can last 30-40 years in high-use, rough, and even commercial environments. Linoleum's integral coloring means that even if you get a gash in the floor, it will look the same as the rest of the floor, as the coloring goes all the way through. Armstrong in the U.S. and Domco in Canada are major suppliers with solid reputations.

One item of note for smell-sensitive people, linoleum will have a strong linseed oil scent in most new applications for many months. Be aware of this if you are sensitive to the smell, as you may want to install this floor in summer when the windows are most likely to be open. For the longest-lasting finish, you want to seal these floors annually.

TERRAZZO

I love terrazzo counters and floors. The look is second to none. It almost appears like granite in some conditions, and in others, it allows incredible artistic and creative license. Terrazzo is constructed of reused glass, tile, and/or stone in a bed of Portland cement. These floors are almost indestructible. Many of the floors in America's houses of state, banks, and businesses from the early to mid-20th century used terrazzo flooring, and despite more than half a century of heavy use, the floors are still in excellent condition today.

EARTHSHIP FINISHES AND DETAILS

Once upon a time, the Earthships were built using everything from their site. Even the tops of oil cans became door handles. While the idea of recycling and reuse is great, many people do not love trying to use these awkward tools to access or decorate their spaces. Making something from nothing is great in principle, but it is only really a good idea as long as people want to use the things we make. So think carefully about what you choose to make into something useful. It is better not to waste time or money doing something twice.

Using reclaimed metal panels found on appliances at junk yards as an exterior finish material is what makes many of the Earthships look so colorful and bright. This is a great option for reusing these items, if you can find them in your area.

The new Earthships use curtains to black out the light in bedrooms especially. Use machine-washable curtains to help keep maintenance costs down.

If you love the look of the metal caps and chimneys and sculptural elements on the Earthships at Greater World, contact their sculptor Christina Sporrong at http://www.spirfireforge.com. Her work is exquisite and she is extremely well-respected in her field. These custom pieces are not inexpensive, but for those that can afford them, these details can make a project go from cool to WOW.

Engaging with the Process: Part 4

What enclosure systems are you leaning towards?

Which do you want to learn more about?

What are the tips and tricks that you already know you want to use?

CHAPTER IX

Mechanical Systems

Mechanical systems help us to make sure we stay warm in winter and cool in summer, and they provide us with adequate water, power, and lighting. The building's mechanical system includes the heating, ventilation, air conditioning, plumbing, and electrical systems. Most of these systems are hidden from view in the walls, ceiling, soffits (drop ceilings), and the floor.

THE MOST SUSTAINABLE MECHANICAL SYSTEMS:

- Let nature do the work for you.
- Aggregate uses.
- Match technology to need.

It is critical to design mechanical systems early and alongside the structure because many times, the systems and structure try to inhabit the same space, and the mechanical system may be heavy enough to influence structural loading. Without careful planning, these systems get crunched and result in details that are not just ugly... but sometimes threaten the way the systems work or inhibit your ability to do maintenance and repair. We also want to make sure we use the latent heat created by the mechanical system in the most beneficial way possible.

Mechanical, solar, electric, and water systems... especially those designed for Earthships and PassivHauses... are somewhat of a high tech solution. There will be maintenance necessary which you can most likely not perform on your own due to the complexity of the system. Most of the systems are designed and manufactured in Europe, and oftentimes they only come with instructions in those languages, and the tools required to repair them may not be readily available. This can be frustrating for those wishing to be self-sufficient.

Previous Page: Figure 46. Standard Earthship Roof Panel System

Mechanical Heating and Cooling

In many, if not most, cases... we really cannot achieve human comfort with only natural means. Passive solar helps. Shading helps. Ventilation helps, but only insofar as it is a) needed and b) in the right humidity range. In order to attain true comfort year-round, we most often need to provide additional heating, cooling, humidification, or de-humidification through mechanical means.

UNDERLYING THEMES OF HVAC

The human body loves to be kept at a temperature of between 75° F to 80° F. As humidity increases, air temperature is more comfortable when it is towards the cooler edge of the 75-80° range.

Heating, Ventilation, and Air Conditioning (HVAC) systems provide us with adequate ventilation when we cannot open the windows. They allow us to move the air around so it does not get stale. They control thermal performance and humidity. These systems also help to control dust and minimize odors.

Regular air movement should be above 10 feet per minute (FPM) to provide the right amounts of oxygenation to our bodies. Air velocities greater than 50 FPM create "drafty" conditions that make us uncomfortable.

Low humidity can create static charges and prematurely dries out wood, so we want to try and keep humidity above 20% and below 50%. High humidity causes the opposite effect - condensation - which we see on many Earthships because they lack adequate ventilation and de-humidification is not provided in humid environments.

EFFICIENCY

The efficiency of a heating system is directly tied to the ratio of air to fuel, and to the system's capability of minimizing heat losses. In the next pages, we will cover the typical systems used in common residential construction and offer up some tips and tricks of how to achieve comfort in a system that works for you.

Peak heating loads range from 20 BTUH for southern locations and 60 BTUH for northern locations. Multiple that by the square footage of the home to determine annual heating load requirements and resulting fuel requirements.

TIPS FOR ALL SYSTEMS

- Use foil tapes and mastic to seal ducts and equipment.
- Change filters every 3 months for best Indoor Air Quality.
- Programmable thermostats are essential tools for sustainability and cost minimization.
- HVAC does not function without power. So you want to be sure you have plenty of operable windows in the home to use for ventilation when the system goes down. Because all systems do go down eventually, even if just for maintenance.

Mechanical Rooms

A mechanical room is more than just a place for all the pumps, filters, pipes, water heaters, hot water storage tanks, electrical, and mechanical equipment to land. Careful design of this space can mean the difference between true occupant comfort and privacy... and too much noise and not enough performance.

Locating the mechanical room is a bit of an art. A central location minimizes the need for long runs and chases and also maximizes the efficient distribution of heat, cooling, and power, but these rooms can sometimes make a lot of noise and the hoses, tubes, vents, and registers can be a mess to look at.

We also try and minimize the number of electrical fields we introduce into the livable space, and mechanical rooms have plenty. Electrical fields are even more prevalent when the room is used for current converters from solar and wind turbines.

We advocate for not placing any mechanical or electrical equipment within 30 feet of a bedroom, for both electrical field and noise reasons.

Our preference is to separate our mechanical rooms from the main body of the home. We recommend placing the mechanical room in a central location towards the north where the sound can be minimized and the latent heat from the systems can be used to condition these otherwise cool spaces. We recommend enclosing mechanical systems behind an acoustically-treated wall accessed by an exterior-rated door with weather-stripping. This solution maximizes beauty, minimizes noise, minimizes mess, and keeps electric fields further away from your body. We design mechanical rooms with vents for combustion and ventilation air, a tubular skylight so there is no need to turn on a light to use the space during the day, a floor drain, and a hot and cold plumbed utility sink.

For sizing, about 6% of the building's total floor area is usually required for mechanical equipment. Another 2% is required for boilers, which must be accessible on all sides for repairs. Plan an easy route through the house for the eventual replacement of these systems.

Note: Some mechanical systems require both indoor and outdoor components. Both should be planned for from the outset.

Mechanical Heating

AIR TO AIR HEAT EXCHANGER OR HEAT RECOVERY VENTILATOR

With most energy-efficient houses being tightly built these days, an air-to-air heat exchanger is often used to provide fresh air into a space. This small mechanical system takes fresh air in from outside, exhausts used air out, and transfers up to 70% of the heat from the outgoing air to the incoming fresh air. An additional humidifier attachment can be used to modulate humidity. This system provides good indoor air quality with minimal cost and fuel input. Prices start at around $500 for this piece of equipment, which can look like anything from an air conditioning unit to a radiator depending on the size, brand, and attachments used.

RADIANT HEATING

Frank Lloyd Wright, in his Usonian Houses, was a proponent of radiant heat. That is part of what makes the homes so charming - the concrete floors with radiant heat means warm toes - that means warm bodies!

Radiant heating can be accomplished electrically, or through a hydronic system that uses water. What is great about radiant heating is that it can be done relatively small, using small baseboard or other heaters that are easy to pipe in, even after construction. A 3/4 inch pipe full of hot water effectively moves heat in the same way a 14 x 8 inch forced-air duct does. So these systems are ideal for tight spaces.

Until recently, baseboard radiators just ran when they ran. No mas! Programmable thermostats are now available for baseboard heat!

Radiant and hydronic space heating systems should be designed in accordance with industry best practices.

Electric Radiant Heating

Electric heating can be derived through two means. The first is resistance-type, which uses electric current through a wire that works much like a hair dryer. When it is used with air, this system is referred to as "strip heat". If it is used with water, it is most often via an electric boiler. Electric radiant is often the least expensive system to install, although it is also the most expensive heating method over its lifetime due to operating costs from fuel.

Hydronic Radiant Heating

Hydronic systems are great because they can piggyback on equipment you may already be using. They can be as simple as a loop added to your hot water heater that distributes hot water to radiators or to a loop in your bathroom floor, and they can be as complicated as using a hot water boiler system for your hot water needs and piggybacking floor or baseboard radiant emitters to warm up the entire house. Wall-hung boilers for these systems are designed small enough now that you can add supplemental heat like this to your mechanical room with very little effort.

Radiant Floor Heating

The hydronic heating idea can be extended to use boilers to heat water and deliver it through copper piping through your floors. The heating performance of these systems is second to none for human comfort, as when we are cold, we tend to lose heat through our heads and feet. Warm feet means we feel warmer faster. These systems can be prohibitively expensive to install, however, and they are best installed by pros. Though installation can be accomplished with laypeople, in our practice we have found that self-installed systems tend to require more maintenance and repair.

Note: radiant floor heating in a thermal mass floor like earth or concrete can cause a home to overheat of the home is super-insulated.

FURNACES AND BOILERS

Combustion heating is another option for heating our homes. This heating is usually provided via a furnace or boiler. The difference between the two is simple - a furnace heats air and a boiler heats water. Furnaces are fine for small areas, but a boiler may be better for a large space, as water moves heat more economically over long distances than warm air. Plus, water piping uses less space than ductwork, and pumps are more efficient at moving heat around than fans.

A safely-installed furnace or boiler requires a continuous supply of combustion air from outside the building envelope; a fire-safe chimney or flue outleting above the roof; a fuel-stopping switch in case of overheating; and a supply of gas that rises above the ground before entering a building to prevent leaks.

Gas, oil, and coal are all suitable fuels for combustion heating. Natural gas equipment is often the most affordable to install because there is no fuel storage required. Oil is the next most expensive because of storage requirements, and coal is most expensive due to ash disposal regulations.

For best performance, use a gas furnace with higher than 88% efficiency rating; an oil furnace with higher than 85% efficiency; or a boiler with a higher than 85% efficiency.

HEAT PUMPS

A heat pump is an electrically-supported HVAC system that takes heat from one environment and delivers it into another. The initial cost of these systems is most often higher than any other type of system, but a heat pump can also be reversed for cooling in summer, which means it offers more overall value for some climates.

As a cooling unit, a heat pump takes heat from the inside of the home and moves it outside, and when it is heating, it brings heated air from the outdoors into the building. A reversing valve switches the flow of the refrigerant. Heat pumps are most efficient as outdoor temperatures increase. This creates a need for supplemental heat in winter, which is often supplied by an electrical resistance attachment. This is an inefficient means of supplementary heating, but it only works when it is needed.

An air-source heat pump uses outdoor air as the heat source or sink. In some climates, this method requires defrosting the exterior coils in cold weather. This is accomplished with strip heater attachments.

A water-source heat pump uses a lake or well as the heat source or sink. Water is almost always warmer than the air temperature in winter and cooler in summer. This makes it an ideal heat reservoir. That is why water systems are more efficient than their air counterparts. A water-source heat pump requires 3 gallons per minute of water per ton of unit. So, you want to plan for a well or grid-tied water supply in most cases.

For best performance, use a heat pump with a SEER above 13 and a Heating Season Performance Factor (HSPF) between 8 and 10.

GEOTHERMAL OR GROUND SOURCE HEAT PUMP

Ground Source Heat Pump, or geothermal, systems utilize glycol loops drilled into the ground to heat or cool a building. These systems can also be used for a snowmelt system to keep ice dams from forming on your roof and gutters, as well as to melt snow at the entry to the home.

A geothermal heat pump is a highly efficient renewable energy technology and it is gaining wide acceptance. The principle is simple, and familiar... the inner-earth maintains a nearly constant temperature most of the time. So, you can easily run tubes of water through it, and the temperature of the water will naturally warm up to the inner-earth temperature. The primary use for this system is heating, as a regulated temperature can be achieved constantly with little variation. Geothermal systems can use a well for a vertical loop. A new system of installing geothermal uses a home's foundation pilings, which will already reach deep into the ground in some locations, as a "backbone" for a geothermal installation. Ponds can be used to provide cooling by geothermal needs as well, though a deep pond is required and beavers have been known to snack on the loops.

Benefits of geothermal heating include nearly free energy after the first initial outlay for installation. There is little or no dependence on gas or electricity for the system to function. The pumps can be run by solar panels if adequate sun is available. There are no emissions.

The challenges of the geothermal system include the cost of installation and a large area of site disturbance, which costs a great deal of time and money and can leave you with a loose landscape that is prone to erosion. If you are re-grading your site to capture rainwater and direct it to your pond, however, this concern is nullified.

On average, a geothermal heat pump system costs about $2,500 per ton of capacity, or roughly $7,500 for a typical residential 3-ton unit. A system using horizontal ground loops will generally cost less than a system with vertical loops, as the well for vertical loops costs about $5,000.

Use a Ground Source Heat Pump with an EER above 15 and use a certified installer.

> TIPS:
> - Install a de-superheater and make sure if cooling is used, that the refrigerant is non-HCFC-based.
> - Install a heat pump water heater and get double the bang for your buck by eliminating the need for additional hot water heating for showers and baths!

Clients in cold climates have shared with us that they no longer needed their wood stove once their geothermal system was installed.

DUCTS AND GRILLES

Avoid placing ductwork in exterior walls and install ducts within the heated and cooled space. This means you should put the insulation on the roof, not in the ceiling, if you are using attic mechanical runs. Insulate HVAC ducts in unconditioned spaces if there is no other option but to put them under the house or in an uninsulated attic.

Many times the metal will amplify sound, so if you install a forced-air mechanical system and the runs are located in the second floor's floor, be sure to have your installer design it so that the sound from the rooms is baffled from the rooms above or below. Sounds transmission can be a nightmare when you are trying to sleep and someone else is banging around cleaning the kitchen, for instance. Also have insulation installed between the floors. On air registers, the amount of noise from the system is directly proportional to how much air is coming out. For quiet zones, use more registers to distribute the air through a space.

Use return ducts and grilles in every room except kitchens, baths, closets, and utility rooms.

Mask all ducts during construction and vacuum them out as much as possible before turning on your HVAC system. This will minimize dust and particulates.

Fireplaces and Stoves

In lieu of the typical mechanical means of heating described above, heating via a centrally-located wood stove or true masonry fireplace is a great option. Fireplaces offer not only heat but a sense of ambience. For many who live in colder climates, having a fireplace going is part of why we love to live here.

We recommend having a wood stove in a centrally-located living space as a backup to traditional heating. The reason why is less about heat than it is about food - we want to be able to keep going if our systems go down. With a wood stove, we can use the heat to warm the space, and also boil water to purify it or make it into bath water, as well as make food easily.

You might want to consider creating an inglenook in front of your fireplace or masonry heater. An inglenook is a small room or "nook" adjacent to a fireplace that keeps much of the heat in so you can warm up quickly. A variation on the inglenook is also used for kitchen fires when cooking.

Alternately, you might want to consider using a double-ended fireplace approach as is used in Georgian architecture. If you head to the east coast, you will see that many old brick homes have a fireplace at each end of the building. These help to create a "zone heating" effect where you can heat individual spaces as they are used and allows the fireplaces in rooms above and below to stack, minimizing the foundation as well as the size of the chimney. This technique is great for warming up the ends of the house. We do that one better, and on long homes, we put a fireplace on the wall between the last room and the next to last room on each end. That way, we keep the heat inside the home and double the number of rooms warmed.

FIREPLACE

A well-designed fireplace will sustain the fire, carry smoke to the outside, make as much heat as possible bounce into the space, and will protect the neighboring materials during use.

A poorly designed fireplace can leave you with a chimney that sucks the heat right out of the house, so its detailing is important. Drafting, or air flow from the fire to the outside, is controlled by a damper, an additional vent tube in some cases, and the flue size of the chimney itself.

Fireplaces require foundations. An open-front fireplace should be a minimum of 24 inches wide and tall by 16 inches deep. The damper width should be a minimum of 10 inches wider than the firebox. There should be a smoke chamber above that is no less than 20 inches tall and the damper width plus two inches wide, and the smoke chamber should have a smoke-shelf of at least 12 inches to deflect downdrafts during windy days. The flue should have an area of 96 square inches or more. A fireplace should be constructed of non-combustible materials like brick masonry or CMU blocks. It should have a hearth that is also non-combustible, is 8" wider than the opening, and is at least as deep as the firebox.

If you have a standard fireplace, you can purchase a fireplace insert which will help you retain up to 60% more heat using less fuel. You can also purchase a wood stove insert for your fire box for even more heat capture.

A final option for making the most of your standard fireplace is to use the proportions of what is called a Rumsford Fireplace. This unique design maximizes the throw of heat from the fire into the space rather than allowing the heat to go up the chimney. This must be designed and installed by a mason.

MASONRY STOVES

Also known as true masonry fireplaces, masonry heaters, Kachelofens, Russian or Finnish fireplaces, Swedish stoves, tile stoves, and contra-flow fireplaces... a masonry heater is basically a really big pizza oven with a bunch of folds in the flue that pass through heavy masonry walls and warm them up. This uses almost all the heat of the fire to store warmth for later instead of immediately shooting it up the chimney. Masonry heaters use about 1/3 the amount of wood of a wood stove and their heat can last for hours after their fire goes out.

Some masonry heaters have built-in platforms that can be used as cozy sleeping shelves. This technique has been used in New Mexico for hundreds of years. In many places throughout Europe, bed nooks had masonry fireplace flues running underneath the bed for heating. The opening to the nook was covered by heavy curtains for warmth retention and privacy.

While a masonry stove can be hand-built, we recommend having yours designed and installed by professionals. They know exactly what to do, and not to do, and this may be required by Code.

ROCKET STOVE

A rocket stove is an extraordinary and simple feat of engineering. Basically, you build a long hollow bench with a hole in the top on one end and another to vent out the other end. You put sticks down into the hole as if you had kindling standing in a bucket. The fire below burns the ends of the sticks, and then blows sideways into a larger chamber along the bench that burns and recirculates the heat. The flue passes through the other end of the bench and the heat from the small fire warms the bench up before sending the exhaust out. The exhaust is just steam and carbon dioxide, though a little smoke is common when the fire is first lit. A rocket stove uses 80-90% less fuel than a standard wood stove and the heat can last for days. Rocket stoves can be built by almost anyone in just a few days. Rocket stoves do require a substantial foundation to be installed. Because of this, retrofitting or adding one later is difficult and expensive. A rocket stove requires a building permit in most cases.

WOOD STOVES

Wood stoves are one of the least expensive and easiest to use heating methods there is. They are great because they let you cook food as well as have a source of primary or backup heat. For best performance, these units should have direct outside air vented into the unit. A flue for a wood stove requires a rain cap, collars at the roof penetration, and 2" minimum clearance from any combustible material it passes through, including floor and roof framing. It should also rise above the roof by 3 feet. A wood stove should be kept away from the walls and ceiling by 18 inches or more at the flue, and 36" or more from the firebox, unless a non-combustible heat shield is used, which can minimize this space to 18". A wood stove should be installed on a non-combustible material at the floor of at least 1/2" thick, and that material should extend to 18 inches or more away from each side and the front of the stove. A stove with a heated air return is ideal. Use EPA-certified wood stoves.

PELLET STOVES

Pellet stoves use a recycled renewable fuel source of reclaimed lumber scraps. They are clean burning, cost effective, and energy efficient. They are considered a carbon-neutral energy source. Pellet stoves should generate 2.0 grams per hour of particulate or less.

FUEL SOURCES

FUEL SOURCE	BTUS PRODUCED
Wood	5,000-7,000
Coal	14,000
Natural gas	100,000 per therm
Propane	90,000 per gallon
Electric	3,400

Mechanical Cooling & Air Conditioning

An Air Conditioning (A/C) system is not just for cooling in the summertime. They also regulate indoor comfort by controlling temperature, providing fresh filtered air, and regulating humidity.

Cooling equipment removes heated air from indoors and puts it outdoors. It accomplishes this by causing a refrigerant to evaporate, which causes heat to be captured, and then it is released again when the refrigerant condenses. These systems require two large parts - an evaporator on the interior and a condenser on the exterior of the building - which must be planned for.

To determine your cooling loads to size an A/C unit, one rule of thumb says to estimate 25 BTUH and then multiply that by your total square footage to get the total load requirement.

We do not advocate the use of air conditioning systems for many cases. A whole house ventilation system with 95% heat recovery may be a better alternative. Check with a local mechanical engineer or installer before choosing your system.

EVAPORATIVE COOLERS

In arid climates, an evaporative or "swamp" cooler is often used in lieu of an air conditioner unit. These units change hot dry air to cool moist air and use 10% of the energy of an A/C unit. They also add needed humidification for occupant comfort.

FANS

In all but cool climates, especially in buildings depending on natural ventilation, ceiling fans should be provided in the largest rooms of the house to move heat and air through the space. A fan also uses 10% of the energy of an A/C unit. Regularly used fans should be permanent, as they will last longer and perform better than their box counterparts. Also, the electrical load is usually smaller.

Using fans in winter is not recommended because while they do move the air around, they also create drafts, which negates the warming effect.

Typical Earthship Mechanical Systems

There are some issues with the Earthship's systems being quite work intensive.

We were told a story recently where a couple had wanted to rent an Earthship to see if they would like to build one. When they went online make reservations, they were sent a link to a YouTube video that explained, over 30 minutes, the process for opening and closing up the house every day. They had to sign a contract saying they would do that, exactly, before they could rent the place. So they didn't.

The first way of fixing the maintenance issues in our new and improved Earthship design is to not use the typical Earthship greenhouse. That may not appeal to many, so the next best way to address this is to use chemical- or solar-powered operators on your operable window systems, which should be located near the bottom AND the top of the greenhouse window wall. The last way to address this is to use high and low windows at the secondary window walls between the greenhouse and the living spaces, so that physics can do its job and encourage air movement through the space. The final tip here, from all the people we interviewed about their Earthships who had figured them out how to make them work, is to include fans throughout the building.

Though, and this is important... if you do not choose to employ an automated system, your home will perform better if you have a schedule for opening and closing vents every day at the same times. There is just no way around it... overheating is minimized when you remember to open windows. Following a schedule makes your building work for you, especially if you adapt the schedule to local seasonal light and heat fluctuations. No two schedules will or should be the same unless you are neighbors.

A fireplace in an Earthship requires a minimum 6" vent from the outside be installed to provide combustion air, because an Earthship is tightly constructed and there is not enough air when the house is closed up to provide oxygen to keep the fire going.

One of the most concerning aspects of the systems design we saw in several Earthships was storing the bulky solar cell batteries, or a bank of 10-12 car batteries, inside the home or in the entrance vestibule of the home. This is a disaster in the making. Solar cell batteries are required by Code to be outside of the structure of the home. The reason for this is because the way they operate results in an off-gassing of hydrogen. Hydrogen is lighter than air so it rises up into the roof. If it is not vented, it gets trapped. Vents fail – they get stuffed with nests, the turbine gets damaged... and hydrogen in a non-vented space can cause explosions!!!! Please, please do not store your solar batteries in the interior of your home!

Earthship systems should be used every day to maintain function. Greywater needs to be re-charged, vents need opening, plumbing needs flushing. To leave the Earthship empty for any amount of time most likely means problems later.

Electrical Systems

Electrical systems supply us with power for lighting, heating, and the operation of the myriad of appliances and equipment we supplement our lives with. The electrical system is one of those places where the building official is likely to have a lot of say. The main reason being that there is a negative and a positive circuit needed to make electrical work, and when those charges are crossed, it can be deadly. For the electrical current to flow, the circuit must be completed, which is what switches do. The circuit board, or breaker box, controls how much of the power goes to what lines and when.

There are three different kinds of circuits coming off a panel board: single outlet lines for major appliances; multiple outlet lines for regular appliances; and a general purpose circuit for lighting and the outlets you use to plug in your vacuum or laptop. Separate circuits are required for cable TV, audio, and intercoms, as well as fire alarm and security systems. A separate circuit is also a great idea if you know where you want to put your desktop computer and peripherals.

Lighting

The point of a lighting system is to make sure you have enough light to do the task you want to do. While it may seem like one of those things where you "put a lamp where you need it", it is in fact a challenging task to accomplish good lighting. That is why there is a professional field of lighting specialists. The art comes through knowing that certain tasks require different lighting requirements. Dining, for instance, may only require 20 foot-candles of light, and you may want to be able to dim that light to create a "feeling" in the space. Regular tasks, like reading or cooking, may only require 50 foot-candles of light. Painting or drafting can require 100 foot-candles of light. Sewing or quilting can require 200 foot-candles of light. How easily these tasks are accomplished depends on the contrast between what we are working on and its background, which we modulate with light. We want to reduce glare so we can work most effectively without tiring our eyes out. For purposes of this effort, let's say that we want our task area to be at least 3 times brighter than the area around it. That will make things as easy on our eyes as possible, and allow us to stay focused on the task at hand.

A mix of directional and indirect or diffuse light in a room is ideal.

UPLIGHTS

Up-lights in a coffered ceiling or from a wall sconce bounce light off the ceiling. This offers indirect diffused light for areas that require less direct lighting, like hallways, offices, or even the living room. This creates more of an "ambient" lighting effect something like daylight coming through windows and lighting up a room.

DIRECT LIGHTING

Direct lights can be pointed from the ceiling or under a cabinet onto our task area or a piece of art. They throw more shadows and therefore are better for anything that requires detailed attention and/or depth perception. Direct lights are better for sculptures, and those times when we may want to emphasize something's color, shape, or texture. Direct lights can be pendant, recessed, or track type.

A LITTLE STORY ABOUT SUSTAINABLE LIGHTING

Even lighting can be more sustainable, and we can achieve that sustainability without depending on light designers to do it for us. Consider this example about my friend Illac Diaz's work for Liters of Light:

When solar lights, or other technological projects like water filtration systems are offered as gifts to third world communities, who oftentimes are off-grid not because they want to be but because it is the nature of that community, the end result can sometimes not satisfy the desire to help that was originally intended in the giving.

Things break. Technology... breaks regularly. It is easy for those of us in first world countries to take that for granted. We pop down to the store and get the missing part and the problem is solved. In an off-grid community, especially one that is not near a social center like a city, when something breaks and there is no repair plan... the technology that breaks may well become trash.

After seeing this happen repeatedly in the Philippines, social entrepreneur Illac Diaz decided to take a different approach. It started out as a source of daylighting. There were entire villages constructed of found objects in some of the poor and disaster-ridden areas of his country. The shanties in these communities didn't even have windows, in most cases. The people living in these areas had no light, unless it was provided by a lantern or candle or some other light producing means.

Illac wanted to try and do something to help. His revolutionary idea was to take an empty clear plastic drink bottle that would otherwise be thrown away, then add water and a drop or two of chlorine bleach, and seal the bottle. Then, they would cut a hole in the ceiling of the shanty he wanted to get light to, and to add a piece of metal flashing at the top of the roof which would hold the bottle of water. A few minutes of assembly, and voila! Instant skylight! It was genius. And catching! The idea took off! Then, people asked for more... they begged for a little light for evenings, something that would not cost them anything, and was as simple to install as his daylight bottles.

Instead of importing expensive solar technologies for his efforts to bring light to the many people without in his country, or those that are trying to recover from disasters, Illac's organization Liter of Light works now with the local community to build fast, affordable solar lighting... within the community. They use the same reused bottle technology that gave them daylight, and add a tiny circuit board of recycled parts that are easily found locally, a high-tech LED lamp guaranteed to last 70,000 hours that works off solar power, and voila! Instant light. Repairs are simple, use locally available materials, and use local hands to create sustainable industries to handle new builds as well as repairs.

In some locations, instead of just having a bare plastic bottle hanging in a hole in the ceiling, the bottles are covered with handcrafted woven shades, offering an opportunity for local basket-weavers to use and pass on their traditional skills.

This approach is really quite genius. Environmental, social, and cultural sustainability fuse into one truly sustainable whole. So, the question becomes... are there ways you can cultivate this kind of forward-thinking and industry-building opportunity in your build? Can you hack making something that you need that you can do better yourself and preserve your traditions at the same time? Does buying everything you need in a box from someone else, somewhere else, satisfy your values? If it doesn't, or if you are looking for creative ways to fund your project, or build an industry, why not consider something like this? Try and solve the sustainability question in a way that works for you and feeds your soul!

TIPS FOR BEST LIGHTING DESIGN

When thinking about where you want to put your lights, we suggest chalking in an outline of the furniture you want to use on your floor first. We do that to avoid placing lights too close to the wall or a tall cabinet, so the light gets where you want it... onto work surfaces especially. Also, think about where lights go in relation to where you will put ceiling fans. You want to be sure that the light is not over the blades. There is nothing worse than accidentally creating a strobe effect when you get the fan installed!

Exterior lights should have light and motion detectors and should, ideally, be solar powered.

Power

Power is one of the core essential elements of buildings. You can live without heat, without plumbing, and without electric lights. But almost nobody these days can live without some power source. Our world just runs on it.

If you are designing your power system around natural and renewable energy especially, you can get the most bang for your buck by maximizing efficiency and minimizing the size of the system. Most importantly, you need to size your system so that it works for your loads. The easiest way to do that is to list every input you will need, and the power it requires. From pumps for the greywater and solar hot water systems, to refrigerators, computers, and phone chargers... catalog everything with a cord or plug you own or will ever use, and size your system accordingly. Do not freak out if the load seems huge. 1,000 kwh/month is normal.

GRID-POWER

Once we confirmed that the most affordable Earthship to build is a grid-tied one, we realized we had to address grid-tied power.

While you may dream of one day affording solar power, and even wire it in so it is easy to add later, the easiest and most affordable way to green your electrical use is to buy "green power" from your local utility. The greener alternatives are powered via a solar farm or wind, most commonly. Typically this service costs up to $20 more a month than traditionally-sourced power, but careful attention to turning lights on and off, and minimizing your electrical load by using natural techniques - employing root cellars, designing your home with passive solar, using a laundry line instead of a dryer, and replacing your traditional lighting with LED and CFL lighting - can make this an attractive and affordable alternative for people who will not be going off-grid just yet. In the U.S., you can find out if this option is available to you by going to the DOE Can I Buy Green Power in My State? Website at:

http://apps3.eere.energy.gov/greenpower/buying/buying_power.shtml_and

Then call your utility company and switch to green power. It will take you less than 10 minutes, and for an extra few bucks a month, you will be putting your utility company on notice that you want better, greener power practices out of them.

POWER LOAD SUCKERS

If your electrical devices have an indicator light, a clock, a power adapter, or a standby function, they are using energy even when they are "off". Put these, and especially your cable box - which uses half the power of a refrigerator! - on a power strip and/or a switch so you can turn it off when you are not using it. This will vastly reduce your loads!

You also might want to find a central place in your home to set up a power strip that is wired to a switch and have the entire family commit to using this location to charge household items like batteries, phones, tablets, etcetera... Just switch off the power strip when it is not in use. If you would prefer not to use a switch, a timer-regulated power strip is now available from Belkin, which will turn itself off after an amount of time that you determine. The ideal place for this is the location people are already setting their phones and tablets when they set them down. Many people find that a central kitchen charging station is a great option, and it provides a perfect place to have a small desk with telephone books, paper, pens, and any other things you might need while using these tools.

THE HOT ROOM

For people with electrical field sensitivities, and those who just want to minimize electrical fields in the home... in the places you can get away with this because they are not subject to permitting, we encourage people to consider eliminating electrical outlets in the home and building a "hot room" separate from the main house with all the electric and telephone connections that they could need, and possibly even locating the kitchen in this space. Something like an artists' studio or a workshop, complete with lots of windows for great ambient light, only that can also work as an office, studio, or workroom space. This keeps the electric and wired connections out of the main body of the home, and allows us to stay connected with the outside world. By building this extra room, we can minimize the exposure to electrical fields. For these cases especially, we advocate the use of small solar arrays.

SOLAR POWER

Photovoltaic (PV) solar electric systems generate electricity by converting the sun's energy into DC current electricity and storing it in solar cells or car batteries. The traditional Earthship Power Organizing Module draws DC electricity from the batteries, inverts some of it for AC electricity, and a standard wiring system supplies it to the home. The POM can be powered alternately from a gasoline generator and can be grid-tied if needed. Without the POM, solar power is just run through an inverter kit you can purchase from your solar supplier. In a typical Earthship, DC power runs all the pumps, critical lighting, and a DC fridge. We leave it up to you whether or not you want to use that system, as it may be prohibitively expensive to use, or you may be required to be grid-tied, which opens up your options.

PV panels are a reliable source of power in places with lots of sun. You can find out generally if they can work for your area by studying the map provided in our Passive Solar Doesn't Work Everywhere section. PV is non-polluting (except when manufactured), decreases dependence on the grid, offers increased energy security, and requires little maintenance.

A GRID-TIED or NET-METERED system uses a power meter that starts turning backwards when the house produces more electricity than it needs. The grid serves as the battery in these systems. These systems consist of a PV array made of solar panels, wiring, switches, and an inverter in the mechanical room to turn the DC electricity produced in the panels to the AC electricity used by modern appliances. The power produced runs through the home's main breaker panel. Many localities offer solar rebates for grid-tied systems.

An OFF-GRID system requires batteries. Because of this, this system can be quite expensive, but this option allows you complete control over your power security.

Some Concerns about Solar Power

We have been convinced by some researchers' arguments that solar power photovoltaic (PV) is not the way to go for everyone. It is up to you to decide what works for you.

HERE ARE SOME FACTS ABOUT PV TO HELP YOU MAKE YOUR CHOICES:

- PV cannot be used at night without some form of storage, usually a deep-cycle battery.
- In areas with mostly cloudy weather, depending on solar energy may mean a struggle to meet energy needs. These systems can be extensive and prohibitively expensive in high latitude locations.
- Most solar cells are made of silicon, and the process of refining it produces wastes like silicon tetrachloride that can damage the environment. Recently released solar cells use other materials like cadmium telluride that are also toxic and require proper handling.
- It takes 5-8 units of bauxite ore to produce one unit of aluminum. The waste often gets dumped into watersheds.
- Today's best solar panels only capture and use about 60% of the sun's potential energy.
- Solar panels are most often placed on the roof, creating a shield of electrical energy over the home. (But, to be fair, in hot areas, this shading can help minimize solar gain on the roof.)
- Severin Borenstein, professor at the UC Berkeley's Haas School of Business and director of the UC Energy Institute, conducted a study calculating the net present value of power produced by a 10 kilowatt PV system, comparing that to the cost of installing and operating the system over its lifetime. His research indicated that the cost for a typical installation ranges from nearly $86,000 to

$91,000, while the value of the power produced is only valued at up to $51,000, thus the cost of solar PV is about 80 percent greater than the value of the electricity it will produce.

Solar Power Cost

Solar Panels cost somewhere in the neighborhood of 70 cents per watt these days. Our local solar supplier told us that he and suppliers like him can develop a payment plan for solar panels that gets very close to the rates one might pay per month for electric service. He also mentioned that the payback period for solar panels is nearing 3 years and that modern solar panels can last 50 years or more.

A selling point: a well-designed solar or wind system can add $10,000 to the home's resale value!

TIPS FOR DOING SOLAR POWER WELL:

- The system should have unrestricted solar access and should be equally non-restricting for other systems. No trees or buildings should be in the way of the panels and there should be no penetrations on the roof where the solar array will be: no plumbing vents, no fireplace vents, and no skylights! Plan for this now and have a much easier install later!

- Photovoltaic panels should be installed within 20 degrees of due south and at an angle equal to their latitude in summer and that plus 10 degrees in winter.

- Have your PV designer be sure to document proper protection to prevent electric islanding in the event of a power outage.

- Use solar power equipment with applicable IEEE and UL certifications.

Alternative Solar Power Collectors

Solar roofing shingles are also available now though they are a bit cost prohibitive for most.

Translucent solar collectors can be used as roofs in greenhouses.

Getting Solar Ready

If PV is desired, but you either cannot afford it yet or want to wait a couple years for panels to be more efficient, consider adding the following while building so adding PV down the line is as easy and affordable as possible:

- Make sure the roof structure is designed to support the solar array. Typical solar panels weigh about 50 pounds each and are distributed evenly across a roof on racks. By dividing the weight of the panels and racks by the area of the panels, we find that the combined weight adds about 3-4 pounds per square foot to the roof's structural load. Structures built after 1970 are engineered to support additional loads greater than this so you should be okay. If your home is not designed by an architect or engineer though, this could be a trouble spot.

- Find out how much solar is required to power the home. Add 15% capacity to be sure. How much panel will that mean? Make sure there is enough south-facing roof area to install that much panel, especially if the roof is pitched.

- Install an electric service disconnect switch and a circuit in the breaker box for the solar electric feed.

- Plan the location for the inverter. This requires a 4 foot by 4 foot square area of wall about 12 inches deep and it is usually located in a mechanical room.

- Install a conduit or wire chase from the electrical panel to where the inverter will be installed and also up to the attic or roof so wiring can be added with ease later.

Making the Most of Solar PV

Using PV for power requires some adjustment to accommodate. Our tips for doing it well include:

- Only vacuum, wash clothes, or use the dishwasher when the sun is shining.
- Do not use any appliances that have a LED clock or other display.
- Skip the microwave.
- And the curling iron.
- And the hair dryer.
- And the electric mixer.
- And the games consoles.
- And the gigantic TV.
- Have all power strips switched and turn the switch off when you are not using them.
- Power down wireless internet routers, anything you are not using, and cordless phones at night and when not in use to minimize power draw.

WIND POWER

Wind power is a viable energy alternative if the land you are working with has an average annual windspeed of more than 10mph. The site should really have a minimum rating of Class 3 winds to be viable. To see if your area works for wind power, refer to the Windpowering America website at:

>   http://www.windpoweringamerica.gov/wind_maps.asp

or look for your own country's wind resource map to determine if this is a viable energy option for your location.

The American Wind Energy Association says that a typical home wind system will cost approximately $32,000 for 10kW. A comparable PV system can cost around $80,000. A 1.5kW wind turbine will meet the needs of a home requiring 300 kWh per month in a location with a 14-mile-per-hour annual average wind speed. The cost of installation will be repaid in approximately 10 years with a 10 mph wind.

We have worked with designers that love the Pacwind and Skystream wind turbines.

In regard to the Dynasphere wind generator some people want to use, we suggest not utilizing this means of wind power generation. In the article Earthship Hype and Earthship Reality on GreenBuildingAdvisor.com, Martin Holladay notes,

> *"In an article on Earthships published in Makezine... Andrew Terranova reports that "The Earthship team has even designed their own vertical-axis windmill, called the Dynasphere."... Since vertical-axis machines are the "insulating paint" of renewable energy equipment, this news is not encouraging. (For a physics-based explanation of why vertical-axis wind turbines underperform their horizontal-axis rivals, see Thoughts on Vertical-Axis Wind Turbines by Robert Preus. In his article, Preus notes, "There is an all-too-common belief that a VAWT [vertical-axis wind turbine] approach will revolutionize the small wind industry. This seems to be a lot of wishful thinking by people who do not understand physics.")*

TIPS FOR MAKING WIND POWER WORK:

- An on-site wind use system most often needs to be constructed in accordance with Land Use regulations. Check your city, county, and HOA for applicable requirements.
- Proper protection to prevent electric islanding in the event of a power outage is required.

The Art and Science of Outlets and Switching

Electrical outlets should be provided for every 12 feet of wall space in the living areas and every 4 feet in the kitchen and utility/workshop/work spaces, unless otherwise required by Code, which can be more restrictive. Outlets and switches should be located between 18 inches and 4 feet above the finished floor. Outlets in wet environments - in baths, utility rooms, and near the kitchen sink - need to be GFCI type. Add foam insulation underneath the wall plate on your electrical outlets and light switches for maximum thermal performance.

TIPS FOR LOCATING POWER OUTLETS

- Do a furniture layout plan early. Who wants outlets behind a couch or a bed? Place outlets where your lamps, radios, and appliances are going to be.

- An outlet just outside the garage door can sometimes be useful.

- If the sink in a bathroom is against a left wall, unless the person using it is left handed, they will still use their right hand to hold the hair dryer, curling iron, etcetera... meaning the cord will be across the sink if the outlet is on the side wall. Put the outlet on the right side of the sink and Voila! Dangerous situation avoided!

- Where will you set your cell phone down when you come in the house? That is where the charger should be, and therefore the outlet.

- Do you decorate for the holidays? If so, strategically locate outlets on top of mantles, next to handrails, and any place where you might have light displays or strings of lights. If you think these things through now, you will not have to rely on an extension cord. A wall switch would be a great asset to this system!

- Is there a workbench in the garage or work room? Did you coordinate outlet #, location, and circuiting requirements with your panel size? Some power tools require separate circuiting and several have high amperage requirements.

- In workshops, locate the switches at 40" above the finished floor if you do not install them directly into the cabinets, or if the cabinets will come later. A backsplash is a great thing to put in a workshop in order to minimize the gunk that collects there, and you will want the outlets high enough to not have to cut the backsplash around the outlets.

- Place outlets a bit higher so you do not have to see the cords under furniture and so you do not have to bend down so far to use them.

TIPS FOR LOCATING SWITCHES

- Walk through every doorway, and visualize that instinctual reach for the switch.

- Locate switches on the latch side of the door, within 12" of the door. Locate the switch on the inside of the room it serves. Though, sometimes it makes more sense to place a light switch outside the door, rather than inside. Just think through how you will most easily be able to reach for it with an armload of stuff. Put the switch in the easy place.

- Stand at the sink. Think about the disposal if you will have one. What direction are the stacked pots and pans most likely going to be? Put the switch where things will not be.

- Imagine doing last rounds before going to bed - what is the sequence of shutting down the house? Make turning it all off easy for yourself.

- Depending the age and abilities of those living inside the home, (think senior citizens, children, handicapped, etcetera...) you may want to place light switches, thermostats and other environmental controls in more accessible locations between 18 inches and 48 inches above the floor.

- Make sure that thermostats are not located in close proximity to lamps or TVs, which create a lot of heat and can cause the thermostat to not read the temperature correctly.

- If there are multiple switches, install the switches in the order you use them. In a living/dining area, for instance, make the first switch the living room since it is most often used, then the dining room lights, then accessory lights. Or whatever makes sense to you. In a bath, do the vanity (forward) light, then the overhead light and/or fan, then the shower light.

- If you have stairs coming off the porch, be sure to provide adequate lighting for the steps and the adjoining walkway, and put the switch in a place that makes sense if you are fumbling in the dark.

- Pocket doors could make it difficult to put a light switch exactly where you want it. Careful attention to this detail will be required.

- Provide a switch for your entertainment center and computers! Switching it off will reduce the extensive power load from these systems when they are not being used!

- Also, if you use heat tape for your gutters in cold climates, provide a switch for this too and save yourself a trip to plug them in!

Appliances

Appliances are the core of how we work these days. They maximize our output while minimizing our effort. They are a necessity of modern life. You want to be sure that you have these items planned for, and hopefully bought, before you size your PV system. It is not at all uncommon for any number of draws to max the system out.

Mechanical equipment and appliances should carry the Energy Star or Energy Guide Label that indicates that the appliance is in the top 25% of the efficiency scale. They should also be UL rated.

The most trusted and dependable large appliance sellers include ABT Electronics, independent (mom-and-pop) appliance stores, and Pacific Sales. For big-box type stores, Lowe's and Home Depot are equally rated in customer satisfaction. For small appliances, favorite stores include Amazon, ABT, Costco, and independent retailers. Kohl's and Bed Bath and Beyond rank highest among chain stores for small appliances.

Doing online research before you head to the store can oftentimes dramatically reduce the time required to choose the perfect appliance for your needs.

APPLIANCE TIPS

If you want to minimize electrical inputs, use appliances without LED displays, as they draw continuous power and will thereby diminish the capacity of your system.

Permanent appliances like refrigerators and dishwashers require dedicated outlets to switches at the electrical panel.

When using gas appliances, including fireplaces, you might want to consider an electric ignition. A pilot light adds heat and uses gas whether it is needed at that time of year or not. If you do have a pilot light, especially on furnaces and fireplaces, consider turning it off in the off-season.

EXHAUST FANS

The bath and laundry/utility room should have an exhaust fan vented to outside or to a heat recovery device if there is a mechanical system installed in order to meet Code. Purchase a fan that can move 100 cubic feet per minute (CFM).

REFRIGERATOR

Typical Earthships use a DC fridge. That may or may not work for you. It all depends on how you want to address your power needs.

For the best performing and easiest to care for refrigerators, look for stainless, black, or white finishes. If the fridge will be exposed to direct sunlight, choose white or stainless which will absorb less heat. Models with split shelves and adjustable door shelves are the most convenient. Skip the fancy technological climate controls available in some models but choose a dual evaporator model if you can afford it, as this will maintain a more constant humidity. Plan ahead for your desired fridge's height before determining whether you will use cabinets above it or not. As far as cost is concerned, a top-freezer model fridge starts at $600 and a side-by-side starts at $1,500.

The top performing affordable new refrigerators requiring the least number of repairs are:

- For top-freezer models with a front ice-maker: Maytag, Kenmore, GE, Whirlpool, and Frigidaire. Haler also makes a value-packed top freezer model.
- Without an icemaker: Kenmore, Frigidaire, GE, and Whirlpool.
- For bottom freezer types: Kenmore, Samsung, and Maytag are great for units with front icemakers and Kenmore and GE for units without.
- For side-by sides: Maytag, Whirlpool, and Kenmore.

DISPOSAL

While many people consider a disposal or disposer a nice gadget, others find them essential kitchen tools. Disposals are differentiated by their price, size, noise, whether they work best as continuous-feed or batch-feed and maybe most importantly - their grind stages. The more grind stages the disposal has, the finer the waste will be when it is sent out to your septic field. Those finer bits degrade more easily.

Other people will prefer to use my favorite method of disposing of food scraps – a worm bin. These great homemade systems require almost no maintenance and make the most amazing compost I have ever smelt!

DISHWASHER

You might be surprised to learn that using a modern dishwasher can dramatically reduce the amount of water used compared to hand-washing dishes. Though, because of reduced water use and increased energy efficiency, a new efficient dishwasher may have a cycle that lasts up to two hours. There is no need to get fancy cycles on your dishwasher. A standard model with light, medium, and heavy settings will take care of almost every sticky dish you can make. Though, if you can afford it, an automatic soil sensor can select the cycle for you and improve efficiency. Drawer-model dishwashers tend to use more water and energy than standard models. A self-cleaning filter makes for more noise, so if you are up for dumping the filter and want to maximize quiet performance, look for a manual-clean filter option. A dishwasher with an 8.5 gallon per load or better efficiency is ideal.

If your home is tending to overheat in the summer, or you could benefit from increased humidity, just set your dishwasher on the wash and rinse setting (with dry turned off) and open the door and allow your dishes to air dry once washing is complete.

A standard dishwasher will start at $600. Technology-heavy versions start at around $1,500. As far as consumer trust in dishwashers goes, Bosch, Whirlpool, and Miele are the most trusted and least repair-prone brands, followed by Kenmore. Maytag, GE, KitchenAid, and Frigidaire, which all score about equally thereafter. Samsung is the most repair-prone dishwasher reported.

HOT WATER DISPENSER

These devices use a small highly-insulated water tank connected to a smaller secondary faucet to deliver instant hot water 24/7. They use less energy than stoves or electric kettles, but they are always on, so they are a more efficient option if you heat water often through the day.

RANGE

In a typical Earthship, the stove is run with propane. That may or may not work for you, so here are some other options:

A range is a single unit appliance that includes both a cooktop and an oven below. Ranges are most often installed in a gap in between floor cabinets. Designing your cabinets around your desired range is critical for insuring the range fits and providing adequate clearance at the sides. Why choose a range over a separate cooktop and wall oven? It is easy to spend $1,500 each on separate unit, whereas a range can do double duty for half the cost.

Electric ranges provide good performance for a better value, and start at $500 for coil type and $800 for smooth-top style. See Cooktop, below, for explanation of the difference and benefits of each. GE, Whirlpool, Frigidaire, and Kenmore make the most dependable brands of electric range.

Gas ranges offer top performance and superior design appeal, but this comes at a higher cost. They start at $750, though professional models can start as high as $3,000. Frigidaire, GE, Kenmore, and Whirlpool are reliable consumer favorites.

Induction ranges use a magnetic field to increase cooking speed and improve efficiency by up to 25% over electric and gas types. Their costs are coming down, but this type of range will cost upwards of $1700.

COOKTOP

A cooktop is a drop-in stove appliance that sits on top of the countertop within your base cabinets or island. A gas model cooktop is preferable if you like to see the flame and immediately have a cooler surface when you turn off the stove. A coil-type electric cooktop is the most affordable type, but it requires more cleaning. A smooth-top electric model is ideal for cleaning ease. Skip the fancy ones with lots of tech attached – they create a continuous draw on your power supply and are not worth the trouble if you just want to cook.

A gas cooktop will start at $1100 for a 30 inch model and $1900 for a 36 inch model. An electric cooktop will start around $800. For gas cooktops, Wolf excels in consumer satisfaction and requires the fewest repairs, followed by GE, KitchenAid, and Kenmore. For electric, GE, Kenmore, Frigidaire, Whirlpool, and KitchenAid all perform about equally.

OVEN

In this case we are referring to a wall oven, which is installed in a framed bump-out designed specifically for that purpose. Oftentimes, cabinets are built-in above and below. We recommend considering not using doors on the cabinets above the oven in order to avoid the inevitable breakdown of the finish there due to the oven's top-vents. Because of those vents, be sure not to store wine or other heat-sensitive products above.

An oven with a smooth bottom or cover over the bottom element is easiest to clean. Choose a knob type oven if at all possible due to touchpads requiring continuous power and being easy to accidentally bump and reset.

An oven will start at around $1300. The most dependable electric oven brands are GE, Frigidaire, Kenmore, KitchenAid, and Whirlpool.

MICROWAVE

We do not advocate the use of microwave ovens. Research done by the U.S. Army indicated that cellular changes occur in humans and animals as a result of radio waves and electrical wires. Where I grew up, an entire neighborhood was found to have gotten cancer from an electrical wires passing overhead. Many of my friends' parents got sick. Most... well, they died. Microwaves are just closely spaced together radio waves. So we do not take chances with this. But if you want a microwave, go for it.

VENT HOOD

An vent hood that exhausts to the outside of the home is required above the range or cooktop, if there is not one integrated into it, to meet Code. These can cost $500.

WASHING MACHINE

Washing machines are a necessity in our home... I just cannot imagine hand washing the four loads I do every week!

When choosing a washing machine, choose one with a porcelain top if possible, as these are the most resilient. Stainless steel and porcelain tubs will not rust and resist getting "smelly." Look for dial controls in lieu of LED or touch controls as these draw less power and last longer. Skip the steam type washer if cost is an issue, as they do not perform that much better. An efficient model washer will use less than 35 gallons of water per load

A decent solidly-built washer will start at $1200. For top-loading type, the most dependable brands are Speed Queen, Maytag, Whirlpool, and Kenmore. For front-loading, choose LG, Samsung, Kenmore, or Whirlpool.

For Zero-Energy options, The Wonder Wash is a $50 crank washing model that many like. The Laundry Pod is a $100 model that also comes recommended.

DRYER

For clothes dryers, electric and gas perform just about equally. Choose a basic model with a choice of heat level and time, and an auto-dry function for most cost savings. Choosing a model with a moisture sensor will minimize energy use and avoid over-drying clothes. While steam dryers are now available, they tend to leave more wrinkles in dress clothes.

A decent electric dryer will start at $1,000, and a gas dryer at closer to $1100, though it should be noted that a gas model will ultimately result in increased cost savings over the long term. For electric dryers, the most dependable brands are LG, Amana, Kenmore, Whirlpool, and Maytag. For gas, LG reigns supreme, followed by Samsung, Kenmore, Whirlpool, and GE.

If locating a washer or dryer on an upper level of the home, you will want to make sure the floor structure can handle the load and vibrations!

Clothes dryers use six percent of all household electricity consumption and 10-15 percent of domestic energy in the U.S. It is totally okay to consider these an annoyance and use a clothesline on the south or west side of your home to avoid using these expensive appliances!

COMBINATION WASHER/DRYER

If space is a concern, you might want to consider a combination washer/dryer. These units can be a bit pesky, as the seals tend to wear out rather quickly, but you can get a under-counter type front-loading dual washer/dryer in the smallest footprint possible for as little as $1,000. Favorite units of tiny house aficionados include LG's $1,500 model and EdgeStar's $1,000 model.

SUPPLEMENTARY HEAT AND POWER

It is always a good idea to know how you will support the function of the home when the gas or power goes out. As we have mentioned previously, we love a wood stove as a backup source of heat and cooking. You might also want to have supplemental heating options, as well as backup generator for your home.

Space Heaters

Space heaters are essential for rooms that tend to be cold when we do not use a central heating system. Modern electric space heaters include several safety features that minimize the risk of fire, though the best ones to choose include an overheat and tipping sensor/auto-turn off control. Always choose a space heater that has a UL, ETL, or CSL rating. Make sure it has a solidly built handle if you want to move it around. Convection models are best for large rooms, and radiant models are best for spot heating. If you can afford it, a model with an integral fan and thermostat will work most effectively and quickly. Fuel burning models are great for backup heat when the power is down, but these are far more dangerous and should only be used as a backup.

A small space heater will cost under $100 in most cases. A more permanent one with a flame display can cost $200 or more.

Honeywell, Heat, and Duraflame brands make the best large heaters; Soleus makes the best radiator type heaters; and Vornado, Dyson, Holmes, and Bionaire make the best small heaters.

Generators

Generators are great during the build and can last beyond the build by being used as backup power. Choose a generator with propane or natural gas hook-ups if you will use either of these fuels in your home, as gasoline is far more dangerous and difficult to store. Choose a model with an automatic low-oil shutoff for safety. Some models have apps that work with smartphones to monitor their function when away. Look for 5,000-7,000 watts to cover most appliances, but go for 10k watts if you want to also power an electric range, heaters, and/or a washer and dryer.

The best portable generators can power your fridge and essentials.

Generators can cost between $600 and $1,500. The larger fixed type, while more expensive - starting at $1800 and running up to $3,000, can power the entire home. These are the easiest to fuel up as well as easier to start when the power goes out. It is also possible to power the electrical box if you choose a model with a $700ish transfer switch.

Honda, Generact, Troybuilt, and Briggs & Stratton all make trusted, dependable models.

Plumbing

A potable (drinkable) water supply is an essential ingredient for long-term habitation. We need water to drink, cook with, bathe in, and clean up with. We might need to treat water if it is hard or acidic to avoid clogging, bacterial growth, or the corrosion of pipes. We want to use soft or neutral water for heating and cooling systems. We might even use water as a form of fire protection.

One of the common mistakes people make is not planning for the plumbing pitch while designing the home. To work effectively using gravity, a plumbing line must have a minimum pitch of 1/4" per foot in order to flow without clogging. That means you need 4 feet of run to accomplish 1" of rise.

Water Flow

If our water is provided by the city or county, we have no control over the flow rate or pressure in the system until it reaches our property. Most often it will come to us around 50 PSI. Wells and rainwater catchment systems require pumps in most cases in order to provide pressure and flow rates consistent with what we need to operate faucets and equipment, which are based on the 50 PSI ideal of grid-tied systems.

Flow reducers can reduce water consumption by up to 40%. These can be great assets on faucets and showerheads that are not already equipped with them. For new plumbing fixtures, we recommend purchasing fixtures with the following characteristics:

Water efficient shower heads	2.5+ gallons per minute (gpm)
Ultra low flow toilets	1.6 gpm/flush.

Especially in areas where it might freeze, but really, everywhere, we recommend avoiding placing water pipes in exterior walls. We prefer chasing them inside the foundation and up under our cabinetry instead.

Hot and cold water pipes should be installed no closer than 6" to one another. Be sure to insulate your pipes with a minimum of 1" insulation, as 15% of the heat of hot water can be lost to uninsulated pipes. Also insulate the first 6 feet of cold water pipes that come into your hot water heater to prevent convective circulation. We also want to insulate cold water lines in unconditioned spaces.

Water hammer is a sound that piping makes as the line re-pressurizes when the water is turned off. We hear this "ka-kunk" relatively often when a toilet if flushed in older homes. To combat this, you can install an air chamber or shock absorber at the branch in the water supply line.

Old homes had access panels to get to the plumbing for tubs and other critical plumbing locations. This useful design trick can save you headaches later.

WHOLE HOUSE WATER FILTRATION SYSTEM

Whether you are collecting rainwater, have a well, or are using water from the city or county, a whole house water filtration system might be advantageous. It can remove up to 95% of impurities in the water. This is especially important in areas with high pollution levels. We cannot help the pollution affecting the water supply as it combines with rainfall or as the rain washes it off our roofs and into the cistern. We can help how much of it goes into our, as well as our plant and animal companions, bodies.

Water Heaters

Hot water is provided from tank-type or instant-type water heaters. These can be gas-fired, electric, or solar powered. Water heating should have a minimum 10-year warranty and the unit should be located within 30 feet of kitchens and baths.

TANKLESS ON DEMAND "INSTANT" TYPE

Solar or electric powered tankless on-demand hot water heaters with a variable-set thermostat are one option for water heating. Install them as close to the point of use as possible.

While we like instant hot water heaters in principle, we find they are often too loud in practice, so we only use those for supplemental heat or in distant baths that are not regularly used. Because these systems can be loud, if you go this route, locate the unit as far away as possible from bedrooms and offices.

If you use an instant hot water heater, make sure it complies with DOE Standard 10CFR420

Alternate option: We prefer installing a simple control-activated re-circulating loop to serve this purpose. Hot water arrives to the fixture 5 times faster than average. It is possible to turn this feature off in summer to minimize overheating of the home.

Note: In Taos, we have seen and experienced installations of instant hot water heating on radiant floor systems. This is a patently absurd idea that illustrates the point of "just because you can does not mean you should." Please do not listen to someone who says this works. After having stayed many times in a house heated this way, I can vouch that the constant and repetitive noise will prevent you from sleeping or working in peace.

TANK WATER HEATERS

Use a tank water heater with higher than 0.60 energy factor for gas heating; higher than 0.90 for electric heating; and higher than 0.55 for oil heating. If you have a Jacuzzi tub, multiple heads in a shower, or multiple bathrooms serving 3 or more people, consider installing two hot water tanks so you never run out of hot water.

SOLAR HOT WATER

A solar hot water system includes a roof-, wall-, or ground-mounted solar panel collector connected to a heat exchanger and/or insulated storage tank.

PASSIVE or DIRECT collectors are the simplest in design and are the most energy and economically efficient systems. They use the water that moves directly through the solar collector. This eliminates the need for antifreeze. However, because of not using antifreeze, these systems are only really effective in locations without freezing temperatures.

ACTIVE systems use solar or electric pumps, electricity, a heat exchanger, and antifreeze to work, or they may use a thermal siphon. Most often, active systems require more maintenance and power.

DRAINDOWN systems pump water from the hot water tank through solar collectors where it is heated by the sun and then returned to the tank. Valves automatically drain the system when they detect freezing temperatures.

DRAINBACK systems use a separate plumbing line filled with fluid to collect heat. These systems operate by gravity. When the temperature gets to freezing, the pump shuts off and the fluid drains back to the storage tank.

One of the challenges of solar hot water is access to adequate sunlight. The system requires unobstructed solar access for 300 days a year to perform correctly. Collectors should be oriented within 20 degrees of south and between 30 and 50 degrees on the horizontal. This system can also supplement radiant heat in floors.

The average person uses up to 20 gallons of hot water each day. That means an average family of four is spending somewhere around $500 per year for hot water. A properly sized solar hot water heater can cut those costs in half.

SOLAR HOT WATER SIZING SUGGESTIONS:

>1 bedroom = 40 square feet of collector + 50 gallons storage
>
>2 bedroom = 48 square feet of collector + 60 gallons storage
>
>3 bedroom = 64 square feet of collector + 80 gallons storage
>
>4 bedroom = 96 square feet of collector + 120 gallons storage

Provide space for the hot water storage tank, even if you will not install it yet. The area required is usually about 4 feet by 4 feet and it should be located adjacent to the hot water heater.

For best performance, use an SRCC rated solar hot water system with a Solar Fraction above 0.3.

You may opt to maximize performance by building a box frame into your south-facing wall with an operable window on the outside and a thermal wall on the inside. Put the solar water heater in here. This will keep cold air off the heater, and will instill a naturally warmer heating capacity. Think: getting in your closed-up car on a really cold day after the sun's been coming through the windows all day... it is usually quite warm in the car, yes? Exactly. An alternative we like is to put these collectors on the south-facing wall inside an attached greenhouse. This will prevent freezing as long as enough sun can be captured.

If you want to add solar hot water later but cannot afford it now, run 2 @ 3/4" lines of copper plumbing pipe with R-6 insulation in an interior wall from the mechanical room to the space under the roof where you will put the collector. Have this end die above the insulation so you can find it later if there is an attic. If there is no attic, penetrate the roof, flash the opening, and cap it off.

HEAT RECOVERY

To make the most of the hot water you already have, install a drain water heat recovery system on your bath and shower drains and install a heat trap on lines to and from the hot water heater.

Drain water heat recovery can increase the temperature of incoming water to your hot water heater by as much as 15 degrees, thereby minimizing the load on the heater and reducing energy needs in the entire home by as much as 10%! Stand-alone systems are cost effective and easy to install. Companies like Watercycles produce 100% recyclable units.

Waste Management

We also need to move fluid and solid wastes from the home. This has an impact on our landscaping as well as the way we orient the building on the site.

The answer to how you choose your means of managing poo may come down to money. A composting toilet can cost up to $2,000 for a well-designed system, but it can be contained in the house. An outhouse can cost $1,000 or more, but it is outside so that may be a better option for temperate climates. A septic system can cost $15,000 or more.

Having grid-tied sewage lines or operational septic is a Code requirement in most locations that require permitting, unless you live in an area where an outhouse is acceptable. Check your local permitting authority to obtain the requirements for your jurisdiction.

We recommend using a dual-flow (big and small) flush option toilet for people who opt for a water-based waste management system like a septic system or a grid-tied system.

SEPTIC SYSTEM

If you have decided that we do not want to connect to the city or county waste lines... or if there are none to connect to... then you need a septic system or outhouse. The bad news - a septic system can cost as much as $15,000. If there is already one on-site from a previous building, you can get that re-certified for a fraction of that cost if it is well-built and still functional.

A septic system is not a line out to nowhere. It is a delicate balance of plumbing and science that directly impacts the pollution of our aquifers and landscape. So we want to do it right.

Use cast iron pipes to 6 feet outside the building; use a three-way valve to move kitchen wastes and laundry machine water to a grease trap first; install cleanouts for any bends greater than 45 degrees; install clay tile or concrete pipes running at a 1% slope (1 inch down per 100 inches over) from 6 feet outside the building to the septic field; use a septic tank at least 4 feet deep; and then run the effluent to distribution boxes. You will also need to keep the septic lines at least 50 feet away from any wells, streams or water sources, and also make sure to locate the effluent fields at least 100 feet away. The septic lines need to be encased in a trench of gravel or broken stone 18 inches wide and 12 inches deep with 12 inches of earthen backfill or more above.

COMPOSTING TOILETS

For centuries in China, human waste has been considered a valuable commodity. There, human poo is collected, composted, aged, and then used as a high quality fertilizer called "night soil."

For some people, the idea of collecting their own poo is really gross. For others, it's not so bad. For those who love this idea, a composting toilet is a great asset. (pun intended) There is no need to connect to city or county sewage lines, nor even to install septic systems when using composting toilets. A composting toilet renders human waste into a harmless substance that helps reduce water pollution. It also reduces our reliance on chemical fertilizers, because we make our own! These units typically use little or no water. Pathogens die off through a variety of processes including predation by other microorganisms. The units do not have to be gross, stinky, or dirty. Commercially available units are self-contained and require a minimum of installation and maintenance. Or, you can also build your own.

The Earthship guys have designed a solar-supported composting toilet that supposedly bakes poo until it is no longer stinky at all. We asked one of the guys how well they work, and he said they haven't ever checked, so we cannot report on the effectiveness of these systems.

Urine is a source of nitrogen, which plants need. A urine-diverting composting toilet will allow collection and utilization of household urine, which helps keep the compost clean and neat.

I offer these tips and ideas here, which I gleaned from friends who have these systems, as a starting place. I do not claim to know how well composting toilets work. They are a little too crunchy granola for me and require more maintenance than I am willing to do. I would prefer an outhouse or a regular low-water flush system paired with a blackwater septic.

NO INDOOR PLUMBING? HOW ABOUT AN OUTHOUSE?

An outhouse can be an asset for those who want to go off-grid, for those who might need a backup potty, and for those who want to use the outhouse for themselves and/or volunteers during the home's build.

Like all accessory structures, an outhouse is limited by the Building Code to be 200 square feet or less without permitting. For zoning purposes, in most locations, an outhouse is also considered a type of simple sewage treatment system. It is a good idea to check with your municipality for local bylaws regarding outhouses, but we will attempt to give you enough info here to make that process as painless as possible.

A good rule of thumb is to build it at least 100 feet downhill from a well or spring and 50 feet from a lake or pond. The outhouse should be at least 10 feet from the property line. The bottom of the pit should be 3 feet or more above the highest groundwater line on the lot (taking into account seasonal fluctuations). The sides of the pit should be reinforced to prevent collapse. The soil at the base of the structure should be raised between 6 inches and a foot above the ground plane. You also want to situate the outhouse downwind from the house.

The process for building an outhouse entails: digging a hole; using 6x6 half-lapped timbers or concrete to frame the hole; and building the outhouse. The critical ingredients here are a roof, walls, floor, self-closing door, an impervious material for the bench, and a screened ventilation duct. Natural light and air streaming through an operable and screened window is often required by Code. A glass bottle wall for extra light is a beautiful addition. The finish materials used in the interior must be able to be sanitized. A well-built outhouse is well worth the $1,000 or so of materials it costs to build one. Using pressure treated wood or untreated wood species that are suitable for your location is key, especially on the floor framing. It is also advisable not the let the soil touch the floor framing.

According to some legends, the traditional moon in the door was once an indication of the outhouse being for women. Supposedly a men's outhouse had a sun on its door. These small openings were once intended as handles to open the door, and a small piece of cloth was nailed to hang over them, with another nail at the side. This cloth was pulled to the side and propped behind the nail as a user left the space, to indicate the outhouse was unoccupied, and the next user would adjust this, letting the cloth fall over the opening to indicate they were utilizing the facility. Many old outhouses were screened by lilac trees in order to help attenuate some of the smell. Many people choose to decorate their outhouses with reading materials, especially catalogs, as was the custom. Once upon a time the Sears Roebuck Catalog was the preferred choice. Many people may not realize that those catalogs were there for a reason other than reading: a smooshed up and hand-worked (read: softened) page taken from a catalog was used as toilet paper! A flashlight or lantern is a great addition to an outhouse's collection of useful tools and distractions.

A handful of wood ash after each poo helps the outhouse work correctly without odors. An outhouse pit should be raked out every couple of months, but that cleaning can result in great compost.

Mindful landscaping can make the trip to and from the outdoor loo a much more pleasant experience. Use a tree-lined path to provide shade, snow fences to minimize shoveling, orient the door to the south so that the snow and ice are naturally managed by the sun, and surround the outhouse with plants and flowers to screen it and make it a destination.

In cold climates, a trip to the outhouse is not too popular in the winter, so often a "privy" is built into a corner of the home. It is really just like the bathroom stalls that we see in public bathrooms, only with a bucket with a seat for a potty, and a bucket of sawdust that you add to the top when you are done. You just dump the bucket into the real outhouse the next day when it is warm!

An exceptional outhouse design, with step by-step-building instructions, is available at:

http://cottagelife.com/files/2011/05/Privy-Plan.pdf

BLACKWATER

Blackwater systems utilize plants and micro ecosystems to purify the remaining liquids after preliminary sewage processing and before pushing the effluent out to the septic field. Where there is no Code to comply with, Earthship builders have used a system called "outlaw septic", which consists of two large side-by-side holes in the ground covered in EPDM, with a wall between them of earth or tires. Poo goes in on one side, is broken down, and its liquid effluent flows on to the other side for further breakdown, then the "water" is delivered to a backwater pond with plants and microorganisms that clean the water before delivering it to the septic field. There are many resources available online about how to do this well.

METHANE

Methane production is viable if you have a large family, a community, or lots of farm animals on your property. Basically, all that is required is an airtight tank with a tight-fitting lid. Oxygen must not be allowed into the tank because it will kill the anaerobic bacteria that produce the methane. Just shovel in some manure, then feed it some organic matter - grass, leaves, weeds, food scraps, hair, wool, etcetera... and add water to create a slop. Seal it up and leave it alone. The anaerobic bacteria that form in the air-tight tank will eat the biomass and release methane gas. Affix the methane tank on an axle and turn it over per the instructions of the kit you used. The thick goo that remains after the production can be used to fertilize your compost heap. Gas piped from this tank can be run straight to some appliances or to a propane-type tank.

Rainwater Harvesting and Collection

As some of the scientific research on Earthships has indicated, not all locations are ideal for rainwater harvesting. Some regions are too arid, and rainwater can only serve as supplementary water to a primary source like a well, where some regions are so wet that trying to capture the rainwater results in an expense that isn't justified. When rainwater harvesting is desired, there are three potential sources for harvesting the rain: direct rainfall, street harvesting, and roof harvesting.

One of the most famous means of street harvesting that you may have heard of is how Tucson, Arizona uses curb cuts to direct storm water to trees instead of sending the water straight in to the underground storm drainage system. The downside of street harvesting is that it is only really effective if your home happens to be in a collective of properties that agree to utilizing the system. However, small scale versions of this water harnessing technique can be used on your driveway and sidewalks to water trees, direct water to planters, or even send it to a pond.

The easier of the two remaining systems to utilize – direct rainfall - falls on your yard. Shape the land around your home to slow and direct runoff where you want it. Raise paths and patios and sink planting areas. Or, reverse that and sink paths and raise beds (though the downside of this approach can be wet toes). Either way, the water will collect and distribute over the site.

On driveways, parking areas, sidewalks, and terraces: use porous paving to minimize erosion and to recharge the groundwater. River rocks or other small cobble type stones; pervious concrete ($4-8 psf); a Hollywood drive of two paved sections separated by grass; or open cell concrete block ($12-15 psf) planted with thymes and grasses are all very effective for allowing water to pass through the paving and back into the earth. This system is beneficial in more than just water control - the paving will not get hot and it will be soft – which is not only perfect for a barefooter or children but it also protects nearby plantings from being overheated. The plastic black turf supports many people recommend are highly functional, though their embodied cost is too high to advocate. People in wheelchairs or on crutches might have a challenge working out access on river rock or highly textured surfaces, so be mindful of that. Also be aware that while asphalt performs better in cold climates than concrete, it is manufactured from non-renewable resources and is toxic. If snow removal is a concern, the simplest, most smooth surface is best. Use of porous paving in areas with soil that has a high clay content is often fruitless. Consult an engineer. Do not pave areas near a well if possible.

In your landscaping, choose native plants that can retain water in their root systems.

The final method of rainwater collection is to collect the rain off your roof, balconies, and patios. The system required to make that happen uses gutters, some screening, a means of storage, and a means of irrigation. In Australia, rain is collected and filtered through a ceramic filter to make it potable. People all over the world are solving these issues. Research the possibilities and find a method that interests you!

Here is a link to a great TED talk about some alternative ways we can harvest rainwater!

http://www.ted.com/talks/anupam_mishra_the_ancient_ingenuity_of_water_harvesting.html

CLIMATE CONSIDERATIONS FOR RAINWATER HARVESTING

In a dry environment like New Mexico, it is often not physically possible to collect enough rainwater to support the home. Many who have Earthships have to get in their cars, drive 30 minutes to town, and buy water just to survive, let alone wash dishes or laundry. If you have more than 12 inches of rain per year that hit the ground, a rainwater harvesting system with a cistern may be a viable option.

Alternately, in well-watered areas like New England, where rural homes commonly draw water from surface springs or drilled wells, installing a cistern to gather rainwater from the roof can be an unnecessary expense.

SIZING UP YOUR WATER COLLECTION CAPABILITY

To calculate the amount of water you can collect on your roof, use the following calculation:

$$\text{Annual Rainfall} \times \text{Roof Area} \times 0.623 \text{ Gallons} = \text{Annual Rain Collection}$$

Roof area is determined by multiplying the length of your roof by its width. So a New Mexico style tiny house casita that is 20 feet wide by 30 feet long will have an area of 600 SF. In Taos, Annual Rainfall is 12.3 inches. Thus, the possible rainwater collection annually is:

$$12.3 \times 600 \times 0.623 = 4597.74 \text{ gallons}$$

For a circular house, the calculation for area will be pi (3.14) times the radius (half of the width of the home) squared. Be sure not to use the diameter, the distance from outside to outside wall across the home.

$$(3.14 \times \text{Radius})^2$$

This calculation also helps determine your cistern size.

ROOFING CONSIDERATIONS FOR RAINWATER COLLECTION

Faculty and students at Cockrell School conducted an in-depth study that was recently published in the academic journal *Water Research*. The study examined the effects of roofing materials on the quality of harvested rainwater. The study, led by civil, architectural, and environmental engineering teacher Mary Jo Kirisits, showed that of the five roofing materials tested, Galvalume (metal) and concrete tile produced the highest harvested rainwater quality for indoor domestic use. The study showed that rainwater from asphalt fiberglass roofs and the increasingly popular green roofs contain high levels of dissolved organic carbons (DOC). Water with DOC is not necessarily dangerous on its own, but Kirisits offered that when it is mixed with chlorine for disinfection, the two substances react to form by-products that could potentially cause cancer and other negative human health effects.

To collect rainwater, clay or cement tile, unpainted but sealed metal, and slate roofing are all viable options. For myself, I will utilize a slightly more sophisticated filtering and cleaning system to address water quality.

SIZING YOUR CISTERNS

The hand-built 3,000 gallon cisterns of yore are no longer used by modern Earthship builders. There are a few reasons for this: they leak, are susceptible to freeze/thaw cycles, introduce humidity where you do not want it, the water leeches chemicals from the concrete, they can get smelly, and they are challenging to clean. It is worth the money, the time, and your continued health to use prefabricated cisterns.

8,000 gallons of water storage is considered optimal.

An average person uses 80-100 gallons per day, and though studies suggest that while extremely bio-conscious consumers can reduce that by half, people who can afford modern Earthships tend towards the higher end of water use. You will want to plan accordingly based on the rain and snow resources of your area. Many Earthship owners now are using an extra cistern to "bank" water from the rare big storms we get, so that they may use the stored water later when our typical drought conditions return. This is a good option for many projects.

RAINBARRELS

Not ready for, or do not need, a full piped rainwater harvesting system? Install a rainbarrel! Rain barrels are a popular way to start harvesting your rainwater, especially in urban areas. The barrels are relatively inexpensive, at around $200 if bought new. They can be installed along the side of your home, under a deck, or in other unused spaces.

WATER BACKUP

The good news is that if you cannot collect enough rainwater, you can still get water without having a well or being tied to the local municipal water system. In fact this is common in Taos, as most homes on the mesa are not able to collect enough rainwater, though it requires a fair amount of planning and effort.

Some of the off-grid communities use collective wells for water. Solar panels are installed to power these deep wells. Without working as a community though, this may be a cost prohibitive option.

Another choice is to pay to have water trucked in. It costs about $100 in Taos for a truck to cart out a couple-month supply of water.

Greywater

Greywater collection and management is essential for a truly sustainable home. Greywater harvesting is a complex system and it can take an entire book to describe all the options. Here, we only want to advocate that you can use used water from your bathroom sink, showers, and baths for use in your planters, in your toilets, or to clean and purify the water, and/or irrigate your land.

In a typical Earthship, the water runs through a grease trap and then to the planters to be cleaned, and is then pumped to toilets. Alternative systems skip the planters and pump that water though a filter and into the toilet directly.

SOME POINTERS FOR GREYWATER HARVESTING:

- Use a strainer on your laundry and sink drains to get hair and particulates out before treatment.
- Greywater systems typically want a slightly smaller pipe than typical plumbing drains. This may be an issue since the Code does not generally know what to do about greywater.
- Never store "treated" greywater for future use. Within 24 hours it will develop microbes that are dangerous. Feed it directly into a processing system and once cleaned, into your toilet tanks and irrigation.
- Do not allow greywater to flow on the bare ground, always feed it from below.
- Do not use un-sealable or un-vented containers for your greywater filter tank.
- It is okay to bury your settling tank but plan ahead for easy access for yearly inspections.
- Do not expose PVC pipes to sunlight or to the interior of the home - UV damages them & PVC creates toxic smoke in a fire.
- Fresh air ensures good system health, so vent the fixtures, settling tank, and leach field.
- Wet soil needs oxygen or it will go sour, so drain and vent containers & planters.
- If you use wetlands for greywater treatment, plants that are known to work in these interior systems include citronella geraniums, basil, mint, rosemary, calla lilies, castor bean and thyme. Keep them trimmed or they may grow gangly.
- If you end up with a pest infestation, use #2 food grade diatomaceous earth to dust plants in greywater-fed planters.
- Heirloom tomatoes evidently love these environments.
- Consider hydroponics for some growing, but exclude hydroponics from greywater treatment.

- The least expensive method of harvesting is a drain-to-mulch system, which uses no pumps and outlets to the landscape.

- Consider constructed wetlands, sand filters, and other alternatives to mechanical means of sewage treatment. Constructed wetlands work best if your location is not arid. They can still work if your soil has low perk and you have lots of humidity.

- Greywater harvesting for irrigation does not always work effectively in cold climates - a solar greywater greenhouse with planter beds is required to make these systems effective. You can, however outlet the overflow to planter beds on the southwest side of your structure.

- Any system which uses pumps will have a price – the electrical load will continuously increase as the pumps wear out and have to work harder to move the water.

- Pumps can be loud.

Maximizing Efficiency in Water Use

- Clean your gutters and downspouts regularly and install screens on them.

- Add a first flush device and filtration system to clean the water if it is to be used for potable water, to reduce the risk of contracting waterborne diseases. A first-flush diverter reduces contamination of the tank water by diverting the first flush of contaminated water after a rain so that contaminants do not enter the tank. Recent research at Massey University has shown spectacular improvements in water quality in storage tanks linked to first flush diverters.

- If you want to use greywater and/or maximize the performance of your septic system, you will need to use biodegradable soaps that do not contain sodium, chlorine, bleach, peroxygen, boron, borax, petroleum distillate, alkylbenzene, "whiteners", "softeners", "enzymatic" components, or parabens ... or use any other products that contain these ingredients... you also do not want to use Drano, most cleansers, hair color, or paint thinner... or you will kill the biological parts of the system that filter and clean the water. A few products that will not muck up your system include Oasis, Bio-Pak, and Aubrey Organics.

- Maintain your plumbing. Dripping faucets and running toilets will quickly drain cisterns.

- Keeping the greywater system functioning property reduces having to use cistern water.

- Collect cold water while you wait for your hot shower water. Use buckets, or flexible piping attached to a funnel to direct cold water to some useful purpose while you wait for the hot water for your shower. In our home, we have a bathroom window right next to the shower, so I direct flexible tubing from the shower head to a rainbarrel outside that window and collect the cold water before the hot gets there for landscape watering.

Options for water conservation range from the most socially acceptable and easy to implement, to some that are "out there" for those who are committed to going 100% off-grid and recycling every aspect of their waste. While this book has attempted to offer a brief outline of what is possible, we recommend you research your options, determine your budget, and seek assistance from the most experienced people in the field locally.

We recommend the websites http://www.harvestingrainwater.com and http://www.greywateraction.org for rainwater and greywater harvest tips, tricks, law, and recommended installers.

Final Notes on Mechanical Systems

Finally, on Mechanical Systems, have a backup plan. What happens if your toilet backs up? Your water pumps fail? Do you have an overflow on your cistern? Where is the water going when the overflow is activated? If you know, you will be ready for whatever might happen!

Chapter X

Imbuing Space with Spirit

or... THE WOO-WOO CHAPTER

Design can be about so much more than just building a building. You may choose to introduce concepts of astrology, douse for locations of power spots or water, consider the creation of Sacred Space, or want to use Feng Shui or Vaastu to supplement your design aesthetic. Here are what I hope are some helpful hints about what all this means, and how it can help you to attain your dream home.

What is Happy, Anyway?

When I started my career in architecture, I had completed many of the classes required for a psychology degree. It was a weird kind of "career accident" that evolved from attending a university with a well-regarded psychology program. I have always wondered how people find happiness. So, I participated in a few research studies. Then I went to classes. I got interested in the subject and I never stopped being. When I transferred to architecture school, the language I used to describe the places I wanted to create used the term "feel." "I want the entrance to feel welcoming..."; "the bath to feel private and secure..."; "and the view to feel spacious..." I was trying to use space to help people feel better and be happier. I knew that space, light, and color could do that and I had learned some of the "how-to" of using space to achieve happiness in my earlier studies.

When I got into my Master's program and started studying the work of Palladio on the villa I worked on for my thesis in Italy, this idea was reinforced. Palladio had borrowed the idea of "firmness, commodity, and delight" from his architectural forefather, Vitruvius, who had lived a millennia before him. Palladio's buildings, to this day, inspire a sense of delight in the people who experience them; nearly 500 years after their architect designed them.

When I started writing this book, I was not at all clear that part of the reason I was willing to go against the Earthship idea as it exists today was because so many of the people that I was interviewing were sortof okay with their homes, but a great many of them were not truly happy - at least not with their space. It took until the last month of writing this book for me to realize any of this was connected to happiness.

According to a United Nations report, the ten key dimensions of happiness that improve all aspects of well-being, not just material standards of living, are: Environment and Nature; Good Government; Material Well-Being; Psychological Well-Being; Physical Health; Time Balance; Community Vitality & Social Connection; Education; Arts and Culture; and finally Work Satisfaction.

Great design helps to address these 10 dimensions of happiness. Access to the environment, great views, warm toes, safety and security, having enough of everything you need, feeling able to move around in your space, having a space you can manage, having privacy as well as opportunities for community, learning by doing, surrounding yourself with beauty... all of these ideas that we have touched on address the ten key dimensions and put us on the path to towards happiness. Where the original Earthship idea revolved around the idea of survival, we are more interested what might be called... THRIVAL. We want us all to thrive, not just survive. That is why we had to rethink the Earthship idea from tip to toe. We decided that happiness leads to healing. For ourselves, and then our communities. We become living examples of what can and does work.

We truly hope that addressing these issues will help you to create a space you love to live in.

Think about how your space can affect your perceptions of the world that you live in. What can you do to increase happiness, joy, and security for yourself and your family through your space? Use the space here to start to write some things down, if you like!

Your Core Desired Feelings

Have you ever heard of the books called <u>The Desire Map</u> or <u>The Fire Starter Sessions</u> by Danielle LaPorte? They are books for coaching yourself into achieving your dreams and goals. I was introduced to Danielle's work a couple of years ago by a girlfriend, and I found that the work offered me something super helpful in my own life: to figure out exactly how I wanted to be able to reflect on my life from the point of view of feelings. The books are a great tool if you are trying to build a new life as you build your new home. They are also great for just rebooting and making sure you are on the path to who you want to be and what you want to do. But an idea they call forth in them – to identify your core desired feelings (CDFs) – also applies perfectly to describing how you want your space to feel… and MAKE YOU FEEL.

The best way to get to your CDFs is to order The Desire Map, which is an outgrowth of the Fire Starter Sessions. The quickest way to start that effort is to visit Danielle's CDF page at her website at: http://www.daniellelaporte.com/cdf/ where she has collected the most common feelings and put them on gorgeous backgrounds so you can print them or use them as wallpapers for your computer. Every few months, I choose 3-5 CDFs that I use to formulate a plan for the coming months. In the case of building a home, you may want to choose some CDFs that you want to print out and keep in your house design binder or hang up in your space so that you always stay grounded to how you want your home to make you FEEL.

Has this made you think about how you want to feel? What delicious emotions are you looking to create in your build and in your space? Write them down here, if you like!

Locating "Power Spots"

Are you one of those people who wants to give Spirit a place to reside on your land? If so, use these techniques to find the "juiciest" spots to build, create, or manifest!

- Go out onto the site you are considering for your build.
- Allow everything else to disappear. Just be still and be with the space.
- Then, when you have plenty of time, just… walk.
- In several locations, you are likely to develop a strange affinity with the land.
- The response you have may be positive or negative. Do not mind that.
- Just mark these spots with a small rock cairn or a branch stuck in the ground.
- Go back to these spots every day for three days and spend, ideally, a half hour in each spot. Some spots will lose their sense of connection and you can redistribute their marker to the land.
- One or two will become power spots for you. You will know because these spots will be the ones you immediately find yourself drawn to.
- This is a sacred center. Mark this place and bring your intentions here.
- Plant a tree, place a bench, hang a hammock, place your bedroom or your office or whatever room matters to you here, or put the center stone of your labyrinth here.

Creating Sacred Spaces

It is often overlooked that the space... represents its place...

The home is a microcosmic connection to the macrocosmic world, and reflects your relationship with both the inner and outer dimensions of your experience. The way you treat the interior and the exterior of your home can be used to fuse your ideals into your space.

With that in mind, we wanted to offer a way of looking at the spaces of architecture through the lens of Spirit. What divine guidance does this inspire in you?

STANDARD ROOM	SACRED PURPOSE
Kitchen	Healing
Living & Dining	Nurture Family and Community
Bedroom	Sensuous places for Dreaming (and Loving, in master)
Bathroom	Purification
Play Areas (in and out)	Stimulate Imagination & Creativity
Greenhouse /Garden	Connection to Nature
?What space for you?	Meditation, Communion with the Sacred

Think about what each of these spaces mean to you, and work with what you discover to manifest your ideal space for each purpose. When you create your spaces in this way, they are more responsive... even alive... they become trained to you and you and the space begin to "breathe" together. This gives architecture that inherently "right" feeling. Then surround yourself with things you love! If it does not serve love, get rid of it. Watch what happens.

Another aspect of creating sacred space is in setting solid boundaries. If you are the type who loves crystals and rocks and honoring the land spirits, you might want to go out to the corners of your property and place a stone and say a blessing to protect the land and all the beings within it. The indigenous Puebloan people of New Mexico use this principle in several layers, with guardian sacred places and sites at several distances away from their pueblos. Various sacred sites are located at the perimeter of the pueblo, others are off at some distance, and still others reach out to a landmark in the landscape - often a sacred mountain, butte, or other distinct landform. Connecting to our place in similar ways to this allows up to form sacred relationships with the land. That is part of what makes us feel at home.

Correct timing

We know how the moon affects tides here on earth... when the moon is full, the tides are highest, and when the moon is new, the tides are lowest. Well, the same gravitational pull between our planet and her orb pulls water up not only into the atmosphere, but into our bodies, the trunks of trees, the leaves of plants, and even into solid rock!

It was once common knowledge that if you wanted lumber to last, you harvested the wood on certain days. Or if you wanted your firewood to burn as long as possible, you would harvest that on certain days too. There is a great book called Moon Time – The Art of Harmony with Nature and Lunar Cycles by Johanna Paungger and Thomas Poppe which goes into many chapters worth of detail about these traditional ways of building. But allow us to offer a brief overview here so you can determine whether you might want to use correct timing to fell your wood and build your home. We will not get into all the "whys" - you can grab the book if you would like to know the details! We will at least give you the "whens"!

For me, the biggest benefit of connecting buildings to the movements of the planets is more about connecting to the cosmos than it is about astrology or right timing. The functional benefits are a perk of setting my intentions!

The moon is waning after the full moon and before the new moon. The moon is waxing after the new moon and before the full moon. As with everything, the ideal wood cutting astrology dates may vary slightly by region. Check to see if your area has its own criteria.

If you would like to find out where the moon is today, or for any days this year, please check out our friend Molly Cliborne Gauthier's free Google Plus Moon Calendar at:

http://www.mollysastrology.com/astrology-tutorials/free-astrological-weather-calendars

TIMBER FELLING EVENT	WHEN TO DO IT
Best days for Cutting Wood	The three days after the new moon each month, in winter when the moon is waning, February evenings when the moon is waning, September 27, December 21.
Non-rotting Hardwood	New Years, January 7, January 25, January 31-Feb 2, the last two days of the moon on the wane in Pisces (usually in March).
Fire-resistant Wood	March 1st after sunset, any day the new moon is in Libra, 48 hours before the new moon in March, the last day before the new moon in December.
Non-Shrinking Wood	December 21.
Firewood	The first seven days of the waxing moon in October, after the winter solstice when the moon is waning.
Planks & Building	Waxing phase of the moon in Pisces.
Floors & Tools	Scorpio days in August (peel the bark immediately).

BUILDING EVENT	WHEN TO DO IT
Load-Bearing Walls, Concrete & Stone, Stairs, Electrical	Anytime.
Site Inspections & Geotechnical Reports	Moon is waning, close to the full moon if possible so the water table is as high as it should get.
Excavation	Moon is waning, preferring earth days ruled by Taurus, Virgo, and Capricorn.
Foundations	Avoiding watery days ruled by Cancer, Scorpio, and Pisces.
Basements & Cellars	During light and warmth signs – days ruled by Gemini, Libra, Aquarius, Aries, Libra, and Sagittarius.
Earth & Concrete Ceilings	Avoid days ruled by Leo.
Walls	During the waning moon.
Wooden Stairs, Windows & Doors, Wooden Floors, Setting the Roof Trusses or Vigas, Ceilings, & Paneling, Paving Stones, Verandas, Paths	During the waning moon, preferable on days ruled by Capricorn, avoiding Cancer days.
Plumbing	Cancer, Scorpio, and Pisces days.
Plaster, Exterior Cladding, Floor Coverings	Moon is waning.
Paint, Varnish, Waterproofing, Gluing	Moon is waning, not on Leo or Cancer days, or Scorpio or Pisces Days either when drying is involved.
Turn the Heater on the First Time	Moon is waning, on Aries, Leo, and Sagittarius days.
Best days to ventilate or "air out" the house	Days ruled by Gemini, Libra, Aquarius, Aries, Leo, Sagittarius.

Vaastu & Feng Shui

Ancient cultures in every region of the world understood the importance of building in concert with nature.

We see this connection between the architecture, the landscape, and the cosmos in the homes and ceremonial structures of the Native American peoples, in ancient temples in Egypt, the Middle and Far East, in Viking longhouses, and British stone circles.

Vaastu

In India, the ceremonial form of these natural traditions was ascribed by the Vedic tradition to architecture in order to align man with nature. *Veda* means "knowledge of natural law". *Vaastu*, or *Vastu*, means "characteristics of site and building". The Vedic traditions have a science of building that has been described as being similar to the Feng Shui of the Orient. In actuality, Feng Shui and Vaastu are quite different, as the Feng Shui practitioner can help to address the ills of a new or existing space and the Vaastu practitioner will cure the ills of the land and site before the structure is completed. You cannot really use Vaastu to "fix" the land or building once it has been developed in the same way you can make corrections with Feng Shui.

While this is by no means the whole of Vaastu, in my time working with it, I have discovered a few rules of thumb that can help you to make your home feel more whole and in alignment with the beautiful principles of Vedic design.

THESE INCLUDE:

- Sunrise – it's vital to have an unobstructed view and alignment with your garden entry and/or front door to the sunrise.
- Land should slope away from the house.
- Thoughtful location and proportions of buildings and amenities.
- A raised first floor, proportionately designed to accent the building - note that this is also an ideal of bio-climatic design in that region.
- An open central square with gardens - this is called a Brahamastan and it is intended to be a silent, essentially empty, space where Natural Law holds and nourishes the space and the beings in it with cosmic life-force.
- Place the head end of bed toward East or South and never towards North.
- Some sort of pointed appurtenance at the top of the building to invite heaven in.
- Natural building materials and energy-efficient construction.
- A good flow of fresh air.
- Generous green spaces around the structure.
- Use of solar, wind, and other cost-effective, self-sufficient, non-polluting energies.
- Use of sustainable organic agriculture.
- Roads aligned north/south, east/west.

The items on this list will allow you to self-align with Vedic principles if that is your desire. In order to accomplish true Vaastu, one must procure the services of a skilled practitioner. If possible, work with one in your area as they will be familiar with your regional building tradition(s) and climate.

Feng Shui

Using universal techniques from Feng Shui can help to create space you will love to live in!

In architecture school we studied the creation of space…. It was a balancing act between the needs of Structural, Mechanical/Electrical/Plumbing Engineer(s), Contractors, and Owners… to bring something beautiful together that met everyone's needs. In the days after I finished my Master's degree, I determined that I wanted to study sacred space… from the construction of the Ziggurats of Mesopotamia… to the missions in Latin America… to Feng Shui and Vaastu from the Orient. I wanted to learn how "sacred" was defined within architectural language.

What I discovered was that… like religions, many of which share some basic tenets, the creation of sacred space in just about every culture involves a simple set of ideals that everybody can use to create spaces that will allow us to become the beings we are destined, and hopefully, determined… to be. The key ingredients:

Clearing

What you collect in your clutter drawer, your closets, and your beliefs represents what stands between you and your real self. Only clearing out what is no longer needed can clear the way for new things to become. The challenge comes in remembering the difference between WANT and NEED.

Before you start "making", you have to "unmake" what you no longer need. Sit with your space, feel what is not right, take it away. Gift it to someone who will love and cherish it, sell it, donate it… but do not put it in a box to deal with later. To put something off until later just means that you have issues you are willingly choosing to repress.

Inside and out, in every nook and cranny… if it does not serve you, be rid of it. Think about why you kept it past its usefulness. Likely you will see a pattern. This pattern will help you identify what you want to change about yourself on the inside, which is ultimately the reason why we do this exercise.

Intention

It is vital that when you begin to create space around you that you understand how you want to use that space.

    WILL IT BE:

- Ceremonial? (often entries and dining rooms)
- Comfortable? (usually bedrooms, living rooms, and patios)
- Functional? (guest bathrooms, guest bedrooms, kitchens, laundries, garages)

What do you want to come from the effort? Will it be the perfect room for romance? An art studio? Do you want to feel less compressed?

Then you should determine which of these rooms you most need to create a space that "sings" for you. This space needs to take priority over all others. Start thinking about what you would really like to see there. Start going to garage sales, flea markets, stores that you love… and fill that space with the things that inspire you. Do layaway if you need time. Just set your intentions and DO IT. You will find your perfect space will start forming without your input just from the energy you used to create your intentions.

Once you have that room done, choose which one should be next. Work down the list until you have gone through every room. Multitask and do multiple rooms if you are fired up. Just listen to your needs and try with all your heart to fulfill these desires.

Secondly, clean it. From tip to toe. If there is anything bugging you about it, fix it. That light bulb has been burned out for a year… that is long enough… change it. Set your intentions to create a "flow". Then manage it so you keep the flow always moving.

Detachment

Our life has cause and effect relationships which we use to create the things we want around us. The most amazing things happen when we want "for the best" rather than a specific outcome. Like prayer, we ask, not for "my mom to be cured of cancer" but rather, for "my mother to accept with ease and grace, the lesson of her sickness, so she can be healed, with as little pain and suffering as possible." That leaves the door open for miracles, because the outcome we are assuming is "right"… may not be the best possible outcome according to the Universe.

BUT WHAT ABOUT THE RULES?

Ask a Feng Shui master in Black Hat Sect, Compass School, Nine Gates, or a Vaastu practitioner what to do about your bad romance luck and you are going to get 4 different answers. Likely, you will get as many different answers as there are divisions within the practices.

Why? Because historically these studies were done within specific politico-socio-eco-systems. In the south of China, the mountains, which in many traditions represent the earth element, are in a different geographical location than they are in northern Japan. Also, emperors, fighters, merchants, peasants… all had access to different levels of education and medical knowledge. So what an emperor could process and afford as far as "fixes" was vastly different than the farmers that lived in the distant regions the emperor controlled. What became clear in all castes and locales, was that the local witch doctors, shaman, and healers… found local and indigenous plants, elixirs, stones, and the like, that seemed to solve problems within their specific system. Thusly, these traditions got passed down within each "tribe." Though the fixes may be different in two locations, they still work.

What does this mean to you?

You can pick the system you want to work within. As long as you set your INTENTIONS, have DETACHMENT, and are CLEAR… you can heal "what ails ya"… yourself.

You do not need any magical mirrors or red cords or juju beads if that is not what you like or not your culture. Bring in light, crystals, crosses, plants… whatever makes your space say, "This is of the best of me, the best of what I believe will grow and protect us, and you are welcome here." Then watch what happens.

Let me give you some basic guidelines to help you on your way:

WATER is a representation of career. A small pond or fountain is a perfect representation of this element. Make sure the water flows inward toward the home. Since metal produces water: black, metallic colors, white, and blues are the way to go to highlight this direction.

EARTH represents love, education, and family. It is represented by crystals, stones, ceramics, and glass. Fire produces earth, so reds, oranges, and yellows will energize this sector.

WOOD is representative of wealth, family relationships, and good health. It is represented by plants, especially succulents, plants with flowers, and/or plants with broad leaves. Its colors are blue and green because water feeds wood.

FIRE represents recognition and respect. You can represent fire with lamps and candles and lights. Wood feeds fire, so woody colored greens are used here, as well as reds of all variations from light peach to deep burgundy.

WIND is luck. Use windchimes, preferably metal ones, to feed the good luck and beat apart the bad luck as it enters through a door or window. Gold and silver represent the bounty of the Earth element and bring good fortune. The colors to use here are white, metallic, and earth tones.

While these guidelines might help, it's really not about rules… think about painting the living room purple if that is what you have wanted to do for forever. There is a reason you want it, and you may not even know why. Then, when you do it, watch what happens, and document it. This will tell you what the doing of it means. What purple means. What living in a purple room means. What changes? What doesn't?

Pick a practice. Buy a book. (I love Lillian Too.) Try some of the remedies. What color represents water to you? Is it blue instead of black? Fine. If the book says put black there, you put blue there. Because it has to matter to YOU. Every time you look at the item or area, think of what you are calling in by putting it out there and acknowledge it. Then watch what happens.

Trust in your inner voice. There is a reason why it tells you to do these weird things sometimes. Take a chance on something invisible that you want to believe in. You want to believe you can change your destiny? Ok. You can only change it if you try, believing that you can.

I have learned from masters in many of the traditional forms of Feng Shui, Vaastu, shamanic forms of space creation, learned sacred geometry… that is my job. What I want is to give you the tools to heal your own space, and know that you can adjust it any time you want. All you have to do is make up your mind, feed the idea of change, and then be open and available.

UNIVERSAL FENG SHUI TIPS

- Use wind chimes and crystals at windows, exterior doors, and decks to prevent bad juju from entering the house.
- If your back door can be seen from your front door, place plants or a beautiful screen of some sort between them so energy can flow around the house instead of through it.
- If your stairs have open risers, put plants under the stairs so the energy can still travel up them.
- Keep your toilet closed and your bathroom door only slightly ajar if at all. If you have a window in your bath, keep it slightly open and keep some cool rocks and crystals or a nice plant there. This room needs to feel as bright and airy as possible!
- Do not put your feet towards the door of your bedroom. (This is the way the dead are carried out). Do not have mirrors facing your bed. Do not do work in your bed.
- Home offices and studies are important for financial flow. These areas should be well maintained and clean at all times. There should be a large comfy chair for meditating on your work. Place something that represents water behind the chair, but visible. When sitting at your desk, try not to have your back to a door. If you do, put a mirror on the desk. Sharp-leaved plants including cactuses thrive in harsh conditions, and that brings in good chi for an office. You want to be able to make it through the hard stuff. So every time you see the cactus… you think about… toughing out the hard stuff!
- If your stove location places your back to a door when working at it, place a mirror over it so you can see behind you. Same with any work space. If your knives are not in a drawer, put them in one. You do not want people thinking you are threatening or ready to assassinate an intruder. You may be. But that should not drive the design of the space.
- Use wind chimes, plants, decorations… anything that will soften… to make beams and gabled ceilings not "cut" through furniture. Especially beds, the family table, and the couch.
- If you have things in your house that are broken, either turn them into art or get rid of them.
- If you have a list of things to do on the house, work on it with all diligence. A list of things to do represents mind clutter.

These few principles borrowed from Feng Shui can accessorize the changes you want to bring into your life. They cannot change your life. Nothing can change your life but you. But they are catalysts, enablers, for us to see ourselves and our lives in new ways. And that is a great gift.

I hope this list of quick tricks helps!

Next Page: Figure 47.
Tile Mosaic in The Phoenix Earthship

CHAPTER XI

Conclusion: A New Set of Earth-shelter Building Criteria

I suppose what all of this comes down to really... is that I like Earthships in principle but I do not like them so much in practice. There are too many ways I can see that they could work better functionally, and I am not married to the design itself, because frankly it does not meet my aesthetic needs - I do not love the look of the Earthships. But I do love some of their details.

Being a design-oriented gal with roots in the Deep South, and of British Isle descent mostly... my people... and my ideas of design... are traditional, practical, and comfy... and trend towards beauty achieved by rich textures and deep finishes. I long for the luxury of sitting with good friends on chaise lounges on a deep and shaded porch, with lightning bugs dancing around like low-flying stars, and sweet teas aplenty to drink as we laugh and make mischief together. Minus the lightning bugs, I have found this ideal in well-designed passive solar homes in Taos plenty of times.

My vision of being at one with my Place includes being knee-deep in streams; walking along or snowboarding down mountain trails with walls of trees and giant views for as far as I can see; treading through tall stands of wildflowers; sitting under spacious shade trees; and enjoying close-up interactions with wild game and horses and farm animals. So, I am looking to build at the intersections of ecosystems. That matters to me.

I have experienced the width and breadth of New Mexico architecture, from Bandelier's hand-dug cave rooms, to many hundred year old puddled adobe kivas carved from the earth and covered with 2 foot deep earth ceilings, to the hogans of the Diné people (Navaho), to Hispanic Period haciendas and casitas, to modern hippie communes and natural building at places like Lama and New Buffalo, and all the way to the PassivHaus and other modern inventions of architecture. Some of these buildings worked well, and others not so much. I learned to trust what I experienced in them... I cannot tell you how amazing the earth smells in a pit-house/kiva on the first warm day after a snow. It is the most exquisite wet earth smell I have ever smelled. I stayed dry and relatively comfortable inside even though it was quite cold outside, and even though I had just walked through a foot of snow and we had no fire... I want THAT.

I discovered through my exploration that I love the feel of Southwest architecture... the thick walls, sun-shading, landscape, views, and most of all... the textures and colors. I want that in my space. That is part of why I shared some of what I love about New Mexico architecture in this book - I wanted to share some other options that might appeal to those who, like me, like the idea of the Earthships but want to do them better. Imagine what we could do if we even started to get into how these themes are accomplished around the world!

The current model of Earthship... with its modern lines, concrete, and dependence on materials that are not natural or sustainable for the long term, and especially its lagging thermal performance... doesn't work for my ideal vision. Evidently, I am not alone in this. In doing the research for this book, we saw countless commentaries about how people are "learning to live with" and "adjusting to" their Earthships, and "making a sacrifice..." This response is understandable, when we are stuck in a situation we cannot get out of. But, we do not really *want* to have to sacrifice *anything*. And we do not have to if we just take the time to make sure what we really want to do works for us and our climate... before we do it. In fact, if we want any idea to be advanced and to help other people, or even just to enjoy a home we created ourselves for the rest of our lives, we must refuse to take the position if "accepting it as it is" if what it is does not work. We must find a better way.

To find that better way, I wanted to investigate what aspects of the Earthships would work for my personal ideals, so I dug deep into the data and then started looking at alternates for the things I did not like. I essentially shared my journey of discovery in this book. I thought I might summarize what I ended up realizing I am seeking. Maybe it will help you to vision your space into being too. I want to meet (really, exceed) the traditional Earthship ideals...

I WANT:

- A home made of natural adobe, timber frame and strawbale, rammed earth, or earthbags - combined with reused and salvaged materials - that has a truly minimal impact on the environment.

- To harvest rainwater and use it wisely, with a greywater and blackwater system; and to discard it with minimal negative impact on the earth and the beings I live here with.

- To have a professional greenhouse attached to my home that works year-round to supplement my food needs.

- To produce my own heat and cooling, through using a combination of earth-sheltering berms and passive solar designed for the climate where I build, plus ventilation, a photovoltaic array, and/or a wind turbine. Or geothermal heating and cooling if possible.

THEN, I WILL DESIGN INTO THE SPACE:

- Windows that meet a passive solar design ideal - maxing out at 7% of the floor area for glazing on the south side, 2% on the west, and 4% on the east and north.

- Skylights maxed out at 2% of the total floor area and I will use a tower skylight in lieu of the versions typically used.

- A giant masonry heater fireplace as the heart of the house, connecting kitchen and living spaces and providing a naturally heated dining/working "nook".

- Flowing water in the home that doubles as rainwater cycling.

- Lots of textures, including colorful earth plasters, tile mosaics, glass bottle walls, and flowing curves.

- A giant bathtub and plenty of hot water to fill it with, heated with solar thermal and/or geothermal hot water.

- A very private bathroom and master bedroom.

- People-scaled spaces.

- Bed nooks instead of guest bedrooms to minimize space.

- A loft getaway space.

- Window seats.

- All major living spaces on a single level.

- Real shutters and an ability to completely block the light when I want to.
- A home that is elevated above the ground plane on a mountain or hillside.
- Sun porches, shade porches, terraced gardens, a sleeping porch, and an outdoor breakfast nook.
- A living space that opens out onto a shaded and protected exterior space.
- A well-designed kitchen with an under-counter washing machine and dryer, and a fabulous large table as a workspace and seating island.
- A super-welcoming front gate and landscaped entrance area.
- A courtyard that connects all the major living spaces and heats/cools the environment.
- Shading, including trees, window overhangs, deep roofs, trellises, and pergolas.
- Landscaping, including swales, berms, and ponds to harness and store water.
- An outdoor shower and/or tub.
- An outdoor fireplace and grill.

When I start building, the first thing I will do is build my masonry fireplace. That way, I will have a place to manifest the feeling of "home" from the beginning as I watch the walls of my actual home come up around me. Each night, as we prepare food for the build crew, I will relish knowing that our memories together will continue well beyond the build. Because every time I light the fire, I will remember the meals there together as we worked to create a sanctuary for friends and family. Now THAT sounds amazing!

I am so glad to finally have a clear vision for exactly what I want in my home.

I hope my report of this journey offers some food for thought to help you design yours.

CHAPTER XII

Overwhelmed? Need Help?

Okay, so this is a lot of information. If it proves to be too much, please consider hiring a professional home designer or architect to help you navigate it all.

One of the great things about the process we have outlined in this book is that it will help you to test drive your designer to find out if your communication styles, values, and approaches are compatible. You can take one of the issues you know you are confused about how to solve, and ask them in the interview how they would solve it. If they give you a solution you like, you will know you are on the right track. In my early career, so many people came into the offices I worked in… and I knew immediately that we were not the right fit. I think they knew we were not the right fit too, but they did not have any tools to judge the firm's approach in regard to their design. Many people have different thinking and working styles. Some people take more time to make decisions. Some clients can go crazy when a designer is changing things all the way up to the millisecond before the inspector comes to give you final approval. It can be crazy-making. If you go through all the design steps here, you will most likely not have these issues because you will know what you want and you will be able to see if the designer will work with you in a way you can enjoy! You can feel confident that it is possible for your designer to translate your desires into results. The bonus is… if you come in well-prepared and your designer is able to help you to connect the dots quickly, it will save you both time… and money.

Our best advice: choose the most qualified design team you can afford.

Previous Page: Figure 48. Tinted earth plaster detail at Carole Crews Workshop Site.

Hiring an Architect or Designer

If you decide to go with hiring a pro to design your home, here are a few tips to help you to make the right choice:

Start with asking friends whose homes you love who the designer of their place was. Look through local or regional art and design magazines and track down the designs you adore. Check with your local chapter of the American Institute of Architects and see who is working in your area, or google "residential design" and the name of your city or region. Then, once you have a list of people to check out, visit their website to learn everything you can about their work. Start with the projects page, which should be filled with pretty pictures. If they do not design things you like, take them off the list.

Do thorough research on the firm, their beliefs, and make sure their style melds with yours. Do not believe that just because someone calls themselves "green" that they are. Many so-called "green" architects are really just slightly greener than average, and they depend on technology and modern materials to make their buildings function. That is okay if chemicals and technology works for you. If you want more than that, ask them about "vernacular style", "natural building", and "bio-climatic design" to manifest a building designed and built for a specific place.

One major tip here: do not trust awards. Awards are for firms that can afford to hire someone to apply for them. More often than not, the award is for the design's pretty pictures and not for its performance, schedule, or budget. This is one of the sad things about how design works in the modern world. Sorry to be the bearer of bad news. But the right designer is the one that inspires you, speaks to you in a way that you look forward to chatting with them (because you may become friends or foes over the life of the design), gives you a building you love and that is permitable, and does so while keeping you from going over budget.

Whittle the names down until you have between one and three people you want to talk to. Then, set up an introductory meeting/interview. Each architect should have 60 to 90 minutes to present the firm's qualifications, philosophies of design and experience.

REVIEW:

- Brief statement on his or her philosophy of practice.
- Detailed statement on contract administration procedure and services.

QUESTIONS:

- Will the Architect's present workload permit them to complete your project on your schedule?
- Will they give your job personal attention from beginning to end or will an associate or employee be designated to manage the project? If there will be a project manager, you should meet with that person to be sure you get along with them as well as you do your designer.
- What form of contract will be used? The A.I.A. Standard Form is used most often and will protect both you and the Architect. This contract is trustworthy.
- How does he or she expect to be compensated for services?
- Will they provide renderings or models?
- Do they expect out-of-town travel, lodging, etcetera… to be included in their compensation and if so, how much of this do they anticipate? Will there be a predictable per diem or will they bill you for expenses? Note: The standard GSA per diem is fair and prevents your designer from going to the best restaurants and staying in 5 Star hotels and handing you an exorbitant bill that you may not have budgeted for. (Yes, that has happened.)
- What is the Architect's track record regarding estimates and construction budgets and what is the firm's method for staying within the approved budget?

- How often will the Architect visit the project site?
- How does he or she insure that plans and specifications are followed?

THIS PROCESS SHOULD HELP YOU ANSWER THE FOLLOWING IMPORTANT QUESTIONS:

- Does the Architect's work show imagination and design skill?
- Does the Architect's work reflect a concern for quality construction and details?
- Does he or she indicate a willingness to devote time to research and programming in order to completely understand your needs?
- Do Contractors find their construction documents clear and complete?
- Do the Architect's references show a spirit of cooperativeness? (And does the architect show a willingness, even eagerness, to have you talk to the people listed? That is telling.)
- Do you have confidence in and feel comfortable entering a business agreement with his or her firm?

Normally, the Architect's Basic Services (this is a contract term) include architectural design plus mechanical, electrical, and structural coordination. Other consultants – for landscape, lighting, and acoustics – are additional services billed directly to you, the Owner, with additional compensation due the Architect for coordination. If any of these services are needed, they should be discussed and agreed on before signing a design contract.

After the interviews are completed, selection of the Architect should be completed within one to two weeks unless you have confirmed that the Architect's schedule will allow for a longer period without penalty. Otherwise, if another paying project comes in before you decide; you may lose your place in line, and then have to be "fit in" when it works for the design team.

After the selection, send a letter of thanks to all of the Architects interviewed, and advise them of the decision.

Tip: Ask the designer to provide plans in 11x17 format. This not only saves paper, it makes working on the drawings on-site easier, as well as reduces the cost of printing.

Stages of Design

If you decide to hire an Architect to help work through the myriad of details in a building project, expect to pay about 10% of construction costs to retain their assistance.

How their fee breakdown will likely work and what you will get as deliverables:

CONTRACT SIGNING AND RETAINER   PAYABLE: 10% FEE

SCHEMATIC DESIGN   PAYABLE: 30% FEE

    Basic concept, uncluttered by detail, but clear

        DELIVERABLES:

- Site Plan with footprint, drive, parking, utilities
- "Sketch" Floor Plan(s) without details
- Two Exterior Elevations (primary facades)
- Budget Estimate

DESIGN DEVELOPMENT   PAYABLE: 30% FEE

    Specs and Details!

        DELIVERABLES:

- Revised Site Plan
- Foundation Plan
- Floor Plan(s) with details
- Four Exterior Elevations
- Electrical Plan
- Reflected Ceiling Plan (if detailed ceilings or lighting)
- A few Interior Elevations
- Finish Schedule
- Building Section(s)
- Wall Section(s)
- Engineering Drawings
- Budget estimate (and meet with Contractor)
- Draft Specs for selected items

CONSTRUCTION DOCUMENTS   PAYABLE: 30% FEE

    The final touches

        DELIVERABLES:

- "Blueprints" (Coordinated with engineering drawings)
- Specifications
- Materials, Finishes, and Performance Standards for work

New Home Design Worksheet

This questionnaire will help you to clarify your goals and can be used to provide your designer the information needed to design your home. It's comprehensive, and not every question will apply to your project.

We will put these Word documents up at http://hackingtheearthship.blogspot.com so you can have all the space you need to fill them out!

GENERAL DATA

    OWNER INFORMATION

        OWNER #1 NAME:

        Mailing address:
        Home #   :
        Work #:
        Cell #:
        E-mail:
        Preferred time and place to call:

        OWNER #2 NAME:

        Mailing address:
        Home #:
        Work #:
        Cell #:
        E-mail:
        Preferred time and place to call:

        If this is for a home design, what is the size of your current home? _____Square feet
        What is it constructed of?

        Will the project serve as your fulltime residence?   Y / N
            If no, months you expect to be in residence:
            Probable months of most frequent use:
            Probable months of least use:
            Will you use a house sitter when away?   Y / N
            Describe your personality(ies) and daily routines:
    Do you have pets?   Y / N
        If yes, what type(s)?
        Are pet doors or rooms required?   Y / N
        Please describe:
        Interests/Hobbies:
            Are additional rooms required for these purposes?
            Please describe:
    Do you work at home?   Y / N   How often?

Do you want an office in the home? Y / N
Please describe:
Active Sports:
Are you sensitive to noise? Y / N
What type of lighting do you prefer?
What areas require the most privacy?
What areas should be most public?
Any special health needs or disabilities?
Will you care for older family members in the future: Y / N
Specific needs:

Are there other houses, places, gardens, etcetera… that you remember having the feeling that you want your house to have? (Please include photos, magazine clippings, sketches, etcetera…)

What have been the principle irritations and inconveniences found in former dwelling(s) with respect to:
Closets?
Bathroom fixtures and layout?
Kitchen Arrangement?
Other concerns?
Remarks:

DESIRED BUILDING

Physical Address of Building Site:
Are there applicable architectural restrictions or covenants in this location? Y / N
(Please provide to designer with this form, if Yes.)
Desired Size:_____square feet
Budget for project $:_____

Desired construction start date:_____

Desired completion date:_____

Will you be seeking construction financing? Y / N
Will your project be owner-built or contractor-built? (circle one)
Will you use phased construction? Y / N
Please describe:
Should we plan for future additions? Y / N
Please describe:
Names and ages of full-time residents:

Is there a special image that you want your home to portray?
What do you want the house to communicate about your lifestyle?

Extra space for storage or other use? Y / N Use(s):

Additional buildings: guesthouse Y / N size: _____ square feet

GOALS

    Please rate the following: (1 = highest   6 = lowest priority)
       ___green building (energy/water conservation, green materials, etcetera…)
       ___beauty
       ___function/performance
       ___health
       ___outdoor orientation (outdoor living areas in addition to views)
       ___economy (hold down size, cost, and maintenance)

EXTERIOR FEATURES

       ___Traditional pueblo/adobe (parapets/flat roof, portals, etcetera…)
       ___Traditional territorial style (pitched metal roof)
       ___Contemporary pueblo/adobe
       ___Contemporary territorial
       ___Alpine
       ___Solar
       ___Custom one-of-a-kind
       ___Other
          Please describe:

EXTERIOR WALL CONSTRUCTION:

       ___adobe / stucco
       ___brick
       ___earth berm
       ___frame
       ___log
       ___pumice crete
       ___rastra block
       ___straw bale
       ___stone
       ___timberframe with infill
       ___wood
       ___combinations as appropriate
       ___leave it to the designer
       ___Other   Please describe:
    Roofing type and color:
       Dormers:
       Skylights:

    Fireplace cladding:

    Windows:

    Doors:

    Remarks:

GENERAL NOTES ON FINISHES:

___budget finishes
___natural and non-toxic materials/finishes
___rustic and earthy
___standard regional finishes
___upscale finishes and craftsmanship
___introduce original or exotic details
   describe:
_____clean & contemporary

Non-toxic materials:
___exclusively
___as much as is reasonable
___don't care

Preferred ceiling heights (common 9'-0' throughout and 12'-14' in great room):
_____feet throughout   _____feet in Great Room

Color Scheme(s):

Favorite Textures:

GUEST INFORMATION:

Do you regularly have guests?   Y / N
   How many guest rooms do you need? (Indicate Number)_____
      Do any of your guests have special needs to get around your home?
                                                       Y / N
      If so, please describe:
Social Activities:
   How frequently would afternoon or evening guests be entertained?
      Weekly   Monthly   Yearly
   Will they stay? (circle all that apply)
   Overnight?   Weekends?   Longer?

   Types of parties most frequently given   (circle and indicate the usual number of guests for each)
         ___Dinners   _____Guests
         ___Bridge/Cards   _____Guests
         ___Garden Parties   _____Guests
         ___Teas   _____Guests
         ___Club Meetings   _____Guests
         ___Luncheons   _____Guests
         ___Dances   _____Guests
         ___Musicals   _____Guests
         ___Cocktails   _____Guests
         ___Buffets   _____Guests
         ___Children's Parties   _____Guests
         ___Television / Movies   _____Guests
         ___Other   _____Guests
      Describe:

DESIGN

ROOM CHECKLIST

Check all desired rooms:
- ___formal entry
- ___mudroom
- ___greenhouse
- ___living room
- ___dining room
- ___kitchen
- ___great room (kitchen/dining/living in one space)
- ___utility
- ___laundry
- ___walk-in pantry or _____ combine w/utility?
- ___Powder room
- ___media/family room (TV, audio, etcetera… We used to call it a den.)
- ___study/office/library
- ___art studio
    Describe:
- ___meditation
- ___wine cellar
- ___basement
- ___ recreation room (billiards, games tables etcetera.)
- ___workout/gym
- ___master bedroom (details to follow)
- ___master bath
- ___master dressing room/closets

ROOM DESIGN CRITERIA

FIRST FLOOR

Guest Lavatory/ Watercloset:	Y / N	
Coat Storage:	Y / N	Area required:

BED ROOMS

Bedroom 1: Master

Bed Size: King   Queen   Full   (2) Twins
Other Furniture Requirements (please provide measurements):
Do you prefer morning sun?   Y / N
Do you read in bed?   Y / N
Fireplace?   Y / N   gas or wood
TV?   Y / N
Safe?   Y / N   Location:

Dressing Area
   Open to bedroom or separate room?
   Relationship to bedroom?
   Do you want built-in:
      Drawer space?   Location:

      Dressing table space? Location:
      Do you want a vanity/ mirrors? Location:
  Closet/ Storage Space
    Spatial Relationship to Dressing Area, Bedroom, Bathroom?
      Walk in   Y / N
      Off Bedroom   Y / N
      Off Bath   Y / N
      Between   Y / N
    Do you want separate His and Hers closets? Y / N

    Indicate the type of storage for each item type (hanging, folded etcetera.) and the space requirement for each (i.e. 3 big drawers, 2 shelves, 2@ 8' hanging rods, etcetera.)

    What type of shoe storage you would prefer: (circle one)
      Shoe rack   shoe bag built-ins
    Would you like out of season clothing storage? Y / N
     Within the room or outside?
    Storage required for Games / Toys / Books / Desk? Y / N
     Please describe:
  Finishes
    Floor Finish
      Bedroom:
      Dressing Area:
      Closet Area:
    Wall Finish
      Bedroom:
      Dressing Area:
      Closet Area:
    Ceiling Finish
      Bedroom:
      Dressing Area:
      Closet Area:
    Windows:
     Window Coverings:

Bedrooms 2-5 (copy and paste for as many as required)

  Bed Size: King   Queen   Full
    (2)Twins Bunk Beds
  Other Furniture Requirements (please provide measurements):
  Do you want morning sun for children's rooms? Y / N
  Do you expect your kids or guests will read in bed? Y / N

  Dressing Area
    Relationship to bedroom?
    Do you want built-in:
      Drawer space?   Location:
      Dressing table space? Location:
      Do you want a vanity/ mirrors? Location:
  Closet/ Storage Space
    Spatial Relationship to Bedroom, Bathroom?

Walk in	Y / N
Off Bedroom	Y / N
Off Bath	Y / N
Between	Y / N

Indicate the type of storage for each item type (hanging, folded etcetera.) and the space requirement for each (i.e. 3 big drawers, 2 shelves, 2@ 8' hanging rods, etcetera.)

What type of shoe storage you would prefer for children's rooms: (circle one)
    Shoe rack   shoe bag built-ins

Storage required for Games / Toys / Books / Desk?
    Please describe:

Finishes

Floor Finish
    Bedroom:
    Closet Area:

Wall Finish
    Bedroom:
    Closet Area:

Ceiling Finish
    Bedroom:
    Closet Area:

Windows:
    Window Coverings:

BATHROOMS

Master Bath

Private or Shared?
Is there access from:

The Bedroom	Y / N
The Hallway	Y / N
The Dressing Area	Y / N

Should the bath area be open or enclosed?

Do you want a bathtub?	Y / N	Type preferred?
Jetted?	Y / N	
Do you want a shower?	Y / N	Type preferred?
Multiple shower heads?	Y / N	
Steam unit?	Y / N	
Bench?	Y / N	

Vanity

Number of basins?
Should there be storage/ drawers below? Y / N
Special fixtures/ faucets/ accessories? Y / N
    Please describe:
Chairs/ stools?   Y / N

Cabinets

Do you want a medicine cabinet?   Y / N

If yes, do you want it built-in?
Do you want a towel/ linen/ toilet article cabinet? Y / N
If yes, do you want it built-in?

Water Closet
Located in the main area or in an enclosed space?
Do you want a bidet? Y / N

Electrical
How much natural light do you prefer and in which areas?
What type of artificial lights do you prefer? (LED, Fluorescent, incandescent)
What type of light fixtures do you prefer? (uplight in ceiling, ceiling, wall, lamps, drop, recessed?)

Finishes
Floor Finish:
Wall Finish:
Ceiling Finish:
Window Treatments:

Bathrooms in other bedrooms

(copy and paste for as many bathrooms as you want, then number them)
Number Required:
Private or Shared?
Bathtub? Y / N Type preferred?
Shower? Y / N Type preferred?
Shower/bathtub combo? Y / N Type preferred?
Will one of these baths double as a powder room for non-overnight guests? Y / N

Vanity
Number of basins?
Should there be storage/ drawers below? Y / N
Special fixtures/ faucets/ accessories? Y / N
  Please describe:
Chairs/ stools? Y / N

Cabinets
Do you want a medicine cabinet? Y / N
If yes, do you want it built-in?
Do you want a towel/ linen/ toilet article cabinet? Y / N
If yes, do you want it built-in?

Water Closet
Located in the main area or in an enclosed space?
Do you want a bidet? Y / N

Electrical
How much natural light do you prefer and in which areas?
What type of artificial lights do you prefer? (LED, Fluorescent, incandescent)
What type of light fixtures do you prefer? (uplight in ceiling, ceiling, wall, lamps, drop, recessed?)

Finishes

Floor Finish:
Wall Finish:
Ceiling Finish:
Window Treatments:

PUBLIC SPACES IN THE HOME

Do you prefer formal/traditional separation between the living, dinging, and kitchen, or an open plan which provides functional and aesthetic divisions but creates a "great room" feel? Check:

___all three rooms separate
___LR and DR open to each other
___Kitchen and DR open to each other
___all three open to each other

KITCHEN

Size:
Shape:
Solar Orientation:
Relationship to the rest of the house:
Walk-in pantry: Y / N
Island: Y / N   Area required:
functions: (e.g. cooktop, eating/bar, prep)
    Table Space: Y / N   Area required:
    Bar Space   Y / N   Area required:
Eating/congregating in kitchen:
    ___stools at island
    ___stools at peninsula
    ___breakfast nook with table for 2-4
    ___country kitchen for 4 +
    ___no seating in kitchen
Minidesk   Y / N
TV   Y / N
Appliances
    cooktop: Y / N   #___burners Finish:
    grill: Y / N
        gas or electric (circle one)
        Finish:
    hood:
    _____range hood
    _____downdraft
    _____microhood combo
            Finish:

    wall ovens:
        gas or electric (circle one)
        single oven   Y / N   Standard or Convection?
            Finish:
        oven above and below   Y / N
            Standard, Convection, or one each?
            Finish:

micro above, oven below: Y / N
Standard or Convection Oven?

Finish:
microwave separate   Y / N   Finish:
refrigerator:
     side by side   Y / N
     French door with freezer below   Y / N
     built-in (subzero style)   Y / N
     water/ice in door   Y / N
     refrigerator drawers in cabinet system   Y / N
     Finish:
separate freezer   Y / N   location:
wine cooler   Y / N   # of bottles:

compactor: Y / N
dishwasher: Y / N   Finish:
sink: double tub: Y / N
     ___stainless or _____enamel or _____composite?
     ___Rim mount or ___undermount?
     Disposal: Y / N
     instant hot water: Y / N
     soap dispenser: Y / N
     reverse osmosis filtration system   Y / N
2nd prep sink: Y / N
     __stainless or __porcelain or__composite?
     __rim mount or __undermount?
     Disposal: Y / N
     instant hot water: Y / N
     soap dispenser: Y / N
     reverse osmosis: Y / N
What other appliances do you require?

Storage

     Under counter storage:
     Above counter storage:
     Pantry:
     Bulk food storage:
     How will linen, silverware, and flatware be stored?

Finishes

     Butcher Block: Y / N   Size:
     Countertops:_____tile_____granite _____
     maple _____copper _____soapstone_____
     Fireslate_____Richlite _____Paperstone_____
     Icestone____Zodiac _____Corian _____
     Floor Finish:
     Wall Finish:
     Ceiling Finish:
Window Treatments:
Remarks:

DINING ROOM

    Size:
    Solar Orientation:
    Relationship to the rest of the house:
    Furniture (Indicate the type preferred, quantity, and finish)
        Table:
        Chairs:
        Sideboards:
    Storage (Indicate the type preferred, quantity, and finish)
        Flatware/ silverware/ serving:
        Table Linens:
        Liquor/ Wine:
    Finishes
        Floor Finish:
        Wall Finish:
        Ceiling Finish:
        Window Treatments:
    Remarks:

LIVING ROOM

    Do you use the living room for entertaining and special occasions, using the media/family room to spend most of evenings?   Y / N
    How many people should the LR seat? _____
    Do you need generous space for wall art?   Y / N
        Please describe:
        Low voltage lighting for artwork?   Y / N
    Solar Orientation:
    Relationship to the rest of the house:
    Size of room:
    Furniture (Indicate size, quantity, finish):
    Fireplace?   Y / N
        gas or wood
    Storage (Indicate type, quantity, finish):
        Do you want built-ins?
        Book shelves?

    Equipment (Indicate how it will be stored)
        Stereo:
        T.V. :
        Computer:
        Distributed audio:
        Other:
    Finishes
        Floor Finish:
        Wall Finish:
        Ceiling Finish:
        Window Treatments:
    Remarks:

FAMILY ROOM

Size:
Solar Orientation:
Relationship to the rest of the house:
What activities will take place here?
What should this room feel like?
Furniture (Indicate size, quantity, finish):
Equipment (Indicate where it should be housed, size, quantity)
    TV/ VCR:
    Home Theater:
    Stereo:
    Recording:
    Computer:
    Integrated Light / HVAC / Theater Controls:
Storage Requirements (Indicate type, size, quantity, finish)
    Books:
    Games:
    Other:
Heating
    Fireplace:
    Wood Stove:
    Alternative Heating:
Lighting Requirements:
    Special Requirements:
Finishes
    Floor Finish:
    Wall Finish:
    Ceiling Finish:
    Window Treatments:
Remarks:

OFFICE

Size:
Solar Orientation:
Relationship to the rest of the house:
Furniture (Indicate size, quantity, finish):
Storage (Indicate type, size, quantity, finish):
Equipment Required (circle all that apply):
    Computer   Typewriter   Files   Audio-Visual   Phone
Special Requirements:
What should this room feel like?
Remarks:

LIBRARY

Size?
Solar Orientation?
Relationship to the rest of the house:
Furniture (Indicate size, quantity, finish):

Storage (Indicate the type preferred, quantity, and finish)
    Hi- Fi/ Stereo/ T.V.:
    Books:
    Display Units:
    Other:
Do you want built-in shelving/ seating?
Do you want a fireplace?
What type of lighting?
Finishes
    Floor Finish:
    Wall Finish:
    Ceiling Finish:
    Window Treatments:
Remarks:

RECREATION / GYM / YOGA

Size:
Solar Orientation:
Relationship to the rest of the house:
Activities that will take place here (Circle all that apply)
    Bar   Kitchen   Ping- Pong   Billiards
    Dancing   Gymnasium   Fireplace   BBQ
    Other:
Should there be bathroom facilities in this area?   Y / N
Furniture/Equipment (Indicate size, quantity, finish):
Storage (Indicate type, quantity, finish):
    Do you want built-ins?
Spa (Indicate type, size, quantity)
    Sauna?
    Hot Tub?
    Indoor Pool?

Finishes
    Floor Finish:
    Wall Finish:
    Ceiling Finish:
    Window Treatments:
Remarks:

UTILITY ROOM

Size:
Relationship to the rest of the house:
What else will this room be used for?
Appliances (Indicate the type preferred, quantity, and finish)
    Washer:
    Dryer:
    Laundry Sink:
    Cabinets:
    Sewing Machine:

Iron Area:
Broom/ Cleaning Closet:
Finishes
    Floor Finish:
    Wall Finish:
    Ceiling Finish:
    Window Treatments:
Remarks:

Garage

Size of garage:
    _____ # cars total
    _____ # Midsize
    _____ # Fullsize/SUV
Should the garage be separate or incorporated in the house?
Solar Orientation:
Relationship to the rest of the house:
Workspace required?   Y / N   Area:
Other uses of the garage (Circle all that apply)
    Woodwork Photographic Ceramic Painting
    Sculpting Model Making Other (Describe)
Storage (Indicate type, size, quantity)
    Gas/Oil cans:
    Paints/Supplies:
    Sporting Equipment:
    Tools:
    Garden Supplies:
    Other:
Garage Door Type: (single, double)
    Automatic Opener:
Finishes
    Floor Finish:
    Wall Finish:
    Ceiling Finish:
    Window Treatments:
Remarks:

EXTERIOR LIVING AREAS

Size:
Solar Orientation:
Favorite time(s) to be outside:
Relationship to the rest of the house:
Type of area:
Furniture (Indicate size, quantity, finish):
Equipment (Indicate size, quantity, finish):
    Barbecue Gas or Charcoal
Additional amenities:
___portals
___courtyard(s)
___fountain(s)
___outdoor fireplace

___shade structures
___roof deck
___vegetable garden
___orchard
___dog run
___chickens or other livestock
___traditional lawn___kid's play area
___basketball hoop
___guest parking   Relationship to the Garage?
___Swimming pool
___dressing rooms / bathrooms
___lap pool
___hot tub
___sauna
___steam bath
___volleyball court
___horse stables
___tennis court
___Other:
Lighting Requirements:
    Special Requirements?
Landscaping: Y / N
  Formal or Informal:
    Any specific gardening needs?
Remarks:

PORCH/DECKS

  Size:
  Solar Orientation:
  Relationship to the rest of the house:
  Relationship to exterior:
  Furniture Required:
  Accessories:
  When will you spend time in this area?
  Will you entertain in this area?   Y / N
  What should this area feel like?
  Finishes
    Floor Finish:
    Wall Finish:
    Ceiling Finish:
    Screened:
    Glassed:
  Remarks:

PLAN REQUIREMENTS FOR POSSESSIONS

Books
    Number to be planned for?
    Are there any oversized volumes requiring special shelving?   Y / N
    Are all to be shelved in one room?   Y / N

Equipment (Indicate built-in or cabinet, size, location)
    I am knowledgeable about technology   Y / N
    I prefer very basic tech   Y / N
    Requirements: (Indicate built-in or cabinet, size, location)
        Stereo/Tuner Amp/Cassette/Turntable:
        Dedicated Computer:
        Surround Sound:
        T.V.:
        VCR/DVD/CD /DVR:
        DVD:
        Computer:
        Video Games:
        Number of albums/CD's to be provided for:

Storage (Please indicate the quantity of each)
    Trunk   Luggage Shoes   Handbags   Hat Boxes

Special Design Considerations
    Special furniture, sculpture, paintings, etcetera. For which the house must be designed: (please provide photographs, indicate where the piece will go, and provide overall dimensions (length, width, and height))
        ___Furniture
        ___Area Rugs
    ___Piano
    ___Billiard Table
    ___Gun Safe
    ___Art
    ___Sculpture
    ___Other   Please Describe:

SYSTEMS

MECHANICAL

Heating (circle all that apply)
___Wood Stove   Location(s):
___Forced Air
___Radiators
___Radiant Floors
___Other

Fuel Preference (circle all that apply)
    Gas Oil Electricity

Cooling
_____Air conditioning   Location(s):
_____Swamp Cooler   Location(s):

What areas would be excluded?

WATER

Filtration or conditioning: Y / N   Location:

POWER

Master switch: Y / N   Location:
Central Surge Protection: Y / N
Central Charging Station: Y / N

COMMUNICATIONS

Telephone: Y / N   Cordless   Conventional   Both
    Locations:

DSL: Y / N   Satellite: Y / N   Locations:
    Wireless or Ethernet or Both

Cable TV: Y / N   Satellite: Y / N   Locations:

Intercom: Y / N   Locations:

OTHER

Security System: Y / N   Type:
Smart Home System: Y / N
Central Vacuum? Y / N
Key rack / wallet / phone desk: Y / N Location:

Radon abatement system (about $1/sf) Y / N

Water test:_____basic ($100) _____comprehensive ($300)

Whole house carbon filter   Y / N
(replaces salt softeners and costs $2,500)

Include HRV   Y / N
(a ventilation system for the environmentally sensitive, about $2.50/sf)

Site Design Checklist

This is a checklist of the factors that may be involved in evaluating a site for construction. Information is usually collected only for those items that are pertinent to the project. We hope this will help you answer questions about what it is you really need and want for your home

OVERVIEW OF DESIGN REQUIREMENTS

Please describe the qualities of your building site that we should know about, include likes and dislikes and any features that should be incorporated into the design.

SITE CONSIDERATIONS

    CLIMATE

        Prevailing winds
           Direction
           Maximum, minimum, and average velocities
           Special considerations (g., tornado, flood, hurricane-prone areas)
        Solar orientation
           Sun angles
           Days of sunlight
           Cloud cover
           Shading of (or from) adjacent structures, natural features, and vegetation
        Temperature
           Variation
           Maximums and minimums for various times of year
        Humidity
           Variation
           Maximums and minimums for various times of year
        Precipitation
           Peak period total
           Annual and seasonal total

    TOPOGRAPHY

        Legal property description, including:
           Limits of property
           Easements
           Rights of way
           North indication
        Topographic maps and aerial photos
           Contours and spot elevations
           Slopes: percentage, aspect, orientation
           Escarpments
           Erosion channels
           Location and configuration of rocks, ledges, outcrops, ridges, drainage lines
           Visual characteristics
           Potential problem areas during construction: silt, erosion, et

Analysis of physical features
    Views and vistas
        Neighboring structures: buildings, satellite dishes, etcetera
        Shading and solar access
        Noise from streets, emergency services, aircraft, etcetera
        Odors

Access and circulation
    Vehicular
        _____Road access to property line existing
        _____Number of Parking Spaces required outside Garage
    Pedestrian

Vegetation

Water bodies
    Location, size, depth, direction of flow
    Water quality: clean, polluted, anaerobic conditions, et
    Use: seasonal, year-round
    Wetlands: ecological features
    Variations: expected water levels, tides, wave action
    Coastal features

Drainages: rivers, streams, marshes, lakes, ponds, etcetera
    Natural and built
    Alignments and gradients
    Pattern and direction

Waterway easements
    Surface
    Subsurface

Surface drainage
    Location of streams and washes
    Proximity to floodplains
        Maximum flood levels
        Frequently flooded areas
    Local watershed areas, amount of runoff collected, and location of outfalls
    Swampy and concave areas without drainage
    Other obstacles that may interrupt or obstruct natural surface drainage

Unique site features

GEOTECHNICAL/SOILS

    Basic surface soil type: sand, clay, silt, rock, shale, gravel, loam, limestone, etcetera
    Rock and soil type: character/formation and origin
        Geologic formation process and parent material
        Inclination
        Bearing capacity
    Bedrock
        Depth
        Type classification
    Seismic conditions
    Environmental hazards

UTILITIES

    Potable water
        ___Municipal
        ___Well
            If a well, is there a well-share?   Y / N
        ___Spring
    Electricity
        ___Public Utility   already at property line?   Y / N
        ___Photovoltaic   location:
    Gas
        ___Natural   already at property line?   Y / N
        ___Propane
    Telephone   How many numbers needed?
    Television
        ___None
        ___Satellite
        ___Cable
        ___Antenna
    Sanitary sewer service
        ___Municipal
        ___Septic
        ___Septic with supplemental blackwater treatment
    Storm drainage (surface, subsurface)
    Irrigation
        _____same as potable
        _____rainwater catchment
        _____greywater
    Fire protection

GENERAL SERVICES

    Fire and police protection
    Trash/refuse removal services
    Snow removal, including on-site storage

CULTURAL FACTORS

SITE HISTORY

    Former site uses
        ___Hazardous dumping / Landfill
        ___Old foundations
        ___Archaeological grounds
    History of existing structures
        ___Historic value
        ___Affiliations
        ___Outline
        ___Location
        ___Floor elevations
        ___Type
        ___Condition

___Use

LAND USE, OWNERSHIP, AND CONTROL

Present zoning of site and adjacent property
___Site Location in Town
___Subject to review
___Site location in County
___Subject to review
___Restrictive Covenants (please provide)
___Subdivision with architectural Guidelines (please provide)
___Subject to review

Adjacent (surrounding) land uses
   Present
   Projected
   Probable effects of site development

Type of land ownership

Function and pattern of land use: public domain, farm type, grazing, urbanized
   Present
   Past

Location, type, and size of pertinent community services
   Schools and churches
   Shopping centers
   Parks
   Municipal services
   Recreational facilities
   Banks
   Food services
   Health services
   Access to highways, public transportation

REGULATORY FACTORS

ZONING CODES

Permitted uses
   By variance
   By special use permits
   Accessory structures
Minimum site area requirements
Building height limits
Yard (setback) requirements
Lot coverage
Off-street parking requirements
Landscaping requirements
Sign requirements

SUBDIVISION, SITE PLAN REVIEW, AND OTHER LOCAL REQUIREMENTS

Lot requirements
   Size
   Configuration

Setbacks and coverage
Street requirements
    Widths
    Geometry: grades, curves
Curbs and curb cuts
Dead-ends
Intersection geometry
Construction standards
Utility location(s)
Sidewalks
Drainage
    Removal of spring and surface water
    Stream courses
    Land subject to flooding
        Detention/retention ponds
    Parks
        Open space requirements
        Park and playground requirements
        Screening from adjacent uses

ENVIRONMENTAL REGULATIONS

Water, sewer, recycling, solid waste disposal
Clean air requirements
Soil conservation
Protected areas, wetlands, floodplains, coastal zones, wild and scenic areas
Fish and wildlife protection
Protection of archaeological resources

OTHER CODES AND REQUIREMENTS

Historic preservation and landmarks
architectural (design) controls
Special districts
Miscellaneous: mobile homes, billboards, noise
Site-related items in Building Codes
    Building separation
    Parking and access for persons with disabilities
    Service and emergency vehicle access and parking

Participate!

We could not have brought so much information together in this exploration of Earthships without the help of quite literally hundreds of resources. From owners, renters, academics, designers, builders, and design and trade professionals… all of the information we share in this book came from the wisdom of people who offered up their experience to help you get an earth-sheltered home that works for you.

You can help us improve future editions too! Ways you can help:

1. **Submit your Earthship's location and website for our resource list.**

    Just email us the following:

    Name of Earthship:

    Location:

    Name of Owners:

    Contact Info:

    Building Use:

    Cost:

    Designer:

    Time to Build:

    # and duration of Volunteers:

    Planning Permission Acquired: (Y or N and with any changes required to obtain it)

    Thermal Performance Issues:

    Issues you have had:

    Tweaks you made:

    Do you have a few photos available? If so, please send them along!

2. **Better yet, TAKE OUR SURVEY!**

    Which you can find at https://www.surveyplanet.com/54571004968d6e492b0e811e

Previous Page: Figure 49. Sculpted earth plaster detail in Taos

Suggested Reading

Visit our website http://HackingtheEarthship.blogspot.com to find direct links to all these books!

BASIC CONSTRUCTION

FRANCIS D.K. CHING
Building Construction Illustrated.

ALBERT DIETZ
Dwelling House Construction.

ROBERT ROSKIND
Building Your Own House: Everything You Should Know About Home Construction From Start to Finish.

SARAH SUSANKA
The Not So Big House.

PASSIVE SOLAR AND BIOCLIMATIC DESIGN

BRUCE ANDERSON AND MALCOLM WELLS
Passive Solar Energy.

MARK DEKAY
Sun, Wind, and Light: architectural Design Strategies.

EDWARD MAZRIA The Passive Solar Energy Book: A Complete Guide to Passive Solar Home, Greenhouse and Building Design.

VICTOR OLYGAY
Design with Climate.

EARTHSHIPS

MISCHA HEWITT AND KEVIN TEFLER
Earthships in Europe.

MICHAEL REYNOLDS
Earthship Volume 1.
Earthship Volume 2.
Earthship Volume 3.

FINANCING

ROB ROY
Mortgage Free: Innovative Strategies for Debt-Free Home Ownership

LYNN UNDERWOOD
Homebuilding Debt-Free: Guide for the Owner-Builder

FINISHES AND MATERIALS

CAROLE CREWS
Clay Culture: Plasters, Paints and Preservation.

LYNN EDWARDS
The Natural Paint Book

LISA SCHRODERA
dobe Homes for All Climates

RICHARD FLATAU
Cordwood Construction Best Practices

JOHANNA PAUNGGER AND THOMAS POPPE
MoonTime – The Art of Harmony with Nature and Lunar Cycles

LIVING A DIFFERENT WAY

JOHN S. TAYLOR
A Shelter Sketceterahbook: Natural Building Solutions.

VLADIMIR MEGRÉ
Ringing Cedars: The Anastasia Series.

VIDEOS

OFF-GRID BUILD
Earthship channel on YouTube
https://www.youtube.com/channel/UC4j-f_5P7ZiC4i-EeqIxNkA

Earthships around the World

THE BEST OPEN SOURCE EARTHSHIP RESOURCES AND BLOGS:

MANITOBA EARTHSHIP, MANITOBA, **CANADA**

    https://sites.google.com/site/earthshipmanitoba/
Use:	Residential
Cost:	$110,000 so far + $85,000 for land INCOMPLETE
Expected final cost:	$220,000 without land
Time to Build:	2012-present
Issues:	Humidity leading to condensation

DARFIELD EARTHSHIP, BRITISH COLUMBIA, **CANADA**

    http://www.darfieldEarthship.com/
Use:	Residential
Cost:	$73,000 +15,000 donated engineering time + volunteer and build time

OTHER EARTHSHIPS AROUND THE WORLD:

EARTHSHIP DEMO STROMBEEK, STROMBEEK, BRABANT, **BELGIUM**

    No website
Use:	Supposed to be a garden shed example project. Now used to house cats.
Designer:	Mike Reynolds
Time to Build:	2000
Issues:	Never used as anything but a cattery! Looks "decrepit".

EARTHSHIP ZEMĚNKA, PRAGUE, **CZECH REPUBLIC**

    http://www.zemelod.cz/en/news/Entries/2012/6/1_An_Earthship_Zemenka_was_born.html
Use:	Demonstration and training center of sustainable buildings
Cost:	$155,000 US
Designer:	Mike Reynolds
Time to Build:	2012 – 21 days initial build by EB, more to finish
Volunteers:	40 from 14 countries

EARTHSHIP REHEMETSA, SAKU, **ESTONIA**

    http://www.sakuvald.ee/
Use:	Demonstration Site for EU
Designer:	Not MR
Time to Build:	2010-present

BRITTANY GROUNDHOUSE, KERNOMBRE, BRITTANY, **FRANCE**

    http://www.groundhouse.com/
Use:	Residential
Designer:	Not MR
Time to Build:	2008-2009
Tweaks:	Vertical glazing, no greenhouse, veggies grown outside, selling additional PV power

EARTHSHIP GER, NORMANDY, **FRANCE**

    http://www.Earthship-france.com
    http://www.off-grid.net/2007/06/22/first-Earthship-in-france/
Use:	Holiday rental
Designer:	Mike Reynolds
Time to Build:	2007-2008

EARTHSHIP ZWOLLE, DRENTE, **NETHERLANDS**

    http://www.doeparknooterhof.nl/
    http://Earthshipeurope.org/index.php/Earthships/performance
Use:	Public Teahouse
Time to Build:	2008-2009
Issues:	Too cold for winter use
	High humidity = mold
	Not enough solar gain
	Cracking in cement around tires
	Water catchment issues from falling leaves
Tweaks:	Built on concrete foundation to address high water table
	North entrance
	Grid-tied

NGARUAWAHIA, **NEW ZEALAND**

    http://gubbsEarthship.com/
Cost:	$30,000, 60% of which was for concrete work
Time to Build:	5 years, completed while working full time
Planning Permission:	Obtained Easily
Temperature:	As low as 14°C (58°F) on cold nights and 23°C (76°F) during summer
Issues:	In-ground floors noticeably colder than above-grade floors
Tweaks:	Used an old glasshouse, split down the middle
	Used single pane glass on greenhouse
	Portable gas heater used for cold nights
	Wears warmer clothing in winter

EARTHSHIP MERTOLA, **PORTUGAL**

    http://www.conventomertola.com/
Use:	The Convento São Francisco de Mértola
Designer:	Not MR
Time to Build:	2009-present

ROMANIA

    http://bhudeva.org/blog/2012/01/17/Earthships-and-ventilation-in-cold-climates-problem/

EARTHSHIP FIFE, KINGHORN, **SCOTLAND**

	http://www.sci-scotland.org.uk/
	http://www.Earthshipeurope.org/index.php/Earthships/europe?showall=1&limitstart=
Use:	Communities Initiatives Building Training Center
Designer:	Mike Reynolds
Time to Build:	2002-2004
Planning Permission:	Permitted
Issues:	Used wet earth to pound the tires with, causing issues later on with rotting in the roof cavity

EARTHSHIP PICTAIL, DEERNESS, ORKNEY ISLANDS, **SCOTLAND**

	http://www.facebook.com/pages/Pictail-Produce/
Use:	Farmhouse and Residential
Designer:	Unknown
Time to Build:	2010-present

EARTHSHIP CUEVAS DE SOL, SORBAS, ANDALUSIA, **SPAIN**

	http://www.Earthship.es
Use:	Residential
Designer:	EEBU (Earthship Europe)
Time to Build:	2007-present

EARTHSHIP VALENCIA, **SPAIN**

	http://oscarlisabuild.blogspot.com/
Use:	Residential
Designer:	Mike Reynolds
Time to Build:	2003-2008
Temperature:	up to 30°C (86°F) during summer
Issues:	Overheating in summer
	Greywater issues
	Under-heating in winter
	Heat gain from skylights
Tweaks:	Vertical Glazing.
	Using awnings at the south windowwall and shades over the skylights
	Removing kitchen sink from greywater
	Adding fireplace

THE MIDGÅRD BLACKSHIP, SKOVDE, **SWEDEN**

	No website
Use:	Residential
Designer:	EEBU (Earthship Europe)
Time to Build:	2007-present

EARTHSHIP VÄXHUSET, MOBODARNE, SODERHAMN, SWEDEN

http://www.vaxhuset.se/
Use:	Eco-Building Education Center
Time to Build:	2005-present

EARTHSHIP BRIGHTON, STANMER PARK, BRIGHTON, UNITED KINGDOM

http://www.lowcarbon.co.uk
Use:	Earthship Community & Education Center
Designer:	Mike Reynolds
Time to Build:	2004-2006
Temperature:	Major issues
Issues:	Requires additional heating in winter and some means to relieve the summer overheating
	Humidity issues
	No insulation at floor

COLORADO, USA

http://www.touchtheearthranch.com/rhome.htm

MONTANA, USA

http://Earthship.com/blogs/2013/01/Earthship-experience-8-weeks-650-tires-thousands-of-pop-cans/

SANTA FE, NEW MEXICO, USA

http://www.hcn.org/issues/118/3776
Use:	Residential	
Cost:	$330,000 US	
Designer:	Mike Reynolds	
Time to Build:	1994-1997	
Temperature:	Excessive heat	
Issues:	Underpowered PV	Roof and window Leaks
	Backed Up toilets – first week	Failed water pump – first week
	No overflow on cisterns	Overheating
Tweaks:	Numerous and ongoing	

Index

acoustic, 164, 172, 237

adobe, 8, 28, 59, 69, 93, 110, 128, 135, 136, 150, 151, 153, 155, 178, 183, 196, 198, 199, 200, 204, 206, 218, 271, 272, 285, 286, 341, 342, 351

appliances, 20, 24, 43, 56, 69, 77, 150, 242, 253, 254, 256, 261, 290, 303, 306, 308, 310, 312, 315, 322, 358

aquifer, 101, 109, 227, 231

asphalt shingles, 229

Assembly Occupancy, 102, 275, 276

attic, 77, 139, 141, 156, 159, 162, 228, 229, 298, 307, 319

backup power, 32, 49, 315

bamboo, 144, 153, 191, 204, 232, 288, 289

basement, 102, 113, 150, 155, 162, 169, 198, 225, 264, 353

baths, 17, 35, 50, 128, 156, 238, 242, 253, 257, 259, 278, 279, 283, 289, 298, 310, 318, 325, 356

beams, 48, 77, 78, 88, 167, 168, 172, 173, 205, 213, 214, 228, 233, 264, 339

benches, 272

berm, 17, 21, 24, 29, 35, 41, 45, 48, 49, 56, 57, 59, 81, 94, 102, 113, 152, 153, 154, 155, 157, 162, 163, 181, 186, 275, 351

blackwater, 11, 14, 17, 102, 109, 321, 322, 342, 369

blocking, 76, 174, 278

boiler, 211, 296, 297

bottle bricks, 21, 192, 207

brackets, 138, 146, 168, 213

building permit, 85, 102, 171, 300

cans, 11, 13, 17, 20, 21, 22, 24, 25, 40, 42, 43, 45, 48, 53, 57, 67, 88, 102, 195, 283, 290, 362, 380

carpet, 76, 158, 287, 288, 289

cars, 44, 60, 263, 323, 362

ceiling fans, 156

cellulose, 161

Certificate of Occupancy, 102

chalkboards, 286

cistern, 13, 22, 29, 46, 73, 130, 158, 234, 250, 275, 317, 323, 324, 326, 327

cisterns, 11, 17, 20, 24, 29, 43, 48, 49, 154, 155, 163, 227, 275, 324, 326, 380

clay, 196, 200, 231, 285, 376

climate, 10, 12, 13, 14, 18, 27, 28, 29, 30, 32, 33, 44, 46, 53, 58, 61, 70, 73, 79, 88, 94, 107, 113, 114, 116, 118, 119, 120, 128, 131, 132, 141, 144, 151, 152, 155, 160, 169, 170, 177, 180, 181, 182, 201, 203, 204, 205, 220, 231, 232, 238, 239, 249, 262, 273, 274, 281, 283, 312, 336, 342

cob, 79, 181, 182, 196, 200, 201, 202, 214, 218

Code, 13, 17, 29, 59, 68, 101, 102, 128, 167, 168, 169, 170, 183, 199, 203, 204, 205, 206, 217, 219, 221, 223, 225, 238, 258, 259, 261, 266, 267, 275, 276, 300, 302, 310, 312, 314, 320, 321, 322, 325, 389

Codes, 51, 90, 101, 102, 111, 171, 201, 204, 205, 209, 216, 221, 267, 370, 371

coir, 288

color, 9, 96, 147, 179, 196, 200, 207, 212, 219, 221, 223, 235, 238, 243, 249, 252, 255, 257, 261, 281, 283, 285, 289, 303, 326, 329, 339, 351

community, 28, 34, 40, 60, 69, 72, 73, 83, 84, 86, 87, 92, 98, 99, 100, 102, 109, 132, 135, 147, 207, 246, 271, 286, 303, 304, 322, 325, 329, 370

composting, 14, 88, 119, 257, 320, 321

composting toilets, 320

concrete, 20, 22, 24, 42, 44, 48, 76, 144, 164, 169, 209, 210, 211, 224, 231, 284

contractor, 77, 92, 94, 102, 147, 173, 199, 203, 211, 217, 222, 224, 225, 287, 350

cooling, 11, 17, 18, 20, 24, 32, 33, 43, 44, 53, 56, 57, 59, 73, 95, 117, 121, 125, 127, 131, 132, 134, 135, 136, 137, 138, 139, 140, 141, 145, 150, 152, 153, 154, 155, 157, 158, 175, 181, 201, 205, 223, 226, 234, 238, 239, 250, 263, 283, 294, 295, 297, 298, 301, 317, 342 cooling tubes, 153, 157

cooling tubes, 20

cordwood, 39, 218, 219, 376

cork, 289

cost, 13, 20, 21, 22, 23, 32, 35, 36, 37, 39, 43, 44, 49, 53, 55, 57, 61, 70, 83, 84, 85, 86, 87, 89, 92, 93, 94, 96, 97, 117, 118, 128, 145, 151, 155, 161, 163, 164, 170, 171, 174, 186, 188, 194, 196, 200, 201, 205, 210, 216, 221, 222, 229, 231, 232, 233, 234, 235, 239, 254, 255, 275, 280, 281, 284, 289, 294, 296, 297, 298, 300, 304, 306, 307, 309, 312, 313, 314, 315, 316, 319, 320, 323, 325, 336, 347, 351, 377

cotton, 161

courtyard, 114, 117, 145, 189, 250, 251, 343, 362

curb appeal, 179, 390

custom design, 13, 36

daylighting, 147

deck, 128, 129, 167, 211, 228, 324, 363

doors, 13, 17, 20, 24, 36, 43, 49, 78, 80, 89, 93, 105, 125, 130, 131, 140, 148, 150, 155, 156, 162, 163, 164, 167, 177, 180, 188, 189, 190, 191, 207, 211, 217, 220, 236, 237, 238, 243, 249, 260, 263, 274, 279, 283, 311, 314, 339, 349

earth floors, 46, 287

earth plaster, 8, 22, 198, 207, 227, 280, 285, 286

earthbag, 196, 206, 207, 208, 390

earth-coupling, 9, 153

earthquake, 45, 167, 168, 208, 220, 221

earthquakes, 45, 112, 132, 180, 199, 204, 207, 208

earth-sheltering, 9, 29, 32, 37, 44, 48, 59, 81, 89, 153, 155, 163, 175, 207, 210, 342, 390

electrical, 9, 32, 55, 59, 61, 83, 85, 102, 162, 167, 172, 179, 180, 210, 211, 237, 245, 253, 254, 259, 275, 293, 295, 297, 301, 303, 305, 306, 307, 310, 312, 314, 316, 326, 347

embodied energy, 11, 42, 43, 49, 70, 72, 161, 195, 196, 204, 223

EPDM, 24, 44, 47, 187, 189, 229, 230, 322

excavation, 20, 117

Feng Shui, 9, 249, 329, 336, 337, 338, 339

fiberglass insulation, 161

financing, 32, 83, 84, 85, 350, 389, 391

finishes, 199, 256, 257, 279, 280, 281, 282, 285, 290, 348, 354, 355, 356, 358, 359, 360, 361, 362, 363, 376

fireplace, 49, 68, 89, 125, 127, 128, 155, 162, 180, 252, 253, 260, 299, 300, 302, 307, 342, 343, 361, 362, 379

flooring, 46, 64, 77, 78, 95, 148, 173, 177, 256, 279, 280, 287, 288, 289, 290

food, 7, 8, 11, 12, 31, 35, 39, 43, 45, 49, 59, 79, 88, 89, 100, 116, 123, 126, 127, 130, 147, 150, 153, 154, 177, 187, 188, 252, 253, 254, 260, 264, 299, 300, 313, 322, 325, 342, 343, 358

footprint, 21, 25, 77, 89, 108, 109, 116, 141, 144, 145, 164, 178, 242, 252, 286, 315, 348

foundation, 33, 38, 60, 61, 67, 77, 81, 86, 87, 102, 112, 121, 125, 128, 130, 136, 154, 160, 162, 163, 167, 169, 170, 171, 180, 183, 201, 205, 206, 210, 213, 215, 216, 217, 221, 223, 225, 227, 259, 264, 297, 299, 300, 317, 378

furnace, 297

furniture, 269, 274, 353, 354, 359, 360, 361, 362, 363, 364

geography, 28, 107, 112, 131

geothermal, 18, 113, 297, 298, 342

glass bottles, 11, 17, 20, 24, 42, 192

grease trap, 17, 34, 50, 256, 320, 325

green roofs, 233, 234

greenhouse, 13, 17, 24, 25, 29, 31, 32, 33, 34, 35, 36, 42, 44, 46, 48, 49, 50, 53, 55, 56, 57, 59, 68, 79, 86, 123, 124, 125, 145, 147, 148, 153, 155, 156, 158, 171, 178, 185, 186, 187, 188, 189, 190, 191, 224, 253, 257, 258, 287, 302, 319, 326, 342, 353, 378

greywater, 17, 111, 302, 325, 326, 379

gutters, 46, 227, 229

hardware, 78, 237

hardwoods, 43, 108, 137, 139, 173, 216

heat pump, 297, 298

heating, 11, 17, 22, 32, 33, 34, 36, 44, 46, 53, 56, 57, 59, 61, 62, 73, 95, 102, 113, 125, 127, 131, 132, 133, 134, 136, 137, 138, 139, 140, 141, 145, 151, 152, 153, 154, 158, 162, 163, 167, 175, 186, 191, 201, 205, 226, 234, 238, 239, 260, 263, 283, 293, 294, 296, 297, 298, 299, 300, 303, 315, 317, 318, 319, 342, 379, 380

hidden hallway, 252

hiring an architect, 346

humidification, 32, 33, 61, 125, 145, 155, 156, 157, 158, 177, 187, 232, 262, 294, 301

inner-earth temperature, 17, 41, 56, 59, 153, 154, 163, 183, 297

insulation, 9, 20, 24, 33, 34, 43, 44, 49, 55, 56, 58, 59, 61, 77, 102, 105, 133, 143, 144, 151, 152, 153, 154, 155, 158, 159, 160, 161, 162, 163, 164, 170, 177, 181, 183, 190, 192, 195, 199, 204, 205, 206, 211, 216, 217, 219, 221, 225, 228, 232, 233, 237, 238, 243, 262, 263, 264, 287, 298, 310, 317, 319, 380

insurance, 8, 39, 83, 85, 87, 90, 94, 95, 96, 97, 98, 100, 102, 108, 205, 210, 217, 233, 389

joists, 172

jute, 289

kitchens, 50, 117, 156, 236, 238, 253, 254, 255, 279, 283, 287, 289, 298, 318, 337

land, 8, 21, 24, 43, 71, 81, 85, 87, 101, 108, 109, 111, 113, 116, 117, 118, 122, 123, 124, 126, 136, 137, 140, 213, 295, 309, 323, 325, 332, 333, 336, 370, 377, 391

landscape, 8, 9, 12, 28, 29, 38, 45, 48, 77, 88, 108, 111, 113, 116, 118, 119, 122, 123, 125, 129, 133, 137, 155, 167, 175, 179, 183, 195, 196, 199, 209, 227, 267, 286, 298, 320, 326, 333, 336, 341, 347, 387, 389, 391

lighting, 29, 73, 78, 80, 119, 127, 147, 179, 185, 188, 217, 238, 248, 256, 261, 273, 277, 279, 293, 303, 304, 305, 306, 311, 347, 348, 350, 359, 361

linoleum, 290

log, 28, 70, 87, 92, 130, 132, 133, 135, 138, 139, 140, 143, 196, 215, 216, 217, 219, 351

maintenance, 8, 29, 32, 35, 36, 46, 49, 50, 55, 57, 59, 71, 79, 85, 93, 109, 118, 121, 124, 126, 129, 155, 157, 158, 174, 177, 180, 194, 199, 207, 216, 217, 225, 229, 230, 231, 234, 238, 239, 242, 247, 249, 255, 274, 280, 281, 283, 284, 287, 289, 290, 293, 294, 296, 302, 306, 313, 318, 320, 321, 351

mechanical, 2, 9, 24, 25, 29, 32, 43, 90, 102, 131, 145, 152, 158, 159, 172, 180, 205, 214, 216, 217, 226, 237, 239, 245, 253, 259, 260, 262, 263, 275, 293, 294, 295, 296, 298, 299, 301, 306, 307, 312, 319, 326, 347

metal roofing, 230

methane, 322

microclimates, 28, 109, 114, 115, 118, 126, 133, 179

mirrors, 148

mortgage, 72, 83, 85, 205, 389, 391

natural building, 180, 281, 336

nichos, 272

nooks, 273

off-gassing, 21, 47, 48, 62, 64, 158, 161, 184, 239, 281, 286, 302

oils, 161, 281, 282, 287

orientation, 38, 42, 59, 107, 113, 137, 145, 151, 351, 367

outhouse, 101, 257, 320, 321

outlets, 217, 254, 256, 275, 279, 303, 305, 310, 312, 326

overhangs, 32, 101, 135, 138, 139, 140, 146, 147, 188, 226, 228, 229, 238, 343

paints, 158, 280, 281, 283, 286

passive solar, 9, 11, 41, 46, 50, 59, 61, 68, 73, 145, 148, 149, 151, 154, 178, 181, 182, 187, 189, 196, 201, 223, 248, 253, 263, 305, 341, 342

PassivHaus, 57, 58, 149, 239, 341

patios, 114, 118, 119, 128, 323, 337

paving, 118, 119, 323

photovoltaic, 11, 17, 84, 306, 342

planters, 11, 17, 29, 46, 141, 163, 187, 253, 259, 323, 325

plants, 17, 25, 31, 33, 50, 55, 56, 108, 109, 111, 113, 114, 117, 118, 119, 120, 121, 123, 124, 125, 126, 129, 130, 137, 138, 141, 148, 158, 159, 183, 187, 188, 189, 190, 191, 195, 223, 233, 234, 235, 259, 287, 320, 321, 322, 323, 325, 334, 338, 339 plumbing, 9, 17, 24, 32, 43, 48, 50, 73, 85, 162, 163, 164, 167, 172, 180, 211, 217, 222, 229, 237, 245, 253, 259, 293, 302, 305, 307, 317, 318, 319, 320, 325, 326

plywood, 48, 76, 117, 158, 172, 174, 210, 212, 225, 255, 264

porches, 116, 119, 128, 133, 141, 145, 216, 226, 238, 243, 249, 274, 287, 343

power, 46, 50, 61, 69, 86, 111, 305, 306, 307, 308, 309, 310, 315, 332

privacy, 23, 35, 40, 50, 87, 107, 114, 121, 122, 128, 164, 180, 189, 193, 211, 237, 238, 242, 247, 253, 257, 258, 259, 260, 295, 300, 329, 350

Propane, 22, 300, 369

radiant, 125, 151, 163, 260, 287, 296, 315, 318

rainwater, 17, 55, 59, 68, 86, 114, 118, 123, 125, 227, 229, 230, 231, 233, 234, 249, 298, 317, 323, 324, 325, 326, 342, 369

rammed earth, 48, 57, 60, 84, 92, 153, 155, 178, 183, 184, 196, 197, 199, 200, 203, 204, 205, 206, 275, 342

reciprocal roof, 247

resale value, 39

research, 4, 7, 8, 11, 12, 14, 20, 22, 23, 26, 31, 32, 34, 37, 39, 40, 42, 44, 47, 48, 53, 54, 55, 57, 59, 61, 62, 70, 85, 87, 95, 99, 100, 117, 144, 155, 186, 187, 188, 190, 203, 204, 205, 208, 253, 260, 264, 306, 312, 323, 326, 329, 342, 346, 347, 390, 391

rigid insulation, 163, 229

roof, 11, 13, 17, 32, 33, 34, 42, 45, 46, 48, 50, 53, 78, 87, 89, 93, 95, 101, 113, 114, 125, 127, 130, 132, 133, 135, 138, 139, 140, 146, 148, 153, 154, 157, 159, 160, 161, 162, 167, 168, 172, 173, 175, 177, 179, 180, 185, 186, 187, 188, 189, 190, 198, 201, 205, 206, 207, 214, 216, 218, 221, 226, 227, 228, 229, 230, 231, 232, 233, 234, 235, 236, 247, 249, 261, 264, 274, 283, 297, 298, 300, 302, 304, 306, 307, 318, 319, 321, 323, 324, 351, 363, 379

roofing, 20, 49, 78, 226, 228, 229, 230, 231, 232, 233, 324, 351

round spaces, 247

rubble trench, 170, 171, 206

science, 8, 9, 41, 68, 69, 70, 145, 320, 336

seagrass, 289

septic, 11, 14, 17, 22, 44, 83, 101, 102, 109, 118, 187, 275, 313, 320, 321, 322, 326

shades, 13, 20, 24, 34, 35, 43, 127, 128, 148, 150, 162, 186, 304, 379

shower, 31, 50, 128, 223, 245, 258, 259, 278, 280, 286, 311, 317, 318, 319, 326, 343, 355

showers, 11, 17, 55, 128, 159, 162, 242, 246, 258, 286, 298, 325

shutters, 78, 130, 132, 148, 150, 179, 251, 274, 283, 343

sinks, 11, 17, 49, 256, 278

sisal, 288

site, 9, 21, 22, 24, 26, 28, 30, 36, 38, 39, 42, 43, 45, 51, 56, 57, 60, 70, 72, 73, 76, 77, 81, 82, 86, 87, 88, 92, 98, 100, 101, 102, 107, 110, 111, 113, 114, 116, 117, 118, 121, 123, 139, 155, 169, 170, 183, 196, 198, 199, 200, 205, 207, 208, 211, 213, 217, 223, 245, 275, 290, 298, 309, 320, 323, 332, 336, 347, 367, 368, 369, 370, 391

skylight, 35, 42, 46, 146, 147, 156, 187, 247, 248, 256, 259, 261, 295, 304, 342

slate, 231

snow, 11, 28, 29, 32, 35, 36, 42, 46, 50, 55, 82, 88, 98, 113, 114, 116, 119, 121, 125, 131, 132, 133, 137, 138, 139, 146, 157, 159, 167, 180, 187, 190, 226, 227, 228, 249, 263, 264, 287, 297, 321, 323, 324, 341

softwoods, 173

soil, 17, 24, 25, 28, 34, 41, 49, 56, 63, 64, 70, 109, 112, 113, 117, 121, 124, 125, 126, 129, 153, 154, 169, 170, 172, 183, 188, 190, 191, 196, 199, 200, 201, 202, 203, 205, 207, 225, 231, 233, 234, 264, 313, 320, 321, 323, 325, 326, 368

spirit, 347

spray foam insulation, 161

stains, 158, 187, 213, 255, 257, 280, 281, 283, 288, 289

stairs, 129, 243, 266, 267

steps, 36, 82, 129, 210, 243, 244, 249, 258, 259, 266, 267, 276, 277, 311, 345 stone, 42, 62, 70, 76, 78, 113, 124, 129, 132, 133, 135, 136, 138, 139, 140, 141, 143, 144, 151, 153, 162, 164, 170, 171, 179, 218, 223, 231, 232, 236, 255, 257, 264, 266, 273, 287, 290, 320, 332, 333, 336, 351

stove, 35, 42, 125, 158, 163, 182, 201, 211, 252, 254, 260, 298, 299, 300, 313, 314, 315, 339

strawbale, 20, 57, 69, 70, 79, 84, 94, 137, 150, 181, 182, 189, 196, 214, 218, 220, 221, 222, 232, 272, 275, 342

structure, 9, 11, 17, 34, 35, 36, 45, 73, 96, 100, 102, 108, 112, 113, 114, 124, 128, 132, 133, 138, 141, 145, 148, 153, 154, 155, 159, 160, 162, 167, 168, 170, 171, 172, 173, 177, 178, 180, 181, 199, 201, 203, 207, 214, 215, 218, 220, 228, 231, 232, 233, 234, 243, 251, 253, 265, 274, 275, 293, 302, 307, 315, 321, 326, 336

swale, 118

swales, 81, 117, 118, 124, 343

switches, 217, 279, 297, 303, 306, 310, 311, 312

tabby 178

tax credit, 91

terrazzo, 255, 290

thatch, 232, 233

thermal bridging, 160

thermal comfort, 33, 50, 55, 56, 70, 113, 116, 119, 128, 143, 144, 238, 261

thermal mass, 9, 11, 48, 57, 58, 59, 125, 148, 151, 152, 154, 157, 181, 182, 189, 198, 200, 201, 205, 206, 210, 287, 296

thermal performance, 9, 31, 32, 34, 41, 56, 57, 59, 68, 114, 115, 144, 146, 149, 153, 155, 157, 159, 162, 163, 181, 186, 189, 193, 210, 214, 236, 237, 272, 273, 294, 310, 342

tiles, 78, 230, 231, 254, 258, 280, 286, 287, 288, 289

timber frame, 214, 215

timing, 9, 174, 334

tires, 11, 13, 17, 20, 21, 24, 25, 34, 36, 42, 43, 44, 45, 46, 47, 48, 51, 56, 57, 62, 64, 67, 73, 99, 100, 102, 154, 183, 184, 207, 208, 322, 378, 379, 380

topography, 113, 367

topsoil, 109, 117, 124, 196, 200

TPO, 230

transoms, 78, 140, 156, 165, 186, 238

trees, 25, 45, 70, 73, 76, 81, 88, 101, 107, 113, 114, 116, 117, 119, 121, 123, 124, 127, 130, 132, 133, 136, 138, 140, 141, 145, 147, 153, 173, 174, 178, 179, 189, 213, 216, 234, 238, 274, 277, 289, 307, 321, 323, 334, 341, 343

trusses, 172

Universal Design, 243, 256, 259, 277

Usonian Houses, 68, 242, 296

Vaastu, 9, 329, 336, 337, 338, 339

varnishes, 281, 282

ventilation, 9, 11, 17, 29, 32, 33, 42, 46, 50, 53, 56, 57, 59, 61, 113, 120, 125, 132, 134, 136, 137, 138, 139, 140, 141, 146, 149, 155, 156, 157, 158, 164, 167, 170, 186, 187, 188, 226, 236, 238, 239, 259, 263, 264, 274, 275, 293, 294, 295, 301, 321, 342, 365, 379

vernacular, 8, 30, 54, 128, 131, 133, 141, 154, 264, 346, 387

views, 2, 8, 28, 80, 81, 88, 107, 117, 127, 133, 137, 248, 249, 251, 252, 329, 341, 351

vigas, 173

Vitruvius, 68, 167, 242, 329

volunteers, 21, 22, 39, 87, 98, 99, 100, 236, 321

waddle and daub, 178

walls, 7, 11, 13, 17, 20, 21, 24, 25, 33, 35, 36, 42, 43, 45, 47, 48, 50, 53, 56, 57, 58, 60, 64, 77, 78, 79, 84, 87, 88, 89, 93, 102, 107, 112, 113, 114, 115, 121, 125, 130, 131, 132, 133, 135, 136, 138, 139, 143, 145, 147, 148, 150, 151, 152, 153, 154, 155, 158, 159, 160, 161, 162, 163, 164, 167, 168, 169, 170, 173, 177, 178, 179, 180, 181, 182, 183, 184, 187, 188, 192, 193, 194, 195, 196, 197, 199, 200, 201, 203, 204, 205, 206, 207, 209, 210, 211, 212, 214, 216, 217, 218, 219, 220, 221, 222, 223, 226, 229, 231, 232, 236, 237, 238, 243, 244, 247, 250, 253, 254, 257, 258, 259, 260, 261, 262, 264, 265, 271, 272, 273, 276, 278, 280, 281, 283, 285, 286, 293, 298, 299, 300, 302, 317, 321, 341, 342, 343, 391

waste, 11, 17, 18, 25, 47, 59, 70, 72, 73, 76, 83, 88, 95, 129, 161, 189, 195, 210, 213, 224, 256, 275, 286, 287, 290, 306, 313, 320, 326, 371

weather

climate, 11, 34, 51, 58, 82, 87, 88, 98, 102, 119, 125, 128, 132, 135, 146, 149, 154, 164, 177, 178, 180, 187, 189, 204, 210, 218, 220, 226, 236, 263, 265, 277, 280, 281, 288, 295, 297, 306, 334

wildfire, 130, 230

wind, 11, 17, 28, 29, 35, 36, 42, 46, 56, 72, 81, 113, 117, 119, 132, 137, 138, 139, 145, 146, 155, 156, 157, 159, 167, 168, 177, 180, 186, 192, 207, 226, 230, 233, 234, 238, 249, 251, 264, 266, 295, 305, 307, 309, 336, 339, 342

wind power, 309

windows, 13, 17, 20, 24, 32, 33, 34, 36, 40, 42, 43, 46, 48, 49, 50, 55, 56, 58, 68, 69, 73, 76, 77, 78, 79, 80, 87, 93, 107, 113, 117, 125, 130, 131, 132, 133, 135, 136, 137, 139, 141, 144, 146, 147, 148, 149, 150, 151, 155, 156, 157, 158, 159, 162, 163, 164, 167, 177, 179, 180, 185, 186, 187, 188, 189, 212, 217, 220, 228, 236, 238, 239, 242, 249, 250, 251, 259, 260, 262, 263, 266, 273, 274, 283, 290, 294, 302, 303, 304, 305, 319, 339

wood, 9, 20, 22, 33, 34, 35, 42, 43, 44, 45, 48, 49, 55, 69, 76, 77, 78, 79, 88, 110, 119, 121, 124, 128, 129, 130, 132, 133, 135, 137, 138, 140, 141, 152, 158, 163, 164, 168, 169, 170, 171, 172, 173, 174, 178, 182, 183, 187, 188, 196, 201, 203, 204, 205, 207, 209, 210, 211, 212, 213, 215, 216, 217, 220, 221, 225, 230, 236, 237, 238, 239, 259, 264, 265, 274, 275, 281, 282, 285, 286, 287, 288, 289, 290, 294, 298, 299, 300, 315, 321, 334, 338, 351, 353, 359

wood shingles, 230

wool, 161, 288

zoning, 101, 145, 321, 370

About the Author

Rachel Preston Prinz is an architecturally-trained American designer, preservationist, documentary filmmaker, and artist working in sustainability and architectural engagement. She graduated with a Master's of Architecture and Certificate in Preservation from Texas A&M in 1998. After working in traditional architectural firms for more than 10 years, Rachel started Archinia in 2007 so that she could live her dream of promoting the craft of architecture and the Genius Loci, or Spirit of Place, especially pertaining to U.S. Southern, Mountain, and Southwest indigenous, vernacular, and modern design.

Rachel has served as a preservation commissioner in Taos, as the host of the UNM-Taos Sustainability Institute, and as co-host of TEDxABQWomen. She has won the Echoing Green Work on Purpose challenge and has been named a Green Guardian and a Wilderness Thinker. Rachel has given multiple TEDx and Pecha Kucha talks on modern applications of vernacular design and critical regionalism, landscape preservation, pattern languages, and photography and Epicureanism. She has given more than 40 presentations, tours, and lectures and written nearly 60 articles integrating archaeology, architecture, place, culture, and emerging trends in sustainability.

Rachel's work has been featured on HGTV's "You Live in WHAT?", NMPBS' "Colores!", "Home made" on Canadian PBS, and she's been a featured guest on radio and television, including CBS Radio Women's Media Center live with Robin Morgan, Women's Focus, New Mexico PBS, PBS, CBS, Good Morning Vail, and KUNM. An emerging leader in the field of sustainability, Rachel's been written about in Prime Your Mind For Confidence; Bermuda Quest; The Girls Guide To Swagger; and Accessing Intuition: Stories from Architects and Designers.

CONNECT WITH ME

Follow me on Twitter: https://twitter.com/Archinia
Like us on Facebook: https://www.facebook.com/ArchiniaDesign
Subscribe to our blog: http://hackingtheearthship.blogspot.com/
Subscribe to my blog: http://rachelprestonprinz.blogspot.com/

Contributors

"I've thrived here not because of who I am but because of the people I have come to know."

- Sherlock to Watson in Elementary Season 2

Debra Bailey   Taos, New Mexico

Debra Bailey is a veteran agent with over 20 years of experience in the field of property and casualty insurance. Debra is the foremost expert in obtaining insurance for your Earthship in the US, and works in one of the only firms who cover Earthships – Brown and Brown Insurance in Taos. Debra will help readers navigate requirements to obtain insurance and will answer insurance-related questions that have a direct effect on your ability to obtain financing.

Carrie Christopher   Albuquerque, NM

Carrie Christopher is founder and co-owner of Concept Green LLC, a national women-owned sustainability consulting firm based in Albuquerque, and Founder of The Soul Clinic. As a practitioner of the Tibetan Buddhist tradition, Carrie continually explores the relationship between mindfulness and sustainability. Carrie's superpowers are communications, training, inspiring, and facilitating multiple perspectives that foster meaningful change in service to the planet and to humanity. Carrie helped us identify ways to improve architecture and landscape in order to achieve a higher degree of sustainability.

Michael Curry, P.E., S.E.   Charlottesville, VA

A licensed Professional Engineer in Virginia and a licensed Structural Engineer in California, Oregon, and Washington, Michael Curry brings his years of experience in commercial, residential, new, and historic construction to bear on every project. He is an innovative, hands-on professional with the expertise to work with Architects, Contractors, homeowners, and public sector clients. Michael helped us to make the chapter on structural systems shine.

Richard Flatau   Merrill, Wisconsin

Richard Flatau built his mortgage-free cordwood home thirty-five years ago in the woods of northern Wisconsin. Since then, he has written books, magazine articles, and has conducted hands-on workshops around the country. Richard has provided consultation to thousands of owner/builders and put on successful cordwood building conferences. Richard shares his Best Practices for cordwood construction with us to help readers get homes that are Code-compliant, energy-efficient, beautiful, and affordable.

Sigi Koko   Washington, DC & Ambler, PA

Sigi Koko founded Down to Earth design in 1998 to provide sustainable building design services. She focuses on projects that are ecologically sensible and on the forefront of sustainable design. Sigi holds a Masters of Architecture degree from UT-Austin. Sigi worked for HOK in Washington, DC, where she provided green building expertise on many projects. She also created their Healthy & Sustainable Product Database and contributed to several HOK publications including The HOK Guidebook to Sustainable Design. Sigi offered chapters for the book as well as feedback on questions.

Shannon Colvin Matteson   Albuquerque, NM

Shannon is an interior designer in Albuquerque who has decorated over 10,000 rooms. Her background includes styling for high-profile social events and retail spaces, as well as set design for TV production. Shannon holds a Bachelor's of Fine Arts & is certified by the Interior Redesign Industry Specialists (IRIS). Her website is http://www.emburinteriors.com. Shannon will be offering readers tips and tricks to make the most out of their spaces as well as helping maximize curb appeal.

Chiara Riccardi   Cisenantica, Italy

Chiara is an architectural researcher in sustainable design and earth-sheltering at the University of Bologna. Chiara worked for several months doing exhaustive research on Earthships and cataloguing the hundreds of pages of data on Earthship builds around the world into a coherent package from which we could build the first two chapters of this book. She also used part of her internship to research and prepare the chapters for Rammed Earth and Earthbag building systems.

Maggie Schlarb   Durango, Colorado

Maggie is a Mindful Life Coach and Nia Black Belt Practitioner. She is the creator of Body Soul Journ. Maggie has spent 16 of the last 27 months camping internationally either in a tent, a pop up camper, or a camper van with her husband, a professional runner, and their three year old son. As part of her contribution to this effort, Maggie will share her insight into simple and sustainable living, living with what you have, and living as a group in small spaces.

Steve Scott   Walnut Creek, California

Steve Scott is a twenty-nine year veteran of the real estate and mortgage industries. Steve has worked in originations, mortgage underwriting, secondary marketing, due diligence for mortgage-backed securities, Broker Price Opinion valuations, and quality control reviews for investors. Steve has held a Real Estate license in the state of California since 2003. Steve has been rated in the top 10% of all RE/MAX agents in California, and was Gold Service Certified by Quality Service Certification. Steve helps readers by laying out a road to get financing.

Craig Schreiber   Leadville, Colorado

Craig Schreiber opened Land Art, his architecture and landscape design firm, in 1977. Craig is an expert illustrator, land planner, Outside Architect, and graphic artist. Craig is frequently on the dreams & schemes teams for development teams with an earthen sensitivity. Take a spin through http://www.landart.info for a glimpse of his style. Craig, an expert not only on landscape but also on block construction alternatives for the tire walls, joined us to talk about Durisol block.

Asha Stout   Taos, New Mexico

Asha Stout serves on the faculty at the University of New Mexico-Taos where he teaches hands-on building and design courses in the Green Technology Program. Asha has experience in conventional to radical off-grid building, sustainable forestry, wildland firefighting, and disaster response. These perspectives inform his view of safe housing as an unalienable right and ecological restoration as a grave necessity. Asha is passionate about the pursuit of *"Lomakatsi"* - life in balance. Asha offered insights into how we could address sustainability in entirely new ways.

Pratik Zaveri   Gujarat, India

Pratik is fluent in sustainable design and site supervision for residential, recreational, cultural, commercial, and urban design. Pratik is a master of merging local materials and traditional technologies with contemporary building practices, and was a Teaching Assistant in the Green Technologies Program at the University of New Mexico-Taos. Pratik works with Building Modelling Consultants in India performing energy and daylight analysis and carbon emissions checks. Pratik helped analyze the research conducted on existing Earthships, and contributed enormous expertise in helping us to make a plan for how to do buildings better.

www.ingramcontent.com/pod-product-compliance
Lightning Source LLC
Chambersburg PA
CBHW040732020526
44112CB00059B/2945